NATURE'S WAY
Observations of a Good Earthkeeper

"A delightful book—the essence of the natural world. Choose a page, any page, and start reading. I was mesmerized."

— Peter W. Stearns, author of *A Journey In Time: Mendocino County Wildflowers*

"This pleasing book reflects the artful collaboration that produced the original "Nature's Way" newspaper columns with their fine illustrations and thoughtful prose. Each column is a ramble into a mystery of nature, investigating a topic that Marion had researched thoroughly. The book is a mixture of science and the expression of joy at being alive in the company of the natural world and its intricacies. Frequently titled by a clever turn of phrase or pun, each ramble presents serious scientific information in compact, easily digested form. Finally, this is a loving husband's heartwarming tribute to a marvelous woman; it records the details of her life and captures the spirit of their mutual environmental ethic."

— Prof. William E. Cook, Ph.D., director, Natural History Institute,
Columbia-Greene Community College, Hudson, New York

"Marion marries the science of nature with poetic elegance in a way that's educational and useful, yet is delivered with her heart, conveying passion, joy, and a love of life. I enjoyed looking at the world through her eyes as I read these pages."

— Linda Stonestreet, Park Maintenance Chief, California State Parks

"Readers of The Independent benefited for years from Marion Dusoir Ennes' perceptive eye, boundless curiosity, meticulous research, graceful prose, and bountiful gift for giving a greater dimension of life to the landscape around us. A new cohort of readers is sure to be entranced!"

— Vicki Simons & Tony Jones, editor and publisher,
The Independent Newspaper, 1986–2001

"Marion Ennes documents the big picture through a small and intimate window— a local sampling with global appeal to all who might feel as close to the earth as she did."

— Taylor F. Lockwood, author of *Chasing the Rain*

NATURE'S WAY

Observations of a Good Earthkeeper

Marion Dusoir Ennes
Edited by Howard Ennes

Cypress House

Nature's Way
Observations of a Good Earthkeeper
Copyright © 2008 by Howard Ennes

All rights reserved. This book may not be reproduced in whole or in part, by any means, electronic or mechanical, without prior written permission from the publisher. For information, or to order additional copies of this book, please contact:

Cypress House
155 Cypress Street
Fort Bragg, CA 95437
(800) 773-7782
www.cypresshouse.com

Cover and book design by Cypress House
Except where noted, all photos and column illustrations by Howard Ennes

Library of Congress Cataloging-in-Publication Data

Dusoir Ennes, Marion.
　Nature's way : observations of a good earthkeeper / Marion Dusoir Ennes ; edited by Howard Ennes. – 1st ed.
　　p. cm.
　ISBN-13: 978-1-879384-73-6 (pbk. : alk. paper)
　1. Natural history–New York (State)–Columbia County. I. Ennes, Howard. II. Title.

QH105.N7D87 2007
508.747'39–dc22   2006024894

Printed in Canada
9 8 7 6 5 4 3 2 1

Credits and Permissions

Material on p. 116 is reprinted from Anna Botsford Comstock: *Handbook of Nature Study,* copyright © 1939 by Comstock Publishing Associates. Copyright ©renewed 1967 by Comstock Publishing Associates, a division of Cornell University Press. Used by permission of the publisher, Cornell University Press.

Drawing and photograph on p. 172 reprinted from Anna Botsford Comstock: *Handbook of Nature Study,* copyright ©1939 by Comstock Publishing Associates. Copyright © renewed 1967 by Comstock Publishing Associates, a division of Cornell University Press. Used by permission of the publisher, Cornell University Press.

Painting by A. A. Jansson on p. 87 is used by permission of the American Museum of Natural History.

Quotation on p. 172 is reproduced from *Down to Earth: A Naturalist Looks About,* by Alan Devoe, copyright © 1940 by Alan Devoe, published by Coward-McCann, Inc., New York. All due diligence was exercised in attempting to locate the copyright holder.

Cypress House is committed to preserving ancient forests and natural resources. We elected to print *Nature's Way* on 100% post consumer recycled paper, processed chlorine-free.

As a result, for this printing, we have saved:
　50 trees (40' tall, 6-8" in diameter)
　21,683 gallons of water
　35 million BTUs of total energy
　2360 pounds of solid waste
　4427 pounds of greenhouse gases

Cypress House made this choice because we are a member of Green Press Initiative, a nonprofit program dedicated to supporting authors, publishers, and suppliers in their efforts to reduce their use of fiber obtained from endangered forests.

For more information, visit www.greenpressinitiative.org
Calculations from www.papercalculator.org

*D*edicated to Marion's children, grandchildren, great-grandchildren—and Howard's, too; and to all our relatives and friends, human and otherwise, whom we have met and loved over the years.

Chula helping

A Note to the Reader

This is a book that can be read in so many ways—dip in to savor, to look up and explore, to read from front to back.

To make it easier, however you may decide, you will find that at the start of each **Season** section is a list of columns by title and topic, with page numbers.

The **Index** gives you a detailed cataloging of the subject of each column by common name and, where applicable, the scientific name. Also, it shows themes as well as tangential subjects contained in the columns singly and as groups. And it spots the topics and names in the introductory and end sections.

Fore Words offers an introduction to the columns. **After Words**, following the four seasons of columns, gives a bit of biography and some sense of how these columns came to be.

Enjoy your travels with the author as she observes and probes into the wondrous natural world in which we are privileged to live!

CONTENTS

Fore Words

Arc of a Life — vii

Acknowledgments — vi

Nature's Way Through the Seasons

Summer — 1

Fall — 43

Winter — 85

Spring — 127

After Words

A Naturalist in the Making — 169

Methods, Models, Mentors — 171

Big Thunder—Then and Now — 173

Index — 177

Barn Owls
Photo by Gene Kirksey

Sandhill crane visits the Ennes home on the East Coast of Florida, 1996

*Great Blue Heron,
Puerto Rico*

Acknowledgments

The first person to whom I am indebted for making this volume possible is, of course, Marion Dusoir Ennes. After her come all those folks who helped assemble and sort out the columns and illustrations, checked facts, and otherwise smoothed the way to publication—for preparation of this *Nature's Way* volume was, like the columns themselves, a collaboration. With hope that none has been omitted, my gratitude to—

Tony Jones, publisher, and Vicki Simons, editor, of *The Independent;* present and past members of the Alan Devoe Bird Club: the late Kate Dunham, Elisabeth Grace, Marion Ulmer, Roland Drowne, Nancy Kern, Susan Scheck, Bill Cook; the libraries of Fort Bragg and Mendocino County and Carol Briggs and volunteers of the Roeliff Jansen Community Library; Bernice Kirksey for photographic equipment and Gene's barn owls.

Special thanks to Marion's daughter, Linda Pack, whose brilliant facilitating role was critical near the end of the project.

To Laurel Aylesworth, graphic artist and granddaughter, gratitude for her insights and guidance in early stages, and for the children and grandchildren who helped along the way.

A particular nod to Medea Minnich for her skill in selecting and assessing the columns, and for her insightful indexing.

And, finally, heartfelt thanks to Cynthia Frank for her sensitive management, and the patient Cypress House staff who carried through despite my interminable "suggestions," with appreciation to Joe Shaw and Mike Brechner.

Howard Ennes

FORE WORDS — NATURE'S WAY vii

Arc of a Life
Howard Ennes

The essays that make up this book mirror the final career of Marion Dusoir Ennes. The 1925–2002 life arc of this Renaissance woman successively and successfully comprised careers as child-student, wife-mother-grandmother, caring professional, responsible executive—then, in "retirement," community activist and amateur naturalist. It was my privilege, as her second husband, to accompany Marion for thirty-seven years of her life, and to watch, in her mature years, as she rediscovered her early vocation as a naturalist.

Marion Dusoir came of a family of Belgian-German immigrants, the youngest of three daughters, the only child born in this country. A "solitary" child—I learned this from her and her sisters—she had a fascination with nature and its wonders. In the absence of close siblings and with few nearby friends during her early days on an upstate New York farm, she found solace and companionship with the creatures of her world, the flora and fauna of nature.

So it was that in 1986 she became editor of the then thirty-year-old Alan Devoe Bird Club's monthly newsletter, *The Warbler*, a post she held for five years. The uniqueness and quality of *The Warbler* under Marion's editorship attracted the attention of *The Independent*, a twice-weekly newspaper for the Columbia County, New York-Berkshire, Massachusetts, area. At the invitation of publisher and editor, Marion created and began writing, in 1988, a natural sciences column under the title *Nature's Way*.

Illustrated, her columns covered a wide range of wildlife and ecological topics—a unique blend of scientific facts and insights. She gave special attention to species found in the immediate northeastern areas, although her writings reflected her observations of nature in many other regions. The column continued for ten years, some 349 essays. About half of these columns are included in this book.

In 1991 Marion's work with *The Warbler* and with "Nature's Way" in *The Independent* caused the Columbia County Environmental Management Council to name Marion for their "Good Earthkeeping Award."

Marion searching the hills above Santa Barbara, California, 1998

Many a paean to nature's mysteries and soul have been written—and the author of these essays was not immune to nature's spiritual side—but Marion's intrinsic approach was factually and scientifically oriented. She sought to give her readers a solid basis from which to observe, to marvel, perhaps to understand a bit, some of the natural world we live in. She tried to answer, pragmatically and accurately, questions her neighbors and us "ordinary" folks have: How do animals, birds, insects keep warm or stay cool? How do they get around, find their way, navigate, know how to find food, communicate? How do they seek and make shelter? What of their family life, of courting, mating, parenting—insects and amphibians as well as birds and mammals and fish? What of the seasons and colors?

Howard and Marion at MacKerricher State Park on the Pacific Coast near Fort Bragg, 150 miles north of San Francisco, 1997

Marion's answers told it "like it is," often with a touch of Colonial or Native American history. Frequently she referenced scientists and naturalists, and her observations were drawn from exposure to a wide universe. During the time she edited *The Warbler* and was writing her columns, Marion and I visited nature reserves and kept our eyes open "naturally" in almost every one of the continental states, Puerto Rico, Hawaii, the Caribbean Islands, Europe, and Asia.

Even while Marion was writing *Nature's Way*, she talked of putting some or all of the columns in book form, as many readers had suggested. But one thing or another always intervened. If she had put the book together, Marion no doubt would have updated the columns, probably also added current comments and observations. Since that was not to be, as editor of this book I decided to let the columns stand as a snapshot of their time—hence, each facsimile shows the original date of publication so the reader can place it in historical context.

What inspired Marion's choice of the column title, I really don't know, even though I was a close collaborator in her efforts. But truly, *Nature's Way* was "Marion's way" from the time she was a child. As demonstrated in these pages, Marion's naturalist career was, to her, rather like coming home again, a renewal and recreation of her down-to-earth experiences of early years.

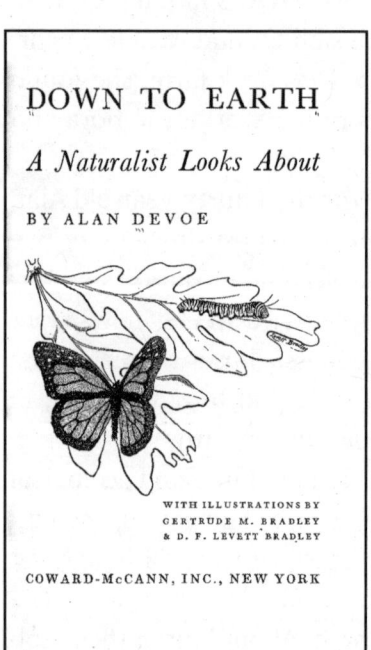

The native curiosity and capacity for illumination which marked the works of Alan Devoe and Anna Botsford Compstock encouraged Marion to share her insightful grasp of the ways of nature.

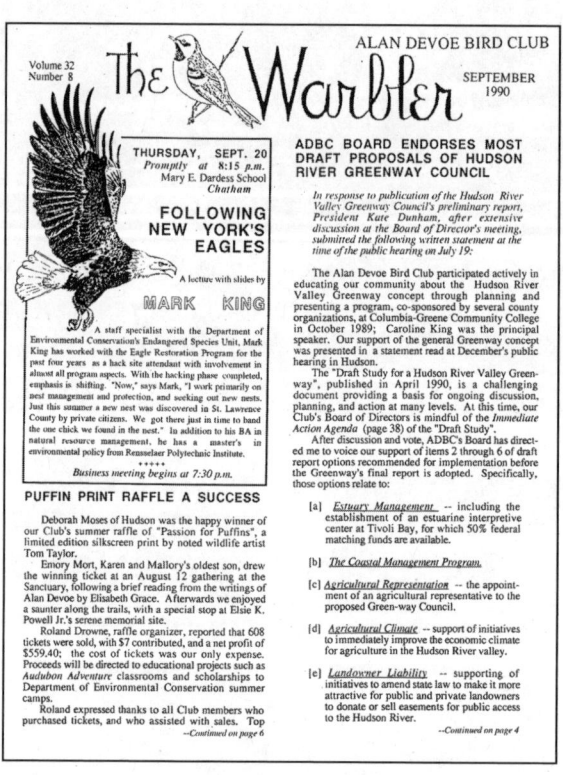

SUMMER

Long days and warm temperatures draw us to the outdoors, teeming with life after what was for our area a rare natural disaster, a tornado (see page 168 for a note, with photos, about the tornado). Peering into nature on all levels, from the star-nosed mole to the bald eagle, we learn the particulars of many species and their air, land, and water habitats—with a late 20th-century view of research and environmental protection.

This armadillo lived under our deck
in Fort Pierce, on the east coast of Florida.

SUMMER

Defending Bluebirds	3	Look Ma, No Hands (bird nest building)	22
Bulbs Are Stems	4	Lessons in the Wild (bird fledglings)	23
Perching Ducks (wood ducks)	5	Painted Turtles	24
"Simple Gifts" (mosses and liverworts)	6	"A Fire of Many Degrees" (animal passion)	25
Orange-tips (orange-tip butterfly)	7	Darwin's Darling (purple loosestrife)	26
Rot is Important (microfungi)	8	Bat Myths	27
Black Bears	9	Flying Squirrels	28
Light Shows (fireflies)	10	Chicken Talk (animal communication)	29
Leopard Frog Friends	11	Wonders Worth Saving (wetlands)	30
Sallys and Jimmys (blue crabs)	12	Corn is Grass	31
Talented Star-nosed Moles	13	Reviving the American Chestnut	32
Meet Shorty (short-eared owls)	14	Fruiting Bodies (mushrooms)	33
My Friend Flicker (Northern Flicker)	15	Finding Fifteen Ferns	34
Ladyslippers in Vitro	16	Cattail Bounty	35
Gentle, Helpful – But Firm (skunks)	17	Underwater Dynamics (ponds)	36
Phoebe, Phoebe	18	Bob – the All-season Cat	37
Estuarine Nursery (Hudson River National Estuarine Sanctuary & Research Reserve)	19	Nesting Eagles	38
		Sandhill Cranes, Dancing Partners	39
Bees as Carpenters	20	Shagbark History (shagbark hickory)	40
Kernels are Fruit (corn)	21	Migration and Freedom	41

NATURE'S WAY
Defending bluebirds

Bluebirds are back, or else they stayed on over the winter. I caught sight of a small flock of males in bright blue coats during the last week in February.

Well-loved as the bird of happiness, this official New York State bird is celebrated in verse and prose. Naturalist John Kieran says "Here is a beautiful, friendly, modest bird with a lovely liquid note and a plaintive song. It has the blue of the sky on its back, the warm color of a hearth fire on its breast and the clear white of soft snow underneath."

These are birds that like field, garden, or farmland habitat. But they need orchard or hedgerow trees with cavities in which to build nests. Lacking these resources, reproductive pressures have forced bluebirds to nest in stove pipes, tin cans, or even cannon.

Though their numbers are increasing in some areas, odds are still against these birds, listed as "of special concern." Loss of farmland, use of pesticides, loss of nest sites to metal fence posts and land clearing, and competition from house sparrows and starlings for nesting cavities have all been heavy deterrents to successful breeding.

The installation of nesting boxes has helped increase bluebird populations, but housing is still scarce for cavity nesters.

Monitors of nest-box networks have learned that a box-hole size of one and nine-sixteenth inch allows bluebirds entry, but keeps out aggressive starlings.

Bluebirds still have to contend with competition from house sparrows, tree swallows, and house wrens, all of whom need the same accommodations and habitat.

Human monitoring has often favored bluebirds, sometimes at the expense of other species. I heard of one person shooting tree swallows so that bluebirds could use a nesting box. It is illegal to shoot any non-game bird, and ill-advised to play God.

Bluebirds can, and need to, defend themselves, and survival is improved for those who make the strongest defense.

Bluebird parent feeding fledglings, soft larvae at first, then insects and berries. Adults 5½ to 7 inches, similar coats, female brownish-gray on back. Juveniles spotted on brown above, white below like a typical thrush.

Long recognized as loving partners, bluebirds are mostly monogamous and rarely combative with one another. Females choose the nest site, build nests inside the cavity chosen, and incubate the eggs.

Males help in feeding the female, the nestlings, and the fledglings. Both guard the nest and babies against predators like snakes and raccoons.

Both also defend their territory and chase other bird species. During nest building and egg laying, male bluebirds fight other male bluebirds, using claws and wings if necessary to keep intruders away.

Ornithologists theorize that the male is protecting access to the nesting cavity so that the pair can breed and prevent copulation with another male. This protects the bird's own gene investment and reduces the labor investment in another bird's offspring.

During the egg-laying period females also defend their nests, engaging in fierce battles with other females that can result in maiming or death. Even so, tests have shown that about one-quarter of the eggs in the nest are not offspring of nesting partners.

A female with fertile eggs and no nest site will try to sneak into another's nest to lay her eggs, leading nesting females to protect their maternity as strongly as the male protects paternity.

Once birds hatch, enmity fades. In cases where a mate dies, the survivor will work hard, and usually succeed in raising the brood to maturity.

Often another bluebird or two of the same sex as the survivor will help by bringing food for the voracious appetites of the growing young.

You can install a bluebird nest on your property. Nests and instructions for installation are available ($6.50 each) from the Soil and Water Conservation District, 828-4386.

THE INDEPENDENT, MARCH 19, 1992

"It is illegal to shoot any non-game bird, and ill-advised to play God."

NATURE'S WAY

Bulbs are stems

A dear friend from Germantown watched her first gift amaryllis bulb grow and sprout this winter. The three-quarter-inch thick stalk pushed straight up from the fat bulb's center, then opened into three six-inch scarlet lily-like blooms.

Her spirit thrilled to the first set of three blooms, and curiosity peaked when a second brilliant trio followed. How did it happen?

Members of the amaryllis family include this hybrid, called Hippeastrum. A house plant here, it is hardy in the hot belt from Florida to Texas.

Most of the world's 800 amaryllis species are tropical or warm-temperature succulents with bulbs or rootstocks. They include large, exotic agaves (ah-gah-vays) like the century plant, which blooms every 20-30 years, and common garden plants, narcissus and daffodils. Like other bulb varieties, they originated in the arid Near East or South Africa. Many garden flowers—including tulips and hyacinth (grown from bulbs), gladioli and crocus (from corms)—are transplanted rootstock plants native to that region.

Except for hybrid versions, species of perennial plants that produce bulbs also have seeds. But bulbs, like corms, rhizomes, and tubers, are a form of vegetative reproduction. Plants with these fleshy rootstocks have large quantities of starchy reserves. These are stored along with a bud that, under favorable conditions, produces a clone of its parent plant.

This non-sexual form of reproduction cuts down on chromosomal variety in offspring, but by eliminating the complex seed-making process and remaining underground through heat and drought, it helps assure survival of the species under rigorous circumstances.

A bulb is an elaborate stem containing a resting bud surrounded by large, leaf-like scales swollen with stored foods, especially thick near the basal disk from which roots grow. In a warm atmosphere, with moisture, the roots elongate rapidly.

When the roots are established, the small bud inside begins to grow. The tip of the shoot containing the flower bud divides and multiplies, pushing upward, carrying the bud up through the soil. Like external buds of woody plants or trees, also covered by overlapping layers of thickened scales, the bud inside contains all the flower parts.

Amaryllis leaves push up after flowers bloom. Tulip foliage emerges along with the flower it has protected within.

Development occurs at the expense of the food starches concentrated in the older, outer leaves of the bulb, causing it to contract. The new fleshly flat leaves of the plant, now above ground, manufacture more food through photosynthesis and pass it down into the bulb. There, single or multiple buds are formed between the base of the flower stalk and the storage leaves. These leaves also share their food with the growing daughter bulb, which replaces the shrivelled parental remains.

Corms, found in gladiolus and hyacinth plants, among others, serve purposes similar to bulbs, but are different in form. They are swollen, underground stems of solid starch, round and covered with a withered, loose, brown scale.

A bud, formed at a corm's top next to the scar of last year's stem and leaves, grows out into a shoot. This produces the nascent flower and leaves which are nurtured by the corm's starch supply. While this starch is used up and flattens out, another corm grows above it, ready to nurture next year's bud.

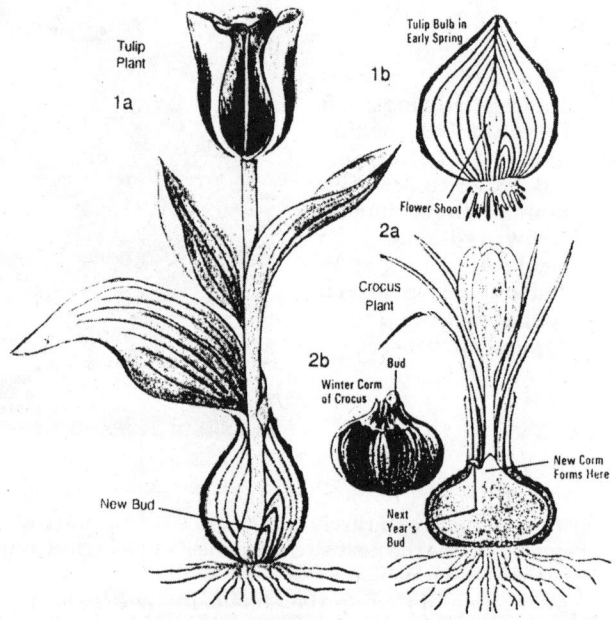

(1a) Tulip plant, root to flower, next year's bud forming. (1b) Early spring tulip bulb, with flower shoot. (2a) Crocus plant, root to flower. (2b) Winter crocus corm, with next year's bud.

THE INDEPENDENT, MARCH 14, 1991

"But bulbs, like corms, rhizomes, and tubers, are a form of vegetative reproduction... that produces a clone."

NATURE'S WAY

Perching ducks

"Loveliest of all water fowl, the wood duck stands supreme. Deep flooded swamps where ancient mossy trees overhang the dark still water, secluded pools amid the scattered pines where water-lilies lift their snowy heads and turtles bask in the sun, purling brooks flowing through dense woodlands where light and shade fleck the splashing waters, slow flowing creeks and marshy ponds—these are the haunts of the wood duck."

So said Forbush and May in the *Natural History of American Birds of Eastern and Central North America.*

These are ducks of amazing color and elegant, compact design. A long crest sweeps from bill to back, with head colors metallic green, purple, and blue, subdivided by lines of white over the head and along the base of the crest. Another vertical white line bisects the cheek, and the throat is all white. The eye and base of the white beak are vermillion.

This easily recognizable marking of the male tops a full, chestnut breast spotted with white. The metallic back is purplish, greenish-brown—colors that go into the wings. The breast is buff.

Female coloration is more subdued; pastel blue and rusty markings on the wing and crest, a marked white eye ring and white faceline from bill to neck.

Colorful wood duck pair. Ducks weigh about 1-½-2 pounds, are between 17 and 21 inches long, with wingspread about 29 inches.

Wood ducks are closely related to mandarin ducks of Asia, both unique for their habit of perching in trees; woodies are the only perching ducks *native* to the U.S.

Most of the world's 15 species of perching ducks have common features. Their claws are sharp and feet webbed, they have long tails that act as brakes for tree landings, and usually nest in holes.

Wood ducks breed in the Hudson Valley, in a wide range of habitats.

They migrated north in small flocks from the southern U.S. early this year, many ready to nest immediately. The site must be near shallow water for food, near trees for roosting.

Large clutches of eggs are common, so they need a large tree cavity. Nests must be 11-12 inches wide inside, a foot or more deep, with at least a 3½ inch opening. Large trees are often hard to find.

Wendy Neefus, wildlife photographer of Hudson, has set out nesting boxes on several country ponds. "On one pond," he says, "I see two wood duck families: one with 17, the other with 8 ducklings. I don't know if they used nest boxes or cavities this year, have to wait till winter when the pond freezes to check it out."

As wood ducks often return to their birth sites to raise their own families, they may use the boxes next year.

Average single-next clutch size is from 13-15 eggs, so it's hard to know if the larger family resulted from egg dumping. Mated females, with or without their own nests, often lay eggs in another wood duck nest, and the owner incubates them too. Dump nests can hold as many as 28 eggs.

Wood duck populations have increased, partly through beavers creating 80,000 acres of shallow water areas over the past 40 years.

This gives hunters access to wood ducks during a controlled season, reducing the populations somewhat and leaving bird lovers and nature watchers the thrill of finding this unique and beautiful creature.

THE INDEPENDENT, JUNE 21, 1990

"... woodies are the only perching ducks native to the U.S."

NATURE'S WAY: 'Simple Gifts'

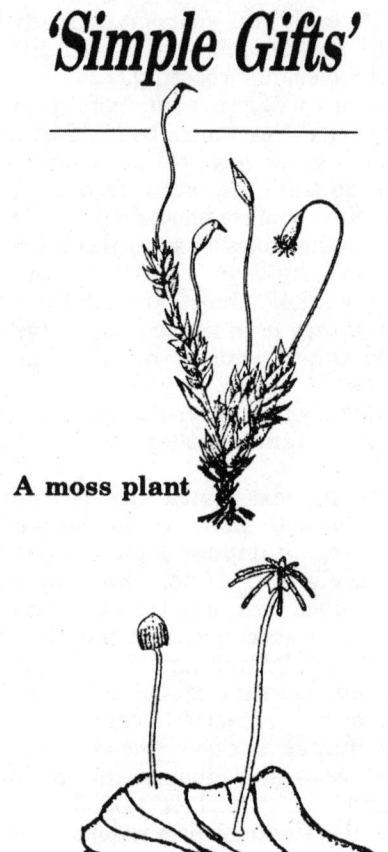

A moss plant

Liverwort plant

Mosses and liverworts are small, inconspicuous land plants, partnered in print as often as they are in nature. Of the two, mosses are better known, probably because of sphagnum, common in gardening for its great water-retentive abilities.

Along with liverworts, mosses are an important link in the chain between simple aquatic algae and more complex flowering land plants, for they make the evolutionary leap to higher embryonic reproductive forms.

Both are called *bryophytes*, and live primarily in boggy or shady moist places where they reproduce by means of spores.

Mosses are low-growing, with thin, light-green leaves attached spirally around an upright stem. We usually notice them as a cushion or carpet on tree stumps or rocks. Dark green liverworts may be found among them. They grow close to the ground and have flat, lobe-shaped leaf-like bases for which they are named.

Both of these primitive flora develop separate male and female sex organs. The mature male sperm is attracted chemically to the female's egg and travels via moisture on the plant to reach her flask-like organ and fertilize the egg.

Gracefully shaped spore cases, small capsules not much bigger than a match head, hold the tiny spores which are sifted out and become new plants.

These simple gifts to the plant world have long been recognized as valuable media in soil development and protection. They support communities in the ecological processes of breaking down tree stumps into humus, or rock surfaces into areas receptive to roots of small vascular plants or grass.

They also stabilize soil to prevent erosion. Researchers have recently been eager to study these plants because of their pollution-detecting ability.

In 1988, Hudsonia, Ltd., a nonprofit institute dedicated to environmental research and education, received a grant from the Alan Devoe Bird Club to be used in work at Stockport Flats in Columbia County.

Hudsonia decided to concentrate on bryophytes. They exist in the moist tidal swamps of the Hudson River Estuarine Sanctuary, of which Stockport Flats is a part. It was recognized that bryophtes are "an integral part of most plant communities,...[but] community composition and rarity or commenness of species are quite poorly known for this plant group."

The preliminary study—the first of its kind in this harsh environment—was undertaken by Eric Kiviat and Lorinda Leonardi. Out of about 10,000 mosses and 14,000 liverworts in the world, their initial identifications included 15 mosses and 6 liverworts. The Sanctuary probably contains a significant number of additional species.

The preliminary report observes that "bryophytes are better pollution indicators than most vascular plants because bryophytes lack a well-developed rooting system, absorbing particles directly from the atmosphere, and do not stay dormant for long periods of time."

Hudsonia has prepared a proposal to the Hudson River Foundation for further research because of the importance of these flora in the estuarine ecological niche. They are "in hopes of continuing the bryophyte survey so that the ecological importance of these plants on the freshwater tidal swamp may be better understood."

THE INDEPENDENT, JUNE 22, 1989

"Researchers have recently been eager to study these plants because of their pollution-detecting ability."

NATURE'S WAY
Orange-tips

The mid-Hudson Valley is graced with the presence of the falcate orange-tip butterfly, enjoying its brief span of life in rocky Catskill uplands as high as 3,000 feet, where it was unrecorded as recently as 1976.

One of only four species in the United States, the falcate is so designated because of the hooked apex of its forewing.

These medium-sized, delicate spring beauties are related to the ubiquitous sulphers and whites, the latter very familiar as the pesty European cabbage butterfly.

Worldwide, orange-tips were called *Auroras* for the glow of early morning; the male carries a sun-orange glow on his forewings. The falcate's early emergence from overwintering pupal case coincides with spring-blooming rock cresses, their host plants.

Adults drink the nectar, mate on or near the flowers, and lay eggs on these plants. Caterpillars grow fat and strong by eating the protein-rich seed pods. So it is not surprising that populations rise and fall according to stands of cresses.

The plants grow in rocky outcrop areas, in open wooded places, on slopes and ledges. The butterfly's design—lower wings mottled in green and white—acts as effective camouflage when it rests on a plant.

A session at this year's Natural History Conference at the New York State Museum introduced me to naturalist Spider Barbour, who has been researching the falcate orange-tip for more than 15 years. His field studies are producing valuable knowledge about their behavior and ecology.

Starting in April, Spider treks to warm woodland slopes where smooth and lyre-leaved cresses are putting out their small white flowers. Here he finds the falcate orange-tip. It is a delicate flyer, not speedy, rarely higher than 15 feet, saving energy by gliding. During its brief life, this ephemeral beauty avoids bright sun and dense shade, staying close to semi-shaded areas at the edge of woods.

After 12 years of exploration, he caught sight of a mating pair. They were hard to see, clinging to a white flower, for the mottled green and white rear wing pattern blended so well they looked like part of the flower cluster.

He left them at twilight. On his return next morning he was surprised to see them still joined, remaining so until almost noon. He described the whole experience in a May 1989 article in *Natural History* magazine.

"Experience proved the behavior was common," Spider says. "I think one-night stands, actually a long relationship for an insect that may live only two weeks as an adult, are not uncommon for orange-tips, and may be common behavior in other spring butterflies, for it is adaptive to the weather of early spring."

Once fertilization takes place, females lay their Day-glo orange eggs on flower buds or pods of the cress plants. Hatched larvae exploit leaves and pods of as many plants as they need.

Once caterpillars fill up, they turn into slender, brown or grey pupae. Almost invisible to the human eye, they hang at a 30° angle suspended by strands of silk, one from the middle and one from the end, to secure them through ten months of fall and winter weather.

Spider Barbour has confirmed the distribution of falcate orange-tips in the Hudson Valley, identifying four different populations in Albany, Greene, and Ulster counties. He is watching their dispersion, and believes this species is pushing northern ecological boundaries.

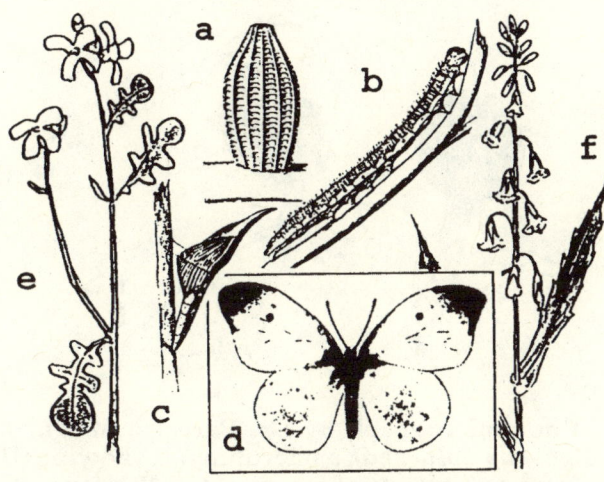

FALCATE ORANGE-TIP BUTTERFLY

[a] Egg—Day-glo orange, ridged. [b] Larvae—Caterpillars reach 1¼ inches, white below, grey to blackish green above, center yellow stripe. [c] Pupa—Brown or grey, attached head up, secured at center and base. [d] Adult male—Body black, wings white, hooked. Forewings with single black dot, orange tip. Female white. Both mottled green hind wings. [e] Lyre-leaved Rock Cress, 1-2 feet. Small white four-petalled flowers. Seedpods up to 1½ inches. [f] Smooth Rock Cress, 2-3 feet. Small nodding white flowers. Pods up to 4 inches. (Illustrations not to scale).

THE INDEPENDENT, JUNE 25, 1992

"Worldwide, orange-tips were called Auroras for the glow of early morning…"

NATURE'S WAY
Rot is important

A walk in the woods in June after the rain is a sure way to see a wide array of macrofungi—delicate-looking mushrooms, jellies, shiny brackets, and more. Several Sundays ago, it was also an opportunity to learn about this special kingdom of lifeforms from Dr. Margaret Carreiro, a Ph. D. in botany with a specialty in mycology, the study of fungi.

Although the walk along Wappinger's Creek on the Cary Arboretum's Institute of Ecological Studies grounds focused on visible fungi, Dr. Carreiro's work concentrates on microfungi that are important in soil decomposition.

As a fellow at the institute, she is looking for new microscopic species and also hoping to discover stress factors on soil fungi coming from soil pollution. Sterile forms of these microscopic fungal species, and/or differences in their numbers and kinds, are possible indicators of environmental stress.

This information is valuable, Dr. Carreiro says, because "rot is important. If decomposition did not exist, we would be up to our ears in dead leaves, sticks, insect and animal bodies.

"The number of atoms on the earth is finite, so atoms and molecules must be recycled to replenish life. Nature provides the means to recycle the elements of old life. Along with bacteria and tiny invertebrates, fungi play a crucial part."

Dr. Carreiro already has several fascinating discoveries to her credit. Her curiosity was piqued about which microscopic soil fungi might be present and active in colder soils. In this temperature region, the upper layers of forest soils are set at or below 50°F five to six months a year.

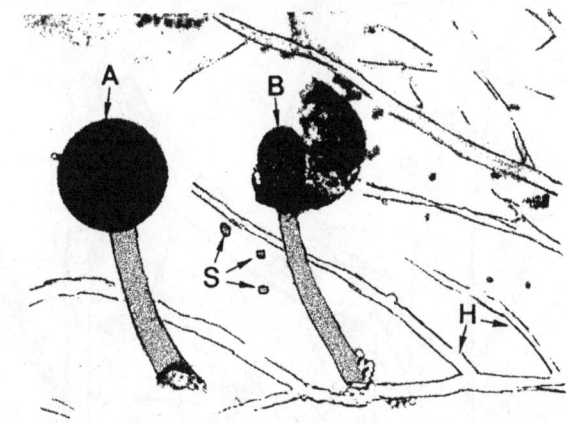

Photomicrograph by Dr. Carreiro of *Mucor* (greatly enlarged), a microfungus, showing (H) *hyphae* (threads of fungus; (A & B) *sporangia* (asexual reproductive bodies), and (S) *spores* (germinating entities). Careful observation of spores and sporangia make possible exact identification of fungi. Spores (S) emerge from (B) broken sporangia and grow into (H) hyphae that absorb nutrients as they penetrate leaf litter and soil.

When she incubated prepared soil samples, half at 78°F and half at 32°F, she found totally different fungal types on the cold plates. She discovered two *new* species, and rediscovered one not seen by scientists for 100 years.

She learned that warm-loving fungi and cold-loving fungi have different decompositional abilities. Cold-lovers break down chitin, the hard substance in insect skeletons, but do not break down plant cellulose.

The institute newsletter explains how Dr. Carriero learned more about how temperature controls the types of fungi in forest soils and their activity:

"She half-filled quart Mason jars with chopped deciduous leaves moistened with distilled water, and inoculated them with soil samples. She incubated the jars for two years, four at 32°F, four at 50°F, and four at 68°F, the maximum temperature reached by soils 4 inches below the surface. She then isolated the fungal species from each jar and measured the dry weight of the leaves to determine how much decomposition had occurred.

"Once again she found that the species isolated from the 32°F jars differed greatly from those in the 68°F jars. The fact that the weight loss at 32°F was 45% of that at 68°F also showed that there can be substantial activity in soils at freezing temperatures."

We'll look for other remarkable discoveries that Dr. Carriero uncovers in the soils we count on for the growth of the plant kingdom and the survival of the animal kingdom.

THE INDEPENDENT, JUNE 28, 1990

"If decomposition did not exist, we would be up to our ears in dead leaves, sticks, insect and animal bodies."

SUMMER — NATURE'S WAY

NATURE'S WAY
Black Bears

The only species of bear we have in the Northeast is the black bear *(Ursus Americanus)* and this is the time of year we might catch a glimpse of one, as Joan Hilton of Copake can attest. She saw a black bear on Route 23 over the Massachusetts line several weeks ago.

Young males, especially, who disperse into new territories in spring, are looking for new food sources as well. They are omnivorous.

Early in April they enjoy succulent young grasses. Their weight fluctuates during the year and they get thinner when young grasses grow tough and berries are not yet ripe. They look for snails on the moist ground areas, and when berries do ripen, they gorge on them.

They flip over stones or tear open logs looking for ants, grubs and other larval insects—and of course they love honey. They pick up and devour combs and bee larvae along with the honey despite the attacking honeybees.

Lou Berchielli, bear conservation specialist of the Wildlife Resource Center at Delmar, says "Bears are curious animals, although they seem to have an instinctive fear of people. They are not just nocturnal, as many people suppose, but keep flexible hours, are solitary and manage to avoid people. Their sense of smell is strong and they may go down-wind to check out who's around.

"If you encounter a bear when you're out hiking through a hilly, wooded area, and you see it stand up on its hind legs, you need not think it is an aggressive sign. It's probably curiosity, so just go on your way."

Over the past 20 years there have only been five to six incidents of people in New York State being hurt by a black bear and these involved either an adult female defending her cubs, or someone trying to feed a bear.

Mr. Berchielli says, "Look and enjoy, but *don't* try to feed them. Remove or *tightly secure* garbage which tempts bears and can make them sick as well as a nuisance."

Black bears walk on the entire foot as humans do. A black bear stands to five-and-a-half feet and is about three feet at the shoulder when on all fours.

It has a smooth, glossy black coat which sheds in spring and fall so it has a heavier weight for winter. Its short tail is hidden in long, black fur.

Bears can grow up to 400 pounds. They have sharp claws which help them climb trees, and they also claw boundary trees to mark territory.

BLACK BEAR

Their sounds include whines, grunts and huffs.

Mating occurs in spring. After a gestation period of seven to nine months, usually two cubs—each weighing eight ounces or less—are born late in January or February.

They stay in the den, usually a cave or a hole in the ground, until they are at least three or four months old. Mother defends them furiously if necessary, but left alone, they play together like kittens.

Steve Williams, wildlife biologist of the Massachusetts Division of Fisheries and Wildlife, affirms the fact that there is a healthy bear population growing steadily but slowly throughout most of the Berkshires and in the northwest quadrant of Massachusetts west of the Connecticut River.

Periodically the bears need to be harvested to have control over their numbers, to keep a balance for human activities, and to perpetuate the species. Bears may be hunted by permit only in the Berkshires.

There is a one-bear limit and any kill must be reported to a biologist, who will check on condition, weight and age of the animal.

For permits contact Massachusetts Division of Fisheries and Wildlife in Boston. The 1988 season is from September 26 to October 1 and November 21 to 26.

Bear hunting in New York State is limited to the Adirondacks, Alleghenies and Catskills. Information can be obtained from the Delmar Wildlife Resource Center, Delmar, 12054.

THE INDEPENDENT, JUNE 30, 1988

"Black bears walk on the entire foot as humans do...they also claw boundary trees to mark territory."

NATURE'S WAY

Light shows

As this week's fireworks displays fade to memories, early night flashes of fireflies create other light shows for us. The fireflies, of course, are playing to one another—male and female.

Fireflies, lightning bugs, glowworms are not flies, bugs, nor worms. Adult forms so named are actually beetles, glowworms their larvae. Both, along with the eggs that produce them, are capable of luminescence.

Bioluminescence is not limited to insects; it is found in life forms from tiny bacteria to fish. There are photogenic (light-generating) protozoa, fungi, sponges, corals, worms, jellyfish, crustaceans, clams, snails, squid, centipedes, insects, and about 100 species of fish.

Yellow, yellow-green, green, blue, pink, and even vivid red are some of the colors. The Central and South American railroad worm has a bright red head, yellow eyes, with green and yellow porthole shapes along the body's length.

What has fascinated scientists and others about bioluminescence is that the light is *cold* and highly energy efficient: between 92 and 100%. Study of the photogenic phenomenon started in the late 1600s, but chemical researchers began unravelling the process in the late 1880s.

The firefly initiates a nerve impulse to a light-producing gland at the lower end of its abdomen. A chalky-white reflecting layer tops the luminous yellow layer, well-supplied with tiny tubes (tracheae) supplying oxygen. Though substances and reactions vary in different luminescent species around the world, the process is essentially the same.

In our local firefly species, *luciferin* is the light-emitting substance. When the impulse is sent, some oxygen is pumped in. An enzyme, *luiciferinase*, and ATP, a common phosphate, join to activate the luciferin and a flash results.

The six common firefly species in the eastern U.S. vary in size from about 1/4 inch to 3/4 inch. **Each species is distinguished by its own flashing system, with variations in intensity, duration, number, intervals between flashes, and flight levels.**

An informed observer—a member of the American Museum of Natural History staff—reports identifying three different species one recent evening, each by its flashing pattern.

One common firefly, *Photinus pyralis*, is active at dusk. While females find grass blades to perch on, males fly about two feet above the ground in an undulating pattern. His flash as he rises comes every two seconds (faster on warmer evenings). Though not as bright, the flash, like a tiny pale yellow rocket, is longer than some other species.

In response, the female flashes briefly every six seconds. After 5-10 minutes of repeated exchanges, he lands and they mate. He is helped to find her by especially keen eyesight; he has 2,500 eye facets, while the female has only 300.

Sometimes a predatory female from another species will lure a male by flashing his species' response. If she succeeds, she devours him.

In an article, "Nature's Night Lights" (July 1971 *National Geographic*), Dr. Paul Zahl, veteran student of bioluminescent creatures, tells of seeing a firefly tree in Malaysia, a "far more spectacular thing than I had ever seen."

First a single beacon flashed, then random lights blinked, without any pattern or rhythm. Soon one cluster of fireflies began "flashing on and off in unison," then others "picked up the synchronization" until most of the fireflies flashed in unison, as if someone were switching them on and off at regular intervals.

THE INDEPENDENT, JULY 5, 1990

> "Sometimes a predatory female from another species will lure a male by flashing his species' response. If she succeeds, she devours him."

Leopard frog friends

NATURE'S WAY

Marion Dusoir Ennes

DESPITE THE HUNDREDS of thousands of leopard frogs dissected in biology classrooms to demonstrate parallel human systems, research about this frog in its natural environment has left surprising gaps. We know little about courting and mating strategies, tadpole behavior or the reason small frogs wander during spring rains.

My fondness for these handsome alert frogs—cheerfully decorated with leopard spots, suffused with iridescence—goes back to childhood. I sought them as companions, easy to find in low meadows, making long leaps just above purple clover and orange butterfly weed. Here they hunted by sight and smell for grasshoppers, beetles, worms or spiders.

I held what I called a "meadow frog" carefully in my hands, feeling the moist skin of its white belly against my palm. The throat's slow pulsing rhythm reflected the regular swallowing that forces air from the nostrils into the frog's lungs.

I carried it to the brook, where I flattened my hand and watched (as I thought then) it return to its "family." It leapt high, arms at sides, legs stretched back, streamlined. Touching nose to water, it slid in without a ripple.

Adult leopard frogs live solitary lives. They return to water on hot days, swim down to where they can dig burrow hideouts with their back feet. Here they take their ease, extracting oxygen from the water through their skin.

If these frogs beat the odds and escape such predators as snakes, fish, raccoons, foxes, herons and many more—like humans who eat frogs' legs—they can live longer than three years.

Leopard frogs emerge from hibernation soon after spring peepers and wood frogs. Males call females with a hoarse croaking call, made even under water, powered by air-filled vocal sacs located at the frog's shoulder between the eye and ear. These sacs balloon as they fill with air. The more air, the louder the call. Sacs deflate quickly when a song ends.

Females arrive, are mounted by male leopard frogs who, though smaller than the females, grow larger thumbs to help them hang on during *amplexus* (joining), then shrink to normal size.

Females lay eggs in elongated masses in the water and seem to prefer communal sites. Each mass has four to six thousand eggs.

Eggs hatch within two to three weeks and tiny vegetarian tadpoles emerge, congregating in shallow water, mouths open. During the next nine to twelve weeks, they eat constantly. Resting only occasionally, they swim rapidly to avoid their many enemies.

Tadpoles are favorite food for the fearsome water-dwelling larvae of various insects. The dragon-fly nymph, with double-hinged lower lip, nails a leopard frog tadpole on its sharp, jagged teeth and swallows it whole. Larvae of the water tiger and the back-swimmer use sucking jaws to get their sustenance.

Giant water-bugs, leeches, as well as fish, turtles, some other frogs and waterbirds count growing tadpoles of various sizes, and small frogs, too, as important menu items.

I have not seen any estimated attrition rates but they have to be high with these and other hungry predators. Frogs are among the amphibians so important in passing energy up the food chain that all have been called the "hot dogs of the animal kingdom."

ADULT LEOPARD FROG: male 3-1/4 inches, female 5 inches. Olive-green or green body, heavily blotched with rounded dark olive spots, creamy outlines, whole overlaid with shiny bronze inflorescence. Two lateral folds, golden from eye to rump. Ivory white below.

INSET, LARGE TADPOLE. Up to three inches, olive or tan above. Born black, about 3/8-inch long with transparent tail fin. Grows rapidly, tail lengthens, body fills out as organs grow and internal gills form.

THE INDEPENDENT, JULY 7, 1994

"I sought them as companions, easy to find in low meadows, making long leaps just above purple clover and orange butterfly weed."

Sallys and Jimmys

When the Hudson's waters warm to 68 degrees or more, Jimmys, adult male aquatic blue crabs in the estuary, look for Sallys, young female adults in their last immature molt.

Sally's skin is soft, her body still slender and triangular.

When Jimmy meets Sally, he picks her up and carries her with him for a few days as "buck and rider." The names come from crab fishers who know this crustacean's habits.

Crustaceans of all kinds abound in the world. Vast hordes include lobsters, shrimps, krill and others which form the base of the aquatic food pyramid, feeding many species, from whales to humans to fish fry.

Along with insects, crustaceans are part of the great order *Arthropoda*, animals with jointed legs, often called "insects of the sea."

Crabs have been known and eaten for centuries, as far back as 2100 B.C. when the Babylonians gave them their own zodiac sign. Aristotle studied them, leaving impeccable scientific data clearly identifying almost a dozen species.

Jimmy hovers nearby as Sally sheds her shell, and turns her abdomen toward him so they can mate. Their copulation lasts up to 12 hours.

Sally will mate only once in a three-year lifetime, and Jimmy will carry her again after copulation, protecting her for the few days it takes for her shell to harden. Now her belly grows round, with ripening eggs and a large supply of sperm inside.

When her carapace is hard again, Sally is a "sook" (or sow), according to fishers. She paddles down the estuary to saltier areas required by the developing young; males favor more northerly waters where salinity is lower.

Of crabs' five pairs of legs, rear pairs are wider and oar-shaped, specially adapted for swimming. Three center pairs, used primarily for walking forward or sideways, also have receptors for smell and taste at leg tips.

Other such receptors are at tips of the crab's pair of antennae. Once food is located the fish or shellfish is grasped by the front leg claws and passed quickly to the mouth parts.

Fertilization takes place within the female's body; ripe eggs from the ovaries join sperm stored in her seminal vesicles. These fertilized eggs are brooded in the female's body for 2 to 9 months after mating.

The female spawns eggs one or more times; up to 2 million eggs. Outside, they form a sponge that remains attached to hair-like structures at the rear of her body.

Eggs hatch as tiny lobster-like *zoea* feeding heavily on microscopic plants and animals. After six weeks, for a few days, it is a *megalopa* until changing into its first crab stage, only one-tenth of an inch wide.

Growth from hatching to mature adulthood takes a total of 19 molts and about a year and a half. By then, at 3½ inches wide it has reached its adult stage.

Blues are now legal size for fishing, and may live another year, an average of 3½ years. Its compound eyes at the end of stalks keep it wary, but can retract into sockets in the carapace for safety. Its hard exoskeleton protects it from predators, and gives it freedom on the sea bed.

Estuarine Reserve Education Director Dennis Mildner does summer crabbing programs at Piermont. Call the Bard Field Station, (914) 758-5193 if you want to see, handle, and ask questions of crabs.

Adult blue crab 3½ to 5½ inches. Hard body carapace, dark blue-green or grey-green, bright blue-green legs with scarlet markings. Underparts white. Male claws blue or grey-green, dull purple fingers. Female claws bluer with scarlet fingers. Larval stages: (1) *Eggs*—1/100 inch, part of sponge containing millions. (2) *Zoea*—1/25 inch, tiny, lobsterlike, with spines and two appendage pairs for swimming. (3) *Megalops*—1/8 inch long, retains tail. Has 5 pairs of legs and stalked eyes like adult. (4) *First crab stage*—1/10 inch wide like miniature crab.

THE INDEPENDENT, JULY 9, 1992

"When Jimmy meets Sally, he picks her up and carries her with him for a few days as 'buck and rider.'"

Talented star-nosed moles

NATURE'S WAY

Marion Dusoir Ennes

WE HAVE HERE IN THE NORTHEAST a mammal for the nineties, a technological "talent." This creature comes as well-equipped for excavation as a steam shovel, yet needs no fossil fuel. It has a complex mobile sensing organ that can pick up electrical signals without being wired. It is the star-nosed mole, an insectivore (not rodent) whose unique attributes make for success in the animal kingdom.

In tunnels under moist meadows, often near water, a brood of 3 to 6 young moles was born in May to a nurturing mother after 45 days of gestation. She prepared an eight-inch nest of dry grasses and leaves in the deeper of two tunnels, taking care to locate it under a tree or stone wall to prevent access from above.

Fairly well developed at birth, with conspicuous fleshy nose fringe, the babies thrive on rich mother's milk. In three weeks they reach 17 times their birth weight, are weaned in two months, well-prepared to cut up worms or dismember beetles for dinner. By three months, fully furred, almost fully grown, they can dig and are ready to set off for a life of underground engineering and tunnel construction.

A mole's life is informed by its cool dark underground, rich with the odors of roots, decomposing litter and earth. With a body supremely adapted, the mole has soft short hair that brushes forward or back and covers all of its cylindrical body except the pink nose and tail. Fur obscures small adequate ears and almost hides the tiny eyes that differentiate light from dark.

The enterprising young star-nose scouts its parents' upper tunnels, laid out much like a downed tree with central trunk, branches and limbs. Finding a likely spot, digging commences.

A mole's heavy-shouldered upper body has large digging muscles which power heavy arms. Huge forepaws are specialized with long sharp claws that scrape and shovel earth at the same time. The sensitive nose identifies the tunnel's route.

The upper tunnel remains six or more inches below the surface for its entire length. As the mole digs, it scoops earth below its body, then back with its feet. After a distance it somersaults and forces the pile up to the ceiling, causing a mole hill in the earth above. Occurring in moist or marshy areas, star-nosed mole hills don't interfere with lawns or farming.

A mole can dig 60 feet of tunnel a day. Fueling the digging are large lungs taking up 20% of body weight. Their blood contains twice as much oxygen-carrying hemoglobin as similar sized animals.

The picturesque star-shaped nose would have delighted Cyrano. It is unique in the animal kingdom, more mobile and complex than an elephant's trunk. Flaring out around the nostrils and constantly wriggling are 22 fleshy tendrils vital to mole functioning in digging, seeking food and finding a mate.

Tendril tissue is dense with receptors, some tactile to augment its sense of smell, others electro-receptors that refine its ability to find food.

The star-nosed often builds tunnels giving access to water. A strong swimmer who uses front paws like paddles and his rather stiff tail as a rudder, he roots in pond bottoms for worms.

By flaring its tendrils, this mole picks up electrical impulses emitted under water from a worm's skin mucosa and pounces on its electrical hot-spot.

With skills like these, under earth or water, the star-nose feeds. It consumes between 1/3 to 2/3 of its weight in worms, grubs and insects daily, thriving in its safe haven.

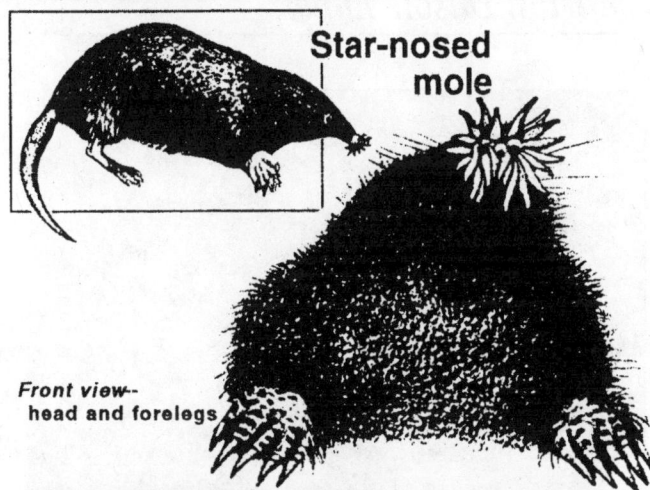

STAR-NOSED MOLE *4 to 5-inch body, 3 to 3-1/2-inch scaly tail (thick in winter with fat storage). Short, smooth black fur. Five toes on front and rear legs.*

FRONT VIEW *(enlarged for detail). Ears not visible, eyes tiny, obscured in fur. Nostrils surrounded by 22 fleshy pink tendrils making star form. Powerful front feet are as broad as they are long.*

THE INDEPENDENT, JULY 20, 1995

"By flaring its tendrils, this mole picks up electrical impulses… from a worm's skin mucosa and pounces on its electrical hot-spot."

Meet Shorty

NATURE'S WAY

Marion Dusoir Ennes

LET ME INTRODUCE YOU to Shorty, one of the resident educators at the Hudson Valley Raptor Center, South Road, Stanfordville. Shorty is my ward, her certificate of adoption identifies her as an adult short-eared owl admitted to the center July 15, 1991. Believed injured by a car, Shorty's wing precludes her ever flying again.

We can't be sure of her age but we can make some good guesses about Shorty's early life. We know that short-eared owls breed in their primary hunting areas, grasslands or marshes near coastlines.

This is where Shorty's mother and father met, as they disbursed in February from communal roosts. His enthusiasm for her was easily discernible in versatile breeding displays, accompanied by a series of three-second pulsing calls, *voo, hoo, hoo, hoo, hoo, hoo.*

In his efforts to excite her, the male makes up for his smaller size by high flying antics. Using oddly exaggerated wing-beats and various maneuvers, he will dive with wings in deep V (dihedral) position, while sashaying (rocking) his body from side-to-side as he loses altitude.

In another aerial display, the male owl climbs with deep beats of his long wings, then plummets toward earth, rapidly clapping his wings together underneath his body before leveling off.

She is won over and lays a clutch of eggs that varies in number according to the availability of prey for food, smaller clutches in lean years. Clutch size averages five to seven eggs, incubated largely by the female while the male hunts.

Short-eared owls nest on the ground in a depression they line with grass. Eggs and young are vulnerable to many predators, from foxes to crows. These owl parents have to be vigilant and are very protective. They will threaten, even feign, injury to draw intruders away from the young.

When all goes well, fuzzy-looking young short-ears hatch after three to four weeks, and grow rapidly. As they grow they beg for food by using calls that sound like *pssss sip* and by wing-flapping. Within two and a half weeks they run as far as 200 meters from the nest, have to be corralled and herded back to the nest area to sleep.

Strong flyers at eight weeks, they remain under parental care, probably for lessons in hunting and other strategies for several weeks more.

Shorty's accident highlights only one kind of hazard facing short-eared owls. Besides road dangers and nest predation, numbers are dwindling from habitat loss and pesticides.

The Hudson Valley Raptor Center reports that short-eared owls are listed as a species of special concern in the state. They are on National Audubon's blue list of declining species. New York's Breeding Bird Atlas confirms some breeding on Long Island, but no longer along the Hudson's shores, though they used to be in Newburgh's Stewart Airport area.

You can visit the Raptor Center on a weekend, see its teaching birds, and learn about those they restore to health and set free. Call the center at (914) 758-6957. For a fee you too can adopt an owl, falcon, hawk, eagle, or vulture, and help with the care and feeding of them all.

With perches placed low to the ground to accommodate her handicap, Shorty shares a a cage with two long-eared owls, Sophie and Lea. She often takes trips to fulfill her obligations as part of the educational team.

Short-eared owl: *12 to 15 inches, 11 to 13 ounces, female the larger. Pale-brown above, dark-brown, boldly-streaked, lighter below. Five blackish-brown bands across tail. Nearly white facial disk obscures true ear openings. Large yellow eyes with black rims. Mobile feather tufts, erroneously call ears, signal owl's intentions, concern about danger.*

THE INDEPENDENT, JULY 21, 1994

"Besides road dangers and nest predation, numbers are dwindling from habitat loss and pesticides."

NATURE'S WAY
My friend Flicker

As a householder recently besieged by carpenter ants, I have extra reason to be thrilled by the call of the flicker and its presence. This bird is a voracious eater of ants.

The Northern Flicker, a member of the woodpecker family that breeds throughout New York State, is a fairly common bird. Even so, it is less common now than in the 1800s, when Thoreau called attention to it.

Starting in early spring, the loud, almost strident call—*wick, wick, wick*—sounds as it flies.

The bird's arrival inspired Henry David Thoreau to write, "how that single note enriches all the woods and fields...this note really quickens what was dead. It seems to put life into withered grass and leaves and bare twigs, and henceforth the days shall not be as they have been."

Flickers share many features with other woodpeckers. They have strong bills capable of hacking out cavities in trees, reinforced skulls to protect brain, eyes, and ears from effects of their heavy blows, and powerful neck muscles that make those blows possible and effective.

Two front and two rear toes clamp evenly to a tree trunk. A stiff wedge-shaped tail props them in place as they work.

But, unlike other woodpeckers, they often feed on the ground, using slightly curved bills to poke into anthills. Their soft, earthy brown colors marked with wavy black lines along the back camouflage them.

To feed, a flicker reaches its prey by extending a sticky three-inch long tongue into the hill. Once the ants swarm over this tongue, they are pulled inside. One flicker's stomach housed 5,000 ants. The total flicker diet includes other insects and, in winter, oily berries like bay, poison ivy, etc.

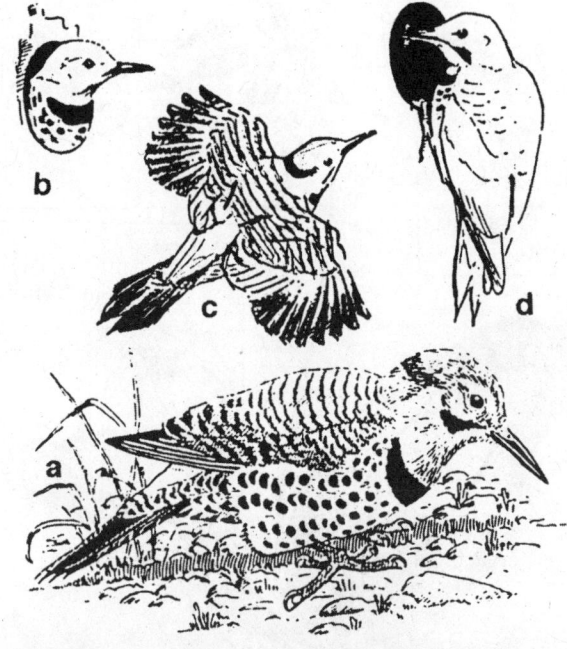

a. Northern Flicker, *colaptes auratus*, 12-13 inches. Brown, black streaked, black neck patch, black tail feathers beyond white rump. Grey head, red crescent on nape. Male has black "mustache." (Eastern version yellow-shafted below wings and tail.)

b. Female oversees view from nest hole.

c. Northern Flicker in flight showing white (identifying) rump patch.

d. Male bringing food for nestlings.

Flickers are found throughout the 49 mainland states, but those east of the Rockies—the Northern Flickers we see—are yellow-shafted, with yellow coloring below the tail and wings that flashes when the birds fly. Western Flickers are red-shafted. Other hemisphere sub-species have variations of these two colors.

Egalitarianism seems the order of the day among flickers. Both sexes use calls and signals and take part in active, dance-like displays that involve head waving, body swinging and bowing. Sometimes the body is twisted as wings are spread and tail waved, and the yellow underwings flash.

Displays are directed at repelling rivals for mates or territory, or they serve to woo and win a mate.

When a rival appears, a female/female or male/male confrontation takes place. Posturing alone may deter a rival, or a brief fight ensues, harmless but effective.

Mates, who return to the same area each year, if possible for life, announce their arrival with a *ke-ke-ke-ke* call, alternating with drumming to announce their presence.

Repeated head-bobbing and *woika-woika* calls provide acknowledgment, yielding to softer *weeta-weeta* calls when mates meet. Sometimes they touch or grab each other's bills.

Seven to nine shiny white eggs are incubated by both parents, each with its own brood patch, a bare space below the breast that makes close skin contact so eggs get maximum body heat. Hatched babies keep parents very busy over 12 days. Each baby is fed by regurgitation, 1.1 times per hour, per nestling.

What important work to raise another generation of elegant battlers against ant overpopulation.

THE INDEPENDENT, JULY 22, 1993

"Egalitarianism seems the order of the day among flickers."

NATURE'S WAY

Ladyslippers in vitro

Mulch was disturbed around a stand of ladyslipper orchids under mixed deciduous trees at Mohonk Preserve. Tracks suggested the presence of a deer, or possibly skunks.

"Deer look for flowers to eat, though blooming is now over. Chipmunks eat the flowers, roots, and rhizomes," said Ilse Biedermann, orchid specialist and preserve research associate, "and skunks pull up such a pile of mulch as this, looking for grubs."

In the dappled June sunlight, she examined each carefully staked and numbered plant, distressed to find two damaged.

"Animal activity is just one cause of orchid loss—and ladyslippers are disappearing at Mohonk."

Paul Huth, research director, explained: "Fifty years ago there were hundreds of ladyslippers in the preserve. We have extensive records of plant numbers, blooms, vigor, and location.

"Loss has accelerated rapidly since the 1970's. On one side of the preserve, for example, in 1967 we counted 177 flowering ladyslippers. By 1983, there was only one plant—and none since.

"We consider ladyslippers endangered at Mohonk, and Mrs. Biedermann is studying the problem. Her experiments include *in vitro* propagation of the plants, for possible reintroduction into the native habitat."

Orchids, numbering around 7,500 species worldwide, grow mostly in the tropics—many as air plants. Northeastern native wild orchids are primarily terrestrial.

The elegant ladyslipper, botanically one of the *cypripedia*, or Slipper of Venus as named by Linnaeus, grows wild in the Northeast, one of 15 species of *cypripedia* from the Arctic Circle to the Carolinas.

A member of the lily family, it has a tripartite arrangement, with three sepals and three petals. One petal is formed into a large, showy bulbous sac.

Reproductive organs carried inside this highly sophisticated structure are normally pollinated by bees.

At the Preserve, Mrs. Biedermann goes from plant to plant inserting a sterilized needle into one flower to retrieve pollen, then placing it in the stigmatic cavity of another. Once pollinated, the flower head withers as the pod grows.

After two months, seed capsules are harvested and sterilized. The tiny seeds, with invisible undeveloped embryos, are placed in a sterile agar gel medium inside stoppered flasks, where water, nutrients, temperature, humidity, and light can be controlled.

Nutrition is complex. Carbohydrates are available from coconut water, containing sugar, vital trace elements, and vitamins.

Unlike other plants that convert starches to sugars themselves, *cypripedia* require help. In the wild, a special mychorrizal fungus, growing like spaghetti around plant roots, performs this function. When this as yet unclassified fungus is absent, plants do not thrive.

In 4 to 7 months of culture, the seed's embryo first sends out a root; leaf shoots come later. After about a year, when baby orchid plants have fully developed root systems and two embryonic leaves, they can be transplanted.

"So far, all transplants die 4 to 5 months after transplanting, for they use up all nutrients already processed and stored during tissue culture," Ilse Biedermann explains.

"The soil where orchids grow at Mohonk has very little mychorrizal fungus that ladyslippers depend on. In the wild, mychorrizae supply many micronutrients, also processing starches, turning them into usable sugars.

"We know from Mohonk weather charts that moisture decreased and temperature increased during the last year, conditions that reduce soil moisture for fungal growth. Changes in acid-alkalinity balance may also act to diminish fungal health.

"Along with this deprivation, other factors, like forest canopy density and changes in human land use may be limiting orchid growth. At Mohonk, we are looking for answers."

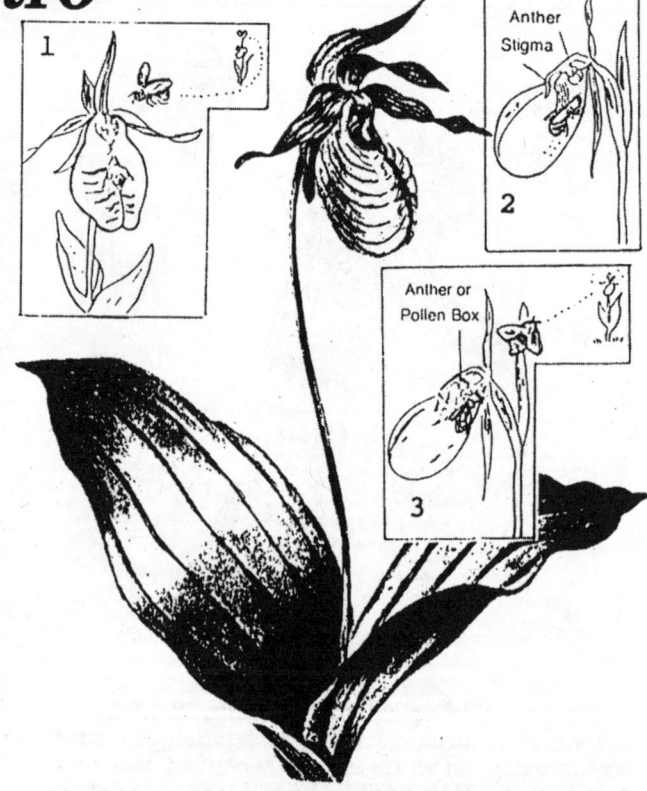

Pink Ladyslipper—1) Attracted by a bright color, bee flies to ladyslipper with pollen grains on back. **2)** Bee falls into cup, drinks nectar, then climbs toward opening at top back of flower. On the way pollen is scraped from bee's back by stigma. **3)** Bee crawls further up, under anther (pollen box) which opens and deposits new load of pollen on bee's back. Bee emerges and flies to next ladyslipper.

THE INDEPENDENT, JULY 23, 1992

"Unlike other plants that convert starches to sugars themselves, cypripedia require help."

NATURE'S WAY

Gentle, helpful—but firm

The scent of skunk that permeates your car on the highway generally elicits a "whew, skunk!" by at least one passenger. Usually the easily-recognizable, cat-sized black-and-white body is nearby, one of thousands killed each year by automobiles.

This non-combative, gentle, slow-moving creature, has met another intractable enemy. But the automobile is wanton, unlike the great-horned owl which makes the skunk its dinner. And that is too bad for this long-time friend of humans whose ecological importance is increasingly understood.

Primarily, the skunk is an eater who travels through woodland, field, and marsh. It's semiplantigrade feet (toes *and* heels on the ground), weight borne by palms and fingers, accounts for the waddling gait, making it slower than animals like fox, deer, and dogs who run on their toes.

In deliberate and thorough fashion it tears apart decaying logs for grubs and beetles with inch-long front claws, tears out nests of young mice and yellow jackets, taking bees as well as larvae. Other larval insects include cutworms that destroy garden plants, grown insect forms like grain-eating grasshoppers and crickets, and other ravenous plant-eating grubs and caterpillars.

Skunks were the first fur-bearing animals protected by law in New York State because they devoured insects destructive to hop plants from which beer is made.

They also like eggs when available—turtle, grouse, and chicken—but secure sheds deter them. Sometimes they are accused of damage done by more aggressive raccoons or foxes who take eggs from nests. Skunks open and lick contents, leaving shells nearby.

Ecologically, skunks do important things: They eat and disburse, through defecation, seeds of berries, wild cherries and plums.

Skunk feasting on turtle eggs.

Their appetite for snapping turtle eggs is an important benefit to duck populations. In one sanctuary, when skunks were removed to protect duck eggs, the snapping turtle population exploded, and gobbled up the ducklings. Skunk *re*population restored the balance.

Its species name—*Mephitis, mephitis*—is redundant, and there is great fascination with its pungent aura.

A powerful sulfur-alcohol compound called ethanethiol, also an ingredient of mustard gas, is the active component of the liquid musk. Produced by two small glands at the base of the tail, each gland has a short nozzle and muscles that can aim and eject a stream or atomized cloud of the oily, strong-smelling liquid 10 to 15 feet. (The skunk itself is a clean animal that usually has no odor about it.) Skunks are trapped for their musk, used as a fixative for perfumes.

The skunk is not eager to discharge its weapon; unless suddenly, seriously threatened, a skunk gives warning.

First, it raises up its fluffed tail. If the threat persists, it stamps its front paws emphatically. If the invader ignores these signals, the skunk swings its rear end around, body in U shape, head and tail facing the target. Tail high, the nozzles protrude. Aiming for the eyes, he lets go. Dogs who get too close may be temporarily blinded. Large quantities of tomato juice neutralize the odor.

Negative effects, like strong musk odor, usually get played up. But the skunk keeps things in perspective, leading a peaceful, industrious life, never attacking, but never accepting abuse.

THE INDEPENDENT, JULY 26, 1990

"Skunks are trapped for their musk, used as a fixative for perfumes."

NATURE'S WAY
Phoebe, phoebe...

In Shakespeare's *As You Like It*, the forest resounds with Silvius' sweet, langorous "fee-bee" as he calls his love's name. That slow high-note/low-note whistle actually mimics the courting song of the chickadee.

Our eastern phoebe—who comes early in March—has an abrupt and peremptory sounding call which puts the early-arriving male in touch with his later-arriving spouse, to whom he shows great devotion. He may repeat her name as often as 20 to 40 times a minute.

Many householders get acquainted with phoebes when the female starts nest building under an eave or on a porch. In open country they build under a bridge or on a rocky ledge. They prefer a horizontal shelf with a protection like a ceiling or other overhang.

Ursula and Peter Marshall of Hillsdale were intrigued when a small grey-brown bird started building a nest on a beam angled 45° upward outside their dining room. Many loads of mud and a great deal of effort were required to fill in this diagonal so that the foundation of the nest would be horizontal.

Once the base was made, weeds, grasses, and other fibers were interwoven in circular fashion and lined with finer grasses, hairs, or feathers. The female, who does all the building, then finished the outside of the nest with delicate mosses, giving it a garlanded look.

The cup is about 2½ inches in diameter, and 1¾ inches deep, big enough to hold the average five eggs and, when they hatch, the five little phoebes of the first, early June, brood. A second clutch of eggs is laid in several weeks.

Mother has incubated the eggs for sixteen days. When she goes off to feed or groom herself, the male phoebe perches nearby. He watches for predators and also cowbirds who often try to lay an egg in the nest. This can destroy a whole brood because the larger fledgling cowbird takes all the food supplied.

Phoebes sit upright near the end of a branch, or on a post or wire, and can be identified by the habit of leisurely wagging their tails downward. They are members of the flycatcher family who consume large quantities of insects—about 90 percent of their diet, the rest being seeds and berries.

When a flying insect is spotted, the flycatcher swoops out and snaps up the bug with a click of its bill. Beaks of these birds are broad, with bristles at the base; these features facilitate aerial capture of insects.

Sixteen flycatcher species are common on the East coast. Most are subdued in color, tending toward greys

Only 5¾ inches long, the Eastern phoebes are unobtrusive in grey-brown coat, darker on the head, white underparts, and black bill.

and browns, with white, and sometimes yellow on the breast or belly.

A brilliant exception is the male vermillion flycatcher. These birds are common in the Southwest, but stray to Louisiana and Florida. Though shaped like our phoebes, vermillions have vivid red coloring on all underparts and on the top of the head. The upper parts, wings, and tail are dusky grey to blackish.

Look around you for the little grey-brown phoebe with its bobbing tail, sitting upright, and flying out to catch as many insects as it can for its own benefit—and ours.

THE INDEPENDENT, JULY 27, 1989

"Phoebes...can be identified by the habit of leisurely wagging their tails downward."

NATURE'S WAY
Estuarine Nursery

The Hudson River National Estuarine Sanctuary and Research Reserve is comprised of four sites and includes over 4,000 acres of prime tidal wetlands and their buffer zones.

Betsy Blair, Reserve manager whose office is at the field station on the Bard Campus, explains that these "sites are set aside as relatively pristine areas for several purposes: research about estuarine life patterns and processes, education about coastal ecosystems, and recreation."

The Saw Kill touches the Hudson at a large area of tidal shallows and reveals an extensive chain of organisms which call the estuary home. A great variety of tiny one-celled plants and animals live there. Interesting worms live underground and eat decaying organic matter by sifting mud through their systems. Others feed by siphoning suspended nutrient material from the water like a vacuum cleaner.

These organisms are bacteria eaters, at the lower end of a food chain that goes way up the line—mollusks, fish, crabs, birds, and mammals. Many tidemarsh creatures are unique to the place, and the documented productivity of the tidemarshes is tremendous.

Underwater plants are also important, providing cover and food for many species. Water celery, pondweeds, watermilfoil, and European water chestnut are some of the vegetation that thrive in the "brackish" water which varies with rapid and wide fluctuations in salinity.

A number of researchers at Tivoli Bays are conducting special projects aimed at filling in pieces of the enormous puzzle still awaiting solution in the estuarine ecology.

Barth Anderson, for example, is exploring the composition and abundance of larval fish communities with special emphasis on the ways in which water chestnut overgrowth affects fish populations. Water chestnut has grown thickly in the shallow tidal areas, choking out other plants, preventing swimming and boating, but the full ecological effect on the tidal community is not yet clearly understood.

It was here I met my first larval fish, collected by Barth and placed in a two-inch vial: The spot tail shiner (¼ inch long) can grow to 6 inches, and the alewife (3/8 inch long) grows to 13 inches or so. Both looked like sperm—with ovate head, two disproportionately large, protruding black eyes, and long tail for speedy swimming.

If these fish grow up—and they may serve the order of things by becoming food for larger species—they frequently serve as bait for fishermen. The alewife a herring, is a popular food fish still being caught in the Hudson.

In exploring his light traps at night, Barth has so far identified nine additional species of forage and game fish that use the water chestnut beds as a nursery.

The banded killefish feeds on zooplankton. It is quite common, grows to about two inches and is used as a bait fish. Killefish can sometimes by seen skittering over the surface of a marsh or mud flat.

The white perch grows to about 8 or 9 inches in this part of the Hudson. It used to be a game fish but is now on the Don't Eat list.

The fearsome-looking fourspine stickleback is a pugnacious, voracious eater too. Aquarium fanciers will remember them because the male builds a nest out of water plants, entices a female to spawn there, and then protects the nest until the eggs hatch 12 days later.

The common carp, which can grow up to 25 pounds in this area, has a long spawning season—from late spring to early August. As water temperature warms, groups of one to three females and two to twelve males swim along in the shallow weedy flats just below the surface.

They are called broadcast spawners. Females thrash as they release their eggs, which then spread and attach to vegetation. Males fertilize these eggs which water-harden in 15 minutes and hatch 55-145 hours later. On-shore watchers are entertained by the carps' great leaps out of the water, a by-product of this crowd activity.

Others in Barth's sample are the red breast sunfish, golden shiner, goldfish, silvery minnow, and inlaid silverside—many used as bait fish.

This is just a small section of the dynamic community Rachael Carson described in *The Edge of the Sea*, "a world that keeps alive the sense of continuing creation and...the relentless drive of life."

Note: Illustrations by Sandra G. Power are from the informative and amusing *Tidemarsh Guide* by Mervin Roberts.

THE INDEPENDENT, JULY 28, 1988

Alewife

White perch

Carp

Stickleback

"The Saw Kill touches the Hudson at a large area of total shallows and reveals an extensive chain of organisms which call the estuary home."

Bees as carpenters

NATURE'S WAY

Marion Dusoir Ennes

SUMMER'S BUZZ AND HUM of bees seem undifferentiated to the human ear, but they include the sounds of many solitary bees. With 3,000 species in North America alone, solitary bees vastly outnumber communal types like honeybees and bumblebees, which only account for about 100 species.

Among the thousands are bees with remarkable skills. Some are masons, other dig underground tunnels and chambers, while some chisel into wood to make nests.

Carpenter bees emerge from hibernation in the warm days of spring, seeking nourishment from the nectar of flowers and the companionship of a mate. Males hover in the vicinity of last year's building sites, sending out a pheromone to entice the female.

The fine sensing devices on female antennae detect the male's sweet perfume from a distance. She is drawn to him and their union consummated.

His job is done, but her labors continue through the summer, for she has the unique skill and determination to make a home for her offspring.

After checking out last year's sites for renovation and finding them occupied, the chubby black-and-yellow mother bee looks for a new location. She chooses dry wood timbers or dead branches of medium-hard yellow pine or cedar in shed rafters, fences and porch rails, or dry tree limbs.

A fence rail attracts her and she starts by boring a circular doorway on the rail's lower side. Using her large, horny mandibles, and working against the grain, she bites out tiny pieces of wood until she has a circular concavity, leaving sawdust and wood pellets below.

In a day or more, a vertical one-inch-long entry is completed. Turning right, she works horizontally (with the grain) to gouge out a foot-long straight cylindrical tube about ½-inch in diameter. One such tunnel reached 16 inches with a 5-inch parallel branch.

When the tunnel is finished, she marks off a section equal to her own length for a single baby's cell.

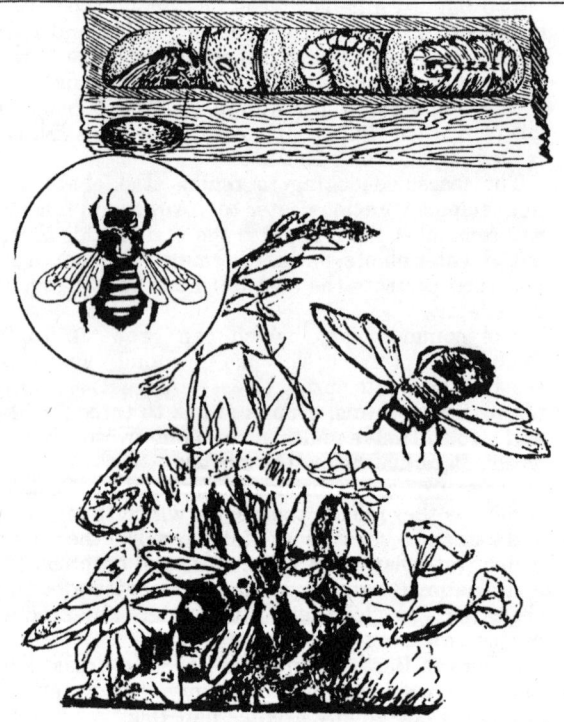

Then, using her mouth and feet, she fabricates a loaf of bee bread—a mixture of collected pollen and nectar—about one-half the cell's size, and lays an egg on top of the loaf.

The individual cell is completed when mother bee seals it. Using sawdust and wood pellets from the excavation, mixed with her glutinous saliva, she forms a fitted circular partition, concave on the cell side and flat on the other, that hardens into a solid composite.

Repeating the process over and over, she nests 12 eggs or more. Eggs hatch and bee bread shrinks as hungry larvae grow larger. At maximum growth the larvae pupates, getting ready for adult life.

The first egg placed inside is the first to become an adult, but it is in a cell at the far end of the tunnel. Now an adult, it has new, strong jaws and uses them to chew through the cell's partition.

Depending on the species, it may wait quietly until the next one hatches, when the mother bee leads them all from the nursery.

In some species—the carpenter bees abound in the world, especially the tropics—young bees will cut the partitions and crawl over other immatures.

After emergence, daughters help mother clean the tunnel, which may be used by a daughter for her first brood.

Many biologists believe that this solitary bee family shows degrees of parental care that ultimately will evolve into more complex social family organization.

Large carpenter bees. *Important temperate zone pollinators. Female above, male below. ¾ to one inch long.*

Female carpenter bee *(inset). Constructs nest and stocks it for developing young.*

Cross-section of nest tunnel *(above). At opening, left, bee sealing off about one-inch chamber with egg and food. Next, larva during growth. Far right, pupa in resting stage.*

THE INDEPENDENT, JULY 31, 1997

"His job is done, but her labors continue through the summer, for she has the unique skill and determination to make a home for her offspring."

NATURE'S WAY

Kernels are fruit

"Hail! Ha-wen-ni-yu! Listen with open ears to the words of thy people. Continue to listen. We thank our mother earth which sustains us. We thank the winds which have banished disease. We thank He-no for rain. We thank the moon and stars which give us light when the sun has gone to rest. We thank the sun for warmth and light by day. Keep us from evil ways that the sun may never hide his face from us for shame and leave us in darkness. We thank thee, oh, mighty Ha-wen-ni-yu that we still live. We thank thee that thou hast made our corn to grow. Thou art our creator and our good ruler, thou canst do no evil. Everything thou doest is for our happiness."

"Thus prayed the Iroquois Indians when the corn had ripened on the hills and valleys of New York State long before it was a state, and even before Columbus had turned his ambitious prows westward in quest of the Indies. Had he found the Indies with their wealth of fabrics and spices, he would have found there nothing so valuable to the world as has proved this golden treasure of ripened corn."

These are opening paragraphs from a "Cornell Nature Study Leaflet" written by Anna Botsford Comstock almost 100 years ago. She goes on to say:

"The origin of Indian corn, or maize, is shrouded in mystery. There is a plant which grows on the tablelands of Mexico which is possibly the original species. But...maize was so long cultivated by American Indians that it was thoroughly domesticated when America was discovered.

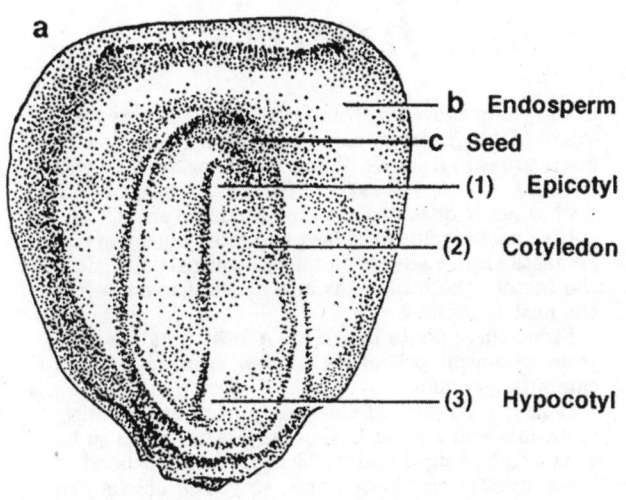

a. Single corn kernel, showing one embryonic plant inside seed. b. **Endosperm**, multicellular tissue containing food supply surrounding seed, pressed close to seed and supplying it with nourishment of starches and proteins. c. Seed in kernel, containing (1) *epicotyl*, precursor of stem of new plant; (2) *cotyledon*, precursor of new plant's leaf structure; and (3) *hypocotyl*, seedling axis that precedes plant's root structure.

"In those early days of American colonization it is doubtful our forefathers could have remained here had it not been for Indian corn. No plowing nor even clearing was necessary for the successful raising of this grain. Trees were girdled, thus killing their tops to let in the sunlight; the rich earth was scratched a little with a primitive tool and the seed put in and covered; the plants that grew therefrom took care of themselves."

At that time European grain staples—rye and wheat—required as much tillage as corn does today—and Comstock believed that pioneers who depended on those grains "might have starved before they had gained a foothold on our forest-covered shores."

Rich kernels containing starches, proteins, and oils nourished them, and still please our palates today. Every kernel is a single fruit with one seed inside. The mature seed contains a well protected, pre-formed plant, waiting for a bed of soil and water to germinate.

Comstock concludes: "It is fitting that a grain which is so peculiarly adapted to be the aid and support of a great civilization should grow upon a plant of such dignity and beauty as the maize.

"The perfect proportions of the slender stalks to the long gracefully curving leaves; the plumed tassels swaying and bowing to every breeze and sending their pollen showers to the waiting skeins of silk hidden below; the ripened ear with its exact rows of shining yellow grains wrapped in silken husks; all these make the corn plant as delightful to the eye as it is intrinsically important to the welfare of nations."

THE INDEPENDENT, AUGUST 1, 1991

"The origin of Indian corn, or maize, is shrouded in mystery."

NATURE'S WAY:
Look Ma, no hands!

The size of a hummingbird's nest is about an inch and 3/4 in diameter, with cup about one inch across and 4/5 of an inch deep.

Some years ago, on a spring-time walk with my four-year-old daughter, we saw a bird fly to a branch with some grass in its beak. When I told her the bird was building a nest, she asked, "How can a bird build a nest when it doesn't have any hands or arms?"

Bird nests include the best and most highly evolved nests known among vertebrate animals. Consider the factors the bird takes into account even before the nest is built.

First, there's site selection. A nest must be safe from potential predators, hidden entirely or in a camouflaged spot.

It has to be located close to appropriate building materials and a good food supply. And it has to be at the right height and in the right neighborhood of trees, bushes, earth, or water, so young chicks can emerge safely and learn their first lessons.

A nest must be size-appropriate, stable, strong, and protected from weather extremes.

Nest linings are thicker in colder climates' there are none in hot climates. The nest must provide sufficient insulation to help maintain the proper incubating temperature for eggs, so parents can save their energy to forage for food.

There should be adequate drainage or a proper roof against rain. The entrance must face away from prevailing winds, and the body constructed so eggs are not damaged by swaying. Materials chosen must be strong, water-resistant, and cushiony enough for the new chicks.

Each bird species builds a particular type of nest, requiring special attributes. Woodpeckers have beaks strong enough to chop holes in trees. Kingfisher's beaks help them dig holes in banks and their feet push out the dirt. Orioles and others that make woven nests of silk and other fibers have fine beaks to help interlace the strands.

The ruby-throated hummingbird flies thousands of miles to the Northeast to raise its young. Smallest of the passerines (or perching birds), it constructs the smallest nest—using plant and animal materials as well as its own saliva.

An inconspicuous place on a twig (at least 10 feet above the ground) is chosen and spread with saliva, which becomes an adhesive wafer to which the nest is glued. The vegetable fibers or cobwebs are laid crosswise on the wafer and coiled clockwise around the twig. Cobwebs are sticky as well as strong.

As the bird flies around, using its bill like a needle, more material is added and a cushion builds up. Loose ends are tucked in and drawn out at the sides as if darned, resulting in a smooth and rounded structure.

The bird then lowers to sit on the cushion and, using her feet, she twists and turns around, bends the edges of the cushion up with her bill and neck until she gets a saucer shape. She then adds more materials, including seeds, plant down, bird scales, hairs until the whole is shaped like a cup.

Then she lies in the center and smooths the edges carefully, using her neck, throat, bill, and wings in a sort of hug. The rim of the nest is curved slightly inward.

This takes about five days and culminates in the laying of two white eggs in the soft bottom.

As a final touch, she decorates and camouflages the outside with bits of lichen tied on with cobwebs, making the nest very hard to find.

The careful consideration, skill and diligence are much to admire—and for the ruby-throated hummingbird, the species' survival depends on these.

THE INDEPENDENT, JUNE 16, 1988

"Bird nests include the best and most highly evolved nests known among vertebrate animals."

Lessons in the wild

NATURE'S WAY

Marion Dusoir Ennes

PEAK TIME FOR BIRDS is now. The outdoors is home to more birds per square foot than at any other time of year. Spring hatchlings have now grown into fledglings—young birds developed enough to make a first flight out of the nest, though they still need parents to survive. Two-thirds of the July-August population are fledglings.

We are most familiar with perching birds and raptors. Known as altricial, they were born naked, blind and helpless, entirely dependent on parental care, needing food and sanitation as nestlings, instruction as fledglings, and protection through their young months.

Fledglings fly as their strength and drive for physical activity grows. Like explosive seeds, they are ready at the slightest stimulus to put the power of air under their wings, to fly several yards or several hundred feet.

Once fledglings are outside, parents lead or lure them to safe hiding places, often as close escorts in shielding flight.

In a pattern observed in other birds, parents pursued a fledgling kingbird on its first flight, flying directly above it until it landed on an exposed branch. Quickly knocking it off this perch into covering foliage, they concealed the conspicuous, vulnerable young offspring.

Now, making the transition to the wide world, life is softened by continuing parental attention. Birds, like humans, are born with certain innate capacities which must be refined and coordinated to survive. Modern research shows that boundaries between instinctive and learned behaviors are not sharp.

Parents of fledglings do much more than follow their calls to feed them. They also instruct in the finding of appropriate, nutritious food.

I watched a lesson in parenting one day at a large wildlife sanctuary that was home to a nesting family of eagles. As I drove along a track running alongside a lagoon surrounded by a hedgerow with a single towering bare tree, an adult eagle flew down and settled on one long empty branch. A dark yearling eagle soon followed and landed in a smaller tree not far away.

I expected the adult to catch a fish to feed the sturdy juvenile. So did the yearling. I watched the adult sitting in a kind of brooding position watching the water.

In the next fifteen minutes the only movement was on the part of the yearling, who changed positions three or four times, once landing precariously on a flexible limb that bounced him into a short flight.

The yearling continued to bounce about, looking at the water more and more often. Twenty more minutes passed, almost twenty-five, before the young eagle suddenly moved. Diving down to the water, it scooped up a sizable fish and flew to a slim bare branch to eat it.

The adult eagle's wings stirred. As the young eagle grasped its prize, the adult raised its wings and soared out of sight.

Fledglings still needing care. Center: Song sparrow offering caterpillar. Insets **Above:** cedar waxwing young getting berry; **Below:** slate-colored junco adult with small worm for eager young.

THE INDEPENDENT, AUGUST 1, 1996

"Like explosive seeds, fledglings are ready at the slightest stimulus to put the power of air under their wings…"

NATURE'S WAY
Painted turtles

An unexpected event for a ridge-dweller like myself is the sight in late spring of a brightly-colored painted turtle, about 5½ inches long, plodding along about half-a-mile from water.

When confronted, the young turtle—older turtles are larger, somewhat paler—came to a standstill, folded the eight cervical vertebrae in its neck into a "U" to retract its head inside the hard shell, pulled in its feet, and sat.

Its journey probably started south at a swampy area, continued across the state road, up a long, steep hill, about a quarter-mile. The nearest northerly water is at least as far over equally difficult terrain.

Turtles sometimes migrate among seasonal ponds, usually looking for a new site near water to dig a nest and lay eggs. Some researchers believe that they locate destination ponds by seeing reflections of them as polarized light in the sky.

Their eyesight is keen; they have good senses of smell and taste. Lacking movable eyelids, they have, instead, protective membranes which cover their eyes from below. Although some seem like amphibians, all turtles are reptiles.

Underwater immersion for long periods is possible because they supplement their lungs by gill-like capabilities in the mouth. When they pull water through their nostrils, oxygen is absorbed within the mouth, and water expelled.

Painted turtle's smooth, oval shell is greenish-black or olive-brown. Carapace (upper shell) edges are ornamented with bright red shapes and black blotches. Black neck, limbs, and tail have greenish-yellow stripes and some scarlet marks. Pastron (lower shell) is pale yellow.

Most often you'll see painted turtles basking at a good-sized pond. When space is limited on a log, tussock, or rock, they pile up two to four deep. The sun's warmth is drawn toward the dark shell to increase body temperature. Digestion improves when stomach temperatures rise.

Painted turtles eat everything; they like moss, algae, grasses, insects, larvae, fish spawn, small mollusks, and will pull apart dead fish or frogs with their claws. Lacking teeth, they use the sharp saw-like edges of their horny jaws to shred food. They do not eat on land, and can only swallow under water.

Painted turtles are strong swimmers, quick and wary. The only way they can protect themselves on land is to retract within their armored shells. When basking, they remain alert, and, if threatened, will slip under water to avoid danger. By using their strong webbed feet, they can swim away or dive to hide in a pond's bottom.

When *Teenage Mutant Ninja Turtles* materialized recently, youngsters started pressuring their parents to buy baby turtles, at costs that reach $100 for safe and proper housing. In times past, baby turtle pets died slow deaths in unnaturally restricted circumstances; small glass bowls with about two inches of water and a rock.

The July 1990 *Audubon* magazine printed a warning from the New York City Turtle and Tortoise Society: "In 1973 it became illegal to sell any turtle under four inches because children were contracting salmonella poisoning from these small turtles. There currently exists an extensive black market in these baby turtles. Society members are positive that sellers do not warn customers that if a turtle is not properly taken care of, it can transmit salmonella bacteria to their children."

Turtles live long lives, currently estimated at about 60 years. So if the painted turtle I saw on migration made it to another pond, it may well survive me as a county resident.

THE INDEPENDENT, AUGUST 2, 1990

"Some researchers believe that they locate destination ponds by seeing reflections of them as polarized light in the sky."

NATURE'S WAY

'A fire of many degrees'

In his short lifetime (1910-1955), Columbia County's distinguished naturalist Alan Devoe lived with and wrote about nature, always generous in sharing his knowledge. His book *This Fascinating Animal World* contains generous answers to queries about animal behavior.

In response to "Do all animals reproduce sexually?" he answers 'yes'—with examples of primal passions elegantly described. Herewith, some excerpts:

"When waxwings are in love, the little birds caress each other tenderly, rub their beaks together after each separation of even a few minutes, and when building up to their final intimacy, often spend long periods side by side on a twig, passing a ripe berry or small fruit back and forth from mouth to mouth."

Egrets perch motionless together for hours, "the female on a twig just below her mate's, her head pressed against his flanks. Every so often, as quiet delight surges into ecstasy, both birds raise their wings, stretch up their long necks, and then with an outburst of love-cries intertwine their necks together.

"The egrets' necks are so long and supple that each of them actually makes a complete turn around the other. The birds are locked together in a true lover's-knot."

"Among mammals the female's role becomes the important one...Female enticement, and intensity of love-making, reach their greatest height in the big cats."

"Then each...takes the fine plumes of the other...in its beak, and nibbles them lovingly, giving each plume a long sliding 'kiss' from its base to its tip. As the egrets' love-play subsides, they untwine their necks and relapse once more into their sharing of a quiet happiness: side by side, always touching one another. The honeymoon of the egrets often lasts as long as four or five days."

"Slowly the female [tiger] walks back and forth before the male. If this lounging provocation does not arouse him she glides closer and pads sinuously in front of him, almost touching his nose each time she goes by. She begins to flick her tail. Now as she passes before him she draws her tail softly, slowly, across his muzzle. She does it again, again, until the growlings start in his great throat.

"She prances lightly away. Now a little wait, while the male stares at her, growling throatily, kneading with his claws. She circles him, rippling her tail down his body, across his muzzle again. She throws herself on her back, four paws in the air, and lies waiting, purring.

"A well-known animal painter who was fortunate enough to see two tigers at their love-making has said that its climax has so furious an intensity that nothing can be seen but a vibrant blur of tawny colors.

"The fire of love burns all through the creation, now bright in passion, now a steady flame of quiet happiness. It is more than just sex. A pair of old apes, long past days of passion, will sit by the hour with their arms around each other, petting, comforting, in the quiet joy of togetherness.

"Love is a fire of many degrees, at which all animals may warm themselves, after their fashions."

Alan Devoe and his wife, Margaret Sheridan Berry, lived at Phudd Hill in Hillsdale, their own 120-acre wildlife sanctuary.

THE INDEPENDENT, AUGUST 9, 1990

"In response to 'Do all animals reproduce sexually?' he answers 'yes'—with examples of primal passions elegantly described."

NATURE'S WAY
Darwin's darling

From June to early October, stands of tall, pink-purple candles brighten roadside ditches, color pond and stream banks, crowd around wet meadows and marshes. Such is the versatility of *purple loosestrife*, which favors moist to wet soil.

Though usually a fresh water plant, it is "common in Hudson River tidal wetlands as far down as Piermont Marsh where salinity reaches one-third or more of seawater strength," says Eric Kiviat, describing this plant's habits.

Mr. Kiviat is director of Hudsonia, Ltd., a non-profit corporation formed to increase scientific understanding of human/environment interaction in the Hudson Valley.

Marked ambivalence stalks *Lythrum salicaria*, invader from the Old World. Two centuries after arriving on these shores, its widespread presence in our country is debated.

Charles Darwin's 1893 book *The Different Forms of Flowers on Plants of the Same Species* recorded his patient researches on genetic variation and gave Lythrum its place in history.

Purple loosestrife is a trimorphic plant; reproductive organs in individual flowers in the heavy clusters show marked variations from one plant to the next.

A female organ (pistil) sends up one style—short, medium, or tall—centered in each flower. Also, in each flower are two sets of three pollen-bearing stamens. When the style is short in a flower, one set of stamens is medium and one high; in other words, whatever the style length, the two stamen sets are of the other two lengths.

Since pollen grains from short stamens are acceptable only to short styles, and so on up, separate plants must interbreed and genetic variation is guaranteed.

Purple loosestrife (3-6 ft.) consists of spiky, herbaceous stalks growing up from a woody root crown; stalks densely covered to tip by reddish-purple flowers. Whorled or opposite lanceolate leaves are spaced below.

Darwin's excitement about the implications of this for his theories is set forth in a letter to Harvard botanist Dr. Asa Gray. He wrote, "I am almost stark staring mad over lythrum. For the love of heaven, have a look at some of your species..."

Cross-pollination of loosestrife is effected by a variety of flies, bees, beetles, moths, and butterflies who appreciate its nectar and pollen. Large tiger swallowtails fly far into the marsh to enjoy a sip.

Its tall, somewhat woody stems support nests for goldfinch, and it is clearly favored as a nesting site by red-winged blackbirds. Loosestrife also feeds and harbors a variety of caterpillars.

Caterpillars of our largest North American silkworm moth, strikingly-colored Cecropia, are found in large populations: bluish-green caterpillars eat leaves, soon pupating inside a large, tough, silk cocoon attached to the stalks.

But other creatures have suffered seriously from this invasion. Muskrats lose food and shelter materials as cattails are crowded out. Nesting marsh birds like the king rail, least bittern, common moorhen, and marsh wren require cattails. American bittern, northern harrier, Virginia rail, and sora prefer it to habitat infringed by loosestrife.

The dense shade of Lythrum is partly responsible for loss of endangered bog turtles, who need protective growth that allows basking. Rare marsh and meadow plants are also lost to shade.

Mr. Kiviat observes: "Flower enthusiasts, apiarists, moth and butterfly lovers, and goldfinch fans may hail the conquest of the New World by purple loosestrife. Managers of wetland reserves for diminishing populations of muskrats, ducks, marsh birds, and bog turtles feel differently."

THE INDEPENDENT, AUGUST 16, 1990

"Two centuries after arriving on these shores, its widespread presence in our country is debated."

NATURE'S WAY:
Bat myths

Recent reports about bats with rabies have put the Health Department on the case, so there is no need for bat vigilantism. On the contrary, with all the myths circulating about this mammal it is time to set the record straight.

Although bats do get the rabies virus, they do not become silent carriers (without exhibiting symptoms). If a bat gets rabies, it gets sick and dies.

Among wildlife, in one report they were far behind skunks in carrying the virus. Of 7,213 animals confirmed for rabies in 1981, 4,480 were skunks, 1,089 were *domestic* animals, and 858 were bats. The estimated rate is between 0.1% and 0.3% for all bats.

Bats have puzzled humans at least since Aristotle, who understood some of their anatomy. They are now recognized in their own mammalian order, named *Chiroptera* from the Greek *cheir* for hand, and *pteron* for wing.

Perhaps it is their centuries-old reputation for being "enigmatic" and "weird-like" that has helped to sustain so many exaggerated stories and untrue reports about them.

Bats are not blind. They are not members of the order of rodents—are not "mice with wings". They are not birds, nor do they get into people's hair. They are not aggressive toward humans and only one species, Keen's bat, is known to bite—when it has been provoked.

Like all bats, the big brown flies on wide membranous wings. The structure that holds these wings consists of the equivalent of our hand, with four greatly elongated fingers. A thin, flexible, leathery skin spreads out from the sides of the body across the "fingers", and, at the rear, across the hind legs and tail. The knees of the back legs project backward, helping to support the membrane.

The chest muscles are strong for flying—the toes of the hind legs are fitted with claws for clinging. When a bat reaches a roost, it secures itself by means of these claws, hanging upside down. When it folds up its wings, it becomes a neat little pendulous bundle.

The four-inch-long native big brown bat is familiar to us as the house bat. If it cannot find shelter in an old barn or other nook or cranny for its daytime sleep, it may live under loose tree bark or in a cave.

For decades, naturalists puzzled about how bats could fly at night without bumping into things. By the 1940s, their ultrasonic abilities were discovered.

While it flies—with its mouth open—the bat sends out a high pressure, high frequency sound wave which bounces back to it from distances of one to six yards. The bat's large ears then pick up the echo from a flying insect, and the bat quickly swerves to devour it. If there's not enough time to catch the insect in its mouth, the bat will swoop it up in its wings, then, into the mouth.

Using these sophisticated techniques, this acrobatic flyer can consume up to 500 mosquitoes per hour—probably more effectively than an indiscriminate electric zapper, which kills bees and other insects useful to humans.

And, if you are fortunate enough to have a bat or two in your attic, you can harvest their guano on black plastic bags. It is a rich fertilizer for your garden, and an extra gift from our friends, the bats.

THE INDEPENDENT, AUGUST 17, 1989

"Using these sophisticated techniques, this acrobatic flyer can consume up to 500 mosquitoes per hour…"

NATURE'S WAY
Flying squirrels

When night settles in under the canopy of a well-established forest and most woodland denizens have gone to sleep, tiny flying squirrels wake to activity.

Although they favor sites fairly close to water in oak-hickory forests, both northern and southern flying squirrels are wide-ranging over New York.

This was news to me, a New York resident for most of my life. I never learned about this "phantom of the night" until now.

As part of my research, I called Peg Hunt, who is not only Hillsdale's town historian, but also a knowledgeable wildlife observer, and squirrel aficionado; we often speak of red squirrel antics and other natural phenomena.

As she is transplanting to central New York, this column is by way of a fond farewell—not goodbye—to Peg.

Unlike raccoons, 'possums, and foxes, flying squirrels are strictly nocturnal and, in the U.S., the only flying mammals.

In 1624 Captain John Smith described the southern species in his *History of Virginia*. Its Indian name was Assapanick, recognized as a flying squirrel, seen to fly 30 to 40 yards. This figure is confirmed today as an accurate measure.

Glaucomys (its scientific name)—the "silver-gray mouse that flys"—remains active all year, preferring to snuggle together with relatives and friends in cold periods, rather than hibernate.

This keeps them busy storing hickory nuts and acorns in the warmer seasons.

One naturalist who kept a squirrel as a pet, actually counted nut-storing capability. He found that between September and January, a single squirrel could store 200 nuts a night for 10,000 to 12,000 a season—probably many more than they could eat. Nuts are stored in holes, in limb forks, and in leaf litter.

Flying squirrels live together in tree cavities, often woodpecker holes, which they line with bark shreds, moss, dry leaves, or feathers.

In February, the mother squirrel builds a separate birthing and nesting chamber where she raises two to six young, born naked and helpless.

During the two months of early growth, she keeps all adult males away from the nest lest the young be mistaken for baby birds, occasional treats.

Sixty-eight days after birth they meet papa, touching noses and sniffing each other all over to get acquainted.

In contact with each other, flying squirrels are playful, chase one another and bother mother when she eats. They issue low chuck-chucks when contented, sharp notes or squeals when displeased, and loud barks when frightened.

Flying squirrels' aerial ability—properly called gliding or volplaning—is innate. They are born with a transparent version of the membrane extending from hind to foreleg. This develops into a furry flair of skin that spreads as they stretch all four legs.

Starting from a tree branch 60 or more feet above ground, the squirrel scans the territory below, leaning from side to side and scouring the dim light with its shoe-button eyes as if making visual measurements.

Then, bunching all four feet together, it leaps into the air, spreading its legs wide so air is caught under the almost 50 square inches of skin surface.

The flight angle is 40° to 50°, and the squirrel may change course to avoid branches or trees by adjusting its limbs or tail.

In anticipation of landing, the tail is raised and the squirrel sweeps up slightly, landing hind feet first to absorb landing shock.

In this way it can travel downward from tree to ground 150-200 feet, to branch or earth below. It can cover 75 feet in 12 seconds by long leaps over the ground, or clamber up a nearby tree for another glide.

Flying squirrels—two similiar species; body and flattened tail grayish-brown above, light below. Northern—larger, 6-1/2 inch body, 5-1/2 inch tail; 3-1/2 ounces. Range, from Tennessee mountains up into Canada, across to California. Southern—8-10 inches overall, including 4-inch tail, up to 2-1/2 ounces. Range, eastern states below northern New England.

THE INDEPENDENT, AUGUST 20, 1992

"Unlike raccoons, 'possums, and foxes, flying squirrels are strictly nocturnal and, in the U.S., the only flying mammals."

NATURE'S WAY
Chicken Talk

"How do you ask an intelligent question of a bird if it doesn't share your language?" asks Dr. Gregory Ball, a behavioral biologist. Part of the fun and challenge to scientists at the Rockefeller University Field Research Center for Ecology and Ethology in Dutchess County is to devise ways to get answers, then to discern what the answers mean and where they lead.

Scientists there are using audio tapes so the birds can hear and respond to calls or songs, mechanical displays that can be manipulated to create simulations of living objects, sonograms to analyze birds' voiced patterns, TV monitors which present other birds under controlled conditions, and more. All this is in the scientific tradition which gets some questions answered—and more fascinating questions raised.

Dr. Christopher Evans, another post-doctoral biologist, is interested in animal communication, the structure of animal sounds, as well as parallels between those sounds and human speech.

At the center he works with golden seabright chickens, a variety native to Pakistan and India, considered progenitors of our common chicken varieties. These birds travel in small flocks consisting of several males and many females.

Early work in animal communication, with vervet monkeys, revealed some startling results. It showed that cries of monkeys were more subtle and specific than people ever imagined.

These monkeys had different alarm calls for different types of predators. Each call had a *meaning*—one for snakes, one for hawks, one for leopards. Tests of individual monkeys (separated from others to be sure they were not imitating) confirmed the reactions. When the snake warning was given, monkeys searched below; at the hawk warning, they looked up, etc.

"Can the humble chicken, often considered stupid and with its small brain," asked Dr. Evans, "make such fine distinctions? And can that be confirmed?"

Conventional scientific belief held that the sounds chickens make are merely reflexive, sort of like the human "ouch" when a toe is stubbed.

Dr. Evans set up a plywood chamber, placed a male chicken in a wire cage with microphones to pick up its vocalizations, and a video monitor in which various stimuli, chickens or other species, were presented.

Overhead were several fishing lines, with pulleys, with balsawood hawk models of different sizes and shapes attached. These were released to fly overhead, manipulated as to size, speed and direction so the birds below did not get bored and pay no attention.

When the television screen is activated a seabright hen is shown about 90% size, walking around and vocalizing. This is about as effective for the scientist in getting a response as if it were a real hen, though it might prove ineffective in studying courting behavior. The male responds to her image by crowing; his tail comes up, and he flaps his wings.

Then, the hawk form is released. The male chicken tilts its head, looks up, then crouches slightly and makes a distinctive, low, slow-onset whistle followed by a kind of slurring gurgle. This brief call is given three times. (When a bob white is on the monitor, and the hawk figure released, the male chicken gives no alarm call.)

The significant thing is that the sound is *never* made in any other circumstance. In real life, the other birds in the flock freeze, then look up for hawk. When it is spotted, they disburse to hiding in tall grass or other cover.

As yet, there is no clear indication that male chickens will call more loudly when a hawk is close, although there is a suggestion that the call may vary slightly according to the predator's height.

Speculation is that the call is not a loud one because the aim is to warn the nearby flock without letting the hawk notice any chicken's location. In the wild, a faint sound like this would be sufficient warning.

In contrast, the warning signal for a ground predator—man, raccoon, dog for example—is very loud.

THE INDEPENDENT, AUGUST 25, 1988

SNAKE

HAWK

"'can the humble chicken, often considered stupid and with its small brain,' asked Dr. Evans, 'make such fine distinctions?"

NATURE'S WAY

Wonders worth saving

"Swamps, once regarded as foreboding, dangerous places, have gained new respect. Along with ponds, bogs, marshes, mudflats, and wet meadows—all now called 'wetlands'—these are considered precious ecological resources. The benefits are enormous."

Anita Cartin of Chatham, executive vice president of the New York Association of Conservation Districts, made this observation after returning from the association's annual Northeastern Regional Conference. This conference put her in touch with representatives of New England states all the way down through West Virginia and Maryland.

Wetlands was a conference highlight.

"Wetlands slow down fast-moving water," says Mrs. Cartin. "Acting like a sponge, absorbing large quantities of water, wetlands blunt the force of major storms. Along shorelines, wetland vegetation slows water currents and buffers against erosion.

"Water purification is another function of wetlands. They break down nitrates and other chemicals and keep them from entering groundwater. Wetland plants filter out silt. Soil erosion means loss of topsoil, loss of farmland as well as prime building land.

"Wetlands are habitats for many wildlife species, including a wide variety of song and water birds, small mammals, fish, amphibians, and insects. At least a third of the nation's threatened or endangered species find food or shelter in wetlands.

"In the past two decades, 100 million acres have been lost to development and other programs. More than half of the wetlands in the U.S. have been lost since colonial days. These losses, along with drought conditions of re-

Wetlands, once known as bogs, swamps and other names that produce a foreboding sense, provide shelter for wildlife and regulatory nightmares for town planners.

cent years, have resulted in erosion, acceleration of groundwater contamination, and declines in waterfowl."

President George Bush has affirmed his commitment to "no net loss of wetlands," says Mrs. Cartin. The question, she adds, is what this will mean, how it will be interpreted in government regulations.

"While awareness of the value of wetlands has become heightened, concern about the impact of wetlands regulations has reached nightmare proportions for town planners, farmers, and others who deal with restructuring of the land," says the former chairman of the Columbia County Environmental Management Council.

"Red-tape and frustration abound while talking with the various state and federal officials on just the simple question: 'What is a wetland?' "

At long last the "Federal Wetland Delineation Manual" was released August 9. Mrs. Cartin says she eagerly awaits publication for public comment in the *Federal Register* to see what the parameters will be in efforts to save wetlands.

As of now, she says, "The U.S. Fish & Wildlife Service is looking for landowners interested in having former wetlands restored. Potential sites will be evaluated by the service at the request of the landowner.

"In turn, the landowner is asked to sign an agreement not to drain or alter the wetland for 10 years.

"Landowners may also be eligible for tax relief for lands taken out of production for conservation. For more information about this program, call (607) 753-9334.

"In addition, of course, we have our own district conservationist, James Calhoun, a federal employee who heads up an important resource in Columbia County. The staff of the Soil and Water Conservation District & Soil Conservation Service can respond to questions about wetlands, 828-4386."

THE INDEPENDENT, AUGUST 29, 1991

*"'Acting like a sponge, absorbing large quantities of water,
wetlands blunt the force of major storms.'"*

NATURE'S WAY: Corn is grass

We walk barefoot in it, sow it, mow it, or pull it up as a weed. But considering its vital importance to all creatures, especially humans, grass is ignored for itself.

My perception of grass was enlarged when my older sister wrote these words from Walt Whitman's "Song of Myself" in my autograph book:

"A child said *what is grass?* fetching it to me with full hands,
How could I answer the child? I do not know what it is anymore than he."

Grasses, found all over the world, cover about one-third of its surface. The fact that grass subsists on great prairies where trees do not grow is still a subject of serious study.

The growth area of a grass plant is not at the tip but at the base of the leaf or shoot. That means it can grow back whether it is burned, grazed, or cut.

During short spurts of growth, perennial grasses send out side shoots directly from their base, or through rhizomes. These help create a densely matted plant, discouraging other plant growth and binding the soil to prevent erosion.

These grass tops dry out or die at the end of the season, but their roots survive. Ninety percent of a grass plant's weight is in its efficient roots, where it concentrates starch and energy and keeps water loss to a minimum.

Grass plants have common characteristics which distinguish them from sedges and rushes, which resemble them. They can grow in dry or moist places, from a few inches to nine feet in height.

Generally, the stem is round and hollow, except at the joint, a visible bulge where the leaf is attached. Long narrow leaves wrap around the stem at the base and have parallel, vertical veins to carry moisture from the soil. Grasses reproduce with the help of an almost ephemeral, inconspicuous flower.

Though the plant seems to consist mostly of leaves, what we usually notice most is the fruiting head. In fields and along roadsides, clusters of these plumes in muted tones of pale green and purple nod silkily in slight breezes. Some may dry to golden tans and browns that soften the cold of winter white.

Annual plants of the *Gramineae* (grass) family—from which the word "grain" derives—have been cultivated for centuries as wheat, rye, oats, barley, rice, and, of course, corn which was as satisfying and sweet to native Americans as it is to us these last several weeks.

And even if you eat only one ear, consider the enormous number of fruits you consume—for each kernel is an individual fruit!

Corn, with wide leaves and fat stem, needs heat and humidity for successful growth. Corn, *like all grasses*, has great water-lifting capacity. In one short growth season a single cornstalk will lift 440 pounds of water, enough to create a five-foot deep lake in a cornfield, if the water remained on the ground instead of evaporating into the air.

"The fact that grass subsists on great prairies where trees do not grow is still a subject of serious study."

THE INDEPENDENT, AUGUST 31, 1989

Reviving the American chestnut

NATURE'S WAY

Marion Dusoir Ennes

ALMOST A CENTURY HAS PASSED since the first American chestnut succumbed to chestnut blight, but efforts to save this magnificent tree are livelier than ever and hopes are higher.

Settlers found these trees in abundance. Every fourth Appalachian tree was a chestnut, some 100 feet tall with trunks 10 to 12 feet in diameter. Taller and sturdier than the European species, the American variety offered a bountiful crop of delicious nourishing nut meats.

They were a mainstay for Native Americans and archeological sites record their use at least 3,000 years before Christ. Bumper crops fed generations of wild turkey, deer, squirrels and bear.

These "sweeter than European" chestnuts, roasted over winter fires, were enjoyed by colonists and carted to Eastern city markets for sale.

Farmers of the 18th and 19th centuries fattened their hogs, turning them out to gorge on the superabundant harvest under yellow-leaved autumn trees. As much valued for its shade as its fruit, the tree was carried west by pioneers, and planted in prairie dooryards.

Growing tall and straight from long taproots, mature trees yielded a wood with straight grain that split and worked easily, making it perfect for split rail fences, railroad ties and telegraph poles. This weather-resistant wood was used to build sturdy cabins, cradles and coffins. Moonshiners liked the logs because they produced a hot, smokeless, therefore undetectable, flame.

In 1905 at the Bronx Zoo the orange blush of a parasitic fungus introduced from Asia was discovered on an American chestnut tree. Carried on the wind, sometimes by bird or insect, the fungal spores invade the tree from a break in the bark. Here the canker fans out in threadlike filaments, attacking the tree's vital inner cambial layer.

In growing trees, the vascular cambium is where new tree cells develop that distribute nutrients—oxygen, sugars, minerals, water—from stems to roots and reverse throughout the tree. Once the fungus encircles the tree it chokes off this vital circulatory process and the tree begins to die.

During our century this unstoppable disease spread rapidly up the Hudson into New England, south into the Appalachians, and west where it is now attacking trees in Oregon.

From the start, government and private organizations tried to fight the American chestnut's destruction. In 1912, Pennsylvania's governor convened a commission "to repel the invader using every means known to science and practical experience." Early efforts included building mile-wide firebreaks to prevent its spread, cutting and burying affected trees, but to no avail.

By mid-century, scientists from here and abroad (the blight also affected European trees) experimented with hypovirulence. Cultures made from healing cankers on European trees were applied to blighted trees, slowly killing the virulent cankers and giving trees an opportunity to build healing tissue.

European chestnuts improved, but here the process was slowed by more than 100 virulent fungal strains, many not responding to hypovirulent intervention.

As efforts to find a hypovirulent key progress, three other techniques, are being investigated. Irradiated chestnut seeds are being cultivated to find a disease-resistant strain. Searches also are under way for standing chestnut trees that have developed resistance to the disease.

And efforts are being made to breed the blight-resistance of Chinese chestnuts into American trees. First cross-bred, hybrids are then back-crossed into American trees and may some day preserve chestnuts with 15/16th the generic inheritance of their grand and glorious forbears.

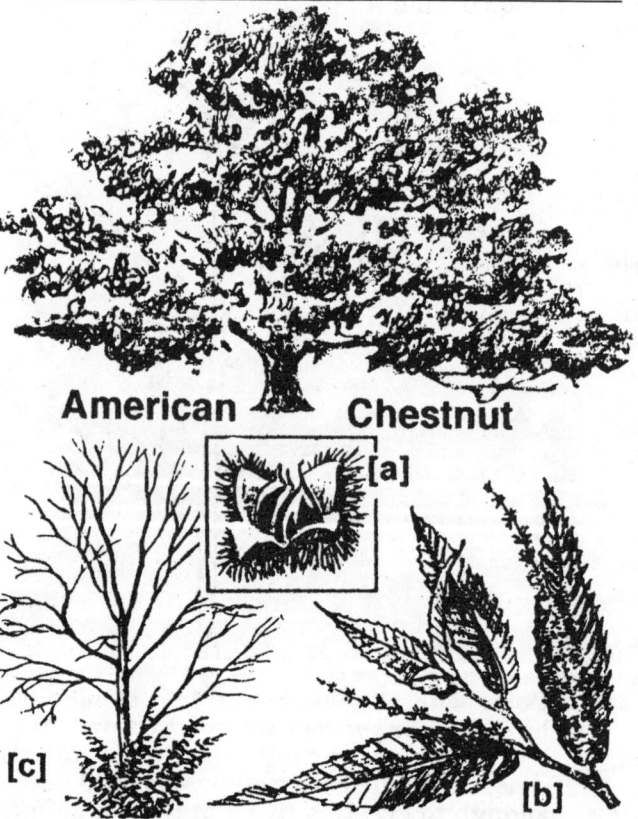

American Chestnut

AMERICAN CHESTNUT *Height and crown diameter each up to 100+ feet. Smooth young dark brown bark matures to broad, flattened, scaly ridges.*

A. Prickly bur, 2 ½ inches, opens to two or three flattened 1-inch tasty nuts.

B. Oblong, sharply-dented leaves 5 to 8 inches long, 2 inches wide, dark green above, paler below. Fragrant flowers, slender, arching from leaf axils.

C. Blight-afflicted tree stands bare, apparently dead except for persistently growing stump sprouts.

THE INDEPENDENT, AUGUST 31, 1995

"They were the mainstay for Native Americans and archeological sites record their use at least 3,000 years before Christ."

NATURE'S WAY
Fruiting bodies

The heavy August rains that seemed so oppressive to us were a great boon to the ubiquitous fungal kingdom. It made possible the emergence of those important fruiting bodies, the mushrooms. On my own grounds I found great variety and quantity, more than a dozen species in many colors, sizes, and shapes.

The evergrowing main structure of fungi is a fibrous mass (mycelium) that thrives underground in meadows and woodlands.

For months or years, fine hairlike threads (hyphae) push through soil to draw nourishment from decaying carboniferus and nitrogenous materials. During growth, these nutrients are converted to cell cytoplasm, nuclei, and the walls that hold them, or stored as sugars, fat, and glycogen—literally, for a rainy day.

This nourishment also produces plus and minus sexual cells that meet, pair, and begin cell division processes of reproduction. This happens at several knobs or tangles in the mycelial network.

Finally—and all this takes considerable developmental time—a compact fungal mass called a button is formed. When the right temperature combines with good heavy rain, the button grows up through the soil, already differentiated to become the mushroom cap, spore plates, and stem, according to its species form.

Mycologists are trying to discover the mechanisms that switch the fungal mycelial focus from loose to firm structuring. Underground, the vegetative pattern spreads threads (hyphae) apart in search of nutrients; above ground the reproductive pattern consolidates threads to build a solid, fruiting body.

My mushroom sortie was exciting when I spotted the round bud of an emerging *Amanita muscaria* on the lawn near some birches, within 10 feet of my front door.

It looked like a creamy knob, about an inch in diameter, wtih orange-yellow top spotted with creamy warts. In the moist weather the stalk stretched tall quickly; dry weather slows growth rates. In seven days,

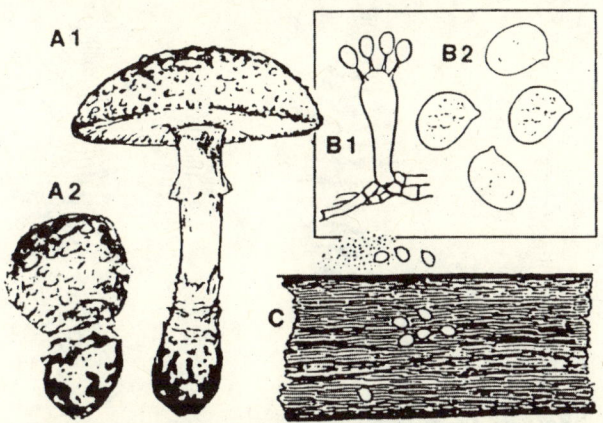

A. Amanita muscaria [1] emerging, [2] mature. B. [1] Club-shaped basidum attached to plates within amanita gills. [2] Spores with nuclei (enlarged). C. Spores compared to human hair (shaft) below, and microscopic bacteria (dots) above.

it was nine inches high, and the elegant domed cap seven and one half inches across at maturity.

Soon the cap flattened. Then edges pulled up. It formed a saucer balanced on the very slender-appearing stem. The white gills, now clearly visible, stretched until the remaining spores could be freed. The structure took on the aspect of winged victory.

Most amanitas, or "death caps," including muscaria, are poisonous. Muscaria, also called fly agaric, contains the active principle muscarin, which is used in small quantities as a ritual hallucinogenic. Years ago it soaked in water with sugar for fly poison.

With their typical mushroom form, amanitas carry their spores inside gills, a structure that looks like a delicate, shalow, circular accordion folder. Fleshy mushrooms of other shapes—cups, clubs, puffballs, and others—have different arrangements for holding spore plates, but all have spore-carrying organs called basidia.

A single basidium looks like a club. Four delicate prongs protrude from each basilium's blunt apex, each prong holding a single, nearly microscopic spore.

This whole crowded structure is covered with a delicate membrane. As the mushroom grows, the membrane breaks, exposing basidia to the atmosphere, and the tiny ballistospores are literally shot into the air.

They travel in air or water, above or underground, or are transported by animals. Some few of the billions released by one mushroom will find a suitable spot and grow, putting out one single hypha that starts a new mycelium.

THE INDEPENDENT, SEPTEMBER 3, 1992

"Mycologists are trying to discover the mechanisms that switch the fungal mycelial focus from loose to firm structuring."

NATURE'S WAY

Finding fifteen ferns

Ten years of independent study have afforded tremendous satisfaction for Roland Drowne of Old Chatham, who modestly describes himself as a well-informed amateur on the subject of ferns.

Intrigued by the elegant leaf-forms of these non-flowering plants, he searches for and identifies them.

Mr. Drowne is a long-time member and officer of the Alan Devoe Bird Club. This summer he led a group of nine on a fern-walk through the club's Powell Wildlife Sanctuary, Old Chatham.

He has generously allowed me to quote his report from the September issue of "The Warbler," the club's newsletter.

Ferns are usually lacy and can be described according to the way the leafy parts divide. Though a few ferns are undivided, most are either

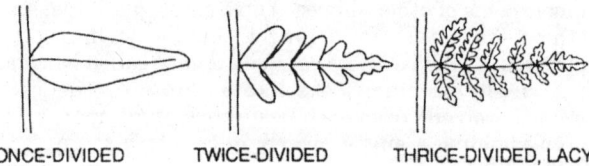

ONCE-DIVIDED   TWICE-DIVIDED   THRICE-DIVIDED, LACY

At the start of the walk, Mr. Drowne explained this aspect of fern morphology so that everyone could participate in identification.

Walkers noticed a large, delicately cut **Lady Fern**, a thrice-cut, vigorous, showy, common fern. Ahead were many large-leafed plants, **Sensitive Fern**, once-cut with a fertile spore case separate from the sterile fond.

"We soon located a scattering of **Christmas, Marginalis,** and **Spinulose Wood** ferns, once, twice, and thrice-cut respectively.

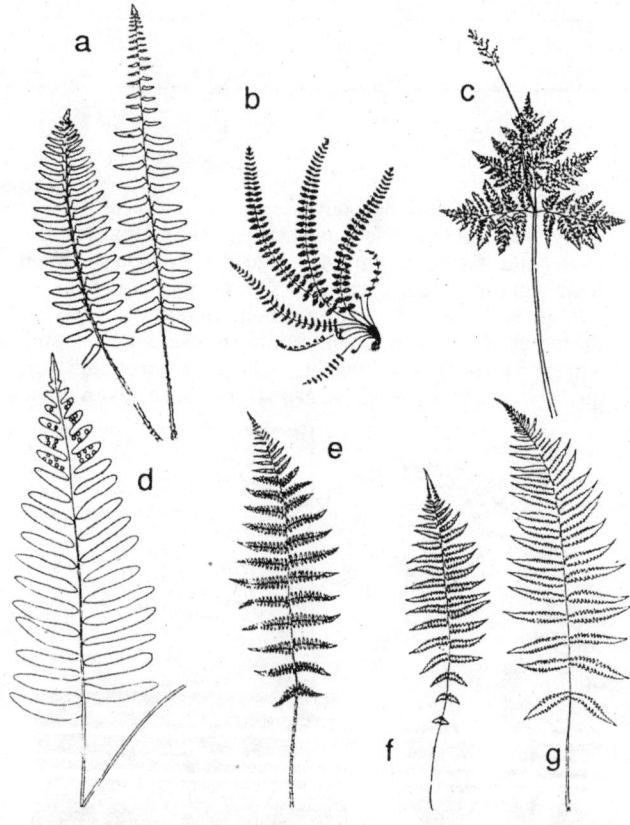

"Back on the trail we came across a 25 to 30-square-foot stand of fern. Key characteristics of ferns were studied at length. Of similiar height, both were twice-cut, one semi-tapered to the base, the other was very tapered at the base.

"Fronds were delicate and lance-shaped, with smooth, slender stalks, but fruit dots on the underside of the fronds were different. The semi-tapered was **Massachusetts**: the very tapered, **New York**, a species we had hoped for.

"A beautiful stand of 18"-high, lighter green fern—delicate, thrice-cut lance-shaped fronds with shiny, brittle chestnut-colored stalks—were indeed **Hay-scented Ferns**.

"Another Lady Fern over the knoll, slightly different from previously-identified one, had a distinctive wine-colored stem known as *Rubellum*.

"We spotted two rather common varieties: small, evergreen **Poly Pody** growing happily atop a rock outcropping; then two-foot plants with broadly triangular leaves, thrice-cut, coarse, leathery **Bracken**.

"Unable to find any **Grape Fern**, we hiked to Dorson's Rock to enjoy **Maidenhair Spleenwort's** delicate beauty. One of the prettiest and daintist of ferns, it survives in rough territory.

"Clinging to the sheer face of the cliff with roots anchored in a small crack, this fern forms dense rosettes about five inches long.

"Sterile fronds usually lay flat against the surface; fertile fronds are more erect. Tiny leaflets are about ¼"-long, usually round or oblong, dark green and evergreen. Everyone who braved the arduous climb down the cliff felt it was a most rewarding venture.

"Leaving Dorson's Rock we found three species in a large patch. **Ebony Spleenwort** may grow to 12" in tapering semi and evergreen fronds. Leaflets are alternate, narrow, oblong, and pointed, once-cut.

"**Rattlesnake Fern**, a succulent of the Grape Fern family, is lacy-cut, bright green, triangle-shaped, and horizonal in form. The erect, fertile stalk grows from the juncture of leaf and main stalk, usually equal in length to main stalk from leaf juncture.

"Last identified was the **Fragile Fern**, a small, bright green, thrice-cut fern with a slender, brittle, brown stalk. Fronds are lance-shaped up to 10" in length, rusty brown during dry spells."

For further study, Mr. Drowne recommends the *Field Guide to Ferns* by Boughton Cobb.

THE INDEPENDENT, SEPTEMBER 12, 1991

"Ferns are usually lacy and can be described according to the way the leafy parts divide."

NATURE'S WAY: Cattail bounty

Plants with brown flowers are not common, but the members of the cattail family make up for the shortage of this color among blooms by producing so many of them.

Cattails, called emergent plants, grow four to eight feet tall, and root under water in marshy areas. Each tall stalk is topped by a brown cylinder often described as looking like a sausage or cigar. This fertilized flower spike remains from the combination flower which appeared in June and bloomed in July.

Broad-leaved cattail flower spikes have a lower female (pistillate) section, crammed with flowerets, waiting to be fertilized by pollen liberated from male (staminate) flowers. Fluffy male flowers grow directly above the female inflorescence. After pollination by the wind, male flowers dry up and disappear. One fruit grows in each fertilized flower.

When I was a child, we broke the stalks and lit the fully mature and spongy fruited cattails for use as punks on mid-September evenings. The aroma was pleasant, and we believed it kept away mosquitoes.

Various parts of the cattail were valuable food sources to Native Americans. The chestnut brown head, which turns into tan, downy cottonwool when the millions of mature fruits are released, was used as absorbent material in baby carriers, or wrapped around a baby's feet in cold weather. Indians also made the long pale leaves into twine, using it for weaving mats and baskets, or patching canoes.

About 25 years ago the federal government sponsored studies to develop delectable foods from various parts of the cattail plant. An article in *The Country Journal* in February 1976 by William Walker describes potential uses.

Cattail plants spread by putting out rhizomes as well as by seeding. Young sprouts growing up through the water to 18 inches in spring can be harvested and cut, eaten raw, or boiled like green beans.

In late May, a golden yellow inverted cone, the male flower, can be cut off, husked and cooked like corn.

If this 'cob' is saved, it will become a narrow tassel full of pollen grains, which can be collected by shaking into a plastic bag. The pollen flour from two dozen plants, says Mr. Walker, makes delicious muffins or pancakes.

The extensive underwater rhizome field can also be harvested—with a potato rake. The rhizome's spongy outer section is cut away and discarded, the core sliced, dried and ground and sifted to remove fibres. The resulting flour is rich in carbohydrates, protein, fat, and minerals.

A one-acre plot, efficiently managed, produces 30 tons of flour per year, at least 30 times more than a midwestern wheat field.

Even without human demands this plant is at the center of its own ecological community. Its population of insects includes aphids that feed on the leaf surface and leaf miners that tunnel through. Larvae of snout beetles feed on the starchy core of the root and stalk.

In summer, the cattail moth lays its eggs in the lower half of the fruiting spike. A silken net is spun around the cylinder by the emerging larvae, fastening the seeds in place. The flower spikes fluff out from one to three inches, keeping the larvae warm and well-fed all winter.

THE INDEPENDENT, SEPTEMBER 14, 1989

"When I was a child, we broke the stalks and lit the fully mature and spongy fruited cattails for use as punks on mid-September evenings."

Underwater dynamics

NATURE'S WAY

Marion Dusoir Ennes

TERRAINS CHANGE. Hills and their slopes become shallower as silt washes down during heavy rains. Low meadows become wetlands where new communities of plants and animals find a place. And sometimes a pond forms, changing what was once a dynamic meadow—replete with land plants and animals—into a dynamic fresh water habitat.

So it is with the substantial pond that came into existence about a dozen years ago in the low land to the south of Route 23 between Hillsdale and Craryville.

Ducks and geese, herons and egrets have found it. A great array of insects, amphibians and other animals thrive among the roots and stems of sedges and grasses.

Life in inland water bodies—lakes, streams and ponds—is the subject of its own science, called Limnology. A valuable part of ecological studies, limnology is concerned with the interrelationship of plants and animals in fresh water environments.

Ponds are quiet bodies of water, shallow enough to sustain rooted plants. Mud covers the pond bottom and temperature remains fairly uniform as water is heated or cooled gradually by seasonal changes.

The large majority of life forms that call a pond home are as captive to its atmosphere as we are to the earth's. Unlike muskrats, water snakes, turtles and frogs, who can thrive in air as well as water, other creatures are trapped for their entire existence. Fish from minnows to trout, crustaceans, mollusks, hydea and flatworms as well as the aquatic stages of amphibians and insects have no place to go. They depend on the resources of this water environment for oxygen, nourishment and growth.

A few of the true bugs—including water boatmen, aquatic beetles, and backswimmers—live in water for their whole lives. But many other insects are hatched from eggs in water and spend the major growth period of their lives within it.

Those that have a complete four-stage metamorphosis—egg to larva to pupa to adult—can only return to air on the wings of their adult form.

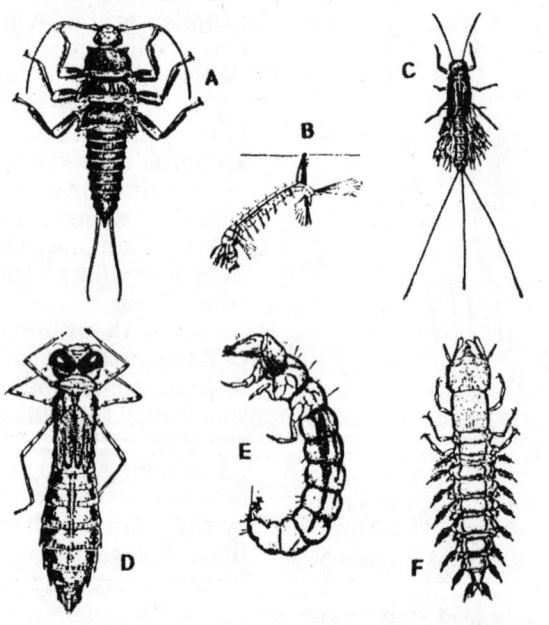

Others, whose metamorphosis is incomplete, grow from egg to a swimming nymph that resembles the flying adult, but spends its time among the stems of waterplants and under rocks and stones, where wings would get in the way.

Not simply fitted out for massive eating like air-breathing caterpillars and larval worms, these underwater larvae have complicated adaptations. Some have tubes to draw air from above the surface. They have elaborate multiple gills, some external, some internal. Some pounce on prey, some fish with nets, and all have their own techniques for rising, sinking and travelling under water.

Six major groups (orders) of insects have specialized larval forms common to fresh water.

Herbivorous orders include stoneflies, mayflies and mosquitoes, whose larvae subsist primarily on various plant materials or dead vegetation. The carnivore orders, with some fierce predatory attackers, include dragonflies, Dobson flies, and Caddis flies.

None of them fly under water, but their highly adapted larvae are functional in the dynamic complex of pond life, along with myriad of other fascinating insect creatures.

HERBIVORES. *Stonefly nymph exists up to three years, reaches one inch. Small mouth, eats fresh and decayed vegetation.*

Mosquito wriggler, 0.2 to 0.5+ inches, exists in this form less than one year. Eats plant material, microbes.

Mayfly larva reaches one inch, one year to adult. Eats vegetation.

CARNIVORES. *Dragonfly nymphs exist 5 months to 5 years, reaches 2½ inches. Eats other larvae including mosquito wrigglers.*

Caddis worm (naked), ¼ to one inch long, exists month to one year. Preys on other aquatic animals.

Dobson fly larva exists up to three years, 2-3 inches full-grown. Fierce predator.

THE INDEPENDENT, SEPTEMBER 15, 1994

"The large majority of life forms that call a pond home are as captive to its atmosphere as we are to the earth's."

Bob—the all-season—Cat

NATURE'S WAY

Marion Dusoir Ennes

ADULT BOBCAT, *28-40 inches long, male 4-6 inches longer than female. Weight: Male 12-48 pounds, average 28 pounds; female 9-34 pounds, average 15 pounds. Coat very soft, short dense fur, buff-colored, darker in winter, spotted or streaked with black, white below.*

Short tail, faint black striping, tip black on top only. Head heavily striped, full mutton-chop whiskers on face, small ear tufts. Backs of ears black with large central white spot. Ears bend forward to create fearful effect of four eyes.

BOBCAT TRACKS *Left, trotting gait stride. Right, walking stride. Rear paws appear ahead of front paws in tracks.*

IF RABBITS are common around a neighborhood, sooner or later a bobcat will notice and help keep the population down. They like our combination of wooded patches, streams, swamps, farmlands, and hilly or mountainous places that provide multiple opportunities for finding food. Somewhere in a large thicket, stump, or cave-like rock ledge, a bobcat has made its unobtrusive home.

Like other members of the cat family, bobcats are agile, curious, clever. They are great climbers and good runners, up to 15 mph. Fantastic stalkers, they can hold a pose motionless for long periods of time, keeping prey from bolting as they measure and calculate terrain, distance, and leap energy needed to make a catch.

Except during early spring mating when adults meet for a brief period, and when the females spend parenting time with their young, bobcats live solitary lives, fending for themselves, noting each other's marks and avoiding one another.

In our corner of New York, a female bobcat defends a range of 5 to 10 square miles, marking its territorial edges with droppings or urine. Normally, feces (or scat) is buried. When left exposed at specific places, it serves as warning to other bobcats to stay away. It also signals her readiness to mate with the local territorial tom.

"One male's territory overlaps a female's two to four times," says Ken Koqut, senior wildlife biologist with the state Department of Environmental Conservation. "Territorial size is directly related to availability of prey for food. In the Adirondacks, where snows are deep and food scarce, one male bobcat can range 80 to 125 square miles and females up to one-fifth that area."

The single litter of two to three babies born last spring is probably still with mother, who is teaching the ways of the wild since weaning them at two months. A dedicated parent, this female carnivore uses her own consummate hunting skill to feed herself and her young.

During their nine to 10-month apprenticeship with her, the curious and adventuresome kits are monitored and protected. She teaches them, by demonstration and example, how to hunt by themselves. Not hibernators, they hunt through all seasons.

Bobcats are endowed with a discriminating sense of smell which augments excellent hearing and sharp vision.

As they generally hunt in the evening or at night, they benefit from the flexibility of the pupils in their eyes. Depending on circumstances, pupils enlarge and/or change shape to admit more light. This helps the bobcat to judge the distance required to effect an accurate pounce.

Once a bobcat spots potential prey, it is at peak attention. Its whole muscular-skeletal system is engaged for careful pursuit.

Body low to the ground, the cat slides forward, keeping its eye focused on its goal. Tension sustains it through long, seemingly interminable waits, until just the right moment.

Then it pounces. Pinning the victim's chest, it braces for struggle by digging its hind claws into the ground.

Now in a state of high excitement, the cat quickly scans the victim's neck, then sinks two fanglike front teeth between two neck vertebrae, bloodlessly snapping its special chord.

Often it carries its dinner back to a safe, familiar resting place or den. Here it uses carefully manicured, razor-sharp talons to rip open the animal's body, eating almost everything, save the head and feet.

THE INDEPENDENT, SEPTEMBER 16, 1993

"Bobcats are endowed with a discriminating sense of smell which augments excellent hearing and sharp vision."

NATURE'S WAY:
Nesting eagles

Bald eagles, young and mature, are flying over the Hudson River once again.

Concern about the possibility of their extinction dates to the start of this century when their decreasing numbers became apparent.

Although they were designated our national symbol in 1792, eagle slaughter by shooting was common. In one report, dating to 1844, between 60 and 70 eagles were shot in Long Island in one season. Later, egg collecting and then pesticide contamination compounded the loss.

By 1976, there appeared to be only one nesting pair of eagles in New York State, and they had not produced a fledgling for several years.

In that year, the Department of Environmental Conservation started its popular bald eagle hacking program. Wild eaglets were captured in Alaska and brought here to be released in the wild (hacked). The goal was to establish 10 nesting pairs by 1990.

This remarkable goal was achieved a year ahead of schedule, according to DEC Commissioner Thomas Jorling. "It took 13 years," he said, "198 eaglets and thousands of hours of effort by our professional staff and hundreds of cooperators. It also took a lot of financial support—nearly half a million dollars—the bulk of which came from the Conservation Fund and federal aid."

The male, and the larger female, similar in marking, are tied to their established territory. They mate exlusively until one dies and another spouse takes its place in the territory.

Mature bald eagles—not bald, but with white-feathered head and tail—build massive nests in the crowns of tall trees, close to the waters where they feed. These nests are added to each year: one reached nine-and-a-half feet wide and twenty feet deep.

The eagles we see in the Hudson nest in the north in March. Although mature birds have a wing span of 6 to 7 feet, their two eggs are less than three inches long.

Both parents incubate the eggs, turning them over as needed. The ungainly baby birds, with large heads, are covered with white down at birth, which changes to woolly brown in the first three weeks and real feathers three weeks later. By the time they are fully feathered—in three months—they are very dark brown and look larger than their parents.

A mature bald eagle weighs 12 pounds and ranges from 35 to 43 inches in height.

The long-term future of eagles in New York rests with these 10 pairs.

"We have reached an important milestone, one that many observers doubted we could attain," said the DEC commissioner. "Our next step is to manage and nurture our growing eagle population. Based on historic records of 70-80 different nesting locations in New York State, our goal is to establish 40-50 nesting pairs by the year 2000."

"One problem we still encounter is the illegal shooting of eagles," he said. "Such indiscriminate killing can have a major impact on our small, growing eagle population. We ask that every New Yorker help us stop these incidents and, if they occur, help to identify the perpetrators."

Persons killing an eagle are subject to fines up to $10,000 and up to two years in jail. Up to $2,500 can be paid to an informant if the person arrested is convicted.

This year DEC wildlife biologists confirmed ten territorial pains for bald eagles in New York, with eight of these pairs attempting to nest. Six pairs successfully produced a record ten young.

The future looks bright now for bald eagles in New York State. Considering the combination of all the young eagles to be fledged by these nesting pairs, as well as 64 hacked eagles that have not reached sexual maturity, things are clearly looking better than they have in many years for our national symbol.

THE INDEPENDENT, SEPTEMBER 21, 1989

"These nests are added to each year: one reached nine-and-a-half feet wide and twenty feet deep."

Sandhill cranes, dancing partners

NATURE'S WAY

Marion Dusoir Ennes

USUALLY TRAVELLING IN LARGE FLOCKS, sandhill cranes stand tall in muddy fields searching for insects, small rodents, amphibians, or plant foods like the underground nuts of the sedges.

Occasionally, in autumn a single stately bird will turn up in the Northeast, to the delight of enthusiastic birdwatchers.

Fifteen crane species exist worldwide on all continents except South America and Antarctica. All are part of an almost unchanged ancient lineage that flew above the dinosaurs. Some reach altitudes today up to 30,000 feet and can migrate 5,000 miles.

All cranes mate for life and are dedicated, attentive parents.

On this continent we have two species—sandhills and whooping cranes. The latter population diminished to just 14 birds in 1941 and a crusade began to protect and enlarge their numbers.

Conservation groups, joined by government at all levels, sportsmen, birdwatchers, teachers and civic leaders worked to restore the population and anxiously awaited word of success. Complex and continuing long-term efforts have so far yielded about 150 whooping cranes in the wild and another 100 in captivity.

Sandhills, seriously endangered in the 1930s, were feared lost by famous ecologist Aldo Leopold, who warned eloquently of their potential demise. They recovered sufficiently by the 1950s to serve as foster parents to whooping crane chicks, their contribution to restoring whooping flocks.

Though most cranes are migratory, local resident populations that breed in Florida have become fairly familiar with humans, who seem to respect the birds' space.

Calling and dancing are important signals that cranes use to form bonds with one another.

In Florida I observed a small flock of sandhill cranes inside a fenced yard at a rehabilitation center. Three other sandhills flew overhead. One called and attracted the attention of a female inside the wire net fence. He landed. They each approached the fence, bowing, jumping, and posturing toward one another from opposite sides.

The male came and danced with her every day, and the staff expected the birds to mate when the flock was released.

Besides bowing, this ritual dance includes nodding and leaping, pirouetting and spreading wings. Sometimes they toss up grass or throw up and catch sticks. Shaking of the tail "bustle" marks then end of display and mating soon takes place.

After mating, parents-to-be together build a large, mounded 3- to 5-foot nest of sticks, mosses, dead seeds, rushes and grass tufts. Located in prairie ponds, marshes or bogs, it rests on crane-built islands 6- to 8-inches above surrounding water. Thick vegetation and wet habitat markedly reduces predation by coyotes and other mammals.

Two eggs are laid, but only one may survive. The other is thought to be an insurance egg.

Family life has great synchronicity. Observers report unison behavior. Couples tend to move in exact-likeness or mirror- image, as if choreographed.

Both parents guard, incubate, feed and teach the fuzzy yellow young for about 10 weeks until they can fly. The family usually remains together for 10 months and young birds learn migration routes in large flocks.

They can mate at four years and live monogamously 18-plus years

There is something special about cranes. Their fidelity and family devotion, their grace and beauty have made them the inspiration for art and dance, paradigms of elegant behavior in many cultures worldwide.

Sandhill cranes. *Height 3.5 feet, gray body feathers stained rusty from iron oxides in mud rubbed on by bird. Feed and nest in shallow wetlands, marshy meadows, prairie potholes.*

Steady high flyer, *7-foot wingspread, flies fully extended head- to-foot. (Herons fold necks.)*

Head has dark red crown above white neck. Bright yellow eye, strong defensive 6-inch bill. Audible one mile distant. Trumpeting, gurgling "gar-oo-oo" call.

THE INDEPENDENT, SEPTEMBER 11, 1997

"The male came and danced with her every day…"

Shagbark history

NATURE'S WAY

Marion Dusoir Ennes

TREES ARE BEGINNING to yield their fruits, among them the nut trees that stand wild in fields or on woodland slopes. Our own shagbark hickory known only in the Eastern United States (though it has a single species relative in Eastern China) still prospers here after more than a thousand years, according to evidence found in the middens of early American archeological sites.

All this time shagbark hickory trees have shared the loamy, well-drained soil of eastern deciduous forests with other nut-bearing hickories and oaks. These rich mast (nut crop) trees tower over an understorey of bushes like mountain laurel, blueberry, viburnum, where spring wildflowers like rue anemone, false Solomon's seal, and pipsisseva announce each blooming year.

This habitat is shared by jays and wild turkeys, and various members of the squirrel family who feed on acorns and hickory nuts, or bury them and reseed the forest.

Shagbarks are easily found among these friends. Their tall straight trunks, sometimes clear of branches for 50 feet, support a rounded irregular crown more than 100 feet above ground.

The bark that announces its name is distinguished by its loose-looking, smoke-gray plates that curve away from the tree. Not as easily detached as they appear to be, each foot-long plate is strongly attached at top or sides.

Naturalist Donald Culross Peattie, describing the tree's overall aspect, says "The shagbark seems like a symbol of the pioneer age, with its hard sinewy leaves and a rude shaggy coat, like the pioneer himself in fringed deerskin hunting shirt."

This great nut-bearer was well known to Native Americans. Fruits were collected in quantities in excess of 100 bushels and stored for use as staple food.

Dried hickory nuts were pounded into a kind of flour and mixed with boiling water. The strained liquid, a sweet nutritious extract the Indians called hickory milk, was an oily cooking ingredient that sparked up the flavor of pumpkins, peas, beans, or was mixed into corn meal cake or hominy.

Ripe nuts encased in woody husks split open into four segments revealing fairly small, almost white nuts, wedge-shaped and thin-shelled. Pioneers appreciated their delicious flavor and ate them out of hand or added them to cakes and cookies.

Native Americans also knew the value of this hickory's heavy wood. Tough, flexible, though close-grained, its center (heartwood) is light brown, while its sapwood (under the bark) is nearly white.

The Ojibway tradition was to make bows from a tree section with one side heartwood and the other sapwood—heartwood at the bow's front, sapwood facing the hunter.

From pioneer days, the hardness of shagbark hickory's lumber made it valuable for wheel spokes and rims, buggy shafts, and it is still used for tool handles for axes, hammers, hatchets.

As a fuel shagbark hickory has few peers. Most of us remember the delicate flavor of hickory-smoked ham, smoked over the coals of slow-burning fires. Aromatic fumes from the green wood permeates the ham, making it a gourmet treat.

When the seasoned wood is used for fuel it gives more heat than any other tree except locust. Shagbark hickory, scarcer now than in pioneer days, has a value related to its own destruction. One cord of the wood is not quite equivalent in thermal units to a ton of anthracite coal.

SHAGBARK HICKORY: *Straight trunk, 100-140 feet high. Gray bark, 1/2 to 3/4 inch thick, peels in long strips. Wind pollinated.*

INSET: *Leaf and fruit: Leaf 8-14 inches long. Compound, 5-7 graduated ovate leaflets. Mature fruit dark red or black, paired or solitary, one inch long. Woody husk, 1/8 to 1/2 inch thick, splits freely to expose white nut.*

"Pioneers appreciated the delicious flavor of ripe nuts and ate them out of hand or added them to cakes and cookies."

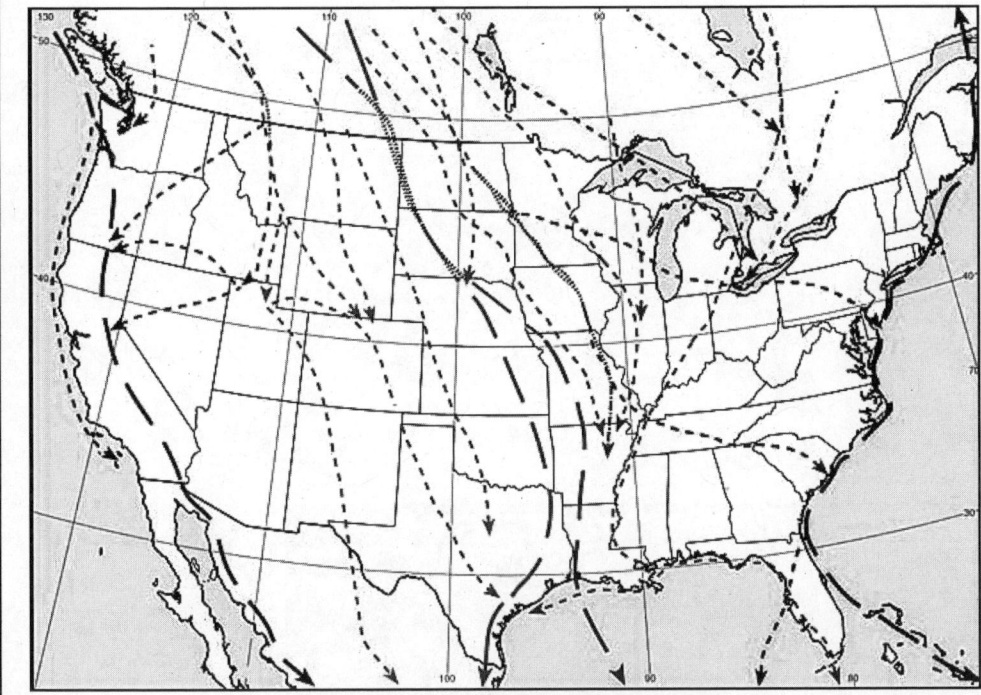

North American Migration Flyways
Map by Julia Pahountis-Opacic

Migration and Freedom

My walls are covered with birds in pictures, and a mobile, and I will doubtless have more. They are the symbols of the sky, and they help us maintain our illusion of freedom. But they tell us something more if we think beyond the obvious, beyond the wishing dream that is a human indulgence.

They remind us that the longest flight of birds are those to which they are least free, when they are drawn by forces they do not know. Every day they may chose to swoop or soar, to dip and dart to find some special prey of their own choice. They may choose the site for the nest which instinct helps them build, still reserving the prerogative of weaving in the shiny silk thread picked from the sewing basket on a sunny porch. Individual intelligence's govern their choices until the time of seasons change.

Then there is no more time for individual decisions, or even for communities. It is time for all to move together. Perhaps they are freed in another way, freed from the individual decision by their universal solar clock.

I will keep my walls covered with birds, and wish and try to find the universal in me which is governed through my knowing and feeling and which might give me that same freedom.

Marion Dusoir
Notebook, 1969

From green to colors at autumn equinox.

The author and colleagues bird watching in the cool of autumn.

FALL

Perhaps autumn is the time of year when the rhythm of the seasons is most keenly felt. Scurrying colored leaves, migrating birds, frenetic squirrels, mammals provisioning for winter—a surge of activity before the great slowing down. Observers to this bustle and hum, we are afforded intimate glimpses of various bird and mammalian species, insects and amphibians, fungi and more.

Mountain stream in mixed woods in fall.

FALL

Migration Mysteries (bird migration)	45
Migration: Fueling Up (bird migration)	46
Migration: The Urge and the Ability (bird migration)	47
Migration: The Flight Path (bird migration)	48
Partners in Flight (ovenbird)	49
Bird Navigation, Cues and Clues	50
Migration: "Angels" Revealed (bird migration)	51
Monarchs' Monumental Excursions (butterfly migration)	52
Great Blues (great blue herons)	53
Flashy, Thinking, Green-backed Heron	54
Learning From Eagles	55
Population Exploders (aphids)	56
Snow Swimmers (river otter)	57
Honeybee Workers Outside	58
Dance of the Honeybee Forager	59
Hidden Thunder-pumpers (bitterns)	60
Wild Canaries	61
Coyote: Myths and Realities	62
A Lot of Lip (dragonflies)	63
Pine Politics (history & the white pine)	64
Battles with Old Bushytail (gray squirrels)	65
The Great Egret Wars	66
Curious Kits (raccoons)	67
Masked Meddlers (raccoons)	68
The Courting Cicada Chorus	69
Well-designed Engineer (beavers)	70
Naturalized Citizen (pheasant)	71
Treasuring American Toads	72
A Third Kingdom (fungi)	73
Honest Foragers (turkey vultures/buzzards)	74
Turkeys in Season (wild turkeys)	75
Recyclers (beavers)	76
Silent Hunter (great horned owls)	77
Woodland Elves and Fairies (butterflies and moths)	78
Green in Winter (mountain laurel)	79
Pileated Crested Woodpeckers	80
Beetles of Our Lady (ladybug)	81
Rebirth of the American Elm	82
"Feeding Birds"	83

NATURE'S WAY:
Migration mysteries

September and early October are peak periods of bird migration, although birds move south in vast numbers from July to December and return as early as February and as late as June. But right now, millions of birds are flying to their winter quarters; 500,000 birds were counted in a single migratory flock of starlings.

Migration patterns are quite complicated and varied. The time, place and rates of migration are species specific and some—like bobwhites, cardinals, titmice, woodpeckers—apparently don't go at all.

Some species go in combined flocks, some birds go as individuals. Within species there are also variations: sometimes sexes go separately or young go first and there are differences according to the location of the bird's main residence.

Take the red-tailed hawk, found in our area and throughout North America: northerly red-tails migrate south in winter and come back in spring; those in middle latitudes go south a short distance, depending on weather; and sometimes populations stay put. It depends on available food supplies, where a red-tail breeds, and the weather.

While migration has been defined as the seasonal movement of animals in search of food or mating partners and the eventual return of the animals to the starting place, ornithologists Don and Lillian Stokes describe the function of migration differently: as a cost/benefit operation.

What benefits derive from flying to a new environment in the winter, instead of staying put? It costs energy to go to a new place and back. To make migration worthwhile, birds have to store up energy for the journey and eat well during the winter stay, so they can return in better condition to breed than if they had not gone.

This analysis helps explain migration variations. The resident downy woodpecker feeds on insects under bark and can get that food in winter or summer—no need to migrate. But the eastern kingbird, which feeds on aerial insects, must go south before the cold exhausts his supply.

In other cases, it is believed that males like the dark-eyed junco stay farther north so they can get back to defend breeding territories successfully in spring. Males may exclude females and young from local winter food supplies, forcing them to migrate south. Some think the larger-bodied male adult junco stays because he can withstand cold better than the smaller females or young.

We'll have more in coming weeks about discoveries being made through bird banding, radio telemetry, radar, and that good old standby, bird observation. Information has been gleaned about internal bird impulses to migrate, flight height and length, bird orientation and navigation, as well as external signals that impel birds on their extraordinary journeys.

Red-tailed hawk

THE INDEPENDENT, SEPTEMBER 22, 1988

> "... ornithologists Don and Lillian Stokes describe the function of migration... as a cost/benefit operation."

NATURE'S WAY:
Migration: fueling up

To prepare for their journey, birds must store fat in their bodies to supply the vast quantity of energy needed for the trip.

The golden plover, which breeds in the Arctic and winters in southern Argentina, makes the trip of more than 2,400 miles south over the Atlantic from Nova Scotia in about 48 hours using less than two ounces of body fat.

A 1,000-pound airplane would have to use *one single pint* of fuel (rather than the usual gallon) for a 20-mile flight to be equally efficient.

The rate of energy use is affected by whether feeding or resting stops are made, the competition for food supplies at the stop, the adverse effects of weather, and errors in the birds' flight plan.

The ornithologist Frank R. Moore says "the migratory strategy of a bird has been shaped by natural selection to yield a mix of programmed and learned behavior well adapted to a bewildering number of factors affecting the safety and economics of the migratory journey."

Many small birds, including the ruby-throated hummingbird, add "fuel" reserves in fall amounting to 35 to 40 percent of their body weight. With that much fuel, the hummers could theoretically fly *twice* the distance between northern South America and the Louisiana coast, so these tiny birds retain a goodly fuel margin when they make the 10-hour non-stop journey across the Caribbean.

Their plumpness is one of the best criteria to distinguish birds who are ready for migration. It is just now being discovered that birds' food selectivity increases during migration time—they make more nutritionally beneficial choices.

The increase in fat reserves is augmented with a change in digestion of foods; fats and carbohydrates are much more efficiently used. This is especially beneficial when birds make migratory stopovers.

Field observations made by Frank Moore—who studies migrant warblers at a stopover site on the north coast of the Gulf of Mexico—finds birds arriving with variable fat reserves. Those birds with enough fat reserves get back into flight on the night of their arrival. The other birds stay over to restore fuel reserves, foraging actively according to their needs.

A 12-gram prothonotary warbler will eat a large enough quantity of food of a quality which results in the addition of as much as 5 to 7 tenths of a gram of fat per day. Even with the food resources available to human beings, it would be difficult for a 120-pound person to add 5 to 7 pounds of body fat in one day. So the birds have a special adaptation which, with their own enterprise, helps them restore their reserves.

This plump bird has stored sufficient food for a long migratory journey.

NATURE'S WAY

Migration:
The urge and the ability

About now birds of almost every species experience "migratory restlessness."

Among some young this urge takes them as much as 100 miles *north* of their original nesting place. The great (white) egret, visiting one of our local marshy ponds, may have taken such a tour before going south.

Other birds adjust their location by only several hundred feet of *altitude*. Aristotle, an early student of migration, talked of this vertical movement: "Weakly birds in winter and in frosty weather come down to the plains for warmth, and in summer migrate to the hills for coolness." Some quail and grouse make these short migratory trips on foot.

The essential message is that birds are looking for maximum ecological benefit in their struggle for survival.

Birds' impulses to migrate are directed by internal stimuli thought to be activated by the pituitary gland hormones.

Many birds, however, make their relocation decisions in the fall depending on the available food supply. Waxwings wander, finches make lateral explorations, and the red-headed woodpecker goes south only in those years when northern corn and beechnut crops have failed.

Another stimulating factor is the change in day length. Long cold winter nights can deplete a bird's fat layers, so birds have a hard time—in the short daylight hours—eating enough to meet metabolic needs, much less to build strength for the next breeding season.

So most of them rely on their magnificent flying equipment, which makes migration possible. "Built to fly," says the National Geographic Society, "a bird is all lightness and strength from feathers to skeleton." Birds walk on their hind legs, and their wings (front limbs) are exquisitely adapted for flight. Feathers, unique to birds, are pliable, yet sturdy and weather resistant.

When a bird flies, the flight feathers of the wing curve so that the air is cupped, lifting the bird and pushing it forward as the wing goes down. Then the feathers spread slightly on the upstroke to allow air to move past.

The bird's body, divided between the head, neck, and trunk, is a combination of flexibility and rigidity. The backbone of the trunk is almost completely fused, giving the skeleton a rigid axis which supports the body in flight.

At the base of the trunk are five or six unfused vertebrae that move the fused tail section, which supports the large tail feathers—the bird's rudder.

The skull is fused into what is essentially one bone, but the head can turn because the long neck vertebrae move freely. The spindle shape of the bird body helps reduce air resistance, expediting forward movement.

Birds have well-developed muscles. They are anchored deep into the breastbone and large, powerful chest (pectoral) muscles control the wing beats, which keep the birds flying. Crow wing-beats are about three times a second, chickadees about 30 per second, and hummingbirds 50 per second—except when they are in a hurry and then the beat can accelerate to 200 times a second.

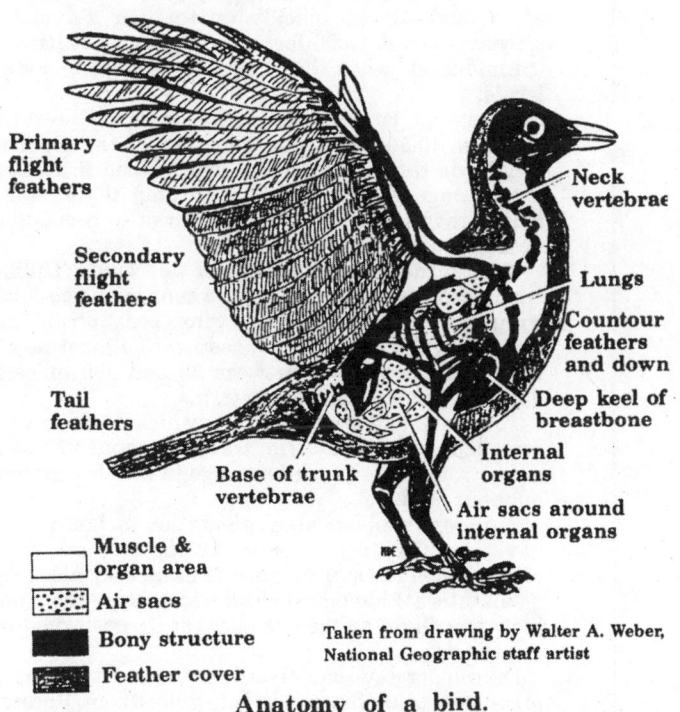

Anatomy of a bird. Taken from drawing by Walter A. Weber, National Geographic staff artist

"Birds' impulses to migrate are directed by internal stimuli thought to be by the pituitary gland hormones."

THE INDEPENDENT, SEPTEMBER 29, 1988

"A flock of geese was seen over the Himalayas by a mountain climber at approximately 27,000 feet."

NATURE'S WAY:
Migration: the flight path

Many species, and sometimes families, of blackbirds, ducks, geese, waterfowl, warblers, swallows, hawks, and others have been gathering into flocks since late July. This flocking behavior brings thousands to staging areas that serve as take-off points for the leisurely autumn trip south.

Birds fly in waves, most at altitudes of under 3,000 feet. You can sometimes see flocks silhouetted against the moon if you focus a telescope up on a clear fall (or spring) night.

Some birds fly well above 15,000 feet. A flock of geese was seen *over* the Himalayas by a mountain climber at approximately 27,000 feet. Birdwatchers travel to local mountaintops to glimpse migrating hawks soaring high on wind currents as they make their way south in fall.

Variations in altitude depend on the species (most songbirds fly below 5,000 feet); weather (warblers often aviod storms by flying over them); geographical aspects of the route (mountains, plains, or oceans); time of year or time of day.

Most small birds fly at night. They take off just after sundown, go quickly up to their maximum altitude—about 1,000 feet—and fly at that altitude 'til midnight, when they begin to descend to lower levels.

In general, larger birds (ducks, geese, turkeys) fly between 40-50 miles per hour, while the smaller songbirds range from 12-32 mph. When in flocks, the average speed is faster. Autumn flights take longer than in spring, when the urge to breed and nest is pressing.

Most birds take advantage of tail winds. Unlike small birds, which have to use a continuous circular wing motion, birds with large wings coast on air currents that can move them ahead with almost no effort. Birds can travel between 30 and 300 miles a day, barring the danger of storms.

The black and white warbler, which nests in this area, takes a leisurely trip; traveling about 20 miles a day, it reaches its winter range in South America in about 50 days.

Birds use sophisticated orientation techniques to navigate. They set a course by the sun, stars, or moon. When the sun-compass is used, they also rely on an internal biological clock which helps them adjust their flight as the sun changes its position during the day.

Diurnal, or day-time, flyers can use coast lines and other specific landmarks to help guide them. Recently it was learned that birds can use the effects of *light polarized by the atmosphere in a clear sky to help them confirm direction.*

Stormy weather and heavy winds will keep birds on the ground, but on a clear autumn night it is very exciting to see as many as 200,000 individual birds *per hour* flying south along a one-mile front.

The summer and winter homes of the black-and-white warbler are illustrated on this map. A very slow migrant, these birds, nesting in the northern part of the country, take 50 days to cross the breeding range.

THE INDEPENDENT, OCTOBER 13, 1988

NATURE'S WAY
Partners in flight

Neotropical migrants—songbirds, shore birds, and reptors included—are birds that winter in the tropics and subtropical regions of the continent and return north to the U.S. or Canada each year to breed and raise families.

Of the 650 birds that breed in North America, about 300 are migrants, and population declines are alarming.

At least 70% of the bird species in Eastern deciduous areas, including forests, grasslands, and wetlands, are at risk. They suffer from increases in human populations, urban expansion, and exploitation of natural resources.

A preponderance are thrushes, flycatchers, vireos, orioles, tanagers, grosbeaks, and warblers. They make long journeys from southern grounds each spring, eagerly searching for breeding grounds that will assure development of the next generation.

Despite its unusual name, the small but feisty ovenbird is a wood warbler. The female builds a cup of dry grass, rootlets, bark, and moss in a slight depression on the leaf-carpeted floor of a mature forest, then arches it over with leaves and small branches.

It looks like a Dutch-oven, with side opening. The roof sheds rain. Leaves camouflage the nest and conceal its precious contents.

Late this summer I heard the ovenbird's distinctive call several times in near woods. "Teacher, teacher, teacher" it called out repeatedly with increasing volume and vigor.

I hope this bird will return to nest here next spring, but chances are not good.

In 1948, Roger Tory Peterson said of the ovenbird that it "must rank near the top of the list of most abundant birds in the East." Not any more.

Even before they arrive in the north next year, their journeys of thousands of miles will offer serious tests. Migrating birds arrive emaciated and exhausted at staging areas, coastal areas or river corridors with varied bush and tree habitats.

Here they find food, safety, and roosting places where they can refuel and rest until fat layers rebuild, strength returns, and they can move farther with a favorable wind.

Ovenbirds, like other warblers, require large forests to raise broods. Fragmented woodlands give predators greater access. Raccoons, skunks, opossums, crows, jays, and house cats demolish eggs and young.

Brood parasites, like cowbirds thriving in these open areas, lay their eggs in nests of migrants.

Many small species, like the ovenbird, may also lack the energy after their long migration to raise another brood.

Neotropical migrant birds face a triple whammy. Not only are northern nesting sites threatened, but also needed waterfront staging areas are increasingly being lost to coastal development for residential and summer vacation use.

Those that do make it back to the tropics are confronted by accelerated deforestation as forests are converted to open grasslands and turned to agricultural production.

Serious concerns about the decline of songbirds and other non-game bird species have galvanized Congress to form the first integrated approach for action. Solutions are known and possible.

Federal and state governments are joining non-profit organizations, corporations, academic institutions, landowners and other private citizens in an all-out push to save these unique and colorful creatures.

Ovenbird: 5½ to 6½ inches; black-lined orange-brown crown; olive-gray above, white below; breast spotted, streaked; pink legs. Courtship includes melodious flight-song, jumble of twitters and warbles (incorporating "teacher" call), also sung at twilight or warm winter nights. Parents diligent in broken-wing displays and flight distractions, luring enemies away from babies in hidden nest.

The Neotropical Migratory Bird Conservation Program will focus efforts on research, monitoring, and habitat management from Canada, United States, Mexico, and Central America through the Caribbean islands down to South America.

To participate, write to Peter Stangel, National Fish and Wildlife Foundation, 18th & C Sts., NW, Room 2556, Washington, D.C. 20240.

THE INDEPENDENT, OCTOBER 31, 1991

"It looks like a Dutch-oven, with side opening."

Bird navigation, cues and clues

NATURE'S WAY

Marion Dusoir Ennes

BIRDS ARE TEACHING OBSERVERS there are no simple answers to the mysteries of bird migration. The hazards of flight are mitigated by a multiplicity of cues—some redundant—to reinforce success and reduce dangers of getting confused, hurt or lost. In this, they are like human pilots supported by radar and radio, magnetic systems and beacons.

Birds' directional faculties show two broad categories of skill— a compass component that helps a bird orient to a particular direction and a map component. This latter skill makes possible a bird's precise return to the bush it nested in last year.

Much more is known and understood about the compass skill than about the map one.

Male and female bobolinks, nesting in northeastern United States, are among the thousands that use the Atlantic flyway, which traces the East Coast during migration.

Birds wait for the right weather. A cold front from the north usually predicts fair weather ahead and its tail wind helps push songbirds whose airspeeds average 20 to 30 m.p.h.

Once down the coast past Bermuda, these birds turn southeast to the tradewinds that carry them over water to the Antilles and South America. The bobolink then traces the northern coastline of South America, turning southwest to head deep into southern Brazil or northern Argentina.

They use the sun as their compass, along with an internal clock that compensates for the sun's changing height and distance from the horizon. They do not get confused in cloudy weather because they see polarized light (vibrations of light waves confined to one plane or direction) and take bearings from that.

Some scientists believe that animals (including birds) navigate by earth's magnetic field. In *National Geographic's* June 1991 issue, Charles Wolcott of Cornell University explains how it works.

If you think of a bar magnet stuffed in an orange, "the earth is the orange and the magnet is the fluid iron moving in the earth's core." The iron's movement creates a magnetic field, hypothetical flow lines that make progressively steeper angles (dip angles) the farther north one goes.

It is theorized that a bobolink going south can judge latitude by sensing the changing angle between a "perpendicular" gravity line and an angled magnetic field line.

Mary and Ken Able conduct experiments in migration at the State University of New York at Albany. In 1993 they showed that birds use help from the earth's magnetic field, but often calibrate the information with other nonmagnetic cues, including natural polarization of daylight.

The Ables used Savannah sparrows, keeping them in cages exposed to the sky. When birds became restless, eager to migrate, they faced their expected migration direction.

Birds were first exposed to a strong magnetic field shifted 90 degrees, changing the reading from north to west. Later, cages were covered with transparent sheets to prevent daylight polarization from reaching the birds.

When the birds couldn't make use of polarized light, they ignored the visible sky and relied on the false magnetic information.

When the transparent depolarizing sheet was removed, birds could then see daylight, at which point they ignored the tests' misleading magnetic information, orienting instead by naturally polarized daylight toward true south.

The conclusion: magnetic cues back up celestial navigation.

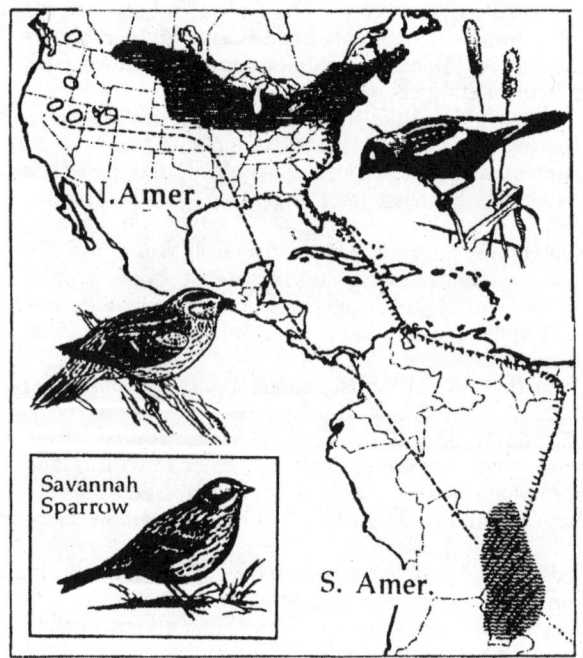

***Following the eastern flyway** (serrated line), the male (above right) and female (below left) bobolinks make a long, long trip from the northeastern United States to southern Brazil, crossing miles of open ocean. The Savannah sparrow (inset) makes the semi- annual trip from the Northeast to the deep South or Mexico.*

THE INDEPENDENT, NOVEMBER 6, 1997

"Some scientists believe that animals (including birds) navigate by earth's magnetic field."

NATURE'S WAY
Migration: 'angels' revealed

The serendipitous discovery of "angels" early in the 1940s opened a great new opportunity to develop a comprehensive understanding of migration's mysteries.

It was the Second World War when radar (radio detection and ranging) was being developed as a coastal defense and anti-aircraft device; later radar was to become important in weather observation. Unexplained clouds of blips on the radar screen—"angels"—were identified as microwave echoes of flocks of birds in flight.

At about the same time, many controlled experiments with caged birds began to turn up information about birds' orientation to sun and stars.

For example, a large round cage was taken into a planetarium where star patterns could be changed. The reactions of birds were documented under various star patterns, confirming that birds use a star compass.

Pre-dating these methods for studying migration was the technique of banding, introduced around 1910. Light "mist nets," usually made of hair, trapped birds and recovered them unharmed. A loose fitting, light metal or plastic circular band was then placed around the bird's leg.

The band was numbered and marked "Notify the US Fish and Wildlife Service. In cooperation with the Canadian Wildlife Service, USF&WS has supervised bird banding in North America since 1920.

It is still used extensively, often in conjunction with other techniques.

Information collected through these methods includes: tracing migratory paths; dating arrivals and departures; noting length of feeding and resting periods for different species; observing the relationship of weather conditions to starting times; the rates of travel for individual birds; and the regularity of return to former summer or winter quarters.

By setting up stations, fascinating data on specific populations has been collected. One concerns the flight of the Arctic tern, which may breed from Massachusetts to as far north as 520 miles from the North Pole.

When the young reach full growth, these terns fly south over several months and end up in the Antarctic—a total of 11,000 miles—where they spend the winter months. They are rewarded for their efforts by enjoying more daylight hours than probably any other bird.

Dr. Kenneth Able, formerly of Chatham, who has studied bird migration for almost 20 years, teaches biological science at SUNY, Albany. He says "with long-range surveillance and weather radars, movements of birds [can] be seen in all directions and at ranges of tens or even hundreds of miles."

Dr. Able sometimes uses a tracking radar unit which can lock on to an individual bird, "giving second-by-second positions of the bird in space. Its height, flight direction, and speed, even the pattern of its wing beats, can be recorded with precision."

His experience has shown that birds actually use multiple cues in their flights and process information about wind, landmarks, sun, or stars selectively, according to need.

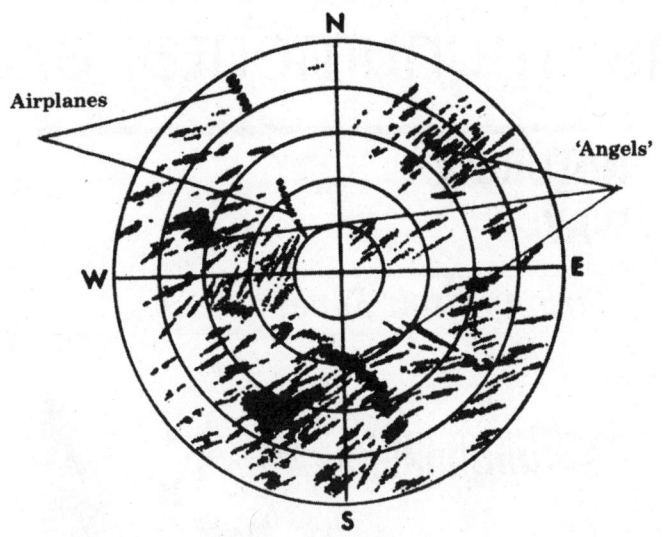

Heavy bird migration shows "angels" on radar screen.

THE INDEPENDENT, OCTOBER 30, 1988

"The reactions of birds were documented under various star patterns, confirming that birds use a star compass."

Monarchs' monumental excursions

NATURE'S WAY

Marion Dusoir Ennes

INTRIGUING QUESTIONS about butterfly migration still tantalize scientists, who have enlisted amateur butterfly lovers who want to help. One of the best known migrating butterflies is the large North American monarch butterfly which every year flies south and west, 2,500 miles or more.

Monarchs introduced to Australia are also migrators, while those native to South America never migrate at all.

The migrators' trip starts in the Northeast, as far north as Canada. In late summer and early fall they start their low soaring flight, roosting by the thousands in particular trees along the way.

One favorite place is Point Pelee in Ontario on the north side of Lake Erie. My husband and I saw them there on a very tall, single, "butterfly" tree.

They were only noticeable when observed flying in to find a place in the crowd or resettling. The rest of the time their folded-wing undersides looked like autumn leaves.

Pelee's Point aims south directly across the lake and serves as a landmark for many migrators.

These eastern travelers were headed for specific fir trees in central Mexico. Western monarchs spend winter seasons along southern California's sunny coast, resting and collecting energy.

Survivors of these monumental excursions head back, mating on the way as weather warms. Each female lays about 200 eggs attached separately to plants. Then she and the male die.

Eggs hatch into hungry larvae that eat and grow for 12 days and nights.

The now two-inch caterpillar turns into a smooth, waxy jewel-like pupa of rich green with shining gold spots.

Depending on weather, this takes an average of 12 days until the striking orange, black and white adult form emerges and then continues on the way back to their families' point of origin.

In late summer, after two or three broods, the last generation born gathers in flocks until huge crowds of migrating monarchs move.

Records show one flock over Washington State's Cascade Mountains in 1928 was estimated at 3-4 miles wide and 10-15 miles long.

Nowadays, scientists are banding butterflies and beginning to get information about their travels.

Monarchs are not the only butterflies to migrate. *Discover Magazine's* Mark Caldwell tells of "The Wired Butterfly" in the February issue.

Apollo butterflies living in isolated Rocky Mountain meadows are tagged with hair-thin antenna wires and superlight radar transmitters powered by solar radiation.

Apollos fly only with energy from the sun. Without it, they are grounded.

Researchers can now follow their migrations from meadow to meadow, recording the movements of, and behavioral differences between, males and females as they meet environmental challenges.

Scientists still have much to learn about phenomenal monarch migration: How do they know when to leave? Why do reproductive instincts turn off going south, on again going north? How do new butterflies perpetually find their way to winter roosts?

The enlistment of "the amateur scientist" in tagging monarchs across the U.S. is reported by Shawn Carlson in the September *Scientific American*. The project, sponsored by the University of Kansas at Lawrence, is called Monarch Watch.

After five years, 1,500 members and school contacts with 100,000 students and teachers captured tens of thousands of butterflies and attached a small coded paper tag to each one marked with the date it was first noticed.

Of 90,000 netted and banded insects, the 137 recaptured so far are already yielding information about butterfly routes.

Monarch butterfly *in its caterpillar stage (top), striped white, yellow and black; in its pupal case (center), smooth, sculptural, bright green with ridge of delicate golden spots; and as an adult (below), 3 to 4" wide, long forewing. Orange wings have wide black margins and white spots, the underside pattern is similar but paler. Distasteful to birds, they contain poison from milkweed. At right is a "butterfly tree."*

THE INDEPENDENT, SEPTEMBER 25, 1997

"My husband and I saw them in Point Pelee, Ontario, on a very tall, single 'butterfly' tree."

NATURE'S WAY

Great blues

The late summer peregrinations of great blue herons take them to unexpected places. On two consecutive mornings recently, I saw one fly up rapidly from a carpet-sized meadow in an otherwise wooded place. The bird's measured wingbeats had grace, power, and elegance.

This time of year great blues, young and old, disperse in all directions before most migrate to warmer southern places on or near our continent. A few winter successfully in the north.

The Spring '90 issue of "The Kingbird," Federation of New York State Bird Clubs publication, reported a 1988-89 study of prolonged winter residency by at least five great blue herons at Collins Lake in Scotia.

This spring-fed lake has open water on the coldest winter days, making fish readily available for food. The area is inaccessible, with enough dead wood for camouflage. It is presumed to be one of, if not *the* most, northerly sites documented for the wintering of great blues.

Throughout history, and for many cultures, the heron has been an important symbol. The Chinese, who often pictured the birds in art, identified their calmness, serenity, and persistence as redolent of nature's ongoing strength, unmoved by human demands.

For almost 1,000 years in China, Japan, India, Persia, and Arabia, the heron was a target bird, attacked by falcons trained for noblemen's sport. Falcons often lost, victim of the heron's skill with its long daggerlike beak.

One of about 120 living species of long-legged waders,

Adult great blue heron. Tall, 42-56 inches, long neck, long pointed yellow beak. Four-pound body, slim, no tail. Bluish-gray coat, white head, neck. Black wing tips. Wingspread 65-74 inches. Sexes similar. Inset: Foot with pectinated second toe.

this solitary bird stands four feet tall on stiltlike legs. In its customary habitat of shallow pond, marsh, stream, or lake bed, it can remain very still for a long time. Guided by practice as well as instinct, it chooses a good spot and waits for a fish or frog to come along. Then, in a blink of an eye, the great blue strikes, impaling or grabbing the prey in its long, sharp bill, and swallows it whole, head first. Occasionally, a bird gets overly ambitious and has to give up on a large fish or eel that won't go down.

Blues can locate and pluck soft shell crabs out of their hiding places. They can plunge into water from a perch to fish, or float on deeper water, wings outstretched as they search.

Mostly, they stand in shallows, raising one foot slowly and setting it down carefully. Their long toes, augmented by a shallow webbing between the second and third toes, keep them from sinking into the mud.

When not eating, herons spend much time scratching and grooming to rid themselves of parasites. Standing on one foot, the bird pulls up the other and literally combs through the underfeathers with the pectinated (comblike) toenail on its second toe.

It is a careful flyer, able to negotiate wooded or open areas at a cruising speed of 18-29 mph and 36 mph when pressed. Because the heron has such a large wing area relative to total body weight, there is less stress on the wings, permitting the bird's slow, stately beat.

When undisturbed, the heron's take-off is graceful. Once airborne, its neck is folded back. The long legs, extended to the rear, will act as a rudder until it reaches its destination. Then with neck extended and legs down, momentum is checked by a few flaps and the bird drops lightly to perch.

THE INDEPENDENT, SEPTEMBER 26, 1991

"For almost 1,000 years in China, Japan, India, Persia, and Arabia, the heron was a target bird, attacked by falcons trained for noblemen's sport."

Flashy, thinking, green-backed heron

NATURE'S WAY

Marion Dusoir Ennes

Green-backed Heron

THE SMALLEST MEMBER of the impressive heron family, the green-backed heron, is recognized in New York's *Breeding Bird Atlas* as "the most widespread and abundant" heron in the state. Not often seen, its secluded life is picturesque with behavioral displays and intelligent tricks.

Normally look-alikes, these herons go into breeding plumage during spring migration in April, making them more easily differentiated. Though both carry strong camouflaging, the male is vivid. His lustrous green head, back, and green wings washed with blue flash atop a buffy-white throat and neck stripe. Bright orange-coral legs and deep-red mouth lining are additional parts of his seasonal display armamentarium.

He's ready to entice a mate, so he carves out a secluded breeding territory, patrols its perimeter, and builds or reuses a nest on a branch 10 to 20 feet above ground. This heron is very serious about keeping intruders—especially other males—away.

With neck pulled in, a green-backed heron is about the size of a crow, but he can stretch his flexible "rubber" neck out to equal his body length. He can also adjust his crest, neck, or back feathers to create threatening displays.

First, facing his opponent in a low crouch, he raises his crest feathers, flips his short tail and starts to raise his back plumage. Then, if he gets no response, he exaggerates his first action. Now, feathers fully-fluffed, tail bouncing, eyes bulging, his large rapier beak is parted to show the mouth's blood-red interior lining.

Usually enough to scare anybody, a stubborn challenger is finally startled into flight by the heron's loud rasping "skeow" call.

This male is so testy he may initially threaten his mate-to-be, but soon wins her over by another complex series of postures. Starting with a short, ecstatic, lurching flight toward her with orange legs dangling and feathers erect in colorful display, he ends by landing and doing a little hornpipe dance before he presents her with a twig for the nest he has started.

Green-backed herons are among a few birds that adopt separate feeding territories. These can be near fresh or salt water, marshy spots or edges of streams, ponds or inlets. Short-legged, with a web between middle and other toes, they swim easily and well when necessary.

On land, they catch crickets, grasshoppers, frogs, small snakes and mammals. In water, they are excellent in fishing and, like other herons, exceedingly patient.

Over several decades, observation worldwide documents the exciting discovery that green-backed herons use bait of various kinds to lure fish. This requires a thinking process.

The birds were seen to drop a small feather, twig, or leaf on water's surface to entice fish within range. If bait drifted away, the heron repositioned it and even carried it to other locations.

One picture story in a 1974 *National Geographic* showed a heron using a dry food pellet to bring in a school of minnows. The bird examined the school of minnows, feinted at them with his beak, and knew they were out of reach. Then, finding the pellet, he dropped it between the fish and himself.

Hunkered down along the water's edge, he watched them move close enough, then, quicker than a blink, pounced, grabbing the fish in a two-inch bill and swallowing it head first. Using bait, this green heron caught two dozen fish—and only missed two strikes.

Green-backed heron fishing. *Grasping pond reeds, luring a fish with bait, ready to strike. Length: 18"*

Inset: *Typical nest, 1 to 1½ feet across. Of twigs, reeds, vines attached to tree branches or aerial roots 10-20 feet above ground. 4-5 eggs (average clutch). Both parents incubate. Young hatched with open eyes, otherwise helpless. In one week, climb around nest.*

THE INDEPENDENT, SEPTEMBER 26, 1996

"... worldwide observation documents the exciting discovery that green-backed herons use bait of various kinds to lure fish."

NATURE'S WAY:
Learning from eagles

The survival and future breeding effectiveness of bald eagles depend on good overwintering grounds with ample, consistent food sources and natural shelter from chilling winds.

Adults and their maturing offspring come down from northen New York and Canada when sub-zero weather freezes up streams and food supplies become scarce.

Dennis Mildner, reserve educator for the Hudson River National Estuarine Research Reserve, reports a significant overwintering bald eagle population in New York State, averaging 55 birds in the Catskill Reservoir area and about 12 birds in the mid-Hudson Valley from December through much of February.

"Prime wintering grounds, like those within the 4,000 acres of the reserve," says Mr. Mildner, "are hard to find." River, marshes, swamps, river islands, and wooded uplands offer diverse habitats and lots of different, available prey.

Mr. Mildner who goes out at 6:30 a.m. in sub-zero temperatures to study the eagles, knows why they come. At Iona Island, near Peekskill, for example, the Hudson River becomes a narrow brackish channel with almost 200 species of fish. The eagles feed on a very small segment of this fish population, taking white perch, striped bass, carp, goldfish, sunfish, and (a favorite) catfish.

Energy-efficient, eagles perch on the shoreline in large, dead or open-crowned deciduous trees watching the tidal surge with keen eyes, spotting dormant fish at the surface, or frozen in ice, or injured waterfowl. At the right time a bald eagle will step from its perch and fly directly to a frozen fish in an ice floe.

When fish are scarce, the broad grasslands and cattail marsh of Iona Island provide rabbits, other small animals, or a deer carcass. Like any predator/scavenger, eagles take what they can get.

Eagle populations concentrate at overwintering grounds, become more gregarious, and abandon breeding territoriality. Novice hunters learn by watching experienced birds, honing skills through competition for fish frozen in river ice.

Bald eagles mature completely to the black coat with white head and tail feathers and yellow beak at four to five years. Immatures have dusky heads and tail and dark bill, with whitish wing linings.

Warmblooded eagles, body temperature around 103°, must protect themselves against wind chill in sub-zero periods. A thick feather coat, 12% of body weight, helps keep them warm, but they find special places for protection.

Nights, they roost in evergreen trees on riverside cliffs; in the morning, their dark feathers soak up solar heat as they perch on the southeast face of a mountain away from cold northwest winds.

"Eagles taught me the dynamics of the wintering area. Morning after morning I saw them foraging over a particular spot in the river," Mr. Mildner said. "One morning I collected a fresh white carcass of an adult catfish an hour after eagles fed on it. But," he confided, "catfish are bottom dwellers. Why was it at the surface where an eagle could catch it?"

"Closer observation told me that the spot was an area of major upwelling, where currents and underwater springs bring a vertical column of water up to the surface. Not only does this concentrate nutrients—phytoplankton, zooplankton, and forage fish—but that rising action washed the catfish out from under a rock, where it was probably hiding out for the winter, and brought it right up to the surface."

"A light bulb went on for *me*—but, of course, *they* knew it all along!

"Novice hunters learn by watching experienced birds, honing skills through competition for fish frozen in river ice."

THE INDEPENDENT, SEPTEMBER 28, 1989

NATURE'S WAY
Population exploders

"How insects do upset our generalizations and our peace of mind! We have heard of feminist reformers who would abolish men. With patient scorn we have listened to their predictions of a millenium where males will be unknown and unneeded—and here the insects show us not only that it is possible, but that it is practicable, at least for a certain length of time, and that the time can be infinitely extended under favorable conditions."

So says Robert Snodgrass in "Insects—Their Ways and Means of Living" in the Smithsonian Institution Series.

He cites aphids, or plant lice, as illustration.

I was on my way to telling about ladybugs when I realized that they could not exist without those ubiquitous population exploders, aphids, who have their own fascinating story.

Any gardener will tell you it is impossible to find a *single* aphid. In the human war with aphids, these bugs' most powerful weapon is reproductive capacity, surpassing all other insects in reproduction rate.

Nine generations of aphids can reach (conservatively) a total of 600 billion individuals.

Tiny soft-bodied plant lice are sucking insects, prodigious eaters feeding on plant juices. Using its flexible hollow beak, the aphid pierces a leaf vein, tapping the plant's vital juices. The liquid food pumped up is rich in sweet carbohydrates with some protein vital to the insect.

The excreted "honey dew," up to 25% sucrose, is eagerly harvested by ants, who actively protect aphids against predators with menacing mandibular gestures or irritating chemical sprays.

Ants also carry aphids to new food sources—other plants of the same species—and sometimes herd aphids or store aphid eggs in their own nests for winter protection.

In autumn, some aphids do reproduce sexually. Before it gets too cold, a male and female mate and eggs are laid in a secure place. Eggs of the apple aphid, for example, are secreted under the tree bark, and young emerge when the weather is right the following April.

Every hatchling is a wingless female nymph with her own reproductive capacity and a very big appetite. Along with her many sisters, she hurries to a leaf or apple bud, sinks her beak into its vein, starts feeding and growing.

After several molts, this aphid is an adult, and virgin though she is, *she* gives birth. Her daughter is born live and kicking, ready to take her place on the bud next to mother and sink her beak in too.

This parthenogenisis is highly economical for the aphid population, eliminating time and energy otherwise expended in courtship and copulation.

Soon the daughter has daughters and granddaughters of her own, up to the fifth generation, each a genetic, but not exact, physical clone of the other. Sometimes generation time is as little as six days.

Crowding produces overpopulation, tactile pressures. Plants lose vitality from loss of their juices, so after a final molt, some nymphs develop wings and fly to new food sources.

Finally, with cool autumn temperatures and reduction of plant sap, the still virgin mothers produce anatomically sexual, winged offspring who mate and fly to the site where eggs will hatch close to their needed food source.

Without mouthparts of his own, the male's only job is to contribute diversity to the gene pool.

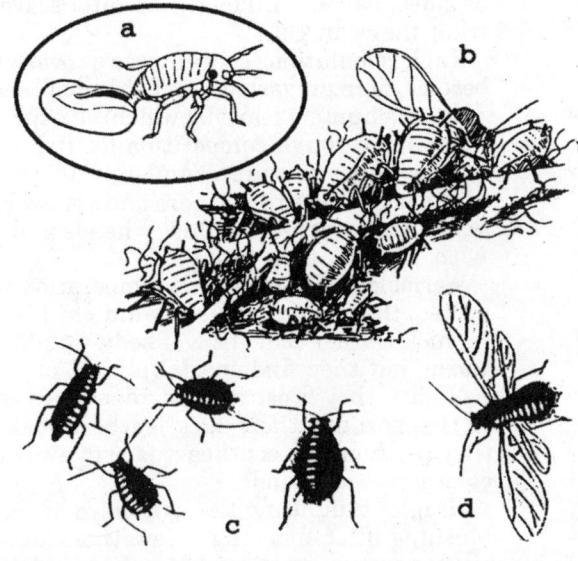

a. First generation aphid hatching from egg in spring. Green, brown, black, red, depending on species.

b. Crowds of aphids on leaf undersurface, feeding at vein.

c. Several generations of virgin female aphids. Adults less than 1/4 inch.

d. Winged sexual form of aphids, male.

THE INDEPENDENT, OCTOBER 1, 1992

"After several molts, this aphid is an adult, and virgin though she is, she gives birth."

NATURE'S WAY

Snow swimmers

Otters are energetic, wary, intelligent, active on land or in water—all of which explains why we see these semi-aquatic creatures so rarely.

That is unfortunate for us, because among mammals, otters have the greatest reputation for enjoyment, alone or with family. Although much activity is nocturnal, observations of daytime play seem to provide almost as much fun for the observer as for the otters themselves.

Curious and enterprising, they play by themselves or together. They often have a game of hide and seek with one another.

They are best known for their love of sliding, a special pleasure they enjoy summer or winter. Any steep waterside bank will do. In summer they make a slide of a grassy bank, climb as far as 25 feet to the top. Giving themselves a push with all four feet and keeping front legs at their sides and rear feet turned up behind them, they bellywop down the slope and land, with a splash, in a pool of water.

They follow one another closely, as the slide gets slicker and faster and their speed picks up with each run. John James Audubon reported watching a pair of otters do 22 slides each while playing together. In winter, this activity transfers to snowy or icy slopes.

Ben Tollar, small game specialist with the state Department of Environmental Conservation, assures us that the otter is resident in this area, although, "they may be more often seen than their distribution warrants. Never actually abundant, their numbers have increased somewhat with the return of the beaver, whose efforts improved the otters food supply."

These elusive, year-round neighbors live near streams, rivers, or lakes and in marshy areas, swamps, and sloughs, often where water is brackish.

The muzzle of the otter's small head is short, with prominent black nose-pad and small ears, both of which close up for swimming. Eyes set high on the head facilitate peeking out of the water, and prominent, sensitive whiskers help catch prey or measure entry into narrow spaces.

During summer months, otter families usually remain in a chosen area on a stretch of river or lake, or around a few small lakes.

There they keep a well-hidden den for resting, under tree roots, rock ledges, or a thicket. They may use an abandoned beaver lodge or enlarge a woodchuck or muskrat burrow, all relatively close to water. Dens open above water in summer, below the ice line in winter.

In autumn, otters begin travelling over their territory. "They have a large home range," says Mr. Tollar, "with a circuit that covers 50 or 60 miles, from here around through Rensselaer County to Vermont.

"Truly nomadic, they travel through streams and lakes on their way. They avoid roads. Their land routes go through culverts or under bridges.

"A family procession, with otter heads and backs high, seems like a long, undulating serpent.

"In snow, they seem to swim almost as they do in water. I followed an otter trail *up* a gradual mountain slope and tracks made the method clear.

"It had humped its body side-to-side, and apparently rode on its rib cage, for the track showed ridged edges, propelling itself with a push from one foot then another as it slid over the snow on its belly. Of course, downhill was a lot easier."

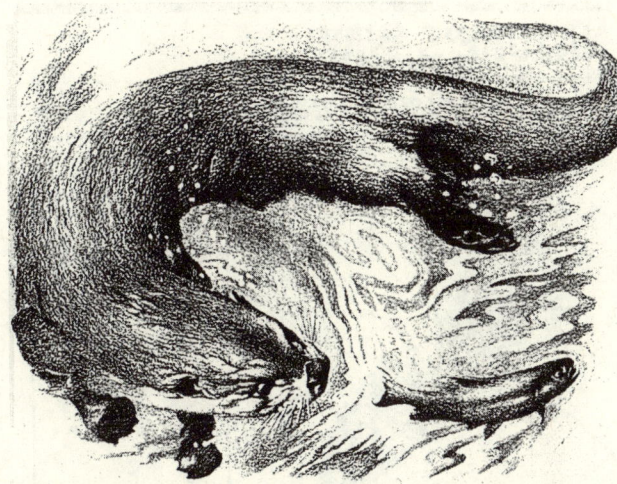

River otter. Long, stream-lined body, dark brown fur, short, stout legs and thick muscular tail, 12-19 inches. Excellent swimmers, up to 7 mph in water, 15 mph on land. Males overall 35-51 inches, weigh 12-25 pounds. Females smaller.

THE INDEPENDENT, OCTOBER 10, 1991

"They often have a game of hide-and-seek with one another."

Honeybee workers outside

NATURE'S WAY
Marion Dusoir Ennes

THE HONEYBEES that go into the countryside to collect nectar and pollen are the oldest, most experienced of the hive. They started as house bees, cleaning cells, then graduated to feeding and nursing young. Then, in succession, they built new wax cells, served as guard and protectors at the hive entrance.

This gradual sequence, lasting about five weeks, included orientation flights in hive environs.

Although task-oriented development stages are accompanied by certain biological adaptations that fit a bee for its job, honeybees are able, in a crisis, to take on jobs out of normal sequence. They switch the biological adaptation according to need, in order to protect and preserve the colony.

Foraging for vital foods that keep the colony alive through all seasons is the toughest, most energy-consuming job of all.

Like all animals, bees need particular nutrients to thrive: sugars available in nectar provide fuel to maintain energy levels, pollen contains protein for growth. Flowers offer nectar and pollen that are converted to honey and bee-bread respectively.

Foraging bees, well-tooled for collecting, are specialists. Some bees collect only nectar, others only pollen.

Whichever type of food they gather, each collector is "flower constant" taking food from only one flower species, ignoring others until supplies are used up.

This singularity helps both bees and plants. Bees learn to probe more and more efficiently as they gain experience, visiting more flowers (up to 500 per trip), many with multiple florets. The bees work faster at greater energy savings.

Plants benefit because the bees' constancy makes pollination prompt and effective.

A honeybee's complex, well-fitted mouthparts hold a long hairy tongue. When inserted in the flower's supply, the nectar rises along the retentive surface. When the bee pulls its tongue back into the suction tube formed by other mouthparts now closed, an airtight connection is made with a pump in the bee' head, activating muscles that cause the nectar to flow down to the honey-crop.

Here it is stored and acted upon by glandular secretion to start the honey-making process. Back at the hive, this new honey is delivered—regurgitated by the forager—then taken into the home worker's crop for further processing before being finally stored in the comb.

A pollen collector has a tough job. Taking along a bit of honey, she settles on the stamen of a flower, usually getting dusted from head to foot. Then scraping up the white, yellow or reddish powdery pollen with her jaws and front legs, she transfers it into the "pollen baskets" on the outside of her hind legs.

While in flight to the next flower, her legs and feet are still busily packing in pollen. First she uses the stiff currycomb on her legs to scrape more pollen from her coat and legs. Then, moistening it with honey, she presses it into the baskets, ultimately unloading it inside the hive for storage close to the nursery cells.

Honey stored in the outermost comb cells, with pollen, is the wealth of this community and the basis for its well-being. Honeybees, who snack on honey as they work, respect its importance.

It takes between 1,000 and 1,500 trips to fill a forager's honey stomach once; 60 stomach loads fill a thimble. Imagine the industry that goes into the storage of more than two pounds of honey a day in a favorable season.

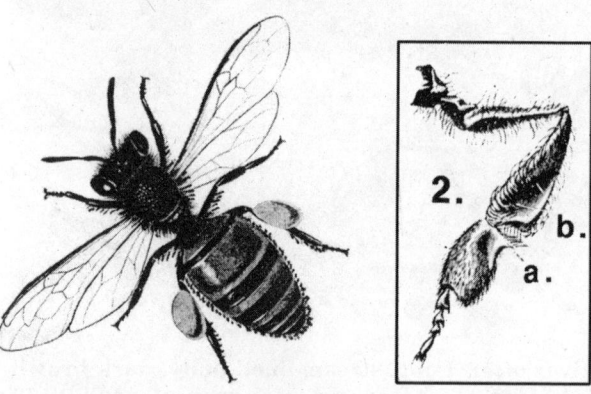
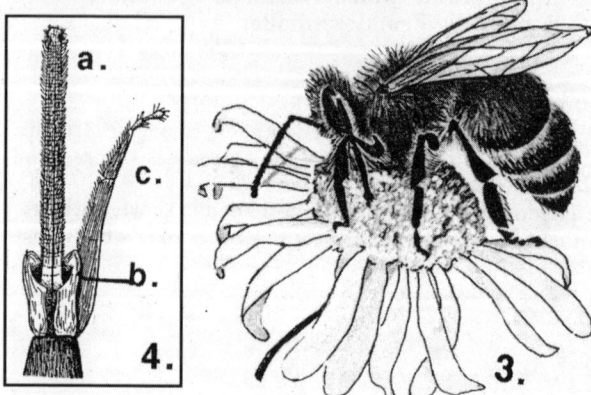

Foraging Honeybees

Foraging honeybees
1. **Pollen collector**, *baskets filled.*
2. **Hind leg** *(outide view)*
   a. *Stiff comb bristles push sticky pollen into*
   b. *basket.*
3. **Nectar collector** *on flower, tongue extended.*
4. **Tongue**
   a. *long, hairy, ending in spoonlike lobe, fits into*
   b. *holder*
   c. *feeling palp (one side shown) alongside.*

THE INDEPENDENT, OCTOBER 10, 1995

"They switch the biological adaptation according to need, in order to protect and preserve the colony."

Dance of the honeybee forager

NATURE'S WAY
Marion Dusoir Ennes

THERE IS A HUMAN SPY in the honeybee home, an electronic robot bee whose activity can be made to conform to the behavior of real message-giving honeybees. Rubbed all over with wax, it matches the hive's scent so residents don't throw it out.

In the darkened hive, mature worker bees watch it closely as it moves in the patterns returning foragers make when they communicate food-finding directions to their nestmates. Its tiny wing mimics real sound patterns and a tube gives out nectar samples.

Like real honeybees who constantly learn from one another, the robot, with computer and operator, learns much from the bees and is telling us.

Mature hive bees are sensitive to messages from scout-foragers who bring information about food sources two to three miles around the hive, or even further. When food is within 100 yards or so, the forager turns its honey over to a worker bee, then reports to the busy colony.

Loaded with scent from the blossoms she found and carrying samples of nectar, she does a "round dance." She moves quickly in one-inch diameter circles, first one way, then the other, attracting other bees who try to touch her with their feelers.

She repeats the dance for one group of bees after another, disgorging samples each time. Persistent dancing indicates a rich source.

Many foragers go out, searching for flowers having the strong scent carried by the scout, then releasing a bee odor at the location to confirm it for their followers.

When honeybee scouts search great distances, they must provide others with more information than is supplied in the round dance. More than just odor and quantity are necessary. Honeybees can overshoot the mark, become lost and die unless they have specific information about direction and distance.

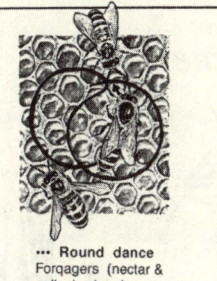
··· Round dance
Foragers (nectar & pollen) signal a valuable new flower find, urge other workers to go out. Followers watch, listen intently.

Waggle dance ···
Other workers watch distant forager's reporting of distance, direction, plus scent & quality. More than 50% make location error less than 15°.

Transmitting honey bee messages

Highly refined sense organs give honeybees excellent information. They are oriented to the sun and its position and have an excellent awareness of time.

Though they only forage by day, they collect food even in cloudy weather. Honeybees know the sun's direction because they detect polarized light. Their acute senses of smell and taste help them zero in on a particular type of flower.

Inside the dark hive, a returning bee positions itself amidst the bee crowds, makes movements, accompanied by sounds, that give workers accurate directions that will take them many miles.

A special "waggling dance" tells them the story. In it the dancer describes a sideways figure eight. Within a one-inch diameter circle, the honeybee makes one loop, then a straight run through the center, finishing with a second loop.

While in the center line, she wags her abdomen rapidly from side to side and beats her wings to send sound signals. Both give information about food location.

These dances are done on vertical comb surfaces, the sun somewhere overhead. If the food is located in the direction of the sun, the bee dances upward toward it on its center line run. If the other way, the bee dances downward, away from the sun.

If food is at an angle to the left of the sun, for example a 70° angle, the dance run is left at a 70° angle. Conversely, if it is to the right, the bee dances to the right at a matching angle.

Distance is indicated by the number of turns: 9 turns in 15 seconds means about 109 yards. A slower, statelier run of 2 turns in 15 seconds means 4,400 to 5,500 yards, shorthand for the amount of energy bees need to return to the hive.

Nobel Laureate Karl von Frisch won the prize in this century for his dedicated work confirming honeybee communication. Today, the robot bee is helping scientists learn more.

THE INDEPENDENT, OCTOBER 26, 1995

"Loaded with scent from the blossoms she found and carrying samples of nectar, she does a 'round dance.'"

Hidden thunder-pumpers

NATURE'S WAY

Marion Dusoir Ennes

IN SWAMPY AND BOGGY MARSHES where mud is thick below, where bulrushes, reeds and cattails grow tall in thick stands, bitterns feed, nest and hide from bird lovers who search them out.

In the 1948 July-August *Audubon Magazine*, naturalists Hayden Pearson reported his own such experience at age 15.

After observing a nesting American bittern pair from an overlooking low cliff for weeks, he and a friend decided to push through a swamp to catch the male in the act of rendering his unique, hollow-sounding *oong-Ka'-choonk* song.

They crawled, belly-down, inching along at 100 feet per hour on their quest. Finally, the mud-covered boys came to rest on a hummock where they could see the bitterns and hoped to hear the song. They were not disappointed.

Feet spread wide, the male stood on his platform of flattened reed stalk and began his serenade. He pulled his head back, then twisted his head and neck, apparently taking in great gulps of air that bulged in his throat as it went down. Then, turning his head forward, the loud *oong-Ka'-choonk* burst forth.

After each bellow he paused to take in more air. The boys heard half-a-dozen calls before darkness pressed their return home.

Bitterns are two species: the bellowing American is about twice as tall as the quieter least bittern at one foot. But unique qualities have brought them many picturesque names.

Descriptively likened to quail or grouse, they were called hog, marsh, or Indian hens, although bitterns are herons, the least bittern being smallest of all herons.

When startled, bitterns point beaks straight up, stretch their necks and pull feathers tight to the body so the bird becomes elongated, its every line stiff and straight as the reeds they stand in. The color pattern of their streaked bellies causes them to "disappear," emerging instead as a dead stump or another dried reed or cattail.

Every mother bird approaches the foot-wide nest by moving slowly, carefully. Stopping frequently, she takes five minutes to travel just five feet to her hungry nestlings.

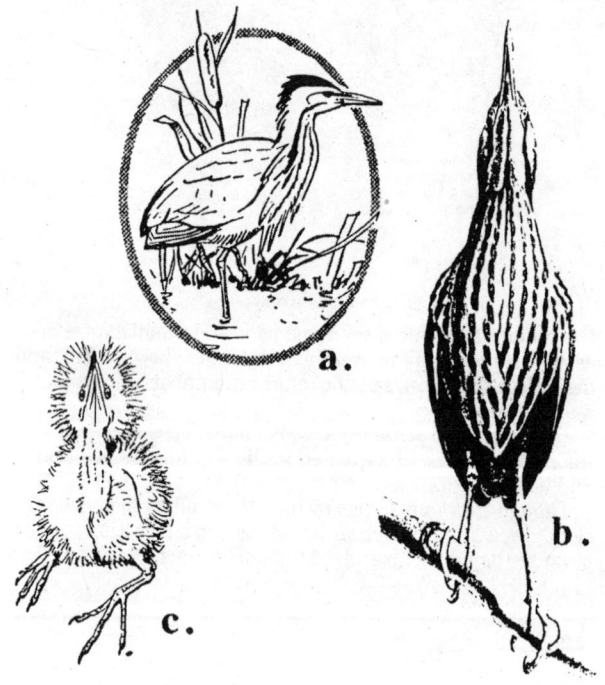

Like other herons, young make fierce grabs at her bill for the half-digested food she carries—frogs, fish, mice, snails, beetles, etc. Each youngster is soon sated with the share she pours into its eager beak.

Mother birds monitor the young birds' explorations, as Jim Sotis learned on a recent expedition. While bird-watching from a canoe, he reports in Hudson-Mohawk Bird Club's August '94 newsletter "Feathers," he heard a female's piercing repetitive alarm cry and saw her clasped to a stalk about 20 yards away.

He turned as he heard the thin responding call of a young bird, realizing he was caught between parent and child. The young bird, still in fluffy down, looking straight at Jim, assumed the stiff, freeze position, eyes fixed, beak pointed upwards. Though visible, this baby bird appeared no thicker than some dried reeds.

Mother flew quickly behind the youngster to a perch 30 yards back, calling again. The young bird turned back toward the clump of stalks, slipped smoothly between reeds and was quickly gone.

Because of the American's song impact, it was called "stake-driver," "thunder-pumper," "barrel-maker," or for the sound itself, "dunk-a-doo" or "plum pudd'n."

For both species, cautious, elusive behavior is augmented by protective poses. All bitterns use a technique called freezing, a rigorous exercise aimed at protecting them when danger threatens.

AMERICAN BITTERN. A. Adult stocky, brown, striped breast, belly, 23 inches tall. Least bittern (not shown) 11-14 inches, brown/tan coat patchier. Both are reclusive marsh birds.

B. Bittern "freezing" head pointed up and neck extension adding about 5 inches to height. Striped breast fully visible.

C. Nestling bittern covered with long, fluffy, light buff down. Unable to fly, threatened young birds "freeze," beaks up, in camouflage position. When approached, they hiss and snarl, spring forward and snap their bills.

THE INDEPENDENT, OCTOBER 13, 1994

"Then, turning his head forward, the loud oong-Ka'-choonk burst forth."

NATURE'S WAY

Wild canaries

A flock of 25 to 50 goldfinch flit quickly from one dry flower to another enjoying seeds in my autumn garden. Their motions are spirited, they riffle grasses and leaves and do aerobatics as they twitter happily to one another.

Every naturalist who writes about goldfinch—a bird about five inches, weighing almost half an ounce—comments on its cheerful nature, sweet voice, and mutual sociability.

Flocks now are in seasonal movement, looking for territories with promising food stores. I hope they have decided that our garden has enough tall weeds to help nourish them throughout the winter.

In fall, males and females, young and old goldfinches look pretty much alike, well camouflaged in dull olive feathers, with dark to black wings, accented with two white wing bars. The birds with blackest wings are probably males.

In spring, the birds undergo a prenuptial molt that markedly changes coloration in the two sexes, called dimorphism. The American goldfinch is highly dimorphic; males are always much brighter than females in dimorphic species and are vigorous territorial defenders.

Duller colored females are safer because they are better camouflaged as they incubate eggs on the nest. Females get new dun-colored feathers in the partial spring molt, keeping black wing and tail feathers.

He courts the female assiduously, first by chasing her with several other males. Having secured her attention by song and special display flights, he circles high in the air, and holding in his wings, goes into a deep dive. He then reverses and coasts upward with wings out, dipping 20-30 feet between peaks. During this roller-coaster flight, he repeatedly sings a warbling song reminiscent of a canary, each burst of song lasting about 30 seconds, with short pauses between.

In summer breeding colors, male goldfinches sport bright yellow coats. A black frontal cap matches black wing and tail feathers.

By the time the goldfinch pair gets serious about nest building and raising a family, it is July. They are the latest nester here; most other birds' young are fledged and flying.

Midsummer, heavy leaf cover offers more nest site security, and brood parasitism by cowbirds is less likely. Perhaps most important, the maturing of vast seed crops, both cultivated and wild, is available to feed the yong. Thistle seeds are especially favored.

The female builds a tightly woven nest, attaching it firmly to the twigs of trees. Almost 3 inches wide overall, its deep (1.5 inch) bowl is 2.3 inches wide. It is waterproof and cushioned with soft, warm thistle or cattail down, with spider silk binding the rim.

She does all the incubating for 12-14 days, taking only brief respites, calling to him for food with rapid, short whistles. He collects a variety of seeds, extracting their contents and predigesting it into a "goldfinch porridge" which he feeds her. For about five days after babies are born, she re-regurgitates the cereal into the babies' mouths.

From mid-September through October, the vivacious dun-colored young fly and flock with adults.

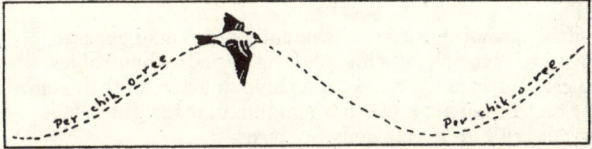

Though hard to see on the ground or among the trees, you can identify goldfinch in their undulating flight over open fields as they sing their characteristic *per-chik-o-ree* song.

THE INDEPENDENT, OCTOBER 18, 1990

"He courts the female assiduously... he circles high in the air, and holding in his wings, goes into a deep dive."

Coyote: myths and realities

NATURE'S WAY

Marion Dusoir Ennes

STORIES ABOUT COYOTES often have the flavor of folk-tales suggesting Reynard the fox fables of European lore. The coyote our indigenous American counterpart, is a begetter of legends as well as fervent complaints.

American coyote lore goes back centuries. Found across the continent, coyote was highly revered by the Aztecs. They immortalized it in stone carvings, passed along the Aztec name *coyotl*, adopted by later generations from Native Americans on.

Among northwestern Indians the Karak religion recognized the coyote's immense cunning, regarding him as a powerful ally. Their tribal mythology includes tales like "How Coyote Made the Indian Tribes," "How Coyote Brought Fire to the People," "How Coyote Made the Columbia River" and many more.

In New York State today, the population of this smallest member of the *canid* family numbers about 13,000, according to Marie Kautz of the state Department of Environmental Conservation.

Mating in late winter, they raise an average five to seven pups in a well-concealed, excavated den or one remodeled from woodchuck or fox burrow.

Before the pups' birth, parents clean and tidy the den. Females ready additional dens, up to a dozen, just in case.

Both parents hunt for food in surrounding brushy terrain.

Although coyotes may occasionally take small exposed livestock, especially during denning periods when babies are growing rapidly, more than three-quarters of their regular diet is rodents and other small mammals. The rest is carrion, fruit or insects, only 3% birds.

Famous for their intelligence and adaptability, coyotes establish themselves, usually unobtrusively, quite close to civilization.

Named for their bark, they are known to humans for their howls—some say for joy, some loneliness, others for communication.

Man continues to be their harshest predator. In a life of constant danger, coyotes risk being shot, trapped or even poisoned. They can be hunted or trapped legally in New York State's long season, from October 26 to February 16.

COYOTE
Canis Latrans
'Barking Dog'

Coyote pelts averaged $14.66 apiece at recent northwestern fur auctions, says DEC's Ms. Kautz. dyed gray, brown, or black, they trim women's clothing.

Hunters and trappers can take unlimited numbers, although trappers find coyotes clever adversaries. Many avoid traps. Numerous reports tell of individual coyotes digging up and dragging traps away, sometimes for release by human friends.

Adversaries of coyotes apparently learned that poisoning of coyotes is seriously self-defeating. Some years back, Western stockmen, who judged coyotes responsible for all their herd losses, started a poisoning program.

Coyotes died. The result, a plague of grasshoppers, but not before the pesky jackrabbit populations expanded and ground squirrels multiplied, digging into agricultural fields, piling up dirt mounds for large families.

Then, insect-eating squirrels needed killing with poison grain, but livestock and poultry died of it, too. With all food chain controls askew, grasshoppers prospered. Ultimately, cyanide guns and poison baits were outlawed.

Human beings can take some credit for the robustly savvy coyote we know today. As human persecution killed the weak and infirm coyotes, trapped the last intelligent, and shot the unwary, natural selection favored larger, more adaptable, more cunning coyotes than those on the continent when Europeans arrived.

In fact, this wild canid enjoys a close and happy family life that parallels our own.

Not an enemy of humans, a healthy coyote has never been known to attack a human being. Intelligent, cautious, he lives discretely, a valuable part of the ecosystem.

1. Canis latrans *describes vocal coyotes, communicating by barking, wavering howls and squeaks. Parents teach pups, using sounds for "freeze," "hide," "run away," "come," "dinner," etc. Young vocally indicate hunger, pain, fear and pleasure.*

2. Adult male *2' tall at shoulder, 44-54" long, including 12-16" bushy, pendant tail. Weight 20-50 pounds, female smaller.*

3. Tracks *(inset, front foot above) measure 7-8". Trotting speed 10-15 mph, gallop average 25 mph, up to 35 mph.*

THE INDEPENDENT, OCTOBER 24, 1996

"... coyote was highly revered by the Aztecs. They immortalized it in stone carvings, passed along the Aztec name coyotl..."

NATURE'S WAY

A lot of lip

Despite this fall's prolonged warmth, local dragonflies—those formidable-looking, diaphanous-winged members of the insect world—have succumbed.

But next year's crop lies in a torpid state, near hibernation, buried beneath the muck of ponds or streams in the insect's larval form, *nymph* (or naiad). Unprepossessing, these nymphs, brown to grayish green, are just as beneficial to humans in their underwater forms as they will be as aerialists.

The order *Odonata*, shared by dragonflies and damselflies, can trace its origin back more than 300 million years, when some achieved a 30-inch wingspan. Today, the largest known is 7½ inches wide.

Such longevity is accomplished with the help of special physical adaptations and skills. After eggs hatch, these insects have only one other developmental stage besides adult, and these nymphs of dragonflies have unique characteristics.

Dragonfly naiads are newly hatched underwater from eggs laid this summer and may winter over one or two season. Most live only underwater, extracting oxygen from their water medium through tracheal gills in the walls of the rectum.

Though it walks sluggishly on six thin legs, it has its own mini jet-propulsion system. When necessary, the nymph can forcibly expel water from the lower food canal and more forward like a rocket.

Dull coloration is a perfect camouflage against the muddy bottoms among the stems of water plants where it lurks, waiting for smaller creatures to come by. Its voracious appetite includes mosquito and beetle larvae, mayflies, small crustaceans and snails, even minnows and tadpoles. Dragonfly naiads are themselves taken by predatory water beetles as well as trout and other gamefish.

The nymph's special capturing device is a complex

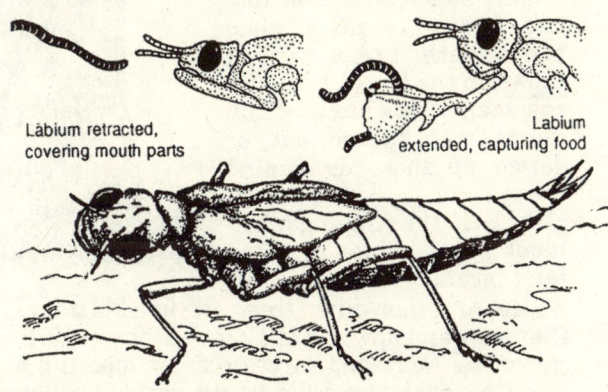

Aquatic nymph of dragonfly, ¾-2", searching for food. Upper schematics show jointed lip (labium) of nymph.

folding lower lip (labium). This jointed organ consists of a kind of arm and at the end a "hand" with several grasping pincers. At rest, it is folded over the mouth parts like a kind of mask. Front on, the nymph looks like a bulldog with great big compound eyes.

When a likely meal comes along, distance is gauged by stereoscopic vision. Then, the lip shoots out in 25 thousandths of a second (a flash much faster than average shutter speed), seizing the prey with pincers and popping it in the mouth. Dragonfly nymphs are so efficient they can dispense with more than 20 mosquito wigglers in one minute.

As such big appetites are satisfied, nymphs grow steadily and shed their skins underwater, molting (depending on species) from 9 to 15 times before they reach adult life. During this time their compound eyes add more six-sided lenses, wing pads develop on the thorax.

Then, on a warm summer day, it propels itself to a water plant and climbs out of the water, supporting itself on a weed, rock, stick, or bank, entering the world of air. The *chitin* (hard covering) of the back splits, the thorax lifts and expands, and the wing pads are visible. The head and forelegs get free, and finally a new insect emerges, nymphal shell left behind.

The body grows now, longer and thinner; furled wings, pleated at the base, begin to unfold. When fully hardened and strong, another colorful dragonfly will fly in the sun.

THE INDEPENDENT, OCTOBER 25, 1990

"The order Odonata... can trace its origin back more than 200 million years, when some achieved a 30-inch wingspan."

NATURE'S WAY:
Pine politics

The history of the white pine in the Northeast was dramatically affected by European colonization and the subsequent waves of change brought about by 400 years of land settlement in this country.

Our first flag was emblazoned with the white pine's image and the first Continental coin, minted in Massachusetts, was imprinted with the pine tree.

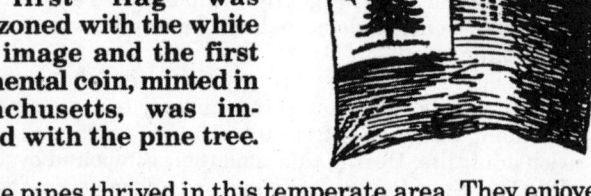

White pines thrived in this temperate area. They enjoyed a growing season of about 150 days; their roots, stems, and needles were saved from freezing by a resinous sap that acts like antifreeze.

As weather warmed, the needle leaves took up photosynthesis with the help of freshly thawed water from the roots, and the pines stretched farther toward the sun.

Colonists and visitors in the early 1600s noticed the value of these rich, prolific forests. They saw tall pines in Massachusetts whose lowest extending limbs started at 100 feet from the ground—with usable lengths of more than 130 feet, weighing 25 tons.

Ralph Austin, a contemporary English orchardist, observed: "England's...forest trees are almost depleted...Nothing is wasted now, but it is almost too late. The ship Mayflower is now the beams and rafters of a barn in Buckingham. Whatever new wood we need for our navy will come from the New World."

The English, expanding and repairing their navy for exploration, trading, and conquest, needed mast timbers to build and repair sailing ships.

The tall-growing white pine—which combined strength with light weight it its supple, resinous wood—was especially desirable for masts but also for spars, planks, and other nautical purposes. The Royal Navy needed reserve supplies to carry on fighting ships for use as replacements when masts were broken by cannon shot.

A 1605 effort made by Royal Navy Captain George Weymouth to transplant the white pine into the mild climate of the British Isles was unsuccessful, so the British government had to count on the colonies for these treasures.

By royal decree, tracts of land in Maine and New Hampshire with tall white pines were set aside, reserved for the crown. But settlers continued to clear land for farming and to use pines themselves for houses, furnishings, tools—cutting trees as they saw fit.

King's men were sent into the forests to mark mast pines with three hatchet blows, in the King's broad arrow mark. This incensed colonists, who burned, cut, or sawed up these designated trees.

By 1761 the King's government put a clause in every land grant "to reserve all White or other Pine trees fit for Masts...of 24 inches Diameter and upwards at 12 inches above the Earth" to the crown, its heirs and successors, for masting of the Royal Navy. No such tree could be cut without a license on pain of forfeiture of the grant and all its lands, along with other British penalties.

The white pine became more and more a symbol of the colonists' determination to be independent. Their response to royal edicts was to take down, with enthusiasm, any timber marked by the King's broad arrow.

By 1775, the Continental Congress recognized the value and importance of these trees and stopped their export entirely. Forty-five hundred pines had been shipped to English naval storehouses by then, but the 99% left were now an unencumbered colonial resource.

THE INDEPENDENT, OCTOBER 26, 1989

"By royal decree, tracts of land in Maine and New Hampshire with tall white pines were set aside, reserved for the crown."

NATURE'S WAY
Battles with old bushytail

Several summers ago, when I took up bird feeding in earnest, I found myself engaged in a war. The shy and playful gray squirrels who had occasionally come out of the woods now appeared in great galloping numbers—eight and nine at a time, jostling each other to get up the feeder pole and gobble up the food.

The feeder opening was about 18 inches long and three inches high—a cozy size for this flexible 18 ½" rodent with its 8 ½" collapsible tail.

At first I made noises and scolded. They quickly ran away, coming back when the coast was clear—first slowly, later more promptly—realizing I was more noise than action.

We moved the feeder, hanging it by a wire from a post that jutted out four feet from the corner of the building, with baffles below the post.

The squirrels studied the situation and quickly found a way around the baffles. They climed up the almost smooth walls, ran across the post, jumped down four feet to the top of the box, then into the feeder and back to gorging. Dominance determined which got the greatest access.

But for us, nothing worked. No matter how quiet we were or how well-shielded from their sight, we couldn't touch them with the garden hose or the handful of pebbles meant to scare them.

Squirrels have sharp hearing and remarkably acute vision. The retina of each eye contains only cone cells, each connected directly to the brain. A squirrel's eye can record 100 separate light flashes per second, as compared with 50 flashes for humans.

They have big black eyes that give them a large field of vision. A 40 degree range of forward binocular vision enables the squirrel to see a great deal without moving its head.

That's why we got the submachine gun. It was realy an enormous, black look-alike that rattled and squirted water, but it really scared our friends.

The squirrels just scrambled out of the feeder, jumped as far as 10 feet to the ground, ran up the nearest tree and into the woods in about 12 seconds—to regroup.

Their ingenuity won. We conceded, adding a short open platform with lots of sunflower seeds, hoping they would share with the birds.

The squirrels knew they had won; they got it all and marked the heap of seeds with urine to designate their new supply.

A strategy session was called for. Tactics were not enough against competitors who had been the cause of the development of the Kentucky rifle, which helped open the frontier—a weapon so accurate it could put "a ball through a squirrel's head at 50 yards."

We installed a new wooden post feeder eight feet from any trees. But it had below it an aluminum cone, pivoted, that truly baffled our plump friends. Another feeder, metal, has a balanced feeding platform. Birds can land and eat, but a squirrel's weight closes it tight.

Now our woodland neighbors get their share by eating below the feeders from a copious overflow.

With their remarkably acute vision and hearing, as well as their acrobatic ability, it is extremely difficult to keep squirrels away from bird feeders.

THE INDEPENDENT, OCTOBER 27, 1988

"That's why we got the submachine gun."

The great egret wars

NATURE'S WAY

Marion Dusoir Ennes

GREAT EXCITEMENT ACCOMPANIES the relatively rare sighting of a great white egret in our county, so it was thrilling to spot two of them at a local pond this year. The last time I saw these tall, elegant, radiantly white birds was mid-October. They were foraging in the shallow waters south of Route 23 between Craryville and Hillsdale.

Great egrets, possibly the same ones, have come sporadically since June, probably visiting from their nearest New York breeding rookery on long Island.

Egrets are members of the heron family, found globally except in the coldest climates. We think of these waders as southern birds. Thousands thrive in sub-tropical, shallow, salt or sweet marshy pools near southern coasts.

But the birds wander, many coming north to breed at established rookeries each spring. Once the breeding process is completed, young and older birds disperse to explore new areas.

Busy rookeries consist of clusters of nests at the tops of tall trees, relatively close to water but remote. Here adults can find small fish, frogs, and small mammals for food, and hope for a reasonable degree of safety for their feisty young.

The three to four bluish-green eggs, laid on successive days, hatch successively. Parent birds feed them four times daily, bringing beakfuls of predigested food. One young bird grabs the parent's bill on its own, drawing it down to the nest, where food is disgorged and each must get the most it can.

Between feedings, the growing young climb around the nest and nearby branches. The older and stronger sibling often attacks the younger, who is knocked out of the nest to its death.

This strange battle for survival is thought by biologists to assure the success of the fittest, who contribute size, strength, and coordination to the species gene pool.

As cruel as it sounds, this battle is nothing compared to the great, and nasty, fifty-year war over egrets fought during the last half of the 19th century.

On the Gulf Coast, boatloads of hunters searched out heronries during spring breeding season, when adult birds—great whites and snowy egrets—were dressed in their gossamer breeding plumage, about 50 plumes per bird. In the siege of their bird cities, adult birds were shot by the thousands, and their young left to die by starvation.

The hunters were an army goaded by the price of plumes offered by the millinery trade, $32 per ounce. In 1902 London, 1,608 packages of heron plumes, each weighing 30 ounces, totaled 48,240 ounces. At four birds to an ounce, these sales alone accounted for 192,960 adults killed, and two to three times that number of young or eggs destroyed.

By the end of the century, the egrets were near extinction.

It was the National Association of Audubon Societies that led the campaign on the side of the birds. Through legislation and education, establishment of sanctuaries and the use of special wardens, plume hunting was stopped. At least two Audubon wardens were killed and more wounded before the war was won.

So the thrill of seeing a great egret close by is not a product of its stately elegance alone. The excitement thrives on the glory of its very existence.

GREAT EGRET. Pure white, three-and-one-half foot tall wader. Long, smooth slender neck, heavy yellow beak. Long black legs and feet. Practices "wade and watch" fishing or hunting. Flight buoyant and graceful on wing-spread up to five feet.

THE INDEPENDENT, OCTOBER 28, 1993

"The older and stronger sibling often attacks the younger, who is knocked out of the nest to its death."

NATURE'S WAY:
Curious kits

About now, most mother raccoons are sending their young into the world to find dens of their own after a summer of serious nurturing and education.

Hollow trees are favorite dens, but a cave or limestone split, an old woodchuck hole, or convenient crevices in barns or sheds will also serve. Raccoons are resourceful animals.

This year's raccoon family was conceived last February. After the female makes her choice of roving males, they remain together for about a week. She stays faithful to him, while he looks for another female to impregnate.

After nine weeks—late March or April—an average of four furry young are born in the mother's den, where she protects them from her mate or any other potential predator.

In 25 days the babies' eyes are open; the black eye mask and tail rings are evident. They stay at home while mother goes out foraging for herself to produce the rich milk which is the kits' primary food.

By June the youngsters' curiosity brings them out of the den, and they explore all aspects of the home tree. They grip the bark and climb over branches and limbs, sometimes walking toward the trunk while hanging upside down.

Soon they are down on the ground, roughhousing, wrestling, growling and squealing or practicing threatening positions with back end hunched up, front end low, ears back, and legs spread. It is hard to get them off balance from this position. When the playing gets too rough, mother comes in and clobbers everybody.

Education begins in earnest in summer when the new family goes out hunting. Mother checks for danger signals, carefully looking around, sniffing the breeze, cocking her ears for any unusual sound—anything that signals danger. When all seems safe, she will climb down, head or back first, young kits following close after.

On their exploratory tour the whole family will investigate just about everything mother finds in their path. Berries, acorns, worms, ground-nesting bird eggs, and other things, all will be studied, sniffed, and handled—then eaten.

My father often told a story about a raccoon family. As he was driving his pick-up, he saw a mother and four kits crossing the country road. He slowed down, because the last little one stopped to examine something while the rest reached the far side. Mother looked around, seeing the car still coming, and raced out to the youngster. She cuffed it soundly and hurried it across to the others. "That little one got a real lesson that day," my father would say.

Mother teaches by discipline if necessary, but more often by example and always with concern for the safety of her young. When a baby raccoon fell off a limb into a quiet stream below and screamed, mother rushed to nuzzle her wet youngster. Baby followed mother more than half way up to the den and then started to squall. Mother came back below the kit, surrounded it with her body, and they climbed back home together.

THE INDEPENDENT, NOVEMBER 2, 1989

"When the playing gets too rough, mother comes in and clobbers everybody."

NATURE'S WAY:
Masked meddler

A full-grown raccoon is universally recognized for its intelligence—sometimes enthusiastically, other times with anger and frustration.

Psychological testing of the raccoon puts it well up on the mammal IQ scale, first below the monkey. The raccoon shows interest in objects of many kinds and is able to learn from experience. A problem-solver, the raccoon can manipulate door knobs, latches, bottle caps, and other closings to achieve its goals.

Native Americans knew this animal well and admired it for its cleverness. Our name raccoon is derived from the Algonquin language. The original, *arakunem*, meant "he scratches with his hands." Indeed, the long slender fingers have remarkable capacity for touch.

The tracks look like baby hand-prints, though in actuality the five digits are all fingers, with no opposing thumb. These dexterous fingers can locate food by touch under water or inside tight spaces. The 2¾" front feet and 4½" rear feet have long, sharp claws and are well adapted for climbing.

Observations of raccoons in captivity and in the wild show that the animal's well-known habit of washing food is not consistent. Some food it swishes in water is already clean and it eats muddy food as well as dry food. But it often holds and touches its food all over, enjoying its well-developed tactile sense, which is intensified when the paws are wet.

Raccoons eat almost everything—except tomatoes—according to season: grasshoppers, crickets, worms, larvae, turtle or birds' eggs, tadpoles, frogs, toads, turtles, crayfish, shiners, minnows, spent shad, baby muskrats, deer carcasses, etc.

In summer, fruits (berries, cherries, melons, plums, peaches, grapes) and vegetables are so popular that they compose up to 80% of the animal's diet. They like peas, potatoes, and of course, young corn.

Farmers despair over the damage raccoons do to cornfields. The pesky animals break stalks, pull down ears, husking and sampling kernels on just about every ear they touch.

The challenge of a presumably secure supply of food seems to be irresistible to a raccoon. They are known chicken house raiders, and have inched through a 3½" chink.

Elinor Mettler of Copake Falls sent along a clipping from a Cape Cod paper about a "masked bandit" who stole a plastic bird feeder eight separate times, each time eating all the seeds. The owners tried new hooks, new cap, baby oil and mechanical obstructions, and only succeeded by hanging the feeder on a wire between two trees. "Raccoons can tightrope the wire, but prefer not to," they noted.

Not a true hibernator, a raccoon's body temperature and metabolism remains the same throughout the year. The animal gets lethargic when temperatures get down to 28° or 26° and will curl up in a den and go to sleep. After all that eating, a full-sized, nearly three-foot long raccoon has amassed about 50% of its body weight in fat, an extra layer on the tail, and an inch thick on the back.

The raccoon's double layer of fur—dense soft underhairs covered by longer coarse outer hairs—is warm and durable. Raccoons stay snuggled up through winds above 8 mph, which deaden the benefits of keen scent and hearing, and deep snows that make it hard to move. On a mild winter night, they may go foraging to augment their insulation layer.

THE INDEPENDENT, NOVEMBER 9, 1989

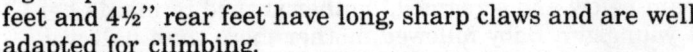

"They are known chicken house raiders, and have inched through a 3½" chink."

The courting cicada chorus

NATURE'S WAY

Marion Dusoir Ennes

AFTER YEARS UNDERGROUND, nymph cicadas, anticipating a whole new phase of life, move to the earth's surface. In early summer's air, cicadas jettison their hard underground cases. Then, with a functional adult body that changes from creamy white to dark brown, they spread diaphanous wings and fly toward sun-bathed treetops.

Not just one cicada, hundreds and thousands emerge synchronously in a temporary explosion reminiscent of heavy fruiting of most nut trees.

This insect food crop attracts a wide range of predators. In their brief season, adult cicadas are never safe from attack.

Birds—crows, kestrels, bluejays, robins, blackbirds—are some that come to the feast, leaving behind piles of insect wings. Plump cicadas are also nutritious snacks for box turtles, skunks, tomcats.

It is one of the few insects that boasts its own insect predator, the giant cicada-killer. Hunting on silent wings, this huge hornet seizes and stings the cicada to numbness. Then it climbs to a higher tree branch and still clasping its heavy burden, glides to the ground.

Finally, the wasp crawls into its deeply-dug burrow, where the female lays an egg on each body captured. Hatched larva feed on the carcass. When fully grown, the larva spins a cocoon and pupates during the winter, emerging as another cicada-killer in spring.

Notwithstanding all threats to its life, each cicada responds to its own biological imperative: to mate and produce a new generation.

Crowds of cicadas now cover the branches of trees. While females wait silently, males immediately begin their luring serenade. As more and more emerge, the original faint trill of the earliest arrivals swells into a resonant, humming chorus.

Once into his song, the male doesn't stop until death, even when caught in the jaws of a skunk or having fallen into the current of a flowing stream.

The choir wanes, then stops in night's darkness, only to start again in morning sun. Then a siesta of quiet until the chorus commences in late afternoon, reaching great volume on long summer evenings.

Unlike other sound-producing insects, cicadas contain their reverberating instrument within their bodies.

Grasshoppers, crickets and katydids, who also produce repetitive sounds, make them by external frictional mechanisms. They rub one body part—a leg or a wing acting as a scraper—across another part fitted out like a file, to make their music.

Cicadas have paired chambers, one in either side of the abdomen. Like musical instruments, each side has a thin tymbal (kettledrum) membrane. Muscles attached to each membrane by struts pull the membrane in, then relax to release it.

This steady in-and-out vibration of the tymbal by the cicada, producing its train of high-pitched clicks, is amplified by several air sacs contained within the abdominal walls.

The sound is irresistible to the alert female waiting for a mate. Wooed, she is now won by the male suitor. Their brief encounter serves to fertilize her eggs.

Now, his job done, his song dies, and he follows. His body falls, becoming just one more of the many in the pile below the tree.

The still active female wastes no time. She uses her needle-like ovipositor to cut deep slits into the tree bark, and deposits her full complement of eggs one at a time until each one is securely placed within. Then, she too, dies.

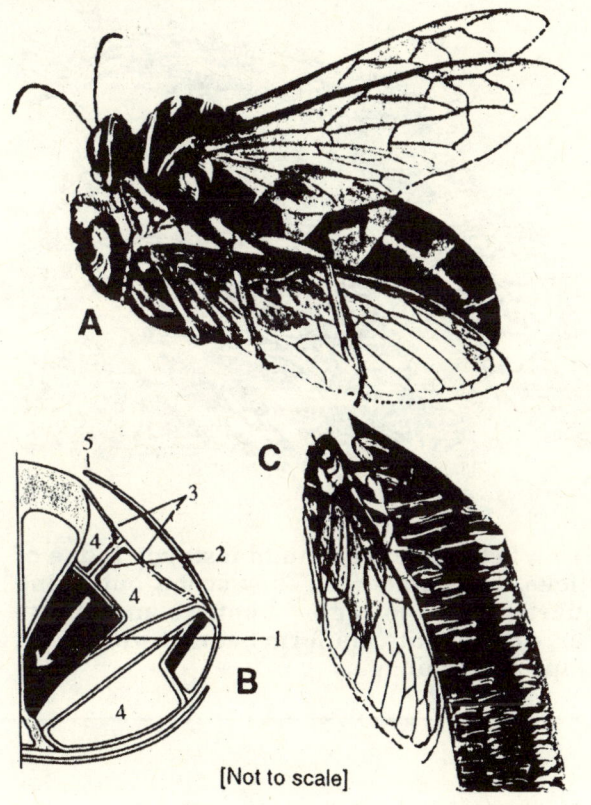

[Not to scale]

A. CICADA-KILLER WASP. *1½ inches long, carrying 1¼-inch adult cicada after inflicting paralyzing sting to body.*

B. *Cicada's sound-producing organ in mid-body (cross section, one side). [1] Muscle pulls in [2] strut attached to [3] tymbal, which buckles, making click sound. [4] Air sacs are amplifiers. [5] External skin (cuticle).*

C. *Cicada female. 1¼-inch, making slits in tree bark to deposit eggs.*

THE INDEPENDENT, DECEMBER 8, 1994

"Once into his song, the male doesn't stop until death…"

NATURE'S WAY
Well-designed engineer

Beavers are hunkering down for winter after a busy autumn collecting food supplies. You may still catch a glimpse of them, as I did, on a visit to Massachusetts Audubon Society's Pleasant Valley Sanctuary in Lenox.

Largest of North American rodents, beavers are superbly adjusted to the water environment where they live, build a home, and raise their young. Even more exciting, they are the only mammals besides humans known to make substantial environmental changes to provide their needs for food, safety, and air.

Beavers live from 10-20 years, usually weigh 25-50 pounds and occasionally reach 80 pounds. A thick coat of brown fur covers a body ranging from 36-41 inches long, including a 4-inch wide, 10-inch long flat tail. Underwater the tail serves as a rudder; on land, a prop as beavers stand to gnaw on trees.

There are five fingers (no opposing thumb) on the short front legs. Large webbed five-fingered rear feet can spread about eight inches, making powerful paddles for swimming.

Underwater, beavers' eyes are covered by a transparent (nictating) membrane which protects the eye and improves vision. Ears and nose are closed by a special veil. Submerged, this mammal's need for oxygen decreases, heart action and respiration slow to half speed, making it possible to work underwater up to 15 minutes.

"Detroit could not have designed a better animal," said Scott Lewis, naturalist, who provided the details. He pointed out several beaver dams and lodges constructed at Pleasant Valley Sanctuary over the years.

In 1932 Morris Pell, a former sanctuary warden, saw the need to add bodies of water to the existing habitat.

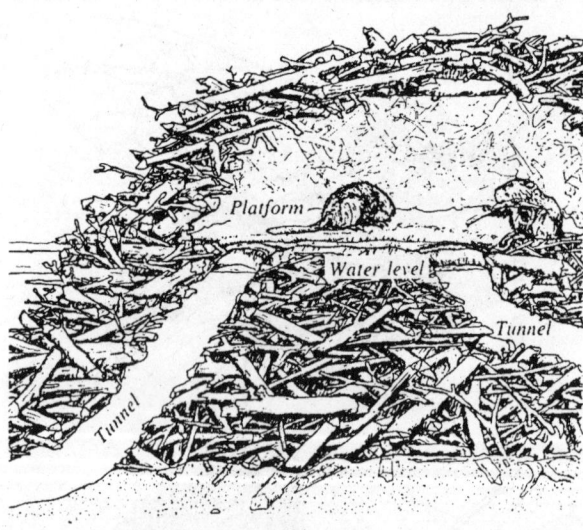

From below, beavers build a sturdy lodge of sticks, mud, and sod. They scoop out living quarters with lower-level entries and an upper, drier family platform bedded with wood chips for drainage.

He brought in engineers Paul and Paula Bunyan, a pair of New York beavers who had lived in Central Park. Since then, their descendants (and others from the north) have spread and become prolific throughout the state.

Amazing engineers, beavers survey the gently sloping terrain around a brook. They they create a pool—three to four feet—deep enough to give them swimming room without freezing solid in winter.

The whole family, except newborns, works from dusk to dawn, the female taking major responsibility. Their construction tools include two pairs of large, sharp, continuously growing incisors with hard orange-colored enamel covering. These wear down and are sharpened as they cut trees, branches, and logs.

Beavers can cut trees up to six-inches in diameter, cutting them into manageable lengths for floating. They drag branches to the water, float them out, placing canopies up-stream to catch debris, then interweave logs and sticks into spaces to complete the construction.

They use their front feet to scoop up mud and stones or sod, carrying it against their chests underwater to fill in the dam.

Beaver dams are built in 48 continental states and Alaska; they range from 15 to 4,000 feet in length.

During autumn, they collected many saplings and branches, floated them to a storage area near the lodge, and stuck them in the mud. There these food supplies will stay fresh during winter, where everything outside (including the lodge covering) is frozen solid.

Inside, the family will cuddle up to keep warm, swimming out to the pantry to cut off a branch for nourishment as needed.

THE INDEPENDENT, NOVEMBER 15, 1990

"Underwater, beavers' eyes are covered by a transparent (nictating) membrane which protects the eye and improves vision."

NATURE'S WAY
Naturalized citizen

As a child, I stroked the smooth mottled feathers of the elegant, long-tailed stuffed pheasant on my friend's mantel. This bird was captured in old-fashioned farm country in the thirties, when pheasants were still populous in the state (200,000 were taken in open season in 1926) and the birds continued to thrive 'til the early 1940s when populations began to decline.

These birds were taken not just as trophies. A brace of pheasants, each about three pounds, made a substantial meal of delicious white meat—reason enough for thanksgiving by a country family during the great depression.

Ring-necked pheasants are naturalized wildlife citizens, imported around the turn of the century. Efforts to establish some of the world's other 48 species failed, but this pheasant, originally from Chinese rice paddies, succeeded.

They are fowl-like birds, similar to chicken in habits and social patterns. Males are territorial, 75% compete with one another for the best and largest areas, the rest freelance or float.

A territory is established in March when a male makes an announcement daily at dawn. He stands erect, flaps his wings, and crows 'skwa-GOCH, hoping to attract neighborhood females. If other males show up, aggressive threatening includes swelling of wattles with head high, chasing, harsh calls, and may end in fights involving jumping and pecking.

Exotic male pheasant, 30-36 inches from beak to long, striped, pointed tail. Beak is yellow, head green with black hornlike tufts, scarlet cheek wattles, white ring neck; body iridescent in browns, gold, bronze, copper, with black-and-white chevrons.

Mottled brown hens gather in harem groups and are wooed individually. Having attracted her with his crowing, the cock swells his bright red cheeks and black tufts, pulls in his head and drops a wing. Sometimes he finds a tidbit for her to eat, clucks and jerks his head toward it.

When enthusiastic, she hops, stretches her neck and spreads her wings somewhat, a signal that she is ready to mate.

By April, egg-laying is under way. The female has chosen a site with good cover in a dense meadow, hedgerow, or wooded area, scratched out a shallow nest, and lined it with leaves and grasses. She lays one egg about every two days and starts incubating when the last egg is laid.

She incubates eggs for 24 days, taking an hour off each afternoon to feed and preen. The female assures warm contact with her body by slipping her bill under each egg and rolling it over at regular intervals. In early incubation stages she will desert a nest disturbed by humans or others and may start all over again.

Mother leads her flock over a wide 5 to 10-acre area, looking for a variety of insects and seeds. She broods them nightly 'til they grow too large and disperse when about 11 weeks old.

Cover is critical to pheasants. Studies have shown that loss of large grassy meadows and hedgerows puts the birds at risk of predation by foxes, great-horned owls, and red-tailed hawks. When good cover is diminished, pheasants have few places to hide, and nesting efforts are doomed.

Federal and state cost-sharing programs encouraged rural landowners like farmers to increase grass habitats. One elegant bird—a challenge to hunters, a joy to bird-lovers—can continue to thrive if efforts are successful.

THE INDEPENDENT, NOVEMBER 21, 1990

*"Ring-necked pheasants are naturalized wildlife citizens...
originally from Chinese rice paddies..."*

Treasuring American toads

NATURE'S WAY

Marion Dusoir Ennes

IN A SEASON THAT ASKS US to count our blessings, let's give thanks for the American toad. Until early this summer, the last time I saw a toad protecting my garden was about 15 years ago. Now, this plump benefactor again devours pests on his insect patrol, and I am reassured.

Concern about amphibian species rises as more and more appear on the endangered list. Their vulnerability, intensified by semiaquatic lifestyles, comes in part from habitat destruction, depriving them of suitable living areas, and from pollution and acidification absorbed by their permeable skins.

Western toads by the hundreds scramble over ice and snow to propagate their species in early May. Each female lays 20-foot-long jellylike strips containing 12,000 eggs fertilized by males.

Within two days, the eggs start to die, victims of the same mid-range of ultra-violet rays (UV-B) that cause sunburn, skin cancers and weaken immune systems in humans. These effects in amphibians and humans are demonstrably increasing since the thinning of the ozone layer.

Some amphibians have a cell enzyme called photolase that counteracts the destructive effects of UV-B. But western toads do not, and breeding pairs in one study dropped from 500 one year to 147 the next, with fewer healthy tadpoles hatched.

In October, our local toad's hind feet dug backward and downward, creating an underground chamber where, sealed up, it is hibernating until April.

The squat toad body, covered by warty skin, records environmental changes of temperature and moisture. Unable to drink, the toad's skin absorbs water from wet plants or damp soil.

Touching a toad does not cause warts, but the toad skin does exude a diluted irritating poison called bufotalin. It certainly discourages dogs from snatching toads in their jaws.

Molting four times annually to accommodate growth, the toad shrugs, then draws its split skin into a wide mouth, enjoying extra nourishement as its shiny new coat dries.

American Toad

Everything about the form and function of a toad serves its own goal as a prodigious eater of insect pests.

The always hungry toad hunts quietly, listening for sounds, watching for movement. His muscles tense, respiration slows. He has no chest muscles. Air inhaled through oval black nostrils must be swallowed.

Though somewhat nearsighted, his elevated eyes shining golden with black centers are so impressive they have often been celebrated in literature. Shakespeare tells us:

> *The ungainly toad*
> *That crawls from his secure abode*
> *Within the mossy garden wall*
> *When evening dews begin to fall.*
> *Oh, mark the beauty of his eye,*
> *What wonders in that circle lie!*
> *So clear, so bright, our fathers said --*
> *"He wears a jewel in his head."*

The toad's short focal length means his prey is always within striking distance. When it moves, he whips out a long sticky tongue connected at mouth's front. Its quick motion wraps the hapless caterpillar, slug, earthworm or insect (including grasshoppers, flies, mosquitoes, cut worms, etc.), eating 10,000 injurious pests every three months.

Overflowing mouthfuls are pushed in by hand, soon swallowed as closed eyes help push food down. Eating incessantly, he only thrives if he fills his belly four times every 24 hours.

Eggs, tadpoles and toads are all vital in the food chain, providing nutrients to various insects, amphibians, reptiles, birds and mammals. American toads can live, happily for us, 30 years.

Adult toad. Throat distended in distinctive spring call, sweet and tremulous, reminiscent of slow opening of Beethoven's "Moonlight Sonata." Body thick-set, short-legged, broad-toed. Warty skin. Color varies brown to brick-red, olive or gray. Light stripe center back. Females reach 4.5 inches, males 3.5.

Inset: a. Sticky tongue extends up to 2 inches to catch fly. b. Shows attachment at front.

THE INDEPENDENT, NOVEMBER 22, 1995

> *"Touching a toad does not cause warts, but the toads skin does exude a diluted irritating poison called bufotalin."*

NATURE'S WAY:
A third kingdom

For centuries and in many cultures, microscopic organisms have been put to life-enhancing use in the brewing of beers and wines, yeasts to bake bread, and cultures to make cheese. All of these agents are *funguses*.

Scientists are now able to describe the special growth patterns and habits of these species—microscopic and visible—and have recognized funguses as a separate kingdom, on a par with plants and animals.

The distinction among these three kingdoms becomes clear in patterns of nutrition. Plants use photosynthesis to *manufacture* organic matter; animals *ingest* solid organic materials; and fungi *absorb* soluble organic compounds.

These clear distinctions were only recently identified. In past times they were considered supernatural in origin, coming from some mysterious earthly process.

Without the typical plant organization of root, stem, leaf, flower or fruit, even serious botanical students like Linnaeus were baffled about where to put these odd mushroom "plants."

A little more than 100 years ago, after Pasteur made some basic discoveries about fermentation processes, German botanist Heinrich Anton DeBary pioneered the science of mycology—the study of fungi.

Examples of 100,000 of these are stored at the National Fungus Collection in Maryland. Now, at least 200,000 species are believed to exist on earth.

A fungus consists of fine, fast-growing threads (up to a half-mile in 24 hours) called *hyphae*, and the tangle they make, called the *mycelium*. They reproduce by means of spores which they produce from various kinds of fruiting bodies by the hundreds of millions. A mushroom is such a fruiting body.

Spores are omnipresent and very hardy. They can dry out or freeze and still return to life, turning into *hyphae* and *mycelium* to continue the growth process.

A fungus does not need light nor oxygen to grow, and it can survive by eating (absorbing) carbohydrates, fats, proteins. Its adaptability is evident, for it can also feed on manufactured products like paint or jet fuel.

Current evidence suggests that fungi lived on earth when the atmosphere consisted of ammonia and methane—no oxygen—more than two billion years ago. In that ancient time their existence and ability to effect chemical changes and release carbon dioxide is now thought to have been a significant factor in the evolution of plants—and, ultimately, of animals.

Today we know that the vegetable kingdom on which animals depend requires much more carbon dioxide for photosynthesis than can be produced by animal exhalation. It is the breakdown of vegetable and animal wastes through decomposition that creates the remaining three-fourths of the billions of tons of carbon dioxide needed. The *hyphae*, travelling through insoluble compounds in forest waste litter, release the extra quota of gasses needed.

Fungi include entities known as molds and mildews, mushrooms, truffles, and brackets, rusts, and blights, and decomposers. Many of these names conjure up negative images for humans.

But on reflection, most people would applaud, for example, the results of fermentation, the benefits of decomposition of wastes, the curing powers of penicillin—challenges readily assumed by these primitive members of the fungal kingdom.

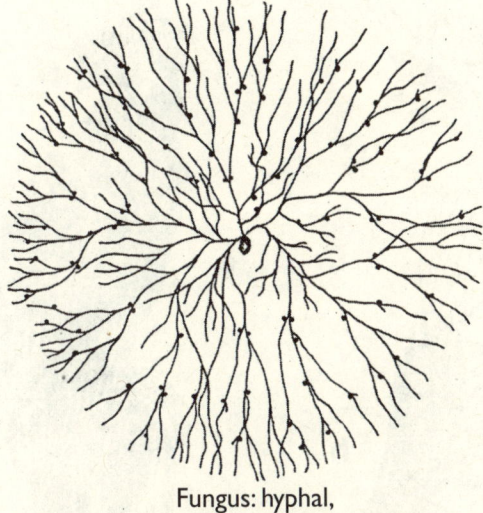

Fungus: hyphal, and the tangle they make

THE INDEPENDENT, NOVEMBER 23, 1989

"In past times [fungi] were considered supernatural in origin, coming from some mysterious earthly process."

Honest foragers

NATURE'S WAY

Marion Dusoir Ennes

LET'S GIVE THANKS for the turkey vulture. Here is a drab-coated bird without a song, a raptor listed with skilled hunting falcons, hawks and eagles, but without their speed or sharp talons. The turkey vulture's talents, though significant, are less romantic.

Turkey vultures (so named for their resemblance to wild turkeys) get a bad rap even from Charles Darwin, who called them disgusting. Today we realize this bird's importance as a scavenger of mammals, birds and fish carcasses—all potential disease carriers.

Coming north each spring to breed, turkey vultures meet in obscure places, old hollow tree trunks, caves or on cliff ledges. One family thrived in a recess at the Wilson Powell Wildlife Sanctuary's Dorson Rock in Old Chatham.

Covered in fuzzy white down, two ungainly chicks hatch after 30 to 40 days incubation.

Devoted parents feed and protect their young, bringing choice bits of aromatic aged meat to the nest site, partially digested by parents, then regurgitated from growing birds.

Nesting areas that shelter young from 8 to 10 weeks before they can fly are not (happily for the birds) popular with humans.

By late summer, fledglings are old enough to join parents and other adult birds at remote night roosts, up to 100 or more at a time. Mornings they rouse slowly, then take part in what seems a ritual.

Naturalists were in awe observing crowds of birds facing the sun with wings spread apart to catch the solar energy. These rays warm their bodies and dry out any dampness in their feathers before they can fly.

All vultures benefit from special adaptations. They have bald, wrinkled skin on head and neck, preventing feather-soiling and accumulation of harmful bacteria.

Their food of choice, carrion, eliminates the need for chase and attack of active live prey. Their broad wings support soaring, energy-reduced flight.

Turkey vultures seek rising columns of warm air (thermals), then glide in slow circles, staying aloft by sinking more slowly than air rises.

Relatively short, broad wings support their weight easily, giving the bird great maneuverability at slow speeds. They avoid drag from wing broadness by separating primary feathers, making slots that reduce above-wing high pressure.

From great heights they search for food, by sight over open spaces, by smell over forests.

Recent studies by David Houston, reported in September 1994 *Natural History*, show that these forest foragers possess a discriminating sense of smell that leads them to carrion. Other vulture species in the Americas, including king and black vultures, without the same abilities, follow them to find food, making turkey vultures the only "honest foragers."

Houston's work, supported by Kenneth Stager of Los Angeles Natural History Museum, clearly confirms that these birds, flying just over the tree canopy, start to circle, then follow the scent trail down as soon as they get a whiff of carrion.

Their sense of smell is acute and refined. Although they prefer fresh carrion, from a distance they can detect scent molecules when meat is only slightly decayed, at least 12 hours old. A 24-hour carcass creates enough of a stench to attract the birds easily.

They reject rancid, badly decayed meat which contains dangerously toxic or digestion-impeding bacterial compounds. Turkey vultures can judge the age of a carcass from above, just as our ancient hunting ancestors did when they scavenged for food on the ground.

A. TURKEY VULTURE, *American native, 26" long, about 67" wingspan. Dark brown body, naked red head of wrinkled skin.*

B. *Sustains flight for long periods without flapping wings. In flight, wings form a V [dihedral]. Silvery underwing feathers visible from below.*

C. *Range includes whole U.S. [above and below borders to South America as well]. Permanent residents in deep Southeast.*

THE INDEPENDENT, NOVEMBER 23, 1994

"They have bald, wrinkled skin on head and neck, preventing feather soiling and accumulation of harmful bacteria."

NATURE'S WAY
Turkeys in season

Flocks of wild turkeys thrive all around us. They are neighbors who love this terrain as much as we do, but keep a wary eye on our behavior and avoid contact.

They lead a busy social life of their own. The autumn brings them together in mixed flocks of males, females, and young.

Favorite haunts are mature forests where the understory is not heavy but thickets provide cover or cultivated fields with open, canopy-like places.

Flock contact is maintained by a language of sounds quickly learned by young birds. Hens control and protect younger birds with signals. This "talking" to one another pervades the turkeys' day and plays an important role in survival and flock development.

Besides a whole repertoire for mating, particular protective calls tighten up the flock, others help a lost turkey finds its way back. There are alarm and warning signals and some, like the hen's cackle that tells the young to join her on the ground and be quiet, are direct orders.

Their food choices change seasonally. They are heavy feeders, especially in late winter as the reproductive season approaches. About 90% of their diet is plant material; one study identified 345 plant species, food variety that strenghtens species survival.

In warm seasons turkeys eat insects, small amphibians, and crustaceans. In fall and winter, protein and oils are gained from acorns, hickory, or beech nuts and other tree seeds, grains like corn, rye and oats. Flocks can often be seen gleaning a cut cornfield.

Berries are favorite food: fatty berries of dogwoods or wild grapes, hawthorns, poison ivy, and sumac s.

Green foods like grasses, plant leaves, sedges, and ferns provide essential Vitamin A.

When scratching over the ground for food there is a regular sequence—once right, twice left, and once right again—then a careful inspection before they peck.

In deep soft snows these birds have difficulty foraging, but can survive without food for several days. They require water daily and will eat snow to satisfy water needs.

Turkeys are birds of regular habits. Arising at or near daybreak, they forage for food mornings and afternoons but take a mid-day break.

Because they are vulnerable to ticks, lice, and mites, they take frequent dust baths to eliminate the vermin and cleanse their feathers.

Sometimes, morning or afternoon, after they eat, they play. Small groups of 8 to 16 turkeys have been observed in their own game, a kind of chase or frolic. Sounding a fierce, strident call, they run forcefully at one another, then dodge suddenly then just before colliding, veering away within inches of contact. Sometimes they skirt through a brush pile as if to hide, or jump as if they were at leapfrog. Then suddenly the game ends, all quiet down.

Turkeys, who sleep in trees, take roosting seriously. They start moving toward roosting trees from 4 p.m. on. A flock can be a mile away from a roost, but at sundown they break into a run toward the chosen roosting tree.

Each turkey tries out several branches before squatting down with breast against the roosting limb, then does a little preening before sleep. The squatting position tightens tendons that pull the toes tight around the limb, the head goes over the shoulder, and sleep follows.

Eastern turkey, 36-48 inches. Plumage metallic bronze, copper and green reflections; tail feathers chestnut-tipped. Upper neck and head naked, bluish, some pink that extends to skin fold under neck. *Inset* Feet, long flexible toes adapted for foraging. Long legs provide wide, eight-inch long scratching span.

On a bright day they rouse at sunrise, sounding soft nasal syllables to one another, offering reassurance that they are all together.

THE INDEPENDENT, NOVEMBER 27, 1991

"Flock contact is maintained by a language of sounds quickly learned by young birds."

NATURE'S WAY
Recyclers

Until the great age of exploration by Europeans in the 1600s, beavers shared the temperate regions of this continent with Native Americans. The relationship was comfortable, there was plenty of room for both and little conflict of lifestyles.

Native Americans greatly admired beavers for their skill, expertise, and determination. An Algonkin legend explains that the Great Beaver invited an Indian brave to spend the winter in his lodge, where the brave learned many useful and wonderful things.

According to Spence's *Myths of the North American Indians*, "they kept him warm by placing their thick soft tails on his body, and taught him the use of...healing arts...tobacco...various ceremonial dances, songs, and prayers belonging to the great mystery of 'medicine'."

The brave returned to his people, bringing a "beaver bundle" with him and began to teach them the mysteries of its "medicine." Ultimately a dynasty of medicine men handed down the beaver medicine traditions and ceremonials.

In fact, natives caught beaver by hand quite easily in winter by waiting near their plunge holes, special underwater entrances to the beaver lodge. Indians used sharp beaver teeth as chisels to shape wood and bone. The pelts were used for clothing and meat for food. In winter, the fatty tissue of the tail was considered a real delicacy, often served to guests.

A musky secretion called castoreum (excreted from a gland at the base of the tail) contains salicylic acid, a principle ingredient in aspirin. It served as a medicament for many illnesses, including colic, frostbite, hysteria, and epilepsy.

Over a period of one million years, beavers have recycled and remodeled wetland habitats as they built dams for their own protection, with domed structures for family life and winter survival.

Beavers were well-known in Europe, where their fur was available only to upper classes. By the 1400s their populations were almost decimated.

Explorers like Henry Hudson and Jacques Cartier opened up the continent and discovered "fur gold." Great trading companies grew up; Native Americans brought in pelts and eagerly traded them for iron tools and implements, weapons, and then brandy. The black stripe count on a Hudson Bay blanket was the exchange mark; four stripes equalled four beaver pelts.

The colonists at Plymouth added branch trading posts in Maine and Connecticut where, among other things, corn was traded for beaver pelts. This earned our forefathers enough money to pay off loan sharks in London who had subsidized their endeavors.

As populations gave out from heavy trapping in the East, activities moved West; Lewis and Clark's exploration was to report on beavers.

Between 1853 and 1877, almost three million pelts were marketed by the Hudson's Bay Company at the rate of 250,000 per year. The enormous profits attracted people like John Jacob Astor, whose great fortune was founded on expanding western fur trades.

Rival companies killed every animal possible, ignoring the most primitive rules of hunting, killing males and females indiscriminately, and almost eliminated beaver altogether by 1900.

Re-stocked now, beavers are back at their beneficial recycling work, building dams that reduce flooding and erosion. Raised watertables reduce fire danger, create improved habitats for insects, fish and waterfowl, raccoons, otters, and mink. New meadows are formed from the silts in old dams, enriched by recycled organic twigs and branches, creating farmland for the crops on which we depend.

THE INDEPENDENT, NOVEMBER 27, 1990

"An Algonkin legend explains that the Great Beaver invited an Indian brave to spend the winter in his lodge..."

NATURE'S WAY:
Silent hunter

One recent early morning—about 5 a.m.—I was roused by a close *hoo, hoo-hoo, hoo, hoo* sound. As I listened, the great horned owl's call sounded about every three to four minutes, receded, and then faded into distant woodland.

Great horned owls, specific to North and Central America, are one of a worldwide family of 134 owl species. It is the only large owl species in this area, and can average one to three pairs per square mile, if the total forest area is large enough.

Owls have always had human characteristics attributed to them. The ancient Greeks dedicated the owl to Athena, the Olympian goddess of wisdom; they were considered symbols of wisdom, luck and victory, and were inscribed on coins.

In the early twentieth century, a new anthropomorphism ascribed negative attributes to this bird. It was described as "lord high executioner of the owl tribe" doing its "nefarious work" by night... with "savage instincts, doing more damage than all other species."

Fortunately, enough evidence was amassed to give this bird its due, and now it is spoken of as a "soldier of fortune."

The great horned owl is a raptor; it gets food by killing and eating other animals, mostly those smaller than itself, such as mice, rats, crows, rabbits, opossums, skunks, house cats, muskrats, gophers, waterfowl and land birds. It will take domestic birds in unprotected poultry yards.

Great horned owls have an acute sense of sight and of hearing well adapted to hunting at night. Large eyes are capable of rapidly, sharply focussing at various distances. Their eyes, rigidly set in bony sockets, look straight ahead, with fields of vision that overlap, giving them excellent binocular vision and good depth perception.

When they need to change their range of sight, they can turn their heads in a 270° arc. Extra neck vertebrae make this extension possible, and contrasts with the 180° arc possible for hawks, or humans.

A large, powerful, nocturnal bird, 18-26 inches long, 2½ to 4 pounds (female larger), 35-52" wingspread, this 'hoot owl' has soft, fluffy, cross-striped plumage over the entire body, legs, and feet. It has strong talons and a sharp, curved beak.

The owl's eyes have a third eyelid, called the "nictating membrane," which closes sideways to protect the eye during jerky head movements and when flying through foliage. They can see well in daylight; their eyes adjust light intake by expanding or contracting the pupil opening. But they need a little light to see at night.

The sensitive, large ears of the great horned owl, under the sides of the facial disc, face foward and are unusually shaped. On one side the external ear's central fold points up; on the other side, down, to help give these birds the capacity to locate sound in a three-dimensional way.

Combined, these agile sensory organs offer little quarter to a chosen prey animal.

And they are adapted for silent flight. Wing feathers are fitted with comblike projections on their top surfaces, fringelike structures at the lower wing edges, and a velvety pile surface, reducing turbulence and lessening flight sound.

With all this, each great horned owl, so well-adapted for hunting, takes about 128 pounds of varied prey per year, which is only about 10% of the total amount taken by all raptors in a given area.

THE INDEPENDENT, NOVEMBER 30, 1989

"Wing feathers are fitted with comblike projections on their surfaces... reducing turbulence and lessening flight sound."

Woodland elves and fairies

NATURE'S WAY

Marion Dusoir Ennes

THESE COLD, SNOWY months encourage rich and lively recollections of summer's pleasures. If really courageous, we can imagine an excursion through a warm, darkened woodland where night creatures like owls, bats, flying squirrels are active—along with moths.

Robert Southey, 19th century English romantic poet, makes this invitation:

"... sorrowing we beheld
The night come on; but soon did night display
More wonders than it veiled; innumerous tribes
From the wood-cover swarm'd, and darkness made
Their beauties visible."

He was referring to members of the lepidoptera family containing both butterflies and moths. Though less familiar, moths actually comprise 93% of this fascinating family.

Butterflies and some moths are daytime flyers, but the bulk of 142,000 species of moths worldwide (12,000 in North America) are denizens of darkness.

During eons of existence, the protection of darkness has helped make moths the second largest insect group after beetles.

On warm nights, moths of many sizes are attracted to night- blooming flowers. Honeysuckle and petunia hold back their fragrances, then pour them into the dark air, along with other white flowers, night bloomers like nicotinia, angel's trumpet, and moonflowers.

Evolving in concert with feeding moths, flowers make nectar available. Moths are pollinators.

Impressive, so-called large silkworm moths have captured imagination worldwide.

Stout-bodied moths whose cocoons have been used for silk (though not related to commercial silk-worms), they have beautifully- patterned wings. One Australian species covers a space of 70 square inches when its wings and tails are extended.

Many observers believe these showy moths are prototypes of the "little people." Quick, solitary, brown-winged moths were equated with mischievous elves, brownies, gremlins, and pixies.

The pale pastels who troop together as gentle, harmless fairies are the benign *luna moths* with flowing wings.

Luna Moth / Cocoon / Larva

All of these moths, so exciting to see in warm dark woodlands, are first recognized by their dark-adapted eyes, with glowing yellow-red eyeshines.

By the time a luna emerges to adult stage from its loosely wrapped cocoon, it has spent almost a year going from egg to hungry caterpillar to pupa.

In early summer it flies gently through the woods on wide, light blue-green, filamentous wings and unique, flowing tail.

Like other large silkworm moths, the luna has no food, no mouthparts, and lives off stored larval. It will live less than two weeks, with one final goal: establish the next generation.

Resting near trees that feed her offspring, the female luna sends her message to the males. Her advertisement: one billionth of a gram of her pheromone each hour.

Males as far as 120 meters away catch the scent with feathery antennae that have 1,700 hairs, each one holding 2,600 olfactory pores. Here her alluring scent is concentrated, sending him flying to her.

On the way he picks up on his body hairs scents of bushes like jasmine or cinnamon, his pheromone bouquet to her. She has offers from many males and the bouquet serves as the measure by which she chooses her mate.

Though she favors hickory or pecan trees as nesting sites, she will attach her eggs on the lower leaf sides of maple, willow, birch, oak, or other forest trees if her favorites are not available.

In the few hours she has, she rests among the leaves that hide her until she dies, feeding her young after she is gone.

Luna moth

Larva. Caterpillar reaches 2-¾ inches. Translucent light green plus red-orange knobs on smooth skin. Distinguishing yellow line along sides. Eats green leaves.

Cocoon. Pupates inside leaf cover wrapped loosely with silk. Brown, 1-¼". Falls and overwinters in leaf litter. Hard to see.

Adult. Five-inch, spectacular, bluish-green, diaphanous wings, with long sweeping tails. Transparent wing eyespots (to frighten predators) ringed in yellow, white, purple, gold, and black. Forewing margins solid purple or yellow.

THE INDEPENDENT, DECEMBER 4, 1997

"Quick, solitary, brown-winged moths were equated with mischievous elves, brownies, gremlins, and pixies."

NATURE'S WAY:
Green in winter

The leathery leaves of the mountain laurel remain shiny-green through the long winter. You can see them as you drive through the higher elevations of New York, Connecticut, and Massachusetts.

This North American plant is a member of the heath family, considered by some as "aristocrats of our native flora".

The heath family contains such useful plants as blueberries, huckleberries, and cranberries; such exotic plants as wild rhododendron, the wild azalea (also called pinkster flower), and rhodora, a flower whose wild beauty was described as "its own excuse for being" in Ralph Waldo Emerson's famous poem.

The worldwide heath family, including European heathers, consists of 2,000 species, mostly evergreen, that grow primarily in temperate to alpine areas. They prefer cool weather and acid soils, both characteristic of hilly woodland where mountain laurel is found.

Heath plants often thrive because their roots work in cooperation with a special fungus, which stengthens plants like the mountain laurel in drawing nutrients from the soil. These shrubs can grow as high as 30 feet and create a dense cover favored by deer.

Mountain laurel's botanical name is *Kalinia latefolia*, named for Peter Kalm, an eighteenth-century Swedish botanist. At the suggestion of Linnaeus, Kalm made a two-year tour in 1748-49 of the American Northeast, going up the Hudson from New York City and on to Lake Champlain and documenting his observations of flora and fauna in a pioneer scientific report.

The mountain laurel impressed him more than any other flower, and he brought plants back to England, where it was cultivated extensively on elegant estates.

Pollination of the flower is almost guaranteed as long as a thirsty bee comes along. The female pistil sticks well up in the flower's center. The male anthers, two to each of the

This is a shiny plant with delicate, ¾-to-one inch flowers set in clusters at the branch ends of oval, dark green leaves. Each open blossom looks like a 5-pointed saucer, but contains a deep nectar well at the center.

flower's five segments, are curved like springs with pollen-filled heads tucked into pockets of the segments.

The bee arrives, brushes the pistil with pollen from previous flowers, fertilizing this blossom. Then he plunges down to the flower's center cup, releasing the stamens like so many catapults, covering the bee's lower body with a good supply of pollen—ready for the next blossom.

Worm-eating warblers like laurel thickets, and one species of swallowtail butterfly lays its eggs on laurel leaves, later eaten by the larvae.

The leaves of these plants, however, were known for centuries to be poisonous to humans and other animals. Apparently they are tolerated by deer, but sheep sicken and die after eating mountain laurel. Native Americans drank a concoction of it to commit suicide.

On the other hand, it was used as an ointment against itching scalp and skin complaints, even for sores of syphilis. Indians also used it in small doses for bowel complaints.

The wood of the mountain laurel is extremely dense and hard; each cubic foot weighs 44 pounds.

An early popular name for it was "spoonwood," for it was made into spoons by immigrants as well as Indians.

THE INDEPENDENT, DECEMBER 7, 1989

"... it was used as an ointment against itching scalp and skin complaints, even for sores of syphilis."

Pileated crested woodpeckers

NATURE'S WAY

Marion Dusoir Ennes

COCK-OF-THE-WOODS is an old country name for the pileated woodpecker, the largest of its tribe. What a thrill it is to catch a glimpse of that big red-crested black-and-white bird.

A friend in East Taghkanic kept several full suet cages attached to her woodland house in winter. I often saw hairy woodpeckers and downies in numbers, but one special day a large pileated woodpecker, naturally curious, came to join the gang for dinner.

The sight was reassuring. Pileateds have had their ups and downs since this continent was settled. Years of clearing forests for lumber and planting reduced its habitat and destroyed the trees needed for shelter and food. Shot as game birds, by 1914 pileateds were uncommon throughout New York State. Now they are coming back, especially in forests but also in some settled wooded areas where they seem to be adapting.

Another sighting occurred in a wildlife sanctuary, when I heard distant but persistent multiple tapping. Steady searching revealed two immature pileated woodpeckers at the top of a tall tree, hitching themselves around the trunk, keeping each other company as they practiced drumming.

Woodworking is their special skill. They hit so hard their heads shake, cutting through bark, ripping off large strips, tossing them over their heads.

Choosing large old, usually diseased trees with relatively soft heartwood, they excavate new nests yearly. This makes them important benefactors of many other cavity nesters, small mammals like flying squirrels and birds like screech and barn owls, nuthatches and chickadees. Short supplies of cavities create fierce competition for them.

Starting 50 to 60 feet above ground, the nest is cut one to two feet down from a 3½" entrance. The entrance leads to a wide 7 to 8" chamber, narrowing to a bottom bowl 6 to 6½" across.

Both parents excavate, the male doing most of it. Mother lays about four eggs inside the unadorned space.

Pileated couples, once established, are year-round residents of their territory. Their ongoing partnership is close. At sunrise they greet each other from separate roosting holes, often foraging together. They start serious courting in April, calling and drumming, waving their heads from side to side, spreading wings

Incubation is shared, changing each hour when the returning mate taps near the entrance to signal the other.

They remain devoted to the babies until they are fledged, never away from them for more than 15 minutes, defending them fiercely if snakes or squirrels attack. Feeding and supervision continue for several months.

At a campground, an energetic pileated scours a grove of big shade trees for food, testing them by listening, then chiseling into the wooden surface with his big bill. Each pause in the action means he is probing the cut with a tongue made extensible by the *hyoid*, a kind of elastic strap anchored in the right nostril, going over the head and coming out under the jaw. Each deep thrust of this flexible tongue pulls out a delicious grub.

My own acres, now peppered with tornado snags, will need many years before they are forest again, with trees marked by characteristic upright rectangular nest holes of pileated woodpeckers. But happily, one flashed in the other day for a snack, probing snags for favorite carpenter ants, but always ready to grab a bark beetle or grub.

Pileated Woodpecker

Pileated woodpecker. *16-19 inches, wingspan 29-30. Body, tail black. Wings black with a few white markings. Head, neck have striking vertical stripes topped by vivid red crest. Male has red "moustache" behind bill.*

Inset: Tongue a. *Normal length.* **b.** *Extended for deep probing.*

THE INDEPENDENT, DECEMBER 7, 1995

"Woodworking is their special skill. They hit so hard their heads shake…"

NATURE'S WAY
Beetles of our lady

From coast-to-coast, indeed worldwide, ladybird beetles are recognized for their help to humans. The French call them *betes de la Vierge*, beetles of our Lady, for these small insects devour aphids that suck the strength from grape vines.

They are good luck talismans in many European cultures, reproduced in illustrations, jewelry, chocolate. Children, delighted by the neat polka-dotted bug, often protect ladybugs that land on them, gently blowing them to freedom.

"Ladybug, Ladybug, fly away home,
"Your house is on fire, your children will burn," is an English folk response to the beetle's danger from the flames in the hop vines, when the fields were cleared each year.

Of 4,300 species of ladybug beetles, 370 are in North America. Except for two—the Mexican bean beetle and the squash beetle, both destructive leaf-eaters—about 40 eat insects. As predators, lady beetles save farmers million of dollars by controlling crop pests. Besides aphids, they consume quantities of scale insects, mealy bugs and eggs of other plant-eaters.

Convergent lady beetles emerge in spring from winter rest in leaf litter and debris. They fly to any of a wide range of plants, from peas and alfalfa in fields to vines and trees in fruit groves. Soon they mate and look for food.

Aphids hatch first generations, and each beetle chews up 50 or more of them a day.

Ladybugs will not produce eggs unless they eat aphids. Their fecundity depends on the numbers eaten. For every batch of eggs laid, anywhere from 10 to 50 at a time, she needs at least 100 large aphids or 300 smaller ones. An average female lays 400 eggs in her lifetime, during the warm days of one busy season.

Six days after they are laid, tiny, six-legged, alligator shaped larvae hatch. The most active of beetle larvae, they move quickly in search of the smaller, newest generation of aphids. Mother attached her eggs close to the food supply.

The larvae eat so voraciously they split their skins and molt four times in the two weeks of their lives. Molting is an urgent matter because the old skin can dry and trap them inside. The process is eased by a molting fluid that loosens the old skin. The larva rests long enough for its new, spinier coat to firm up.

Soon the larvae attaches its tail to a branch, converts to a pupa. Transformation to an adult beetle takes a week. As summer progresses, the previous generation begins to die off. Young adults only need about a week of eating before they are ready to mate and lay eggs.

Entomologist Kenneth Hagen studies convergent lady beetles in California, where the insects are an important link in a chain of integrated pest control that is reducing the amount of chemical spray needed to protect crops.

He reports that at May's end, the newer generations of ladybugs take off for hibernation in the Sierra Nevada mountains. Raising their hard wing covers, they open diaphanous wings that flutter 75 to 91 times a second. He has tracked them in a plane as they rise quickly from fields to a 55° temperature zone in the air and ride in great swarms with westerly currents.

They fatten up by feeding on pollen, congregating in millions, sometimes 30 million to a quarter-acre, for a sleep of nine months. If they don't get scooped into gallon containers by collectors who sell them, they will fly back to feed in the valleys the following spring.

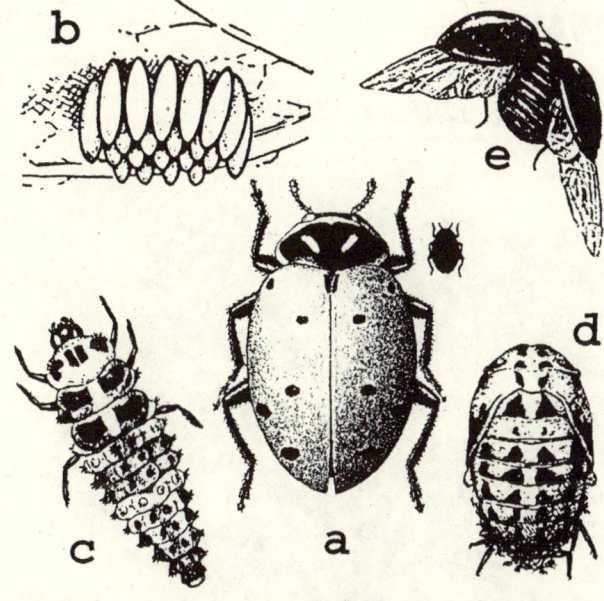

A. Convergent lady beetle, elliptical, 1/6 to 1/4 inch long. Black thorax showing converging white lines conceals black head. Domed shiny wing covers over abdomen, orange-red with 12 black dots.

B. Egg mass, 10 to 50 yellow-orange eggs attached to leaf underside.

C. Larva, 1/3 to 1/4-inch, dotted. Active.

D. Pupa, hard dotted cover, attached to stalk.

E. Adult beetle, flying. Hard wing covers (elytra) raised, exposing finely veined wings.

Illustrations not to scale.

THE INDEPENDENT, OCTOBER 15, 1992

*"Ladybug, Ladybug, fly away home,
Your house is on fire and your children will burn."*

Rebirth of the American Elm

NATURE'S WAY

Marion Dusoir Ennes

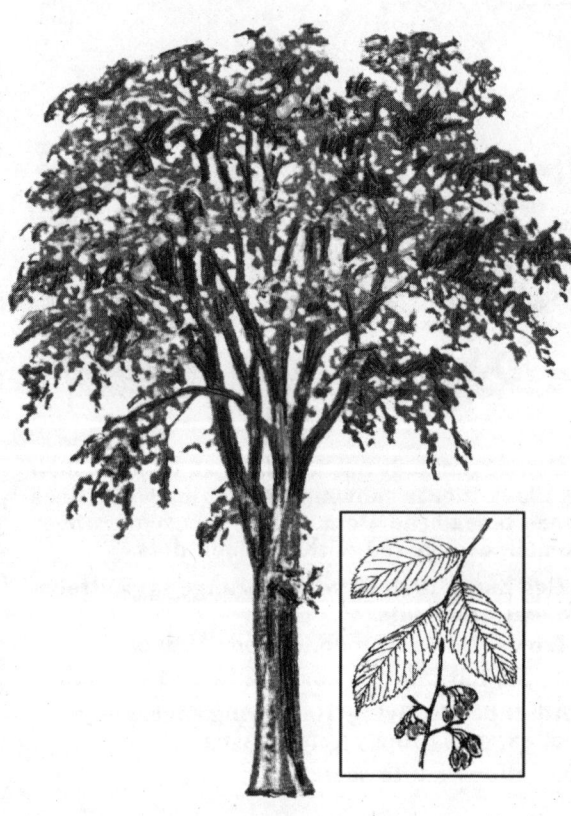

GOOD NEWS: RESCUE of the American Elm from destruction by Dutch Elm disease is imminent. Rows of sapling elms, each cloned from disease-resistant trees inoculated with a million virulent spores, grow sturdily in our National Arboretum.

Plans are to release them for sale in about two years.

Almost two generations have grown to adults since the Dutch Elm plague took hold in the 1940s. Trees were dying then and continued to succumb—an estimated 77 million lost to date.

Those generations lost out on the pleasures and history of this elm. Gone were the tall, beautiful, vase-shaped trees with umbrella-like canopies that arched over hometown streets, shading tall Victorian gingerbread houses.

Many of the greatest trees that grew over 100 feet tall, with branch-spread of 150 feet, and a trunk eight feet or more in diameter, became famous.

Oliver Wendell Holmes' poem, "Under the Washington Elm, Cambridge" was written April 27, 1861, as a call to arms for the North at the start of the Civil War.

The first stanza reads:

Eighty years have passed, and more,
Since under the brave old tree
Our fathers gathered in arms, and swore
They would follow the sign their banners bore.
And fight till the land was free.

Elms became living monuments, not just for Colonists, but before them. Historic councils between Native American tribes, treaties and historic pronouncements linked to our heritage were made under the American elm's eminence.

Settlers taking quick-germinating seedlings to their Western homesteads sought to reproduce the atmosphere of towns they left behind. Elm trees spread across the country as far as the Rockies.

Often, they repeated the close street planting that laid the groundwork for the trees' destruction.

Rachael Carson explains that "the beauty they hopefully created is threatened as disease sweeps through the elms." It would have had only a limited chance "to spread from tree to tree if the elms were only occasional trees among richly diversified plantings."

Dutch elm disease is a fungal infection which arrived on elm logs imported for veneers from England in the 1930s.

This parasitic fungus invades the tree's water-conducting system, produces poisonous secretions, and clogs vessel circulation, yellows outside leaves, wilting branches, and causing trees to die.

The elm beetles feeding on the inner tree bark became spore-carriers, infecting nearby trees. The closely intertwined roots of closely planted street trees picked up the reproducing fungal spores underground, transferring the disease with increasing rapidity.

Experts despaired, believing that chances to save the American elm would be fruitless.

Early efforts to stop the disease (described in Rachael Carson's *Silent Spring*) by killing elm beetles with DDT resulted in poisoning or death to countless woodland creatures, in turn killing birds of many species, including robins.

She believed that the disease could be contained through forest genetics and development of a resistant elm hybrid.

The clones from two venerable elm trees that have shown continued resistance—one at New Harmony, IN, the other at Valley Forge, PA—are the progenitors of the new commercially suitable, disease-resistant American elms.

Planted singly, these specimens prosper in woodland or garden sites, their leaves dropping each fall to return nitrogen and sugar to the earth, feeding the earthworms and other decomposers.

In spring, only eight weeks after a multitude of flowers have covered the crown with a purplish gauze, the seeds will be eaten by bobwhites, grouse, many songbirds, and small animals.

A full-grown American elm commonly reaches 100 to 120 feet, trunks 2 to 6 feet diameter. Trees known to reach 140 feet and 11-foot diameter.

Sharp double-toothed leaves 2 to 5 inches long, 1 to 3 inches wide, slightly lopsided.

Inconspicuous light-green, red-stamened, perfect flowers (containing both male and female organs) bloom February to April.

Greenish, wafer-like fruits, ½ inch, with papery wing surrounding center seed, mature along with unfolding leaves, March to June.

THE INDEPENDENT, DECEMBER 18, 1997

"Dutch elm disease is a fungal infection which arrived on elm logs imported for veneers from England in the 1930s."

Flocks at the Raspberry Ridge pole feeder as winter approaches.

Feeding Birds

The birds watch me fill the feeder,
putting some black seeds on top to entice them.
Do they wonder why I do this,
or do they think I do it to satisfy myself,
or do they care about the reason?

They have survived centuries.
My donation is just another windfall.
What if it does sustain them?
They probably would have found
another way.
They are resourceful, energetic,
and take what they can find.

I want them to thank me,
They will not.
They may trust me a little,
but guard themselves,
making the most…

—*fragment from Marion's manuscripts, 1999*

A lawn at Raspberry Ridge beneath winter's silent cover.

WINTER

The inevitable slowing of winter causes us to reflect on those creatures who live their lives outdoors. What happens to them as the temperatures drop and fresh food becomes scarce? Wonders still abound as we consider the cycle of forests and foliage and mistletoe, of lynx, deer, snowshoe hare, and the mysteries of hibernation. And we focus on the adaptability of nature in the face of a burgeoning human population. Wintering birds give us hope, we dream of butterflies, milkweed, and maple sugar.

Snowy owl in his comfort zone.

WINTER

Catching the Sun	87	The Witch That Isn't (witch hazel)	107
Frozen Safety (painted turtle)	88	White-footed Mouse	108
Snowshoe Hare	89	Deer in Winter	109
Welcome Snow	90	Winter Waterfowl	110
Sky Snow	91	Marvelous Milkweed	111
Raiders of the Landfill (seagulls)	92	Nesting Bluebirds	112
Tail in the Air (red squirrel)	93	A Tale of Two Tails (cedar waxwings)	113
Energy Efficiency (animal insulation)	94	Eating to Survive (short-tailed shrew)	114
Northern Saw-whet Owl	95	Where Did They Go? (insects in winter)	115
True Mosses	96	Tapping Nature (maple sugar/Anna Botsford)	116
The Forest Blanket (forest floor)	97	Bird Study	117
Lynx – The Well-equipped Cat	98	Seven Sleepers? (hibernation)	118
Great Treasure (soybeans)	99	Freshwater Eels — Ocean Travelers	119
A Scientist's Gift (mycological herbarium)	100	Cooper's Hawk	120
The Grouse Family	101	Sturdy Birds (downy woodpecker)	121
The Grouse Who Learned	102	The Furry Builder (muskrat)	122
Thrushes, America's Nightingales	103	Saving a Tradition (Christmas trees)	123
Signs of the Season: Late Winter	104	Mistletoe	124
Trees in Winter	105	"Springtime"	125
Same Time, Next Year (northern goshawk)	106	"Spring is Creeping Over the Landscape"	125

NATURE'S WAY

Catching the sun

We may not have noticed the shifting path of the sun at this autumn equinox, but Algonkin Indians, who made these lands home over many centuries, took careful note of earth signs, developing myths around things difficult to understand.

Glooskap was a favorite spirit in their pantheon. He was cunning, crafty, and a giver of beneficial things. His adventures were passed along to wide-eyed youngsters on long, stormy winter evenings in eloquent stories like epic poems.

The native myth that follows is from Lewis Spence's *Myths of the North American Indians*. It conveys the people's view of winter as a giant to be mastered and the small, though powerful summer as one to be cherished and remembered.

"A long time ago Glooskap wandered very far north to the Ice-country, and, feeling tired and cold, sought shelter at a wigwam where dwelt a great giant—the giant Winter. Winter received the god hospitably, filled a pipe of tobacco for him, and entertained him with charming stories of the old time as he smoked.

"All the time Winter was casting his spell over Glooskap, for as he talked drowsily and monotonously he gave forth a freezing atmosphere, so that Glooskap first dozed and then fell into a deep sleep—the heavy slumber of the winter season.

"For six whole months he slept; then the spell of the frost arose from his brain and he awoke. He took his way homeward and southward, and the farther south he fared the warmer it felt, and the flowers began to spring up around his steps.

"At length he came to a vast, trackless forest, where, under primeval trees, many little people were dancing. The queen of these folk was Summer, a most exquisitely beautiful, if very tiny, creature. Glooskap caught the queen up in his great hand, and cutting a long lasso from the hide of a moose, secured it round her tiny frame. Then he ran away, letting the cord trail loosely behind him.

"The tiny people, who were the Elves of Light, came clamouring shrilly after him, pulling frantically at the lasso. But as Glooskap ran the cord ran out, and pull as they might they were left far behind.

"Northward he journeyed once more, and came to the wigwam of Winter. The giant again received him hospitably, and began to tell the old stories whose vague charm had exercised such a fascination upon the god. But Glooskap in his turn began to speak.

"Summer was lying in his bosom, and her strength and heat sent forth such powerful magic that at length

An Eastern Algonkin encampment.
[Picture from C. Wissler's *Indians of the United States*]

Winter began to show signs of distress. The sweat poured profusely down his face, and gradually he commenced to melt, as did his dwelling.

"Then slowly nature awoke, the song of birds was heard, first faintly, then more clearly and joyously. The thin green shoots of the young grass appeared, and the dead leaves of last autumn were carried down to the river by the melting snow. Lastly the fairies came out, and Glooskap, leaving Summer with them, once more bent his steps southward."

THE INDEPENDENT, OCTOBER 4, 1990

"Glooskap was a favorite spirit in their pantheon."

NATURE'S WAY
Frozen safety

In secret places, inaccessible to the appetites or curiosities of marauders, thousands of creatures maintain their security over the winter.

Painted turtle hatchlings are well hidden in an earthen nest, which mother dug, then deposited her eggs, last summer. She chose a site favored by sunlight—in a bank or field—laid a clutch of 7 to 9 eggs and covered it.

The young hatch late in summer. Here, in the northern part of the painted turtle range, they remain, 2 to 3 inches underground in the nest cavity, not to emerge until the *following* spring.

Much research into the biochemical functioning of non-human creatures is done because of their potential applications to human biomedicine. This was the basis for research on painted turtle freeze-tolerance done by Janet and Kenneth Storey, reported in the January 1992 issue of *Natural History*:

"As an animal that has evolved natural freeze tolerance... the painted turtle can show us some of the cellular and molecular adjustments needed for organs to endure freezing or sustain a long dormancy.

"At present no mammalian organ has ever been restored to a viable state after freezing, and organs removed for transplant can be held on ice for only a few hours before their metabolism degenerates irreversibly.

"The knowledge gained from studies of painted turtle organs could, therefore, have important applications for the advancement of medical organ transplant technology."

They started by measuring occupied hatchling nests insulated by earth and under a thick snow layer. Temperatures inside ranged from 18° to 28° Farhenheit throughout January and February—cold enough to freeze and kill any warm-blooded animal. But the young turtles emerged in April, alive and well.

Then, in the laboratory, they cooled the hatchlings in a temperature-controlled incubator. Normal turtle blood freezing point is 31°F—but body fluids were liquid down to 26.5°, when the animals froze. Even when these young turtles were kept frozen at temperatures lowered to 25° for 11 days or more, they survived freezing and recovered fully when thawed.

As the animal's circulation slowly shuts down, muscles, lung, heart, and blood flow stop, and there is minimal brain activity. When they thaw, vital signs return sequentially.

"Turtles, as well as other animals that endure freezing, can survive only if ice formation is restricted to *extracellular* body fluids (such as blood plasma, abdominal fluid, urine). In fact, we found that even in painted turtles, only 53 percent of their total body water froze at 25°F. The water *within cells* must remain liquid, however, because intracellular ice crystals will irreparably damage the internal organization and structure of cells."

Turtles have special biochemical adaptations to help them protect their cells. First of all, when temperatures drop, special proteins developed in the liver are distributed to all extracellular fluids to keep ice crystals small and not damaging.

At the same time, this icing outside cells stimulates production of special sugar compounds—glucose, glycerol, lactate, and a special amino acid—called cryoprotectants, that act like antifreeze.

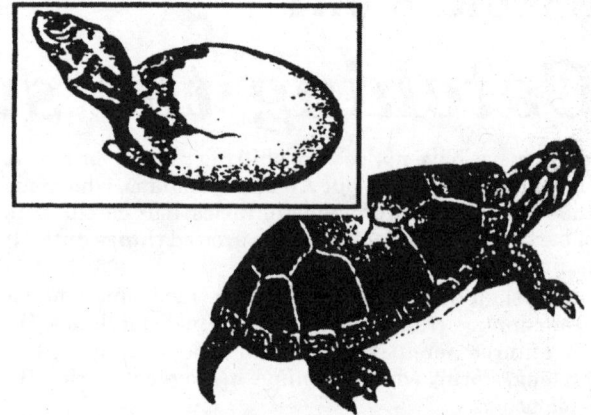

Painted turtle, with colorful marked shell, common to shallow, weedy waters of Eastern and Central states, 5-7 inches long. INSET: Hatchling, young turtle emerging from egg.

These protect cell membranes and proteins from damage and prevent the water *inside* cells from freezing. The well-developed abilities enabling them to tolerate freezing are lost to painted turtles after their first winter.

Adult turtles cannot endure freezing. They have other special metabolic adaptations to help them hibernate at temperatures as low as 37°F in shallow pond bottoms.

THE INDEPENDENT, DECEMBER 31, 1991

"... this icing outside cells stimulates production of special sugar compounds... that act like antifreeze."

NATURE'S WAY
Snowshoe hare

Winter or summer, the wary snowshoe hare can hide by just standing still. Its coat is tailored to the seasons, helping it blend into the background.

John Mettler of Copake Falls spotted one in its white coat on Shepherd Hill in North Hillsdale earlier this winter, calling my attention to the fact that snowshoe hares inhabit heavily wooded areas of Columbia County and western Massachusetts. They are hunted in New York State.

Man is only one of a long list of predators of the snowshoe, relative to the rabbit but more closely related to the many species of hares that live in bogs or hilly, wooded areas up to 4,000 feet, ranging across our country from Newfoundland to Alaska, into Canada, down to the Rockies and the Sierra Nevadas.

What distinguishes hares in general are their long ears—for excellent hearing ability—and their long, strong legs, used for flight, maneuverability, and battle.

In late spring and summer, male and female snowshoe hares wear a cinnamon-brown coat with black guard hairs. The darker back, rump, and top of head graduates to white on the belly and under the tail.

By mid-September, this first coat is molted and a separate, second white pelage (coat of fur) starts growing from the feet, ears, and legs to the back.

The medium-size snowshoe hare averages 19 inches in length with a two-inch tail, weighs between 3.1 to 4.4 pounds, female largest. Short front legs have five toes on short feet, the long hind legs, four toes and large feet.

From November to spring this animal, also named 'varying hare' because of these color changes, wears a white coat with black ear-tips and eyelids.

The hind feet, about 5½ inches, develop an inch-thick coat of fur on the soles as weather turns cold. This is important to the hare, which counts on its prodigious running ability to avoid predators. The whole foot acts as a warm snowshoe. When the hare spreads its four rear-foot toes, it can travel safely over deep snows.

Active from twilight to dawn, it spends most of the time eating quantities of vegetation—clover, grasses, dandelion, berries, ferns, vetches, tender bush and tree shoots and leaves in summer; twigs, buds, seedlings, bark of many bushes, deciduous and evergreen trees in winter. The snowshoe's fondness for tender shoots and for girdling saplings makes it the bane of foresters nurturing new growth trees. But this brushy woodland growth is favored as cover by this hare.

The snowshoe hare is heavily hunted. It provides food for such carnivores as man, foxes, lynx, bobcat, weasels, coyotes, great horned owls, snowy owls, goshawks, and red-tailed hawks. It also succumbs to autos, fire, ticks, fleas, parasites and disease.

Its strengths lie in its carefully learned familiarity with its home territory. The hare makes its own trails, decoyed by multiple sets of tracks ranging around them.

It is reported to travel up to 25 MPH in open areas, and its prodigious legs make it an acrobatic leaper. When startled it can jump directly into a run from a resting position; when pursued, it can leap 8 to 10 feet; and when a predator closes in it can turn in air, changing direction to end up at the rear of the pursuer.

THE INDEPENDENT, DECEMBER 28, 1989

"In late spring and summer... snowshoe hares wear a cinnamon-brown coat with black guard hairs."

NATURE'S WAY: Welcome snow

> "Once a substantial snow falls, the winter sheet becomes a ledger on which is inscribed a record of local animal activity."

Not all land has a protective covering of fallen leaves or dry grass, and the gleaming white snow layer adds an important carpet of protection to forest floor, field, and hill.

The billions of tiny pockets of air trapped in snow create insulation that holds in earth's warmth and encourages life in the leaf layer.

Tests have shown differences of 50° or more between the air above and under the snow surface. When the air above registered 32° below zero, the temperature dropped to only 1° below zero one inch under the snow surface, and 31° above zero one foot down.

This differential benefits the small, furry creatures who count on snow as a protective cover in the cold season. It offers them a soft, wind-free area under the surface in which to tunnel and hide, as well as sound-proofing when they are on the surface.

Ultimately, snow, which also protects the roots of plants and bushes, melts, providing needed moisture and fertilizer to the soil. Snow's virtues are summed up in the old farm saying, "A year of snow is a year of plenty."

Once a substantial snow falls, the white sheet becomes a ledger on which is inscribed a record of local animal activity. You can read these marks in your yard—especially cottontail rabbit and squirrel tracks, each with large front feet and small rear ones, although the rabbit tracks are longer and narrower than the squirrels'.

If you take a walk through a field near a hedgerow, you may see the small, 7/8-inch fingered tracks of the deer mouse, with a tail mark in between, or the smaller, 5/8-inch meadow vole's tracks.

Weasel tracks have four toes and a pad clearly marked, and a lightly depressed foot outline. Bobcats also show four toes and a pad, but no foot outline. Raccoons' feet are 4-1/2-inch-long, sharply pointed five-digit prints, deeply indented.

Some animals take advantage of the snow's understory. Rabbits often hollow out depressions in drifts. Their body heat melts the snow which solidifies into "forms" where they sleep several nights.

Shrews, voles and mice all tunnel in the snow. Close examination of their tiny tracks often shows them disappearing into a hole and reappearing at some distance from the entrance.

They need this protection from several predators.

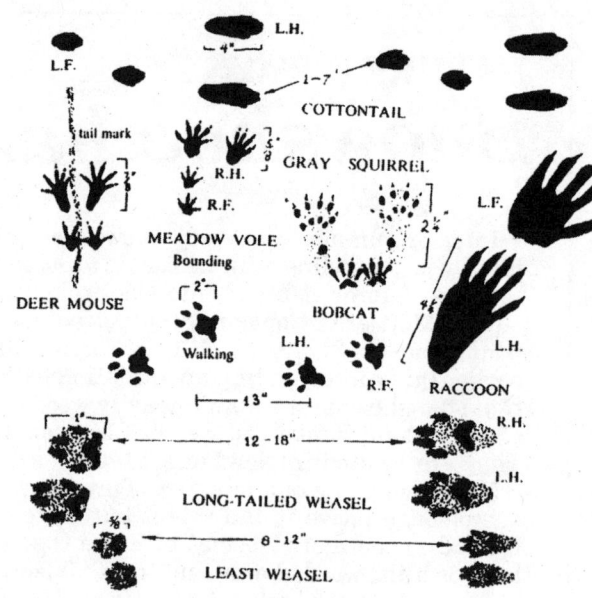

Tracks in the snow

Weasels and foxes sniff them out under the snow and make short work of them. Owls and hawks watch from above and pounce whenever they can.

One such drama was depicted in the 1984 Jan.-Feb. *Conservationist:* "Tracks of a meadow vole began at a hole (in a snowy field) where he came up through the snow to feed on weed seeds...His trail (led to) a disturbed spot in the snow which showed wing marks and a small spot of blood...The vole had become a meal for one of our wintering red-tailed hawks."

But the snow makes a happy ending possible, too. I spent one morning watching a busy deer mouse popping up out of—and then disappearing under—the snow around our bird feeder, obviously making a hearty meal on the seeds trapped in his subway under a foot of snow.

THE INDEPENDENT, JANUARY 19, 1989

NATURE'S WAY

Sky snow

Water vapor is the stuff that snow is made from in the free air of the upper sky. Rising warm air carries plenty of moisture, cooling 5½° for every thousand feet it goes up.

When the air cools to 20° or less, some water vapor finds a microscopic particle of dust, or salt, or a spore, and starts its crystalline growth as one of millions and millions of snowflakes.

This growth capitalizes on water droplets in clouds through a chemical process called sublimation: the water evaporates to its gaseous state and then is grabbed by a flake to become part of the crystalline complex. Air, too is added, folded around the crystals as they grow into delicate designs.

To those who study them, the term "snowflake" has a special meaning: an assemblage of individual snow crystals that have collided and remained fastened together during their fall through the atmosphere. A snowflake goes through many changes in its lifetime.

What distinguishes a snow *crystal* at its birth is its single *crystallographic orientation*.

This orientation is possible because of the characteristics of the tiny, unique water molecule, H_2O. When lots of these molecules are in liquid form, the three atoms that form water—one oxygen and two hydrogen—are only partially structured.

When water becomes solid—freezes—the molecules "assume an *orderly* arrangement with fixed positions for the oxygen atoms." At the same time, strong hydrogen bonds link water molecules to one another in bundles of three to six at a time. The frozen water vapor forms into a *crystal lattice*—the famous hexagonal pattern of snowflakes. The plane showing this hexagonal symmetry is at right angles to the snow crystal's central axis.

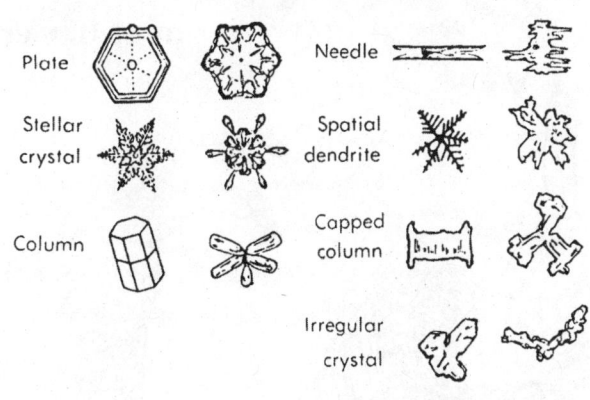

Examples of the seven basic crystal forms in snowflakes. Taken from the *International Snow Classification Chart for Solid Precipitation* (with additions from Mangono and Lee) for falling snow.

In our century, snow crystals were photographed in and out of the laboratory. Okichiro Nagaya of Japan actually grew snow crystals in his lab and was able to document the combinations of temperature and moisture concentration required to produce various types of snow crystals.

In high, dry altitudes, tight shapes like needles or columns form. Lower down—where temperature is warmer and moisture high, more complex—lacy, fern-like crystals are common.

The fact that essentially perfect snowflake forms have been photographed at ground level is remarkable in view of all that happens to them in the atmosphere.

They spiral and spin, sometimes adding twigs, branches, or bumps. As they fall or rise with the wind, delicate branches break off; other times, several attach in clusters or lines. Some flakes become coated with rime or hoar frost.

Each design is a record of its origin and travels—main branches elaborated in moist air, twigs in dry.

According to Guy Murchie, in his book *Song of the Sky*, "There is a whole world in this tiny skyborn gem... (It also) gathers sound waves and magnetic forces of its own as it floats, even broadcasting dainty music from its own radiolike sending station as if to tell the big world below of things it never dreamed—if only, if only, it could hear and understand."

THE INDEPENDENT, JANUARY 11, 1990

"... essentially perfect snowflake forms have been photographed at ground level..."

Raiders of the landfill

NATURE'S WAY

Marion Dusoir Ennes

WHERE FOOD IS FOUND in massive piles, there you will find some species of seagulls. Where there are plagues of locusts, or outbreaks of field mice destroying crops, a huge arriving gull flock will eliminate the menace, aiding people for whom crop success means life or death.

Where massive mounds of garbage are found, including stale raw or processed food wastes and fast food remnants, gulls in astounding numbers will gather to feast. The way of this omnivore is to hunt or scavenge, in company or alone. It is said gulls never forget a handout, never miss the big chance.

But sometimes these birds come afoul of human plans. Years ago, during canning season, Western gulls trailed barges hauling fermented fruit parings for dumping in San Francisco Bay.

Prohibition was in force, and federal authorities, overloaded with confiscated liquor, needed to dump it. Offering a dollar a ton, they contracted with the nearby City of Oakland, and the first barge was loaded with 250 bootleg gallons, smelling marvelously fermented to local gulls.

Screaming their delight, they attracted others; newspapers reported 50,000 gulls drunk, 30,000 of them killed—buried under loads of wet garbage, hundreds more around the barge dazed with hangovers. The contract was canceled.

Nowadays landfills are gulls' great shopping centers—piled high with free goodies. At New York's Albany and Colonie landfill sites, herring gulls fly over in enormous flocks. Two to three thousand birds swoop in great circles, a pattern called towering, before landing to feed selectively among the filth.

Landfills are often sited near airports, where slow-flying gulls could, and have, collided with planes, causing death and damage.

Two local residents protecting against these dangers are wildlife biologists Ken Preusser of Martindale and Dan Beaudo, recently moved here from Michigan. They are employed by the U.S. Department of Agriculture to do animal damage control.

"What we aim at is to resolve human and wildlife conflicts that pose health, safety, or economic hazards," Dan Beaudo explains. "Herring gulls that touch down and feed in Albany and Colonie landfills are vectors for disease carried to human areas.

"We have cooperative agreements with landfill operators to keep the sites free of gulls, and we use non-lethal methods to do this. First we broadcast recordings of a herring gull distress call. If it's quiet around the landfill, those calls alone frighten birds into leaving.

"Landfill machinery is noisy, though, what with dumping and earth-moving, so we may need to use 'bird bangers' to scare gulls away. They are like flare guns. We shoot one up, it explodes with a loud bang.

"But after a while the birds get used to them and we may have to shoot one or two birds in sight of the others. Then some of the circling birds drop down to check out the bodies—and soon they cut out with the flock following."

Dan and Ken are local USDA team members on the front lines. Other USDA scientists are learning that landfills provide a protected social center, like a huge mall, where herring gulls can party or nap without fear of predators, with a handy snack nearby.

Parent gulls, on the other hand, avoid landfills during breeding season, according to recent studies, and avoid feeding their young putrid landfill food. A report of a Lake Erie colony showed that parents demanded a higher quality of food for their young, catching freshwater fish 80 percent of the time.

As long as landfills exist, however, there's no preventing young birds from joining the grown-ups at their social centers.

Towering over dinner

THE INDEPENDENT, JANUARY 2, 1997

"…landfills provide a protected social center…
where herring gulls can party or nap without fear of predators…"

NATURE'S WAY

Tail in the air

This year's prolific crop of pine cones has brought a red squirrel close to our house. It quickly located the squirrel-proof bird feeder, but enjoyed a feast from the overflow of sunflower seeds on the ground.

Even if this frisky fellow was not busy in the pine trees clipping pine cones and carrying them away, its middens (large trash piles) of pine cone clippings were clear evidence of its presence.

There is something about the red squirrel that elicits human comparison among naturalists as well as country folk. Turn-of-the-century moralists mention its many "vices" and few "virtues," describing it as quarrelsome, noisy, thieving, and mischievous. Yet, said Stone and Cram in 1902, "Few people realize what a thoroughly practical, thrifty, and ingenious little animal they really are; for, unlike most thieves, they are not in anyway shiftless or lazy, but are steady, hard-workers the year 'round."

Red squirrels are one of five members of the squirrel family, which includes the grey and flying *tree* squirrels, chipmunks and woodchucks, and *ground* squirrels. Reds favor conifer woods, but subsist in mixed forests too.

They can take over a territory as large as five acres, often chasing away grey or flying squirrels.

Usually half to one acre will serve as space enough to breed and raise young, to eat and harvest their principal foods: pine or spruce cones and hickory (or other) nuts. Caches of closed young cones have been reported up to five bushels in size and 1½ bushels of hickories stored against a log or stump, moist enough to keep seeds inside.

Red squirrels eat constantly, capitalizing on whatever food a season provides. In spring, it nibbles on tree buds; it taps maple or birch trees by gnawing a small saucer-shaped depression atop a horizontal limb, then laps up the collected sap.

As summer unfolds, it samples berries, strawberries, cranberries, wild or not, and mushrooms, subterranean or on ground. These are spread on tree bark to dry or stuck in crevices. Red squirrels eat, and enjoy without ill effect, mushrooms poisonous to humans, like the parson's or fly amanita.

Though truly not hunters, a variety of insects are also taken, along with flowers, leaves, grass, and weed seeds. Bark, roots, and carrion round out their menu, probably in leaner years.

They are diurnal (daytime) animals, active all year, and equally at home in trees and on the ground. In winter they tunnel under snow to food sources. Their curved and sharp claws are well-adapted to climbing. Feathery tails, usually carried at a jaunty angle, serve as excellent flight stabilizers for long jumps from tree to tree.

While on territorial rounds—checking out or working—this energetic animal makes itself heard. It chatters, barks, nickers, wickers, and wumps. These noises have seemed scolding, or gay, or just companionable to human woodland visitors, but taken together with a red squirrel's actions, the best-suited word is exuberant.

Not surprising, then, that countrywide red squirrels have earned picturesque names. Ojibway Indians call them *Adjidaumo*, "tail in the air," in the Midwest, "piney squirrels," the West, "chickaree," other places, "boomers," and in West Virginia, "fairy diddles."

Rufous-backed red squirrel, whitish underparts, 11½ to 13½ inches overall (tail 5 inches), weight about 6 ounces. Tracks show 5-fingered hind feet (about 2 inches) placed before smaller 4-fingered front feet.

THE INDEPENDENT, JANUARY 3, 1991

"It chatters, barks, nickers, wickers, and wumps."

NATURE'S WAY

Energy efficiency

In sub-freezing temperatures, when we drive by deer browsing in a snowy hayfield's green patch, my husband always says, "I just don't comprehend how they stay warm out there!"

My most eloquent descriptions of the animals' thick fur coats leave him unconvinced.

In fact, in extreme cold, the special insulating qualities of hair and fur are, by themselves, inadequate to protect the organs that perform internal body functions.

Heat deserts the body in four ways: by conduction, convection, radiation and evaporation.

Conduction takes heat from skin to air, foot to ground, by molecular transfer. We all know how fast our fingers get cold when we pick up a cold metal tool.

The movement of air (or water) around an animal transfers heat through *convection,* known to us as "wind chill."

Any warm body emits heat into the environment through *radiation.* And a small amount of heat is lost in breathing by *evaporation* when internal moisture changes to vapor.

As we know, a thick winter fur coat, made heavier by the animal's physical efforts, is a crucial external insulating barrier.

But when cold temperatures begin to challenge fur's effectiveness, internal systems turn on to provide heat from within.

Small animals, with relatively short hair, become extremely vulnerable to cold long before temperatures reach freezing.

As autumn days shorten, their bodies begin to adapt to this with an increase in metabolic rate, for a quicker physiological response to turning food into heat.

Most crucial, however, is the development of brown fat deposits, laid down near the body's vital organs. This protective "embryonal" fat is also abundant in young mammals—including humans.

Brown fat is densely packed with tiny elongated organisms (*mitochondria*) that make it capable of consuming more oxygen, and thus of producing more heat than ordinary white fat does.

Besides mitochondria, brown fat contains more nerve cells to transmit messges about urgent thermal needs and more blood vessels which supply oxygen to process into heat.

The brain, sensing a heat deficit, sends a nerve signal from its hypothalamus via the sympathetic nervous system to the adrenal gland, located near the kidney. This gland produces noradrenaline and stimulates the tiny micochondria to start heat production.

In his book *Life in the Cold,* Peter Marchand says, "...so effective is this tissue in generating heat that temperatures measured by the skin just over brown fat are sometimes higher than core temperatures."

Appendages present unique problems. Each leg, foot, tail requires oxygenated blood for nourishment and to prevent freezing.

But with its characteristic large exposed surface compared to a small internal mass, the appendage could act as a radiator, draining heat from the animal's core.

This drain is avoided in the beaver's tail by the use of heat-exchanging system with veins and arteries closely paralleling one another.

When it's cold, tiny veins in extremities constrict. Venous blood is shunted into vessels lying close to arteries carrying warm blood, heating venous blood as it passes toward the body core.

The arterial blood in turn gets to the extremities precooled—and heat is saved in the system.

Of course, frigid temperatures may be relentless. A small mammal like the red-back vole demonstrates that its muscles increase production of a substance called *myoglobin* in fall.

This hemoglobin-type chemical is believed to make oxygen transfer and storage easier, so that the animal can more efficiently produce heat through shivering.

So valuable is shivering that it is involuntary, an animal's final resort in its defense against death.

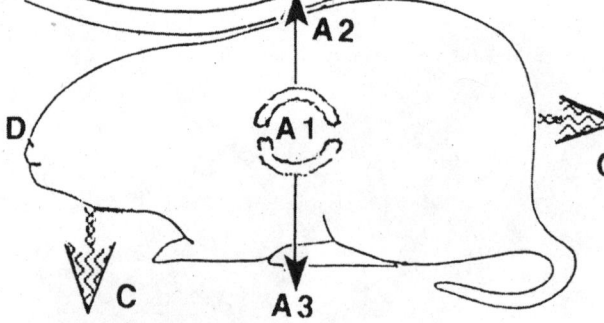

Schematics of small mammal.

Above—Forms of heat loss: A1, molecular conduction, from core to outer surface; A2, to air; A3, to ground. B, convection in moving air. C, radiation to surroundings. D, evaporation.

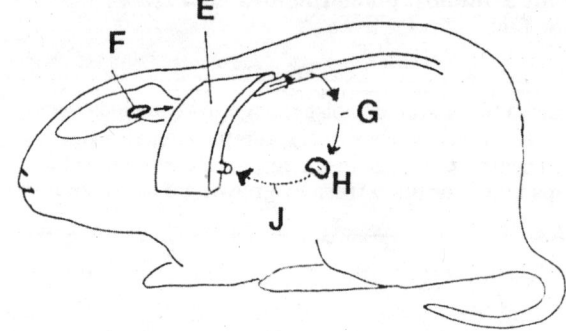

Below—Internal heat production; E, brown fat. F, hypothalamus sends signal via G, sympathetic nervous system, to H, adrenal gland, producing J, noradrenaline going to brown fat via bloodstream.

THE INDEPENDENT, JANUARY 7, 1993

"Most crucial, however, is the development of brown fat deposits, laid down near the body's vital organs."

NATURE'S WAY
Northern Saw-Whet Owl

The tiniest of our Eastern owls, called by one naturalist the "mighty adorable" and admired by most writers, the Northern Saw-Whet Owl may be more common in our area than first thought.

Last February, Department of Environmental Conservation wildlife biologists who conducted a deer wintering survey at Blue Hill in Greenport, came upon a large number of raptor pellets on the forest floor, along with a conspicuous amount of whitewash on the ground and in the foliage of a nearby tree. The site was near an apple orchard and irrigation pond.

Inspecting more closely, they spotted a Northern Saw-Whet Owl on a branch about six feet up in the tree. It had been feeding on a short-tailed shrew, half of which remained on the roosting branch.

Although the Saw-Whet has been described as a fairly common breeder in the Adirondacks, it is rarely spotted in the rest of the state. The 1988 *Breeding Bird Atlas* lists only one probable breeding location in Columbia County.

A report of this exciting Greenport sighting—"Winter Roosting and Food Habits of Northern Saw-Whet Owl in Columbia County, N.Y." by Karl E. Parker—and the discoveries associated with it, appeared in the Summer '91 *Kingbird*, the journal of the Federation of New York State Bird Clubs.

The DEC surveyors collected 11 of the 17 grayish-black, cigarette-butt-sized pellets found at the location. Owl pellets are diagnostic tools for ornithologists, offering all kinds of information about what an owl has been up to.

Owls eat their prey whole or by halves. Once the soft parts have been digested in strong stomach secretions, the indigestible hard parts—fur, bones, teeth, etc.—are regurgitated and remain as discards. Pellet size, color, and shape are often characteristic of a particular species.

Careful examination of pellets was made and taxonomic identification of bones inside them were done by the staff of the NYS Museum Science Service. Results of these efforts indicate that a wintering Northern Saw-Whet Owl probably consumes 1.0 to 1.5 prey items a day.

The cache of 17 shows that the owl was present from 9 to 18 days, eating a range of food—three short-tailed shrews, seven field mice, and one meadow vole, all probably available from the nearby mowed apple orchard.

This tiny nocturnal owl, difficult to locate, is now thought to be more common in New York State than was originally thought. It is probably overlooked because it hides in dense foliage and remains very still and mute.

The unfamiliar Saw-Whet's vocalizations, which sound like grasshopper stridulations or a saw being sharpened, occur before dusk or at night from March through May, their breeding season.

The Greenport Saw-Whet seemed fearless. Without moving, it allowed itself to be observed by six DEC field workers.

The owl's breast feathers are light brown below, darkening to rich lustrous brown on the upper head and back, the tail chocolate brown with marginal white stripes.

The proportionately large brown head is crowned with faint white stripes. The center facial disk is accentuated by a white feather band from the bill's base, up over each eye to form V-shaped "eyebrows."

The Saw-Whet gazed down at the observers, eyes brightened by lemon-colored irises, under questioning "eyebrows," for almost five minutes, and then flew deeper into the woods.—**Marion Dusoir Ennes**

Northern Saw-Whet Owl, above, almost ½-size, 7-8 inches high.

THE INDEPENDENT, JANUARY 9, 1992

"...Saw-Whet's vocalizations, which sound like grasshopper stridulations or a saw being sharpened..."

True mosses

When the ground is without its comforting white blanket and the world seems dull and brown, look again. Tiny moss plants, pale or deep greens or golden yellows, are growing on rocks, logs, or stumps. You have to go close up, though, to see what the poet Ruskin says of mosses: "To them, slow fingered, constant-hearted, is entrusted the weaving of the dark eternal tapestries of the hills."

A quick exploration of the rock wall in my front yard yielded three separate moss plants, each with spore capsules standing tall among the cushioning "leaf" growth. They were so intriguing, I spent an inordinate amount of time trying to identify them without achieving certainty. My references led to three good possibilities (illustrated).

Mosses are in the plant kingdom because they contain chlorophyll. But true mosses are *Bryophytes*, 10,000 species of small, flowerless land plants that breed by spores.

Mosses love moisture, thrive and respond in its presence, and may lie dormant in drought, waiting for rain to revive it.

Common in Ireland, their growth can be seen covering castles and cottages, curbstones and stone walls, trees and stumps. It has been said that they are the proper home for the "little folk."

Each moss is tiny, best held in tweezers, examined with 10X magnification. In the three specimens I found, the leafy part ranged from less than ½-inch tall to 1½ inches, though some species grow 15 inches high. A few species grow underwater, some have adapted to deserts, but many do not mind cold and grow profusely in the tundra.

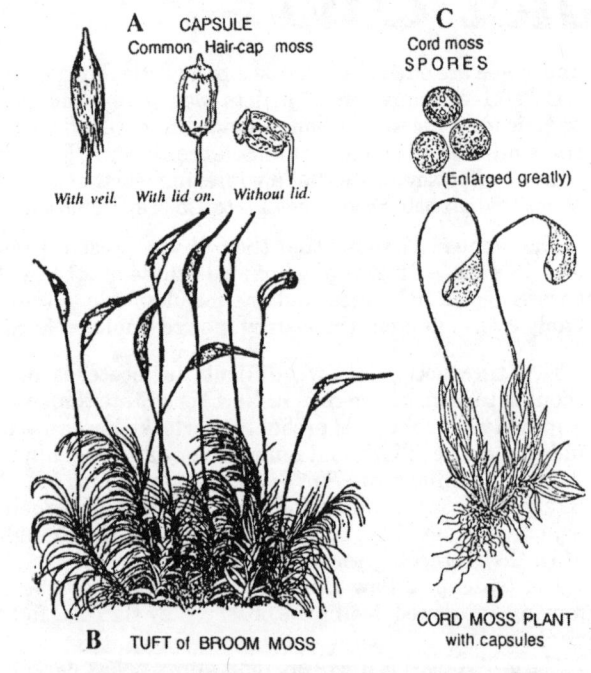

A. Common hair-cap moss, named for veil on capsule, earlier called "virgin tresses." B. Broom moss, named for bristling look of foliage. Years ago children called capsules "ducks in flocks travelling toward water." C. Cord moss spores swell and germinate into branching base. D. Cord moss plants growing from base, with spore cases atop wiry pedicels (stalks). Named for pedicel's habit of twisting around each other when moist.

A moss plant starts growing from a spore (its equivalent of a seed). But this spore lacks elements contained in a seed so it needs two generations to create a new seed.

In the first generation, spores divide to send out a leafy branching structure with buds at intervals. These buds grow into stalks with a spiral of thin pointed leaflets around the stem. *Rhizoids*, thin rootlike structures, secure the moss plant to its surface, drawing in water and dissolved minerals.

Though the leaflets contain chlorophyll, moss plants lack a vascular system of pipes or tubes to transport water or food any great distance. This keeps plants close to the ground; my samples ranged 3/8, 3/4, to one-inch tall.

In the second generation, leafy stalks put out male and female structures, sometimes on separate plants. When the sperm and ovum join, a capsule forms, growing up above the leaves on a wiry stem no thicker than a human hair.

The capsule, often chestnut-brown, unique to each moss species, contains thousands of dust-speck-sized spores. Some capsules are as small as 1/16 of an inch long, others reach 1/4 inch.

Figure A shows the common hair-cap moss first with its hairy veil. Once the veil falls off you can see the tight lid that holds in the growing spores. When they mature, pressure from a swelling ring of cells below the capsule lid pushes it off. When humidity is low, spores shake out through a grating around the rim case, distributed by air currents to new germination sites.

THE INDEPENDENT, JANUARY 10, 1991

"It has been said that they are the proper home for the 'little folk.'"

NATURE'S WAY
The forest blanket

By the time autumnal winds have knocked down the leaves, each acre of woods has been covered by a blanket of 10 million leaves. Along with twigs and limbs, dry flowers and plants, animal remains and wastes, they make a blanket which weighs almost two tons per acre.

This heavy layer of plant and animal clutter is the site of a great community of recyclers. In one square foot of floor, three inches deep, there are about 104 billion living plants and animal organisms.

Most are microscopic; the macroscopic comprise only .000004 per cent of the total and are usually well camouflaged or live in darkness. They are not as cuddly as furry animals nor as flashy as birds, but they are as important to the health of forests and the viability of soil.

High levels of humus formed on the floor of the great undisturbed forests in this country prior to settlement. After these forests were cut down for farming, the rich soil supported agriculture for many years.

The forest floor is well-protected: in summer, the upper canopy of leaves filters light and heat; in fall, the dead leaves offer an insulating blanket.

Between the layer of air and the deep earth is a wind-free, moist, cool environment. In this micro-climate, the temperature varies less than two degrees Fahrenheit even as air temperatures above vary more than 30 degrees.

The leaf-mold medium is home to a wide range of creatures, predominately microscopic bacteria, fungi, and protozoa. The visible creatures, only about 300 million an acre, are tiny, and about three-quarters are sightless invertebrates.

The vertebrates include mites, springtails, pseudoscorpions, and sowbugs. Reptiles and small animals live in and above the forest floor, bringing oxygen below by burrowing and nitrogen through their waste.

Through hundreds of thousands of intestines or other "digestive" processes, important elements like nitrogen, carbon, and oxygen are released. Tough materials are softened and ultimately converted to a soft colloidal mass, called humus, which combines with soil where tree roots grow.

The cycle consists of: (1) microscopic decomposers, fungi, and animals such as millipedes, sowbugs, and earthworms who eat litter. (2) Predators, some microscopic, some small animals—mites, larvae, beetles—who eat decomposers. (3) Secondary predators, "the lions and wolves of the forest floor"—snails, spiders, pseudoscorpions.

And above all these, the small reptiles, birds, and small mammals snack on the insects and worms at the top of the food chain.

The humus that remains mixes with and enriches the soil for the plants and trees.

Those who explore this fascinating world of the forest floor adjust their perceptions to a "slow motion," so they can study the full life cycle of each tiny animal or plant, to make a richer connection to the great ecological cycle in the forest blanket where a great deal is happening, summer and winter.

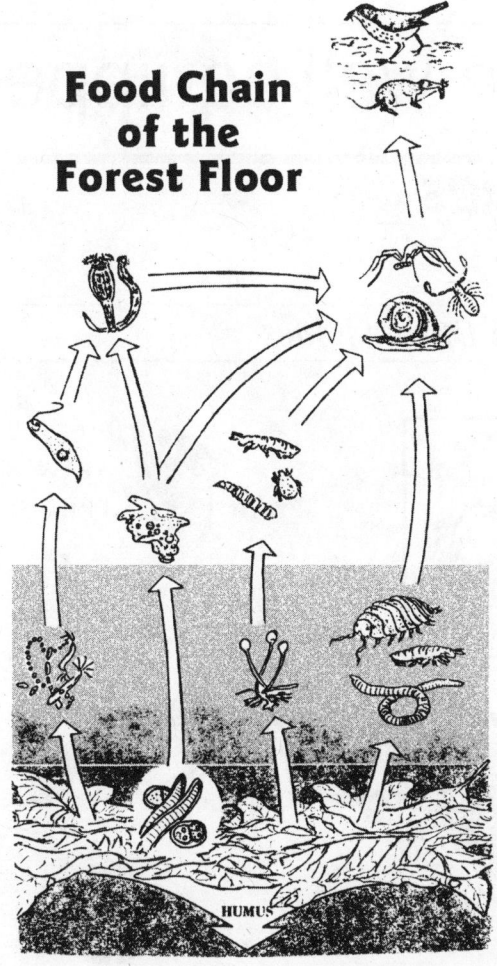

THE INDEPENDENT, JANUARY 12, 1989

"... they make a blanket which weighs almost two tons per acre."

Lynx—the well-equipped cat

NATURE'S WAY

Marion Dusoir Ennes

THE LARGE, ROUND TRACKS of a Canadian lynx progress across snow-laden woods, feline style, in a single line. This excellent hunter is still occasionally found in cold remote areas of the Adirondacks and may live in western Massachusetts and northern New England's dense forests where snowshoe hares live. Common in Canada, it is still hunted for its soft, thick, lustrous mauve winter pelt.

Thriving in temperatures that dive down to minus 30 degrees F, this lynx makes a living even in heavy snows, using special adaptations provided by nature, and skills taught by its mother.

When autumn temperatures drop, the lynx changes to its light-colored winter coat from its darker, silky 3 ½-inch summer version. The fur thickens with dense underfur and 4-inch guard hairs to help protect against icy winds and shed water.

Acting like snowshoes, massive 3 to 4-inch-wide feet are covered with such thick fur that they can walk atop snow. The abbreviated black-tipped tail is too short to convey heat away from the body. A sturdy muscular body is topped by a broad face decorated by a picturesque ruff and prominent black ear tufts. Hard yellow eyes are especially adapted for night hunting.

Hiding by day on the branch of a tree or inside a dense thicket or windfall, the lynx satisfies its hunger at night. Although it will eat mice, moles, grouse, squirrels and occasionally fox, deer or carrion, it favors snowshoe hares.

In general, it uses a "still hunt" style, lying in wait alongside a game path or dropping from a ledge or tree. When stalking prey, it slinks along the ground with shoulders and hips above the dragging belly. Its nose twitches and muscles tighten just before a pounce.

In a good year, 70% of its diet consists of snowshoe hare—about one every other night. Heavy reliance on this one food leads to a 7 to 10-year cycle of starvation for the lynx. Enlarged snowshoe populations means diminishing food supplies for hares. The resulting reduced hare count causes starvation for the lynx, who take several years to recover and breed again.

This ecological cycle is documented by fur sale records going back 200 years that show fluctuations of the lynx population from 2,000 to 36,000 per year.

Adult males are territorial, scratching and marking posts regularly by scent on night patrols as long as 12 miles. They keep scents fresh to reduce—though it doesn't prevent—confrontations with other males. Fights are fierce but usually end in one turning tail, and the winner gaining the local female's company.

Mating follows, preceded and accompanied by loud yowls, not too different from alley cats. The pair may stay together briefly, but she wants him gone by the end of her two months gestation, and he has other females to woo.

The nursing kits look as adorable as domestic kittens, but with great big feet. Their eyes open in two weeks. Curious and playful, they tumble and tussle with one another, hide, seek and pounce. Mother brings meat or juicy bones to the den to strengthen their jaws and give them the taste of prey.

They grow quickly, wearing brown-dappled, buff summer coats by spring, when they catch small prey like mice. By fall they are full size, grooming themselves and hunting with mother. When winter wanes, their skills allow them to disburse and face survival on their own.

Canadian lynx: long legs, large feet support muscular, feline body, 36-40 inches long, 19-24 inches high at shoulders. Weighs 18-25 pounds.

Face is long, ears sharp, prominent black ear tufts. Layered ruff, long brown-tipped hairs widen face. Powerful jaws, sharp teeth.

Paws are front five-toed, rear four-toed, densely covered with thick furry hairs.

Eyes are yellow, has excellent night vision. Iris slits in daylight (see picture) expand to admit maximum light in dark. Sees only black, white, gray.

Canadian Lynx — Front, Rear PAW PRINTS, Eye

THE INDEPENDENT, JANUARY 15, 1998

"Thriving in temperatures that dive down to minus 30 degrees F…"

Great treasure

NATURE'S WAY

Marion Dusoir Ennes

PART OF THE TWO BILLION BUSHEL soybean harvest in this country each year is grown in Columbia County. Steve Hadcock of the Columbia County Cooperative Extension estimates that 2,000 acres are used for soybean cultivation annually, most used as protein supplement for livestock.

The harvested beans are roasted, he says, "to improve the quality of available protein. Roasting changes the bean so that a greater percentage of its protein bypasses the rumen where it tends to ferment and is digested in the animal's lower gut."

Today's tall, bushy soybean plants are descended from a wild, sprawling vine which produced small hard black or brown beans. Chinese farmers first planted these seeds 3,000 to 5,000 years ago, and by 1100 B.C. had, by selection, an upright plant with larger, more useful seeds.

As years passed, this legume annual proved itself. Easy to cultivate, it was a high protein food with great versatility: soybean sprouts, steamed green beans, roasted soy nuts, soy milk and soybean oil. Fermented products included soy sauce, *miso* (a paste), *tempeh* (a soybean cake), and *tofu*, a cheese-textured substance made from coagulated soy milk which, in turn, is the basis for ice cream and candy, or used shredded, sliced, deep-fried or steamed in a wide variety of dishes.

Named variously "great treasure" or "yellow jewel" by the Chinese, it was revered and designated one of five sacred grains along with rice, barley, wheat and millet.

Like other green plants, soybean's tri-foliate leaves create carbohydrates through photosynthesis to nourish the plant. In time, depending on the genetic patterns and environmental conditions, white or purple flowers form.

The hairs on its roots pull in *rhizobium* bacterium that lodge in root nodules. This symbiotic partnership makes it possible for the plant to fix atmospheric nitrogen gas.

Converted first to ammonia, then into amino acid, the nitrogen ultimately becomes unusually rich in protein with seven out of eight essential amino acids.

Soybeans require short days before they flower. When the plant is large and vigorous with enough leaves and root nodules, it produces a large crop of fruit.

Soybean farming progressed slowly from East to West. Swedish biologist Carolus Linnaeus named the plant botanically in 1737. Almost 150 years later French scientists discovered that soybeans contain almost no starch and recommended it for diabetics.

Nutritionists quickly began to discover many other virtues of the bean and established that it had a higher protein content than beef.

Though grown primarily for cattle fodder, enthusiasm for soybean remained limited until the end of World War II. Then human consumption of meats of all kinds increased, so fodder needs expanded from beef to chicken, hogs, shrimp, catfish, eels, and trout. Animal feed was needed for mink, foxes, bears, bees and silkworms.

The U.S. Department of Agriculture responded by forming cooperative research arrangements with states. Studies of plant breeding and genetics, plant physiology and pathology, agricultural engineering and entomology produced substantial results.

Yields increased. Soybeans were refined into soy meal and flour and produced six gallons of soy (vegetable) oil for each American every year.

And it oiled the wheels of commerce as well. Soy extracts are used widely in glues, cardboard, tires, paints, caulk, gasoline, wallpaper, fire extinguisher foam and lecithin.

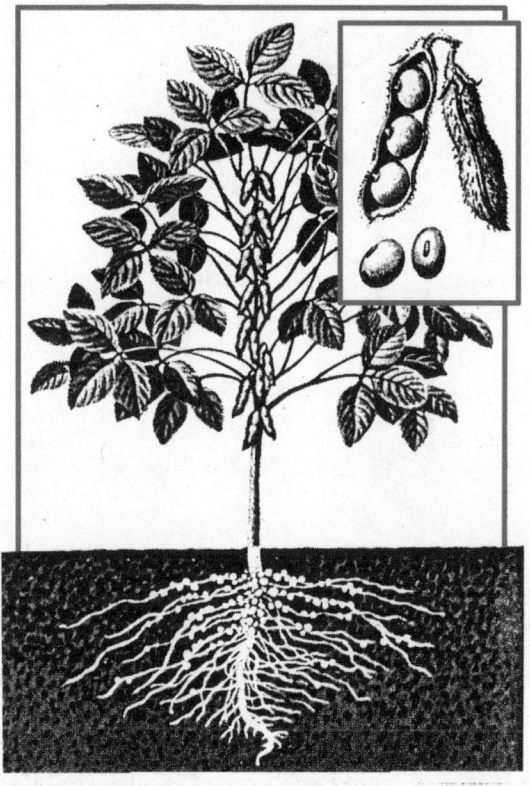

Soybean plant *2-4 feet tall, covered with fine hairs. Large tri-foliate leaves. Pods grow close to stem. Nitrogen-fixing nodules on roots.* **Inset:** *Hairy pod with 2-3 almost spherical seeds (beans). Individuals show* **dark** *hilum (seed scar).*

THE INDEPENDENT, JANUARY 19, 1995

"Named variously 'great treasure' or 'yellow jewel' by the Chinese…"

NATURE'S WAY

A scientist's gift

A lot more goes into the work of the scientists at the New York State Museum than is dreamt of in our excursions to see their elegant exhibits.

Behind those walls scientists are collecting field specimens, preparing them, and adding them to the state biological and geological collections mandated in the 19th century.

Recognition of one of these biological collections was recently conferred by the National Science Foundation through a grant of $67,000, awarded to preserve the state's mycological herbarium, one of the most important scientific collections of dried American fungi.

Today the collection contains more than 83,000 fungi, including the familiar mushroom forms, along with many less known fungi that act as decomposers, parasites, or symbionts of other organisms.

All are vital functionaries in the ecological scheme of things.

The collection's curator, Senior Scientist and Mycologist Dr. John Haines, speaks enthusiastically about their value: "These specimens, many going back 125 years, are important today because the rules governing the naming of organisms dictate that the first name and specimen used to create the first published description becomes the standard for a species.

"These standard samples are called 'type specimens' basic to any environmental inventory or ecological study. They are used to gather or check new information about a species, compare species, or settle disputes over use of a name."

The 3,500 critical early 'type specimens' are a baseline for research identification of new organisms—and now, with DNA, possible organism development.

In 1868, when the state government hired Charles Peck at $1,500 per annum, he was New York's first full-time mycologist.

Peck was born into a rural Rensselaer County farm family. At 18 he left Albay Normal School (SUNY's forerunner) to study college-level botany and classics, earning a master's degree from Union College.

While teaching school, he began serious botanical study of mosses, quality work which earned him, within five years, the mycology appointment.

When he completed his work 47 years later, in 1915, his inventory of fungi described 2,700 new species for the New York State herbal collection, in addition to thousands he identified.

He collected persistently, gathering local specimens in early summer and making longer trips from July through September, covering most of New York by 1913.

From late fall through early spring he worked up dried specimens from correspondents around the country and answered voluminous mail from the U.S. and abroad.

His clear, detailed records appeared in the state's annual Natural Science Report — and justified his salary appropriation.

Dr. Haines, whose field work has added to the 'type specimens' files, is himself involved with various fungal studies, some exploring ecological, others human health-related problems.

His pride in the well-organized files, mycological specimens, drawings, and notes prepared by Dr. Peck was abundant when I visited his Museum office, and I, too, was impressed.

Today, with the help of the National Science Foundation grant, this well-organized data will become part of a computer catalog of information on the 'type specimens' — using Peck's files, letters, and field notes.

This already popular collection will be more accessible to mycologists worldwide more quickly, as they undertake basic as well as applied scientific studies.

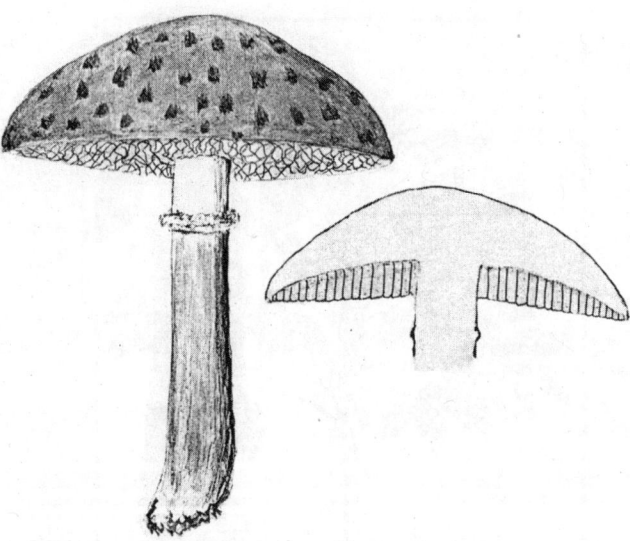

Boletus spectabiles —'Type specimen' collected in the Adirondacks, 1870's. Line drawing and watercolor, showing Peck's detailed observation. Rose pink cap with darker rose protuberances. Yellow-colored gills. Dark stem. Cross section detail describes gills. Signed 'PK', 'K' faded.

This illustration, reproduced courtesy New York State Museum, from Peck's own file, also contains dried specimens of the species.

THE INDEPENDENT, JANUARY 21, 1993

"Today the collection contains more than 83,000 fungi, many going back 125 years."

NATURE'S WAY:
The grouse family

Listen for the thunderous drumming sound of the ruffed grouse in early spring. Somewhere in the woods he jumps on a log or a stone fence and starts beating his wings, inviting a female grouse to check him out.

Films of this activity reveal that the male produces the sound by rapid wing movement alone, not by striking his body or some other surface. This takes practice—with lots of trial and error.

After a powerful upward and forward beat, the wings are quickly reversed. In that moment of motion, a vacuum is created, air rushes in, and a small-scale sonic boom results.

The male struts, raises his ruff and crest and spreads his tail, shakes his head, and drums again—striving for the most impressive effect.

The choice is up to the female, and if the male display is not to her liking, she moves off. If she likes him, she may fluff up her ruff feathers, move and posture in ways inviting mating.

After copulation, she takes on single-parent status and goes off to make a nest while he drums for other hens.

She hollows out a nest two and three-quarters of an inch deep with a six-and-a-half inch diameter in the woodland floor, next to a tree base or other protection, with a clear line of visibility at least 50 feet.

The clutch of about 11 white/pale brown eggs incubate in 24 days. The new born chicks dry their wet feathers close to the warmth of their mother's body.

Although the fluffy tan chicks are covered with down and active, they cannot fly and are dependent upon the hen for the skills they need for survival. The many efforts to propagate and stock these birds artificially have been unsuccessful; they have to learn in the wild environment.

Mother teaches them to eat insects at first and to drink dew from leaves. If they are wet or cold, she gathers them under her for protection; at night they sleep together.

Leaves, pine needles, and some grouse feathers are used for lining the ruffed grouse hen's nest. The hardy eggs survive the hen's food-breaks even in cold weather.

She stays alert and wary and keeps them close as they travel through the woods, warning them of danger; they disappear when she gives a sharp cry.

She will threaten an intruder, ruff and crest erect, flying toward or away from the enemy. She may affect a broken wing or cry and run to draw attention to herself to protect her young.

By two weeks they have learned to fly and roost in low branches. She teaches them to take dust baths to eliminate lice and other vermin.

As summer wanes the young grouse learn to feed on berries, nuts, fruit, acorns, seeds, catkins.

The brood stays together until September. The strongest take the best territory, with good cover and food supply and the better chance to survive longer than the three-year average estimated for the regal ruffed grouse.

THE INDEPENDENT, FEBRUARY 2, 1989

"After copulation, she takes on single-parent status and goes off to make a nest while he drums for other hens."

"The bird's own regal demeanor is heightened by a crest and a chocolate brown ruff..."

NATURE'S WAY:
The grouse who learned

Several winters ago I was thrilled to watch for about three-quarters of an hour as an agile ruffed grouse ate every bright-red barberry from a well-fruited bush at the lawn's edge.

Though the bush has been full of fruit each intervening year, no grouse returned. This year, when there were several sightings on our hilly property, I began to wonder why the barberries had lost their allure.

A fascinating bird personality emerged from my inquiries—a bird whose history and longevity are a testament to the survival of the fittest, whose beauty, gallantry, and ingenuity elicit paeans of praise from biologists, ornithologists, and hunters alike.

Archaeolgists confirm the ruffled grouse's existence in eastern North America during the Pleistocene Epoch 25,000 years ago. It prospered through the centuries to become an important food source to Native Americans. The Canadian explorer Jacques Cartier referred to it in his 1535 journal and probably even enjoyed a meal of grouse, still a gourmet treat.

In colonial times, the ruffed grouse was called the 'fool hen'—so populous and tame it could be killed with stones or easily snared. Later, it was gunned down in large numbers by market hunters.

By the first quarter of the nineteenth century, survival had favored the wariest of these birds and the ruffed grouse developed its current reputation as the 'king of American game birds.'

Ruffed grouse is an indigenous American species which lives in 34 states from New England to the Pacific and throughout Canada. This terrestrial bird, related to the domestic chicken, likes hilly woodlands with bushy cover.

It's about 17 inches long from beak to tail, with a 23-inch wingspan, flies on small rounded wings, and can reach speeds over 65 mph.

At rest the tail of the ruffed grouse is square and straight out, but in courtship display, or in flying maneuvers, the tail fans out to a banded design ending with a dark brown and white stripe. In 1672 high fashion ladies carried these feather fans in the court of Louis XIV.

It is well camouflaged by a thick coat of mottled feathers that range from golden brown to light silver.

The bird's own regal demeanor is heightened by a crest and a chocolate brown ruff which raises like a fur collar when it displays for courtship or for defense of territory.

To hunters, the ruffed grouse is a respected and daunting adversary. Aldo Leopold has written, "there are two kinds of hunting, ordinary hunting and ruffed grouse hunting."

Hard to find, when flushed it uses surprise and intimidation, along with speed and calculated evasiveness, to escape. But it is so ubiquitous in it vast range that six million birds are taken each year.

THE INDEPENDENT, JANUARY 26, 1989

Thrushes, America's nightingales

NATURE'S WAY

Marion Dusoir Ennes

FOR MUCH OF MY LIFE I believed that there was only one nightingale and that it sang for poets and emperors on other continents—but never on ours. Immortalized in Hans Christian Anderson's *Wonder Stories*, the nightingale comes to visit the Emperor. His glorious song moves the Emperor to possession, and the bird is caged.

In the excitement about the arrival of a bejeweled artificial nightingale, the real one escapes back to the forest.

The sweet-singing nightingale is a member of the thrush family, all known for their glorious music. The good news is that 13 species of thrush breed in the U.S., many praised for their moving musicality by poets, writers, and naturalists. Three of these—the wood thrush, the veery, and the hermit thrush—breed regularly in this area.

The bad news is that, countrywide, many thrushes are threatened with extinction through fragmentation of woodlands by logging, agriculture, or development, putting nesting young at high risk.

Cornell's Laboratory of Ornithology is using trained citizen scientists to survey maximum size and conformation of habitats needed to support viable populations. Their focus is on seven finch species nationwide, all but one declining significantly.

Plump wood thrushes, slightly smaller than our robins, are perhaps most familiar. They like damp woods, but also nest 3 to 12 feet up in trees along wood edges and in gardens. In early morning or at dusk, you will surely hear its song—a series of rich, flutelike phrases of three to five notes, connected by L sounds—the famous ee-o-lay.

Dedicated parents, thrushes build deep cup nests similar to robins, lay 3 to 5 blue eggs. They feed their babies small insects and defend them vigorously against predators.

The veery nests along stream banks, wooded swamps, or low moist woodlands. A ground-nester, it often needs to place the nest cup on a thick pile of dry leaves against the moisture.

This slender bird, described as one of the sweetest songsters, takes its name from the spiraling call of bell-like notes descending—vee-ur, vee-ur veer—to a resonant, yet soft, indescribable sadness.

Most eloquently praised for its song is the inconspicuous hermit thrush—retiring denizen of dense woodlands where it, too, nests on earth. This bird is aptly called the American Nightingale, for its song has a dream-like quality.

In F. Schuyler Matthews lovely book, *Wild Birds and Their Music*, he compares the two birds in musical notation to show the hermit's capacity for improvisation.

"What a consummate tone artist he is! Not content with a single key, he deliberately chooses several in major and minor relationship, and elaborates these with perfectly charming arpeggios and wonderful ventriloquous triads. And what a wealth of melody!"

It seems like an outpouring of the heart, at dawn or in the darkening woods.

Thoreau called it more American than the plaintive European sound, for "whenever it is heard a man is young, it is a new world, and a free country, and the gates of heaven are not shut to him."

The Emperor's nightingale flew back to the palace to restore the dying ruler's health with a song of comfort and hope.

Loving his heart more than his crown, the nightingale promised to sing to him again as he did for peasants and fishermen.

Having discovered our own nightingale and its cousins, will we allow them to continue singing in our woodlands?

American Nightingale

1) **Wood thrush,** length 7 ¾". *Bright reddish-brown above fading to olive-brown tail. Whitish below, large dark spots. White eye-ring.*

2) **Veery,** length 7". *Reddish-brown above, white flanks, face grayish. Small spots on buffy chest.*

3) **Hermit thrush,** length 6 ¾". *Brown above to gray-brown above. Breast, flanks buffy, spotted, and tail reddish. Whitish eye-ring.*

THE INDEPENDENT, JANUARY 29, 1998

"It seems like an outpouring of the heart, at dawn or in the darkening woods."

NATURE'S WAY

Signs of the season: late winter

February has been described as "stern and unrelenting" with morning temperatures expected to average from 15°-20° F. It may be snowy, but balmy days remind us that spring is just seven weeks off, and even in February a lot is going on.

Winter's dark is beginning to yield to changes in the sun's position in the sky. Light has increased steadily since December 21, when the earth's orbital movement caused the rising and setting points of the sun to move northward. By March 21, the vernal equinox, days and nights are of equal length as the sun rises due east, setting due west. The higher arc makes the angle of the sun's rays more direct and, therefore, hotter.

The flow of sap in trees is one sign that spring approaches; the opening and closing of valves controlling water flow is governed by light. During winter, the small roots close to the surface and side roots draw up moisture from small rains or snow melt.

Warmth makes underground frost melt, root pressure from the absorption of water pushes up. Sap, for example maple, rises inside the trunk where it can be tapped to make syrup and sugar.

By February, many of the medium-sized mammals that were more or less active in cold weather begin to feel the urge to procreate. Raccoons, opossums, skunks, and squirrels begin to look for each other.

You can see the five-fingered tracks of mature male raccoons, who may travel up to eight miles a night to find a mate. He searches all possible den sites—especially hollow trees—for a female.

Once he finds her *and* she accepts him as "her

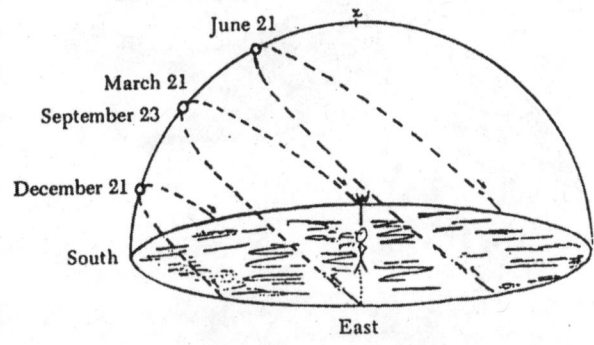

Sun positions as they appear at noon in this latitude. The sun's arcs from rising to setting during spring and autumn equinoxes and summer and winter solstices are also shown.

one and only," he stays in her den, where they cuddle until she is ready to mate. This happens over three-four days. Ten days later she returns to a half-sleep as he goes on to find another responsive female.

In the woodlands' upper story, many birds, large and small, are courting and beginning to nest. Great horned owls started in January and are already incubating eggs, even in heavy snowstorms.

The call of the barred owl—"who cooks for you, who cooks for you all"—is probably a signal to a female. The male eastern screech owl whinnies or hoots to call his beloved's attention to the nest sites he wants to show her.

Foxes also go house-hunting this time of year. The pair starts mating activity by fast runs together over meadows and hills. They locate several den sites: caves, hollows, or old woodchuck holes. These are cleaned and prepared for the female's laying-in, when the male brings her food.

Red-tailed hawks, northern goshawks, kestrels, and peregrines; woodpeckers, nuthatches, jays, starlings, and titmice are all pairing off, now protecting territories and making special gestures to each other.

Listen for the high-pitched whistled phrase of the tiny, crested, gray, tufted titmouse—"peter, peter" or "peeyer peeyer"—repeated loudly to establish territory, and softly to one another through the quiet of the lengthening February days.

THE INDEPENDENT, FEBRUARY 1, 1990

"By the time of the vernal equinox, days and nights are of equal length as the sun rises due east, setting due west."

Trees in Winter

NATURE'S WAY

Marion Dusoir Ennes

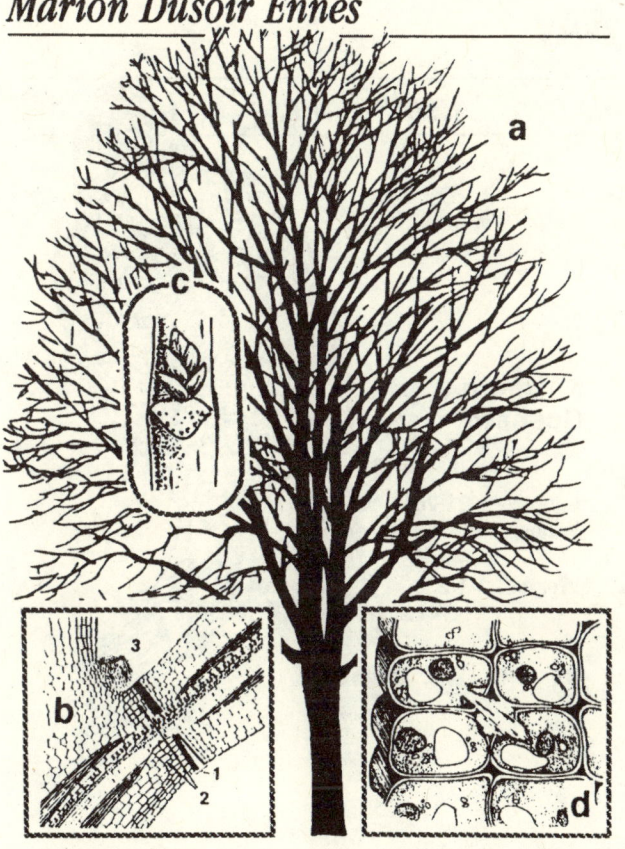

DECIDUOUS TREES, WHOSE rustling leaves offer us renewal in spring, the comfort of shade in summer, and oxygen throughout the leafy seasons, are silent colleagues with us in the ongoing battle to survive winter's cold.

Bare now, they are far from dead. Their suspended animation masks a careful struggle deep in their cells to withstand freezing.

We hated seeing the brilliant autumn leaves disappear last fall, little realizing that this loss was only part of a much larger plan for self-preservation.

Trees plan ahead. From the time their leaves emerged in spring, these green plants worked hard at photosynthesizing sugars and starches.

At first, this food was used to assure growth, to push out buds and flowers and form seeds. Seeds are a tree's fail-safe mechanism for survival. They are tiny fertilized embryos wrapped in multiple laminated tissue.

Each mature seed goes into the world with its own food supply. At first dormant—sometimes for long periods—it is finally triggered into germination by moisture, oxygen, and/or temperature.

By the time summer peaks, leaf production stops and twigs stop growing. Now a large proportion of a tree's annually manufactured food is already stored inside twigs, branches, trunk, and roots. Some will be saved for winter rations, the rest allocated for next year's growth spurt. But a substantial portion will feed the current formation of buds for next year.

Close examination of twigs on a bare tree reveals its "resting" buds. These may hold leaves or flowers or both together—all already formed and prepared to emerge next spring.

For protection during winter, they are tightly enclosed in bud scales—designs specific for each tree species. All buds are now completely waterproof against outer moisture damage and—very important—water loss from within.

Most of the year, trees can draw water from the soil through their roots. But when water freezes they are subject to great danger from drought damage. One important way they cut water need is to drop their leaves.

So in autumn, when day length and light intensity decrease, and temperature and precipitation levels change, a hormone called *abscisic acid* triggers loss of leaves and dormancy begins.

An abscission zone forms where the leaf stem attaches to the twig. A separation layer divides the leaf stem from the tree, and the leaf falls. A leaf scar made of tough, corky cells forms to seal tissues up tightly—and to prevent further water loss.

Now, with tall, woody frame watertight, trees face winter's lowering temperatures. Trees vary in freezing tolerance—some safe only at local minimum temperatures. Red oaks, sugar maples, white ash, yellow birch die at minus 40 to 45 degrees. Along with evergreens, the poplars, aspens and paper birch tolerate low temperatures to minus 80 degrees.

The danger is to thin layers of live cambium tissue inside the trunk. Here, the vital cells are each enclosed in green cellulose membranes holding cytoplasm. This plasma cradles tiny crucial organs that do the cells' work; they must not freeze or the tree will die.

Cells cooperate, acclimate. Cell walls remain intact, becoming increasingly permeable during autumn, able to allow water—which would freeze at 32 degrees—to flow out of the cell into intercellular space. Ice crystals can form there without damaging internal organs.

Cell liquid, packed with salts, protein, sugars, and alcohol, freezes at temperatures lower than water. Inside, cytoplasm gets stickier, more viscous, but vital organs survive the danger.

Tree defenses.
a. Red maple silhouette, tree bare of leaves.
b. Twig showing 1) abscission layer; 2) protective corky layer below; 3) next year's axillary bud.
c. Bud sealed by protective scale.
d. Cells inside cambium layer; ice outside cell walls.

THE INDEPENDENT, JANURARY 18, 1996

"Their suspended animation masks a careful struggle deep in their cells to withstand freezing."

Same time, next year

NATURE'S WAY

Marion Dusoir Ennes

Northern Goshawk

Length: 21-26"
Wingspread: 40-46"
Weight: 1-1/2 to 1-3/4 lbs.

THE GLOW IN THE CRIMSON IRIS of a northern goshawk, its shrill scream and sudden swoop as it lunges toward an intruder, is a serious warning: Stay away from our nest, our eggs, our babies!

Gray and white parent birds, solitary through the fall and early winter, are forming a serious partnership that will last until late summer.

Each February, they return to last year's territory, a mixed forest of mature trees strong enough to support a large nest up to five feet across and two feet deep, one they build or redecorate from a past year.

Northern goshawk nests are found in all but 11 New York counties. These birds prefer secluded mountain sites where they require a territory of almost two square miles to assure security as they nurture the next generation.

On arrival, they seek each other out, call politely to one another early each morning. The high-pitched *keek* is repeated hoarsely in a long series four to five times a second.

Soon there are courting displays. Partners engage in glides interspersed with exaggerated wing flapping, undulating flight, fluffing white undertail feathers and sometimes diving, while giving a shrill signal call. Each step strengthens their bond, though they still roost up to 100 yards apart.

The nest takes its final shape slowly, the female lining it with feathers and decorating it with evergreen boughs.

Like most raptor pairs, females are larger, goshawks strikingly so. She is one third heavier, with wingspan broader than her partner's. From this time on, she stays close to the nest. he ranges far, hunting for himself and, with a call to let her know he's back, bringing all her food.

As tree buds open, she invites the male close to the nest. Here she perches on a branch, droops her wings, lifts her tail. He accepts this invitation to copulate frequently for two weeks before the first eggs are laid.

She incubates the eggs about five weeks, turning them daily, keeping them warm as needed. She leaves them only briefly, to eat the food he brings while he guards them. Occasionally she collects green sprigs to drop on the nest.

Both birds are skilled hunters. They have relatively short, rounded wings and a long tail that acts as a rudder. With amazing maneuverability in wooded areas, they can turn on a dime. Over open fields they reach 60 mph.

A goshawk generally hunts from a perch well above an open area frequented by ground birds or rodents. He waits patiently, hours at a time, watching till a prospect appears.

Then, wings spread, taking rapid beats, it is off its perch, sailing down swiftly. Pouncing hard on its next meal and grasping it with the four talons of each foot, it hangs on, squeezing it to death.

When the male brings his catch back for the newly hatched babies, he stops first at the "butcher block," an arched-over tree or stump where he (or she) plucks feathers from prey birds before eating or delivering to young.

The young birds are eager eaters, but Papa is a great hunter, so Ma stores some of the babies' unused meat in a tree crack or hollow.

In 10 weeks fuzzy hatchlings reach self-sufficiency, five weeks on, five off the nest, with parents feeding regularly, defending constantly.

Though the female seems the dominant partner, she couldn't do it all without him. It's the partnership that leads to success.

THE INDEPENDENT, FEBRUARY 2, 1995

"… he stops first at the 'butcher block,' an arched-over tree or stump where he plucks feathers from prey birds…"

The witch that isn't

NATURE'S WAY
Marion Dusoir Ennes

THIS IS A GOOD TIME to think about flowers blooming. Only a brief time ago, the witch hazel bloomed, in late October or early November. Not only did it bloom, but well after its yellow autumn leaves dropped, this aromatic tree had its own seasonal party, adorned at one and the same time with flowers, last year's ripening fruit capsules, and next spring's leaf buds.

Nowadays, few people recognize witch hazel, a moderate-sized tree, sometimes with multiple stalks. Because of its large, asymmetrical leaves and interesting habits, it used to be a popular northern ornamental, and is still considered a curiosity in English gardens.

I remember the sweet-sour aroma of its extract, a commonly-used astringent years ago that served my father, as it did so many other gentlemen, as an aftershave.

This tree reminded early pioneers of true hazels familiar to them in Europe. Actually, the witch hazel's family is indigenous to eastern Asia as well as eastern North America, where it was well known to native Americans who distilled the extract. They made a tea to relieve sore throats and colds, stronger solutions as liniments for muscle cramps, still stronger to stem bleeding from wounds.

Our notions about witch hazel trees, the name given to them by early settlers, derive from European beliefs about the magical properties of true hazels. Those trees' legendary abilities included finding witches or helping witches find water, or even gold.

In the science of philology, the witch in the tree's name derives from *wicken*, to bend, in Anglo-Saxon, or *wick*, quick or living in Old English.

The tradition of magic persists, as the name does. The forked branches of the witch hazel tree, those whose points carry the sun's influence by growing toward north and south on the tree, were regularly employed by dowsers, and probably still are, to locate underground sources of water.

If you walked into the woods now to a normally damp place in the understory, you might identify a witch hazel by a few remnants of its yellow flowers, or its woody two-beaked seed pods, quite unique on the tree's zig-zag branches.

Flowers grow in clusters of three. Each one consists of a small *calyx* (outer protective coating) that opens to show the inner lining of its four sepals, orange-brown, yellow or red. Springing from the cup-shaped center are four long bright-yellow strap-like petals. When weather turns very cold, the petals curl up tight until the sun's warmth returns to unfurl them.

The long petals, like so many strands of ribbon confetti, twist and curl above their ovaries, the better to catch the favor of late autumn insects.

They do a good job. The flowers are fertilized, their ovaries swell on the calyx, building a pad that will become the seeds' home. This pod develops into a woody, two-chambered capsule, fitted with valves in its outer wall.

Once the flowers have bloomed, these last year's fruits join the celebration with noise and action. When the fruit is ripe, the valves contract with a loud "pop," literally exploding the container, as two slender, shiny dark-brown seeds are ejected. They are catapulted 10 to 40 feet from the parent to start another tree.

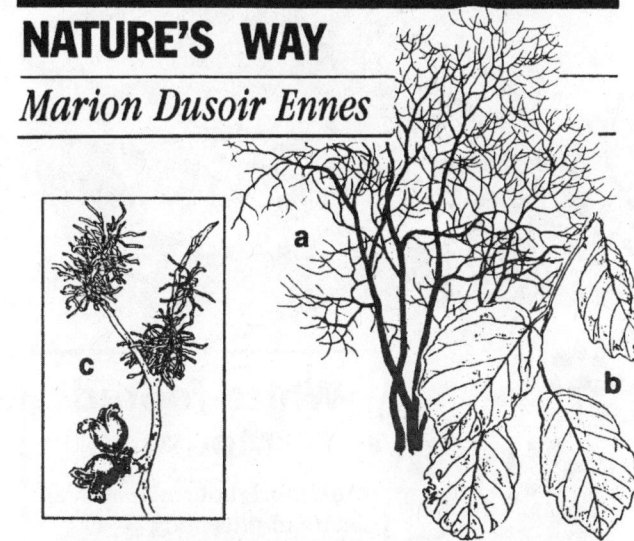

A. Witch hazel silhouette showing canopy spread at 20-30 feet. Trunk reaches 12" diameter.

B. Large alternate asymmetrical toothed leaves, 4-6 inches long. Dull dark green above, pale lustrous below.

C. Above: three-clustered flowers, yellow-petalled, orange-red at base. Below: two empty, woody seed cases, each minus two chestnut-brown seeds.

THE INDEPENDENT, FEBRUARY 3, 1994

"Those trees' legendary abilities include finding witches or helping witches find water, or even gold."

NATURE'S WAY
White-footed mouse

We have neighbors in the winter woods. Along the edges, and in other brushy places, white-footed mice survive the coldest of winter in cozy self-insulated nests.

But, like us, they are out and about, leaving little tracks in the snow as they search for food.

These small mammals have certain characteristics we like to regard as human. They have great curiosity, are industrious and acquisitive, and live basically individual lives—cooperating primarily for safety and protection.

The white-footed mouse that thrives in the eastern U.S. is closely related to other deer-mice, whose coloration and large eyes and ears are reminiscent of white-tailed deer.

Vermont naturalist Ron Rood knows about white-foot's curiosity first hand. He had company while checking pipes in a country home.

"Every turn of the wrench, every move of my hands was followed by two liquid-dark eyes, two alert, tissue-thin ears, and a twinkling set of nose whiskers attached to a grayish-brown body.

"And when I stopped for a moment, the ears and whiskers poked right into where I'd been working."

In the wild, this kind of thorough research means that the mouse is well-acquainted with its well-defined territory. It is aware of all the hiding or nesting places and of all the food supplies waiting to be gathered from trees, bushes, or dried plants.

And in the less frequented parts of your house, it knows where you keep your supplies of sunflower seeds, or where to find soft fabric to shred for a nest, or a little-used drawer to build it in.

From early spring to fall last year, white-footed mice did what rabbits are famous for: They reproduced.

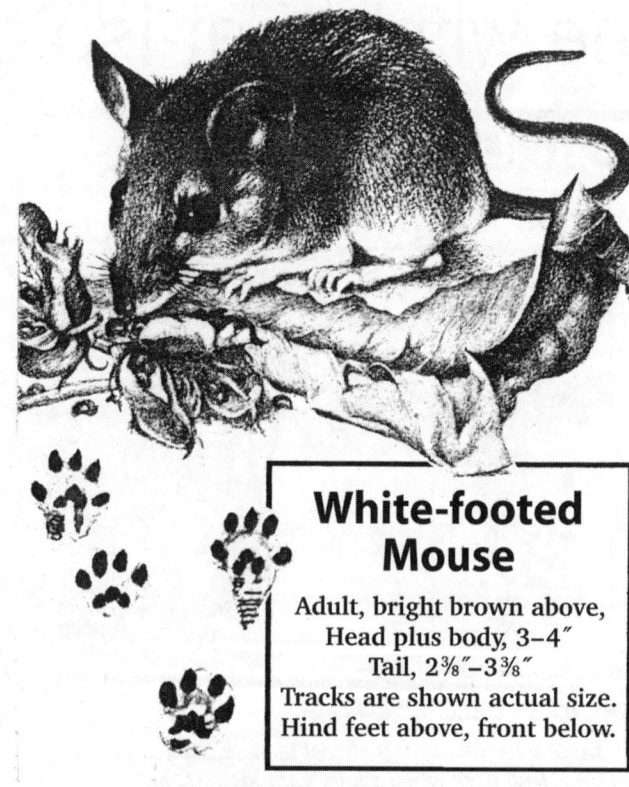

White-footed Mouse
Adult, bright brown above,
Head plus body, 3–4″
Tail, 2⅜″–3⅜″
Tracks are shown actual size.
Hind feet above, front below.

The dedicated and protective mother had four or more broods last year, averaging four or five babies per litter. She prepared a newly-located nest each time.

She nursed each litter, then schooled them in finding seeds and other delicious plant materials, insects, and small mammals to eat; and supervised their earliest tree climbing and ground tracking before sending them out to make families of their own.

Before reaching 10 weeks, young begin breeding; by mid-summer, populations are growing by leaps and bounds.

But a white-footed glut is unlikely. This nocturnal rodent, foraging at dusk, early evening, or just before dawn, is a favorite meal for owls, hawks, weasels, foxes, bobcats, snakes, and—when swimming, even fish.

A community of mice is not totally defenseless, however. They can hear sounds well above the human middle range of 3,000 cycles per second (cps). A mouse's warning scream is emitted and heard by others up to 100,000 cps—out of our range and that of cats as well.

By late autumn, the white-foot is busily preparing for winter, scampering up trees on specially adapted foot pads and clambering out on fine branches to collect seeds in amazing volume and variety—all carried to hiding places in cheek pouches.

Beechnuts are a favorite—collected by the peck, clover in quarts. Maple, pine, viburnum, chestnut, acorns are stored, along with seeds of blueberries, raspberries, shadberries, and turquoise endosperm of jewelweed seeds.

Now the white-foot's fur coat increases by one-third in insulative value in preparation for increasingly cold weather. Brown fat accumulates around inner organs, ready to supply extra internal heat.

And inside the safe haven of a well-insulated winter nest, a cluster of mice gathers together for mutual warmth in coldest weather.

THE INDEPENDENT, FEBRUARY 4, 1993

"These small mammals have certain characteristics we like to regard as human."

NATURE'S WAY
Deer in winter

Somewhere nearby a group of deer has found a winter "yarding" area, a protected place where the deer have cover and, most importantly, protection from winter winds. Many seek out lower terrain, like swamps. Others use gullies, often on the southeasterly slope. The "yard" on our property faces that way. It is located under a wide spreading red pine tree, surrounded by brush.

During winter, a deer's bottom line is survival against the vagaries of temperature, wind, chill, heavy snows, and, to a lesser extent, reductions in food supply.

A yard is usually in a dense stand of evergreens. Under the trees the snow cover is thin, and snow trapped in the umbrella of branches helps keep heat inside. Warmth from the sun, absorbed by the tree trunks, is given off as the tree's own thermal radiation.

In the deer's well-patterned existence, autumn is the season of refueling as well as reproduction. All year long they look for high protein foods. In November, they seek high fat content as well. Acorn consumption in that month can reach 80%, the balance of diet in browse, buds and bark from twigs. If their habitat is rich in these supplies, they put down a heavy fat layer as a reserve for the winter.

Where food is plentiful, a six-month-old buck fawn can reach exceptional weight going into winter. Fawns of that age average 90 to 100 pounds. In one Illinois county with a superabundant food supply, buck fawns reached weights from 164 to 176 pounds.

By standing on their hind legs, a buck can reach food supplies up to seven feet, a doe usually up to six feet. They seek fine twigs, no thicker than a matchstick. These are covered with the newest bark and have the highest protein content.

If they are starving, deer will take twigs as thick as 5/8 inch, but these are less nutritious, with less bark in proportion to volume.

Fawns are most vulnerable in winter, especially when autumn body weight is low. From 60 to 70% of dying deer in winter are fawns. They die of dehydration and starvation when heavy snows prevent access to water and food supplies.

Barring a sudden sharp temperature drop in early winter, which can cause shock and death, deer acclimate to cold weather. The animal's adrenal, pituitary, and thyroid glands reduce in size and activity, remaining largely inactive during the coldest months of January and February.

The deer's basic metabolic rate—about 1,140 daily calories per 100 pounds in 32° air temperature—drops at below freezing levels. This lower metabolism causes deer to lose 12 to 15% of body weight. They could not use more food even if available.

The basic drill is to seek cover, keep activity to a minimum, and fast through the coldest months, conserving energy and body heat.

A cushion of air is trapped in their dense winter fur, giving them a heavy coat of insulation. They lie down in a heavy snowstorm, even a long one, and are often buried in snow. Their own body heat is so well-contained the snow does not melt.

During active winter periods, they forage during daylight for twigs and buds, grass, pine, mushrooms, and fruits and domestic crops like corn, rye, alfalfa, and winter wheat. But they don't travel far, and return to the yard where they remain bedded through the long cold nights.

A hearty 90 to 120-pound doe and buck up to 200 pounds head into winter. Seasonal coat is dense, tweedy, grey-brown.

THE INDEPENDENT, FEBRUARY 6, 1992

"A cushion of air is trapped in their dense winter fur, giving them a heavy coat of insulation."

NATURE'S WAY

Winter waterfowl

To birders, the great excitement and satisfaction in finding birds is intensified when their sightings contribute to the birds' welfare.

The annual mid-January Waterfowl Count sponsored by the Federation of New York State Bird Clubs presented just such an opportunity to members of the Alan Devoe Bird Club.

According to Kate Dunham of Old Chatham, trip leader and president of the county-wide club, "we monitor winter waterfowl by listing each species seen *and* their numbers.

"When all data are compiled, we have a broad picture of the number and range of birds. Comparison of the figures from one year to the next delineates changing patterns to species types and group sizes. It is one way to see if populations are rising, remaining steady, or declining."

For the 1991 foray, a group of six searchers met at 9 a.m. on a cold day and made a sweep of the Hudson River. "This year," Ms. Dunham says, "we started at Stuyvesant Landing and, for the first time, included the former Ice House site recently acquired by the state at Nutten Hook."

"Wading through crusted snow from Route 9-J to the river brought a special reward: an adult bald eagle. It was one of two called by Professor William Cook of Columbia-Greene Community College as the group worked down-river, checking for waterfowl at access points at Nutten Hook's Ferry Road, Stockport Landing, the Roe-Jan Kill, Germantown Landing, Cheviot, and Clermont Historic Site."

This year birders found eight waterfowl species, five dabblers: Northern pintail (2), mute swan (8), Canada

...In flight   ...Dabbling

Colorful male mallard: green head, narrow white neck-ring, ruddy breast, greyed back and body, short tail, white rump feathers between black, some upcurled. Secondary wing feathers (speculum) violet-blue with white borders.

goose (1,405), American black duck (478), mallard (24); and three divers: gadwall (1), goldeneye (7), common merganser (16). Northern pintail and gadwall were new to the count this year.

Since the local bird club started counting in 1984, they have reported 12 species. In past years other diving birds—canvasback ducks, greater scaup, buffleheads, and red-breasted mergansers—were also counted.

Figures contributed by bird clubs from all over the state, compiled and reported annually by the federation, reflect changes in distribution, such as the statewide population shifts in the number of American black ducks and mallards.

Over a period of about 50 years, mallards have gained in numbers as black ducks diminished. More recently, black ducks show an upward trend.

Both species are dabblers or surface-feeders who skim insects from the surface or upend in about two feet or less of water, paddling furiously as they probe for edible roots and seeds. Grains and acorns are favorite foods on land.

Both species use a variety of habitats but need grassy wetland sites for nesting not too far from open water. Mallards are essentially birds of fresh water; American black ducks can handle coastal salt marsh.

Brightly-marked and colored male mallards outnumber females. Crossbreeding between the two species, often on the same breeding grounds, has occurred. Offspring are fertile, and efforts to monitor these hybrids are difficult.

In this century waterfowl populations across the country have been decimated by wetlands drainage, pesticide and herbicide pollution, lead poisoning, disease, and predation. Humans, who created at least two-thirds of these problems, are beginning to correct some of them.

THE INDEPENDENT, FEBRUARY 7, 1991

"... the great excitement and satisfaction in finding birds is intensified when their sightings contribute to the birds' welfare."

NATURE'S WAY

Marvelous milkweed

Some sturdy stalks of milkweed still stand in the meadows, their yellow-lined pods split open, a few wisps of silk still showing. It seems a long time since last spring when I enjoyed the taste of their delicate green shoots at Vivian Rosenberg's home in Germantown.

The milkweed is a prodigious plant, serving a wide range of insects at different stages of their development. It is a valuable source of food, fiber, and medicine to humans—and a life-saver as well.

In a September 1987 *Audubon Magazine* article, "Underachiever of the Plant World," David M. Schwartz calls it "the plant that outscored all others on the 'Gee Whiz' scale."

Milkweed shoots, a favorite early food of Native Americans and settlers, put out strong, erect fibrous stalks three to five feet. Large fleshy ovate leaves, smooth above and hairy below, are alongside the stem, filled with a sticky white latex containing cardiac glycosides (heart poisons).

A host of insects make a living by feeding on the milkweed plant. Some—like the milkweed leaf beetle, the larva of the queen butterfly, and the red milkweed beetle—know how to enjoy the greens without ingesting a bit of the bad-tasting latex. They cut the leaf veins that store latex so it flows away, then eat outer leaf sections.

Monarch butterfly larvae, which use milkweed as their host plant, feed exclusively on these leaves, latex and all. This protects the larvae *and* the later emerging butterfly, making it unpalatable, if not poisonous, to bird predators.

The good-tasting viceroy butterfly, an orange,

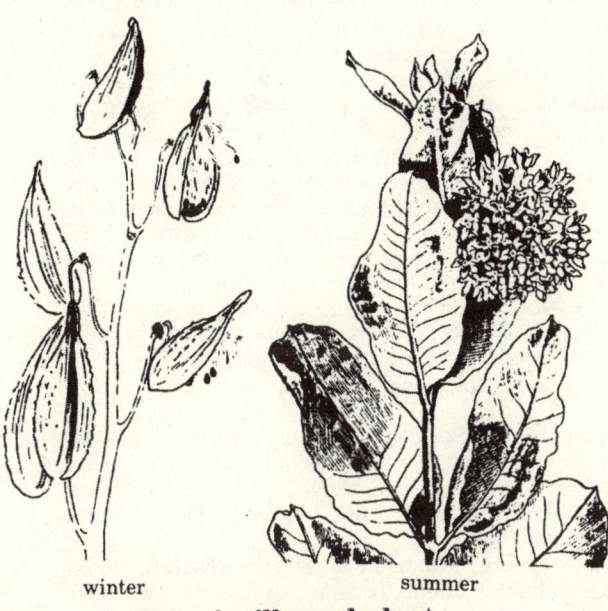

Top of milkweed plant.

black, and white look-alike of the monarch, coasts to freedom on the monarch's reputation.

Green flower clusters and early green seed pods were a culinary treat (comparable to okra) for Native Americans. In the 1700s, French Canadians gathered the dusky pink flowers at dawn and boiled them down for brown sugar.

The milkweed's fibrous stem has been used for centuries by indigenous peoples of several continents to make a strong hemp for netting or rope, and to weave into baskets and textiles for clothing.

Often used in artistic dried flower arrangements, elegant two-three inch milkweed pods, warty and brown outside, smooth yellow inside, split lengthwise in late summer to expel hoards of seeds. Each seed is attached to a flossy filament which acts as a parachute.

Efforts between 1800 and 1940 to spin and weave these fibers, though producing lustrous cottony cloth, were discontinued.

World War II produced the most dramatic success in the use of these fibers, when milkweed actually became a lifesaver.

When the Japanese cut off the supply, the U.S. needed a substitute for buoyant, light, water-resistant kapok, which grew in the Dutch East Indies. The Department of Agriculture recruited school children and scouts to scour the fields for ripe milkweed pods and "Pick-a-Weed—Save-a-Life." They collected 25 million pounds. When processed, the pods yielded the hollow, air-enclosing floss, resembling kapok.

Many a serviceman owed his life to the 26-ounce "Mae West" life jacket filled with milkweed silk that "could keep a 150-lb. man afloat in salt water for 48 hours."

THE INDEPENDENT, FEBRUARY 8, 1990

"When processed, the pods yielded the hollow, air-enclosing floss, resembling kapok."

NATURE'S WAY:
Nesting bluebirds

Bluebirds are the 'delicate' members of the thrush family, known for lyrical songs and speckled breasts.

The male Eastern bluebird, only seven inches long, sports a bright blue coat, a rusty breast over a white belly; the female and young wear a brownish coat. The young show the characteristic 'thrush' speckles on their breasts.

The almost 90 percent decline in the bluebird population, extending over 50 years, is now beginning to reverse, but still has a long way to go.

These birds use fields, bogs, and meadows for breeding. In the past dead trees or wooden fence posts served as nesting sites. Clearing of dead trees and reforestation of farmlands created strong competition from more aggressive birds like house sparrows, house wrens, and tree sparrows.

The North American Bluebird Society started in the late 1960s to preserve and increase the population of bluebirds "through education, the building of nest boxes, and the establishment of bluebird trails."

By 1975, the Society's founder recorded the fledging of more than 200 bluebirds out of his own 85-box bluebird trail. The 1986 report from the Nest Box Network showed that 7,068 bluebirds fledged from 2,138 nest boxes.

Last spring, Kenny Preusser, a Taconic Hills High School student, took us to see the two nest boxes he mounted. One nest was not used because it was too near brushy areas. But the other box produced three broods in 1987 and a pair was already nesting early in the '88 season.

Increasingly, bluebirds are over-wintering, and there have been several reports of flocks in the county this winter.

Nests should be placed on a post from 3 to 10 feet off the ground on a large lawn or a field with low ground cover. No pesticides should be used. Bluebirds like the nest opening 25-50 feet away from a bush or tree. If more than one nest is put up, it must be 100 yards from the first.

Early March is a good time to get nests ready for installation. They should be cleaned out, the inside sprinkled with rotenone against lice and blowfly larvae. Blowfly larvae, which feed on and ultimately kill nesting babies, can be eliminated by inserting a folded platform of wire mesh at the box bottom. The legless larvae cannot climb through this barrier.

About once a week boxes should be monitored. Watch to see who is nesting; then take out house

Adult Eastern bluebird feeds a fledgling

sparrow or house wren nests to leave the box free for bluebirds. As soon as the bluebirds have fledged and left, the nest should be removed to encourage another brood.

The Soil and Water Conservation District (828-4386) is accepting orders for nest boxes ($5) to be delivered in April, still early enough for bluebird breeding. The February order of 100 boxes has already been filled.

The Nest Box Network of the Audubon Society of New York State invites people to enroll in their organization so that data on bluebird nesting can be collected and disseminated. Details are available by writing: Bluebird, P.O. Box 127, Delmar, 12045.

THE INDEPENDENT, FEBRUARY 9, 1989

A tale of two tails

NATURE'S WAY
Marion Dusoir Ennes

SOME TIME AGO Jack Hurley of Hillsdale brought me the bodies of two waxwings that died after flying into a plate glass window as they tried to reach berry branches inside the house.

From the same flock, the waxwings had similar typical brown and black coloring with red waxy wing tips. But only one had a traditional yellow tail band while the other's was bright orange. Jack wanted to know why they were different.

This year's winter issue of *Living Bird*, Cornell Laboratory of Ornithology's magazine, has the answer. In "The Telltale Tail" by Mark Witmer, the mystery is solved.

Bird banders and ornithologists first became aware of cedar waxwings' orange tail tips about 30 years ago in a Pennsylvania reserve. Until 1971 only 5% of young birds had orange tail tips, which increased to 25% by 1985.

Scientists, puzzled by the phenomenon, studied pigments in feather tips and reported that "both yellow and orange feathers contained yellow carotenoid pigment; orange feathers also contained a red carotenoid pigment called rhodoxanthin."

Waxwings are named for the red-colored waxy substance that exudes from several secondary feather shafts on an adult bird's wing. These tips are composed of lipid molecules called carotenoids. Not produced within a bird's body, the pigments must be obtained from foods the birds eat.

Waxwings are voracious feeders. Always in flocks—up to 100 in size—they wander restlessly, looking for food. Although the flock occasionally takes insects—one flock of 30 can devour 90,000 cankerworms in a month—they actually prefer small fruits, about 80% of their diet.

Traveling in close formation, a flock wheels and, almost simultaneously, lands atop a tree or bush loaded with berries. The birds twitter in incessant, high-pitched whispers, gorging themselves, sometimes till they can hardly stand.

Naturalists write enthusiastically about cedar waxwings, referring to their sociability, their gentle disposition. Observers give many accounts of watching rows of birds sitting on a cherry tree branch, passing a whole cherry bill to bill down the line and back. Apparently appreciating closeness, these birds also call to each other continuously while flying.

In late summer, some get drunk from eating fermented fruit. In all seasons, they eat a wide variety of berries, disbursing seeds of numerous fruiting plants.

Looking for the source of rhodoxanthin pigment in young birds' orange-tipped tails, scientists sought nestlings' summer food.

Morrow's honeysuckle, an increasingly common shrub introduced from Japan in the sixties, filled the bill. In summer, its bright red berries containing rhodoxanthin were fed to young birds who grew orange tail tips.

Mark Witmer tested seven experimental adult birds during their molt. He gave four only Morrow's honeysuckle berries. The other three received honeysuckle only until half the new tail feathers started to grow. Then these berries were discontinued.

The results: birds given the berries throughout the molt showed bright orange tail tips. Those deprived midway grew half orange, half yellow.

Morrow's honeysuckle affects other birds, too. Yellow-breasted chats, Kentucky warblers, and locally common white-throated sparrows may be replacing yellow feathers with orange.

The consequences of introducing alien organisms into an ecosystem can't be easily predicted and caution is indicated in adding exotic imports to eastern landscapes.

Bright color is an important factor in reproductive success. Now, adult waxwings with more red waxy wing tips mate with similar adults. They breed earlier, have larger clutches and fledge more young—all survival advantages. Will a bright orange tail tip in addition be icing on the cake?

Cedar Waxwing

Cedar waxwings. *6½ to 8 inches, 12-inch wing spread. Silky chocolate-brown coat and crest. Black mask and chin. Yellow flanks, whitish under tail converts. Red wax-like appendages from secondary quills on wings, sometimes tail quills.*

Inset. *Tail section showing brown tail feathers ending, at arrow, in lighter color tips—yellow or orange.*

THE INDEPENDENT, FEBRUARY 15, 1996

"Not produced within a bird's body, the pigments must be obtained from foods the birds eat."

Eating to survive

NATURE'S WAY

Marion Dusoir Ennes

OUT THERE, under all that insulating snow, a tiny mammal scurries about looking for food. It is one of several hyperactive shrew species. They are common to wooded areas and edges, rarely noticed or mistaken for mole or mouse.

The short-tailed shrew, a whopping one-ounce, lives in burrowed tunnels in leaf debris. This cool, moist microclimate protects worms, insect larvae, snails and hosts of invertebrates that form the diet of these voracious omnivores.

Shrews, with heart rate of 780 beats and 800 breaths per minute, have a high body temperature and such a high metabolism that they must eat 50 to 100% of their own body weight daily just to replace the energy they burn. Anything less means starvation.

Even with enough food, they die from burnout within 18 months. And at the rate they eat, their set of 32 fine teeth wears down and becomes useless.

The senses and body form of this small, ancient, warm-blooded animal are carefully adapted to its active, ravenous lifestyle. Its long, slender body with wedge-shaped head and long pointed nose travels easily through leaf litter as it makes tunnels at the soil line.

Its plush fur coat, hairs attached to skin so they move in any direction, means a shrew can move backward or sideways as readily as forward.

Tiny eyes provide only poor vision. Ears hidden in fur are fairly helpful. But shrews, like bats, echo locate, sending impulses that bounce back, radar-like, clueing them to blockages in their tunnels or measuring distances to obstructions.

Senses of touch and smell are acute. Tough bristles at the end of the shrew's nose are constantly deployed to find local bits of food, while a keen sense of smell draws them in the direction of larger prey.

Considering this necessary preoccupation with its own survival, it is surprising to find so many negative qualities ascribed to the shrew. The Inuit (Eskimos) thought it could burrow into the human heart, the Romans that it made horses and cows lame, and and one 17th-century English cleric described this little four-incher as "a ravening beast...feign(ing) itself gentle and tame...it biteth deep and poisoneth deadly. It beareth a cruel mind, desiring to hurt anything."

We derive many words implying mean behavior from this animal's name, attributing nasty behavior to a human "shrew," always a woman, possibly because of the animal's high-pitched squeal. In the past, a "shrewd" person was more crafty than clever.

Shrews don't burrow into hearts or make cattle lame, nor do they bite and poison humans. But, unique for mammals, their bite is venomous. The toxic venom they inject in prey comes from glands at the base of their incisors. Similar in composition to snake venom, it kills or paralyzes. These little animals can capture mice (larger than themselves) with a bite at the back of the neck.

Supplies of immobilized prey, still fresh, are sometimes stored for leaner hunting days. One lab shrew had a pantry stocked with 80 frogs.

Shrews are ancient mammals, part of a group called insectivores, that evolved in the age of dinosaurs. Though still primitive, these "tough critters" are believed by evolutionists to be the ancestors of humans and almost all other mammals that exist today.

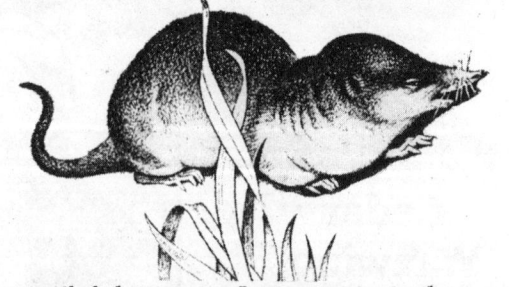

A. Short-tailed shrew, one of seven species in the Northeast. Lean one-ounce body 3 3/4 to 5 1/8 inches long, covered with velvety dark gray fur. Sharply pointed snout with *vibrissae* (tough whiskers) on narrow one-inch wide head.

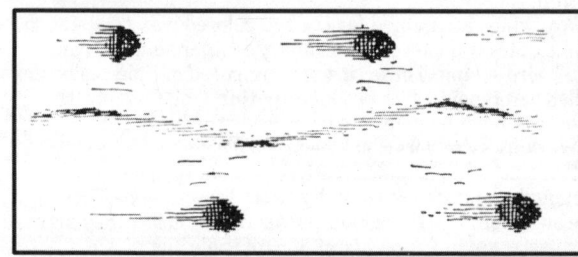

B. Tracks 5/8 inch wide. Gait in soft snow (smart shrews stay underground in winters like this), unpaired, evenly spaced footprints, one-inch intervals. Curved central line made by tail as short-legged body sways side to side.

THE INDEPENDENT, FEBRUARY 17, 1994

"These "tough critters" are believed by evolutionists to be the ancestors of humans and almost all other mammals that exist today."

NATURE'S WAY

Where did they go?

In winter woods' silence, the rustle of a leaf is enough to remind us of summer's sounds and their absence. Where did everyone go?

Large numbers of birds migrated, of course, leaving behind a winter coterie of hawks, owls and some perching birds—seed-eaters (mostly) and bark-probers looking for eggs and larva. A large number of crawling or flying insects have disappeared.

Many birds, frogs, toads and salamanders count on this insect crop for its food. Reptiles, fish and small animals also take their share.

With no food supply and cold weather, each of these must protect itself from freezing. Frogs—air breathers at temperatures above 40°—hibernate, often in large numbers, under the floor of the pond. At temperatures below 40°, they can absorb oxygen from water through their skin, as long as the water does not freeze.

In general, turtles, toads, salamanders, snakes, lizards, and worms burrow into the soil, many below the frost line. Snakes or worms often ball up together to prevent heat loss. Snails hide under rocks after glazing over the shell's opening. The hardened glaze makes a tight, waterproof cover.

And what about insects, who contribute so much to making summer hum and to feeding so many of the foregoing?

Their several stages of development give them options for survival not available to other creatures.

Starting as eggs, they go through various phases before achieving adult, or reproductive, status. Some first assume larval form—as grubs or caterpillars—and then go on to an encased pupal (or chrysalis) stage.

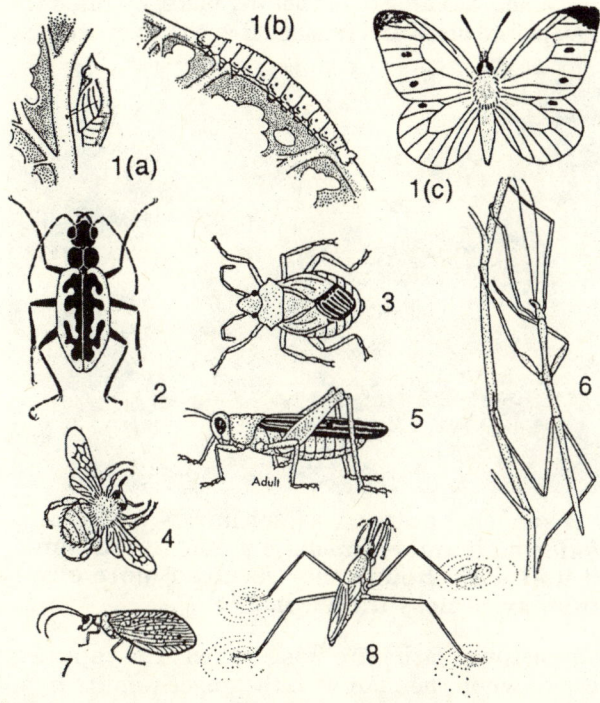

Winter patterns of insects: [1] Cabbage butterfly (a) overwintering chrysalis, (b) next season's larva gorging itself, (c) adult, [2] tiger beetles, [3] stinkbugs, and [4] bumblebees all hide as adults. [5] Grasshoppers and [6] walking sticks lay eggs and die. [7] Lacewing and [8] water strider adults stay over and may come out.

Others skip the pupal stage and become nymphs, sometimes looking like smaller versions of the adult, other times becoming fantastic interim personae with their own lifestyles. The underwater naiad (nymph) of the adult aerial dragonfly is a good example.

Though many insects die with the onset of cold weather, they leave a new generation in the form of eggs. Walking sticks, grasshoppers, crickets, and others deposit winter-hardy eggs on or in the soil. The praying mantis attaches walnut-sized balls of froth to a plant stem. These solidify to become waterproof housing for 125-350 eggs. Katydids cement flat eggs in overlapping rows on a leaf or twig. Garden spiders leave an egg sac in a web center.

Eggs of many beetles, flies, and some butterflies hatch before autumn. Their larvae (caterpillars) find hiding places, some underground, some in leaves or litter, some underwater. The regal fritillary butterfly's caterpillar wraps itself inside a leaf.

Unique pupal cocoons shelter luna, polyphemus, and promethea moths. Swallowtail and cabbage butterflies each place a chrysalis near its species' food site. The following season, when the adult breaks out, it lays many eggs on a host plant, specific food for the larvae which emerge from hatched eggs.

Monarch butterflies migrate, but adult mourning cloak butterflies hibernate, hiding in crevices. Bumblebees, wasps, ladybird beetles, stinkbugs, mosquitoes, termites, tiger beetles are among some favorite and not-so-favorite insects that find places to hide through the winter.

Only a few show themselves. The sturdy water strider may be out on a pond surface. The lovely lacewing, hardy enough to overwinter, is one flier you may encounter outside on a mild winter day.

THE INDEPENDENT, FEBRUARY 21, 1991

"The hardened glaze makes a tight, water-proof cover."

NATURE'S WAY

Tapping nature

The welling of sap at maple sugaring times does not call us to the woods as it did when humans knew a close interdependence with nature. Nineteenth-century naturalists, like Anna Botsford Comstock, nurtured by her early involvement in things of the earth, preserved these experiences in her writing and teaching.

Born in 1854, she was the first woman professor at Cornell, where she founded the nature study department. Recognized and honored during her lifetime, her massive 1911 book, *Handbook of Nature Study*, was used nationally until the 1930s and translated into eight languages.

Herewith her 1860s recollections of sugaring time:

" 'Tapping the sugar bush' are magical words to the country boy and girl, when the south wind blows blandly and bare trees show a flush of living red through their grayness, and every spray grows heavy with swelling buds."

The sap buckets were brought down from the stable loft and washed. Children remembered long winter evenings when they "fashioned sap spiles from selected stems of sumac."

"When the momentous day came, the large, iron cauldron kettle was loaded on a stoneboat, a large oxdrawn sledge, together with the sap cask and log chain, the axe and various other utensils, and as many children as could find standing room; and then the oxen were hitched on and the procession started across the rough pasture to the woods.

"When we came to the boiling-place, we lifted the kettle into place and finished it with two great logs,

"When the auger was withdrawn, the sap followed it and enthusiatic young tongues met it half way, though they received more chips than sweetness therefrom."

against which the fire was kindled. The **tapping** began when the man with the auger went to bore holes in maples which had bled sweet juices in years gone by. Spiles, were driven in tightly with a wooden mallet."

Next day, the largest children put on neck yokes and brought in pails in sap, and **boiling began**. At twilight "how delicious was the odor of the sap steam permeating the woods farther than the shafts of firelight pierced the gloom!

"As the evening wore on we drew closer to each other and told stories of Indians and bears and panthers that had roamed these woods when our father was a little boy; and our hearts suddenly jumped into our throats when nearby there sounded the tremulous, blood-curdling cry of the screech owl.

"The most fun was to gather sap in warmer mornings; then we looked critically at the tracks in the snow to see what visitors had come sniffing around our buckets. Rabbit, skunk, squirrel, mouse, muskrat, fox; we knew them all by their tracks.

"After about three days of gathering and boiling the sap, came the **syruping down**. When it threatened to boil over we threw in a thin slice of fat pork. The odor grew more and more delicious, and finally the syrup was pronounced sufficiently thick. The kettle was swung off the logs and the syrup dripped through a cloth strainer into the carrying pail.

"Now [in 1904] the old stave bucket and the sumac spile are gone, and the old cauldron kettle is broken and lies rusting in the shed, but the maple molasses of today seems to us a pale and anemic liquid and lacks just that delicious flavor of the rich, dark nectar which we, with the help of cinders and smoke and various other things, brewed of yore in the open woods."

THE INDEPENDENT, FEBRUARY 22, 1990

"'Tapping the sugar bush are magical words to the country boy and girl, when the south wind blows blandly and bare trees show a flush of living red through their grayness..."

NATURE'S WAY:
Bird study

On exhibit at the Natural History Museum of Columbia-Greene Community College, bird study skins lie on their backs on large trays. They are in phylogenetic order—the more primitive species (mostly larger birds) first, moving to those more specialized.

Row after neat row of soft feathered bodies, delicately patterned and subtly colored, stimulate the urge to stroke. William E. Cook, curator of the museum, explains how to handle the fragile specimens: "They can be broken," he says, "and need support under the back when they are picked up or turned over. Avoid holding a specimen by the head, feet, or pulling the tag.

"The curator's problem," Bill explains, "is twofold: to protect the collection's integrity and to make it most useful. This affects the amount of handling of specimens. We try to find the middle ground."

He teaches a credit course in museum bird study in which students practice handling study skins, always with white gloves. They record size and weight measurements and tag each bird. Then they skin, clean, dry, stuff with cotton, and sew a specimen skin—using birds brought in with insufficient information or of poor quality.

Through examination of the birds in the collection, they sharpen their skills. Each bird is tagged with vital information: date found, location, condition, weight, sex, breeding status, skull status, collector, and other data.

Study of the skin with tag data round out knowledge of a bird. Cardinal bills, for example, vary in length according to season. The bill is longer in summer when the bird's diet is predominantly insects; in winter, it becomes shorter as fruits and seeds are eaten.

Special features or adaptations are found on each bird's body. Close examination of the brown creeper, for example, reveals that its feet have little pins which help it climb trees.

"Feathers are modified for sound or silence." Bill picks up two corks, each attached to a long string and stuck with three or four feathers. "This one has

Northern cardinal with a winter's shorter beak

feathers from the wings of a screech owl. Now listen as I spin the cork," and he twirls the string around in a wide arc. There is no sound.

"These are woodcock feathers. Now listen." A high pitched whistle grows more vibrant the more vigorously the cork twirls.

"You see the difference between the feathers on these corks. The screech owl's has comb-like projections at the end of the vanes which break up the air vortex over the wing. The owl's wing is adapted for silence so it can surprise its prey.

"The male woodcock, on the other hand, makes a whistling sound with its wings on courtship flights. The narrow feathers are adapted to create this whistling sound as the birds fly higher and higher on rapid wing strokes."

Groups with a serious interest can make arrangements to view the collection with Mr. Cook, scientific studies department, Columbia-Greene Community College, Box 1000, Hudson, 12534; telephone 828-4181.

"Special features or adaptations are found on each bird's body."

THE INDEPENDENT, FEBRUARY 23, 1989

NATURE'S WAY

Seven sleepers?

In time past, common lore held that among northeastern mammals, there were seven sleepers, or hibernators: chipmunks, woodchucks, jumping mice, some bats, raccoons, skunks, and bears. We know now that only a few mammals are true hibernators.

Of the seven, chipmunks are seen during winter, collecting and storing large quantities of seeds and grains. In elaborately tunnelled dens, they curl up on piles of nuts and sleep deeply much of the time. They can wake quickly to take food from the pile and come out to bask in the sun, as our resident chippy has on recent balmy winter days.

True hibernation involves marked physiological changes. Just as in cold-blooded animals, body temperature, respiration, and heart rates are markedly reduced in woodchucks, jumping mice, and some bats.

That heavy eater, the woodchuck, doubles its weight between May and September. Its body is covered by a thick layer of white fat. Specialized brown fatty tissue between the shoulder blades has its own blood supply, proteins, and respiratory pigments that can generate enough heat to keep small animals warm when their muscles, in repose, are not producing any.

The hypothalamus in the woodchuck's brain has a specialized temperature-regulating mechanism. By October, when there have been enough cold days and the woodchuck is obese enough, its biological clock triggers the deep sleep of true hibernation—even though the green and grain harvest is still bountiful.

It crawls into a small, tight, grass-lined chamber in the burrow, tucks head between hind legs, and covers the curled form with its tail.

Once into profound hibernation, the woodchuck's temperature drops from about 98 degrees to 40-57 degrees. Respiration decreases to a breath every 4 to 6 minutes and heart rate falls almost 95% from 80 beats per minute to 4 or 5 per minute. In experiments, when a toe of hibernators like the jumping mouse or bat is cut off, circulation is so sluggish that little bleeding occurs.

If outside temperatures drop to life-threatening levels, a hibernator wakens. They also need a breath of fresh air every 8-10 days to help exhale metabolic byproducts that would otherwise be toxic.

A wakening woodchuck takes several hours to get it all together. Heartbeat increases slowly, constricted vessels expand; blood circulates to heart, lungs, and brain, and then hindquarters.

The male emerges in early February to check other dens for females so they can mate, but then each goes back to sleep. By late March they may have lost up to 40% of their autumn weight.

Raccoons and skunks keep a normal temperature and heart rate as they sleep through some cold winter days, but both come out on mild winter nights, looking for sustenance.

Bears fall somewhere between the true hibernators and heavy sleepers. A black bear's body adjusts so that its digestive system becomes inactive. It maintains a lean body mass without taking in food or water or defecating or urinating. Its heart rate slows from about 45 to 8-10 per minute (an 80% decrease). But its body temperature drops only 7 or 8 degrees, still warm enough to melt snow drifting over its bed.

Bears can wake up and become quickly active. This rapid arousal is enough to keep inquiring naturalists *very* careful when they attempt to take a black bear's rectal temperature in its den.

The black bear is a deep sleeper, sleeping long if it is heavy with fat when bedding down. It is not a true hibernator because it rouses and quickly becomes active.

THE INDEPENDENT, FEBRUARY 28, 1991

"They also need a breath of fresh air every 8-10 days to help exhale metabolic byproducts that would otherwise be toxic."

Freshwater eels — ocean travelers

NATURE'S WAY

Marion Dusoir Ennes

THE VIGOR OF THE HUDSON RIVER, dramatically highlighted by ice floes this season, supports up to 206 species of fish in its deep, according to Dennis Mildner of the Hudson River Estuarine Research Reserve. Among them is the elusive and unappreciated freshwater American eel. One of the unique *Anguilla*, these eels live up to 20 years, part in fresh, part salt water. Right now, adult females are hibernating in local lakes and creeks.

Unfortunately, our image of eels describes a snake-like slimy creature, a pest if hooked because it can tangle a line with muscular adroitness and then, with defensive instinct, cover itself with protective mucus, making it too slippery to grasp.

European species, by contrast, are valued as an important food resource. My Belgian cousin served eel as a traditional part of Christmas dinner, crediting eels with saving many from wartime starvation. Eel industries include eel farming in Japan and eel fishing in other countries worldwide.

The mystery of where eels bred and how they got here was partly solved earlier this century. It starts with full-grown, large-eyed eels easily traveling downriver with the current. Females up to four feet long meet males half their size near Atlantic shores.

From here they swim together, making the thousand-mile journey to the warm Sargasso Sea waters, southeast of Bermuda. Here, females shed loads of 5 to 13 million eggs each, males fertilizing them about 1,300 feet below the thick weedy covering of Sargassum, the exact spot where they hatched two decades earlier.

A newly hatched larval American eel, pinhead-plus size, is transparent except for its dark eyes, primitive spine and tiny needle teeth. Floating in the warm Gulf Stream waters with the European *leptocephali* (larval eels), all travel north before separating. Europeans go 3,000 miles east, Americans 1,000 west to adult home coasts.

The whole journey takes 12 to 18 months for American eels, about three years for Europeans. Growing as they float, these willow leaf-shaped larvae reach almost three inches before consolidating, metamorphosing into two inch glass eels, with true spines, fins and swim bladders to help them rise and sink.

Finally, as elvers (young eels), they enter fresher waters, bodies adapting to the change, skins darkening to greenish-yellow or brownish. They grow a second set of teeth, develop adult food tastes for insects, worms, invertebrates and fish, sometimes carrion.

While young males remain in brackish coastal waters, females travel up the Hudson River through rapid currents, over boulders, over dams.

Using stored oxygen, or absorbing it through skin and gills, eels even travel over mud or moist grass to circumvent obstacles. Destinations reach as far and wide as the Adirondacks and the Finger Lakes in New York.

Thick muscular bodies give eels great maneuverability. Tapered bodies give them digging tools at both ends. If no underwater crevice is available, they dig a burrow with snout or tail. Here they rest, hide, and grow by day.

Foraging by night, their slow serpentine movement followed by a quick snatch yields size-appropriate animal foods. When necessary, an eel may grab a larger bait, hanging on tight. With jaws too weak to snap, its muscular body rotates lengthwise 6 to 14 spins per second for about four seconds. This breaks off a bite or opens the skin to softer flesh inside.

During 15 or more years in fresh water, female eels must grow large enough to carry their substantial egg supply, strong and fat enough to journey back to where warm Sargasso waters will cradle their young.

American eels. *Adult female 3½ to 4 feet, about 4 pounds, males half that size. Full-grown are greenish-brown, silvery side, white below. Elongated body 1/8 head, short pectoral fins; dorsal and anal fins surround 2/3 of body.*

Larvae *(leptocephali) willow-leaf shape, transparent, flattened. Dark eye, primitive spine visible.*

Inset map *shows relation of Sargasso Sea to U.S. coastline.*

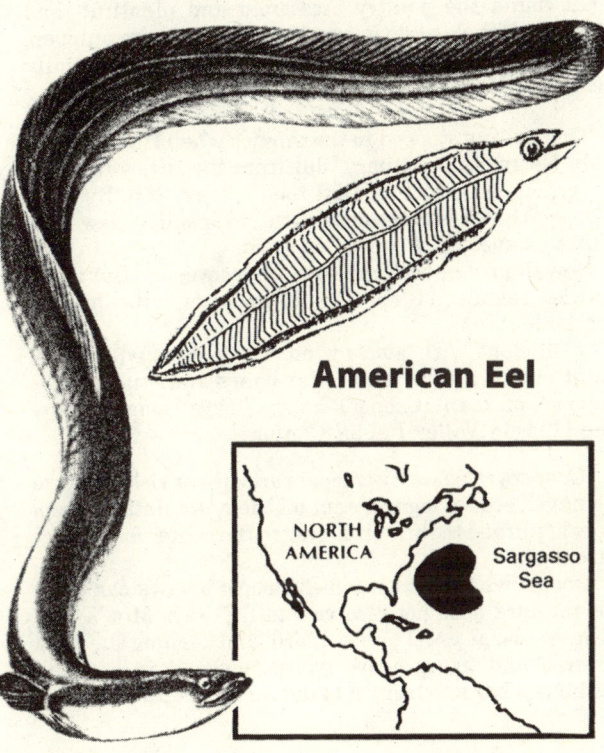

American Eel

THE INDEPENDENT, FEBRUARY 29, 1996

"Using stored oxygen, or absorbing it through skin and gills, eels even travel over mud or moist grass to circumvent obstacles."

NATURE'S WAY
Cooper's hawk

It is March, and the northward migration of the Cooper's hawk has begun, some birds returning from southern Florida or Mexico to breed in the woods of our Taconic Highlands.

The Cooper's hawk is one of three Accipiters (bird hawks) native to North America. These powerful birds have relatively long tails and short, rounded wings which give them great agility in their forest habitat.

The Cooper, about crow-sized, is alert, strong, and dauntless, making a living by hunting in forests and adjacent lands.

They have to be quick and stealthy to catch their primary prey, smaller birds, poultry or ducks, rodents rabbits, snakes, frogs, and insects.

Recent radio-telemetry research shows they forage in "stop-and-go" fashion. Transmitters on birds recorded one sound when vertical (perched), and another sound when flying (horizontal position).

The birds, capable of quick landings and strong, immediate speed when taking off, make 1 to 3-minute flights to a new perch every 8 to 13 minutes.

Though not successful on every try, a Cooper's skill at maneuvering can yield prey larger and heavier than itself.

These days we know that predators have an important place in the balance of nature. As naturalist Roger Tory Peterson explains, a Cooper's hawk can be viewed "as another device in the intricate system of checks and counterchecks that may keep bird populations under control. Predators crop surpluses. They do not eat capital."

From an early time in history, the survival of Cooper's hawks has *not* been left to nature. Instead, it has been severely skewed by the attitudes and actions of humans.

At the turn of the century, when birds were characterized as either virtuous or damnable, Neltje Blanchan Doubleday said of Cooper's hawk that it "lives by devouring birds of so much greater value than itself that the law of the survival of the fittest *should be enforced by lead* (italics mine) until these villains...adorn museum cases only." That goal was almost achieved.

For more than seven decades it was open season on all raptors. Farmers eagerly shot "chicken hawks"—Coopers that found the poultry accessible and plentiful—and destroyed whole nests in breeding season. Large numbers of Coopers were among the 5,000 a year shot annually at Hawk Mountain during fall migration.

That killing stopped in the thirties when Hawk Mountain became a sanctuary. But from the fifties into the seventies, the effects of DDT took a heavy toll. By 1983 Cooper's hawk was one of nine raptors listed in New York State as species of special concern.

Now their numbers appear to be recovering. But these hawks remain vulnerable to contacts with human settlement.

"Collisions with house windows, or cars, while they hunt account for broken collar bones and other severe injuries on many Cooper's hawks," says Dona Tracy of the Hudson Valley Raptor Center.

"Coopers released by trappers are also at risk of severe damage because leg traps cut off their circulation. Trappers are urged to turn birds over to the center for prompt attention."

Anyone who finds a stunned Cooper's hawk can help. "If the bird does not recover and fly," says Mrs. Tracy, "throw a large towel over the bird, and keeping the head covered and using heavy gloves, place it in a towel-cushioned box and bring it to the center in Rhinebeck."

Cooper's hawk, named for New York ornithologist William Cooper. Length: male, 15", female 18". Wingspread: male 29", female 33". Eyes red, plumage similar for both sexes: back and wings bluish-gray, crown dark blue-gray, contrasting lighter nape. Cheeks reddish. Underparts white, barred with cinnamon. Cross stripes on tail.

THE INDEPENDENT, MARCH 5, 1992

"Recent radio-telemetry research shows they forage in 'stop-and-go' fashion."

NATURE'S WAY

Sturdy birds

The drum roll coming from a hollow tree at our woods edge is an early signal of impending spring. It is the rapid-fire pecking of the downy woodpecker that makes the staccato sound, announcing territory and enticing a mate.

From the end of last summer to now, each downy has used its remarkable physical adaptations to make a living alone.

Almost 200 species of woodpeckers range around the globe, except in Australia. Black and white striped downies, well-established in New York State, are among the smallest. The largest in the U.S. was the 20-inch high, ivory-billed woodpecker, native to forested river bottoms from Florida to Texas and now believed to be extinct.

The body adaptations of woodpeckers are unique among animals and fit them from head to toe to find food and shelter.

They are the only birds able to drill into live wood. In its characteristic position, with body parallel to the tree surface, the woodpecker's straight chisel-like beak points directly at the tree bark. The bill has a horny, hard covering at the tip, and an extra tuft of feathers at the bill's base, to keep sawdust out of the bird's nostrils.

What keeps the bird from getting a headache from all that beating into wood? A thick skull, designed like a helmet, protects the brain from shock. A hinge at the bill's broad base connecting the bill to the skull helps spread the shock of pounding.

When looking for food, a downy climbs up a tree in short, jerky movements, tapping as it goes. By tapping, it test the wood's soundness. Once a grub is located in a hollow-sounding spot under the bark, the downy concentrates its sharp blows right there.

The action is quick, a hole is made, and the bird inserts its very long, efficient tongue. This tough tongue can be extended 1½ inches beyond the end of the bill, deep into the hole and all around the now exposed insect's tunnel system. Downy's tongue is equipped with short barbs like a fishing spear that catch the insect morsel licked up by the bird.

One observer watched a downy climb and inspect 181 woodland trees for 2½ hours. It made 26 excavations to find and eat wood-boring ants, an enormous asset in the maintenance of healthy woodland growth.

This constant activity requires strong muscles, so that the bird can hold its position as it works. A tough skin withstands the stresses of all this muscle activity and heavy pounding and also protects against insect bites.

Downies have a stiff, tapering tail, used as a brace against the tree's bark. The legs are short, but two pairs of opposing toes, two facing front and two rear, are long, with sharp curved claws to hold fast.

In addition to drilling for food, downies carve out shelter and nest holes in decayed tree stubs or branches.

On their own during the fall-winter season, each downy gouges out one or more roosting holes to serve as shelters on cold nights. The energy they put into excavation of these small wooden caves serves the community at large, helping chickadees, titmice, white-footed mice, bees, and others survive cold wet weather.

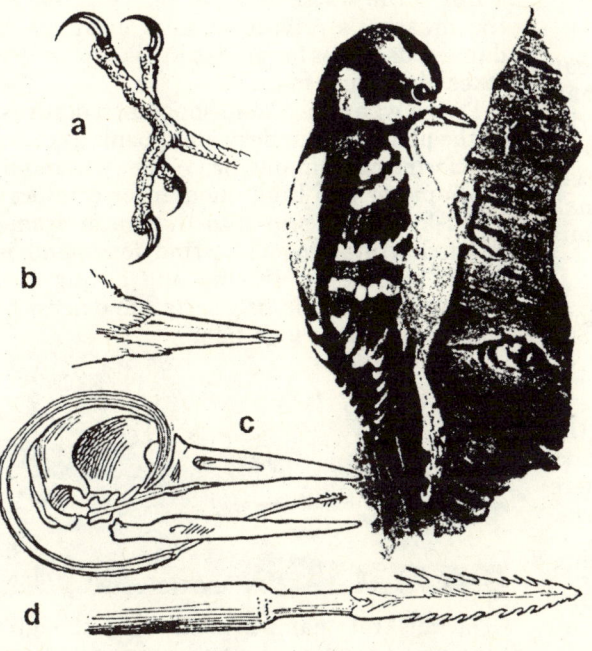

Downy woodpecker: 6¼ to 7¼ inches, black and white striped, male has red top-spot. [a] Foot: two pairs of long opposing toes, sharp claws for gripping. [b] Beak: short, sharp for chiseling. [c] Skull cross-section, showing long coiled tongue. [d] Tongue tip with barbs.

THE INDEPENDENT, MARCH 7, 1991

"They are the only birds able to drill into live wood."

NATURE'S WAY
The furry builder

I came to appreciate the industry of the American muskrat this October and November when four earthen humps began growing on the surface of a favorite pond.

A silver streak of motion in the water called attention to this quick-swimming, amphibious mammal, who carried mouthfuls of vegetation and mud to pile atop the two-foot high lodge he was building.

Muskrats are accomplished builders and prefer to make their homes in the bank of a pond or slow-moving stream.

In an ancient Indian legend, the Sun god offered the muskrat any place he chose to live in return for services provided during a flood. The animal tried the lake first, then the grassy banks, but could not decide. So the Sun god designated the "between land" where grassy vegetation and fresh water come together—where the muskrat can prosper and be happy.

The cuddly-looking muskrat is shaped like a smaller version of the beaver; its foot-long tail is pointed and flattened vertically. From nose to tail it's almost two feet long, weighing up to four pounds.

It is distinguished by a dark brown or black fur coat of longer guard hairs, and a mostly waterproof layer of soft and dense gray under fur. The hind feet are about 3½ inches long, slightly webbed; well-adapted, along with the tail, for swimming at speeds from one to three miles per hour. The forefeet are short but with four sharp claws and a thumb used for extensive digging.

Muskrats burrow up and deep into a bank, creating a small complex of tunnels and a main chamber. The entrance hole is usually under water and the tunnel has an exit hole to land as well. The chamber is about as large as a bushel basket, well padded with vegetation, and kept clean. They are fond of their homes and reluctant to abandon them.

But if the water level sinks, as in our local pond, the muskrat's private aquatic entrance becomes a dangerous access for predators like raccoon and mink, foxes, dogs, and man.

That's when the dome-shaped structures are built in the pond, with underwater openings directly below. Platforms contain one or two chambers about a foot in diameter and high enough for comfort.

Muskrats can slip into the water from these insulated winter rooms to find food—and may build another dome for storing and eating food, mostly aquatic plants including cattail and arrowhead, some small crustaceans, or fish.

Muskrat

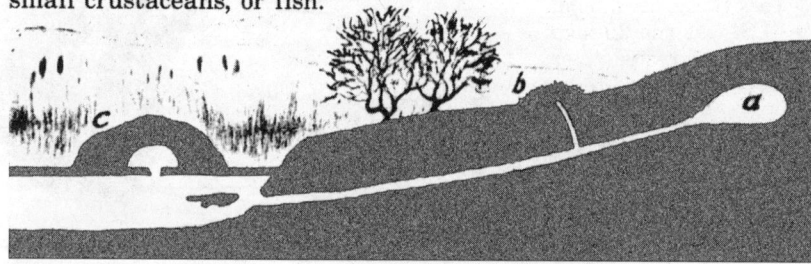

The muskrat's name is misleading; though a rodent, it is classed among voles and lemmings. In the 1600s, the French, who favored the musk odor (from glands near the anus, and important in mating) were reminded of their rats at home—so named it 'muskrat.'

In our area they have two to three litters of about six young every year. This is fortunate because up to 20 million are caught yearly.

Muskrats exceed all other furbearers in numbers trapped in the U.S.—and they don't even get any credit! Their soft fur, durable and adaptable, is sold as "Hudson seal," "river 'mink' or sable,'" or "Russian otter."

THE INDEPENDENT, DECEMBER 8, 1988

"In the 1600s, the French, who favored the musk odor, were reminded of their rats at home—so named it 'muskrat.'"

NATURE'S WAY
Saving a tradition

The evergreen you bring to your home this Christmas is a diminutive relative of great conifers that make up the northern hemisphere's boreal forests. This continuous green belt—called the *Taiga*—covers 5,000 million acres, from New England across the US and Canada to the Pacific, through the USSR and Japan to Scandinavia.

Great firs of the north—Douglas and balsam, blue and Norway spruce, red cedar, Scotch pine and white pine, which grow anywhere from 40 to 300 feet—are the trees whose smaller counterparts are decorated with ornaments and lights.

These conifers (cone-bearers) engage in photosynthesis all year through their green, needle-like leaves, which they shed a few at a time all year long.

The fine waxy leaves hold moisture in the face of freezing weather; the trees' spire-like shapes and downswept branches facilitate the drop of heavy snow.

You will probably choose between a popular spruce; that fragrant old favorite, the balsam fir; or the increasingly favored Scotch pine.

The Christmas tree custom came from Germany. Records of table-sized trees appear as early as 1820 in Lancaster County, Pennsylvania. By the 1860s the uniquely American custom of floor-to-ceiling-height trees was becoming popular. Until about 1850, most trees were cut by families themselves or were ordered from a farmer.

In 1851 a Catskill man loaded two ox sleds with young firs and spruces and took them downriver by steamboat to New York City's Washington Market. He sold out for good prices.

Within 30 years more than 600 tree dealers were competing for selling sites for more than 200,000 trees in the NYC market and additional space had to be rented from the city.

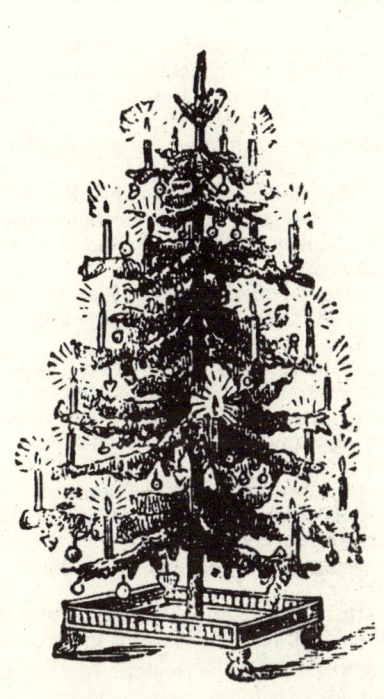

been cut, topsoil was washing away, native birds and mammals faced extinction.

White House celebrations had included the Christmas tree since 1856 and the custom was well-established by 1900.

But Theodore Roosevelt, who championed conservation and lent the power and support of his presidency to the preservation of natural resources, banned the Christmas tree from his White House and urged everyone else to do the same.

His exuberant children, Archie and Quentin, responded to this deprivation by smuggling a tree into a closet in Archie's room. On Christmas morning, Archie invited the whole family in for a look and a present.

Their father lectured his two boys in private and sent them to speak to the great conservationist Gifford Pinchot, then Secretary of the Interior.

It was under Sec'y. Pinchot that the U.S. Forest Service accelerated a combined program of research, forest management (including planting of trees), and extensive, effective public education. He explained to the boys, as he would to the public, that, through understanding of forest growth needs, proper thinning could strengthen forests and still make Christmas trees available.

So Archie got to put up a secret tree in his room each year, while President Roosevelt maintained his commitment to conservation as well as his model of official restraint.

Trees came to cities from the northern part of our country and beyond. When Theodore Roosevelt become president in 1901, conservationists were seriously concerned about the indiscriminate cutting of Christmas evergreens. Natural resources had been depleted; almost half of all U.S. timber had

THE INDEPENDENT, DECEMBER 22, 1988

"Theodore Roosevelt... banned the Christmas tree from his White House and urged everyone else to do the same."

Mistletoe

NATURE'S WAY

Marion Dusoir Ennes

THE SMALL BUNCH OF MISTLETOE, crowded into its see-through packet at a local florist, is an introduction to a plant of enormous historic consequence.

Wherever your ancestors came from—old world or new—chances are the growing patterns of this hemiparasitic plant provided the spiritual sustenance they needed to cope with fear in the cold dark season of the winter solstice.

Mistletoe actually grows on trees. Its sprouting seed sends specialized rootlets through bark into tree tissues. There it taps vascular fluids, water enriched with minerals, that keep the plant alive. Our familiar mistletoe species, growing from New Jersey to Texas, only hurts its host tree during serious drought.

Once roots are secure, mistletoe grows like other plants. A shoot grows up, eventually putting out pale-green, leathery leaves capable of photosynthesis.

Slowly, for one mistletoe can live 400 years, the plant gets bushy and produces sticky whitish berries popular with birds. While rubbing this sticky substance from their beaks, birds often force seeds into bark crevices, effectively planting them.

Picture humans in centuries past, well-accustomed to a forested world, making life from the bounties of, and surviving the adversities of, nature. When leaves fell from nurturing trees, solar energy diminished and winter darkness crept in.

Then was mistletoe most noticeable. A pale green to golden bushy plant, not just alive but thriving and producing berries, seemingly rootless in the treetops. At solstice it was filled with magic, above witches' earthbound spells, below the clouds in human sight.

For centuries, at winter solstice, Druid priests cut the sacred plants from oak trees with golden sickles. They kept plants from defilement by catching them before they could touch ground. Today, mistletoe is still often harvested without human touch by shooting it out of trees.

Priests gave each tribe member this talisman, a mistletoe sprig, power against disease and evil, good fortune's emblem.

For pagan peoples, it protected against witchcraft and disease, helped crops grow, strengthened swords in battle, cured barrenness. It was variously also believed to prevent conception, nightmares and epilepsy.

Scandinavians hung mistletoe in the doorway, inviting a kiss as a pledge of friendship. If combatants met under mistletoe outdoors, they would throw down their weapons and embrace.

Sir James Frazier named his renowned book on universal myths and magic *The Golden Bough*, after Virgil's description of the plant. This Roman poet, writing in the *Aeneid* in about 40 B.C., tells of two doves guiding Aeneas through a gloomy vale. They alighted on a tree "whence shown a flickering gleam of gold."

It was the mistletoe, "a plant not native to its tree, is green with fresh leaves and twines its yellow berries that seemed upon the shady holm-oak, leafy gold; so rustled in the gentle breeze the golden leaf."

Charles Darwin, whose *Origin of Species* was published 1,800 years later, described mistletoe as a plant "which draws nourishment from certain trees, has seeds which must be transported by certain birds, has flowers with separate sexes absolutely requiring...certain insects to bring pollen from one flower to the other." This clear example has helped establish co-evolution as a mainstay of modern ecological thought.

In its history, mistletoe has served humans as magical symbol, as scientific example. In this season, these days, it inspires affection and goodwill.

Winter profile of tree, showing mistletoe plants in branches.

INSET: *Mistletoe plant. Small, pale-green leathery leaves. Male, female plants separate. Flowers yellow, in strings. White waxy-looking berries hold a tough seed within a sticky fluid that helps seeds adhere to tree bark.*

THE INDEPENDENT, DECEMBER 22, 1994

"At solstice it was filled with magic, above witches' earthbound spells, below the clouds in human sight."

Springtime

In Spring we look for flowers
That peek above the ground
Forsythia and daffodils
are just the ones I found

They're both a pretty yellow
Like sunshine and the dew,
I wish that I had lots of them
to share the whole day through.

*by Linda Pack (age 6)
with Marion Dusoir Pack, 1956*

Happy Warbler singing of wonders of emerging Spring.

Spring is creeping over the landscape.

The bare stalks are slowly covering with buds, in marvelous occult colors from pale greens to rusty burgundies. The shad bush is blooming with small, fluffy white petals — and send their message that the shad fish are running in the Hudson River. Even cloudy days are redeemed by the bright yellow flash of forsythia. The birds come to the feeder in pairs, and I know the secret entry to the purple finches' house in the tall, tall spruce.

*Marion Dusoir Ennes
From a letter to a friend in California, 1986*

Colorful blossoms appear among new Spring foliage.

Spring's bluets abound on the forest's floor.

Wood ducks cruising and foraging.

SPRING

The cycle of life renews as ponds, bogs, frogs, moths, and flowers flutter awake, along with the peregrinations of mating birds in the brilliant rush of an East Coast spring. Observation of these renewals in our natural environment are woven together with little-known facts and occasional commentary of naturalists to give us an armchair glimpse of nature as man's enchanter—with a tornado to remind us of nature's awesome power.

Floating islands of water lilies brighten the woods.

SPRING

Awakening Ponds	129
Spring's Colored Eggs (birds' eggs)	130
Ready, Willing, and Able (porcupines)	131
Taconic Revolution (regional geology)	132
Wings for Flight, Ornament, 'Love Dust'	133
Spectacular Scales (butterflies)	134
Long Before Flowers (ferns)	135
Sky Dancer (woodcocks)	136
Downy Partners (downy woodpeckers)	137
Spring Garters (garter snakes)	138
Skunk Cabbage	139
The Outdoor Conspirators (nature lovers)	140
Grass Subways (meadow voles)	141
Small Creature – Big Signals (salamander)	142
Spotted Salamanders	143
Nature's Last Word (white ash trees)	144
Well-featured Nests	145
Sylvan Leaper (wood frogs)	146
Beautiful Behinds (underwing moths)	147
Feeder Watchers (grosbeaks)	148
Foxy Neighbors (red fox)	149
Vagabond Birds (cowbird)	150
Pigeons' Milk (mourning doves)	151
Ancient Loons – Submarine Divers	152
A Local Sphinx (sphinx moths)	153
Denizens of the Dim World (sphinx moths)	154
Sturdy Bluets	155
Quaking Bogs	156
Pleased to Meetcha (warblers)	157
Some Rare Birds	158
Our Home Team (birding competition)	159
Red Efts and True Newts	160
Creatures of Air (dragonflies)	161
Weatherfrog (gray treefrog)	162
Flashy Flyer (kestrels)	163
The Timber Rattlesnake	164
Snakes Are Lovers, Too!	165
After Tornado – Song Sparrows	166
"Run in the Meadow, Child"	167
Tornado 1995	168

NATURE'S WAY

Awakening ponds

As warmth and sunlight increase in spring, the rich complement of plant and animal life in a pond awakens. Many forms of plant life, from single-celled diatoms of higher submerged plants proliferate and grow. These photosynthesizers draw energy from the sun and provide the food base for all animals.

In a pond, these range through microscopic creatures to hydras, sponges, threadworms and flatworms, leeches, crustaceans, water mites, water insects and their immature forms to snails and mussels, fish, amphibians, turtles, snakes, and sometimes muskrats.

Of these, insects are often most fun, each so different, with special adaptations for breathing, traveling, feeding, or protection.

In early spring, half-inch-long scavenging whirligig beetles emerge from bottom ooze to gather in surface companies, resting or skimming around each other in circles. This action is facilitated by fringed, paddle-shaped hind legs that are used like oars in rapid sculling. The lower head is immersed in water, and its compound eyes are divided, half above the waterline for looking up, half below for looking into the depths.

The mayfly nymph, another bottom hibernator, has leaflike gills along the abdomen and three long feathery tail appendages. One species keeps featherly gills moving as it burrows through sediment, creating a current of water that replenishes oxygen for respiration.

This nymph feeds primarily on living or dead vegetation. Quickly maturing, it first changes into a gray-colored flying "adolescent" and within 10 days into a shiny adult.

A mature mayfly has no functioning mouthparts and only exists a few hours or a few days, just long enough to mate. Hundreds of males take part in rhythmic dancing flight over water. Then a dozen of these mate with the few females who lay eggs immediately and then die.

One female can lay up to 1,000 eggs at a time. With three to four generations in a summer, populations can reach 125 billion. Dying mayflies and mayfly eggs are eaten by many others in the water.

Among them are several species of diving beetles which, like many insects, carry oxygen underwater when they dive. Oxygen is collected according to each species-adaptation, some through club-shaped antennae, others through the abdomen tip. Air trapped beneath wings or in body hairs provides their oxygen.

Leaflike water-scorpions live underwater. Two long-tailed filaments at the abdomen's end serve as a breathing tube, replenishing air when projected through the surface.

Water scorpions lurk in pond grasses and seize prey with the pincers on their strong front legs. Small insects to tadpoles are fair game. Water scorpions use hollow mouthparts to pump digestive juice into the victim's body, then suck up the contents.

The sturdy backswimmer travels on a keel-shaped back. Its third pair of legs is fringed and longer than the others, well-suited as oars to sweep this insect through the water. Air captured between the hairs of its lower surface act as external gills, making it buoyant and inclined to float up, unless it hangs onto vegetation.

When necessary, this bug rises to draw in oxygen from its abdomen tip. It is tough, active, predaceous, and, like other water bugs, has a jointed sucking beak of needle-like sharpness that can inflict a painful sting.

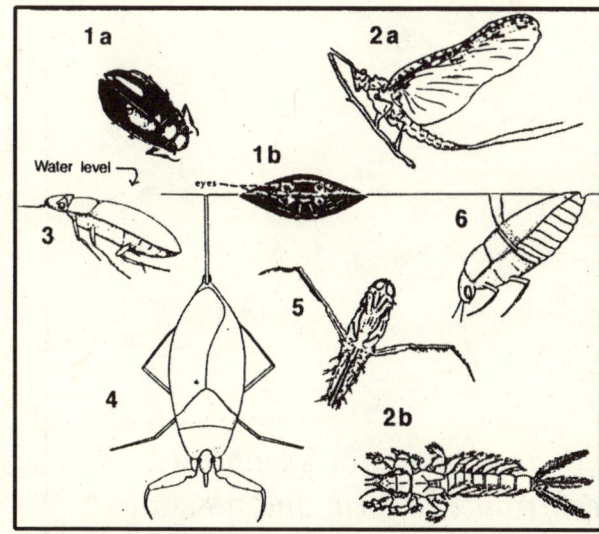

1a. Whirligig beetle, ½", blue-black, oval, flattened. Middle and hind legs short and fan-shaped for water skimming. Scavenger.
1b. Whirligig face view showing double eyes.
2a. Mayfly, pond adult, 1" or less.
2b. Mayfly pond nymph, 1", vegetarian.
3. Great silver water beetle, 2", dark greenish-black. Herbivorous.
4. Water scorpion, 1½", brownish, oval. Predaceous carnivore.
5. Backswimmer, 6/10", green and brown, legs and abdomen face up. Predaceous.
6. Great diving beetle, 1½", smooth, dark brown, streamlined. Carnivorous.

THE INDEPENDENT, APRIL 2, 1992

"...scavenging whirligig beetles emerge from bottom ooze to gather in surface companies..."

NATURE'S WAY
Spring's colored eggs

In this season of rebirth, the birds are already busy. Owls are brooding, crows are building nests, cardinals courting, and other birds are streaming north for their seasonal regeneration.

Soon our woods, fields, marshes, and hedgerows will become neighborhoods to dedicated bird couples, each pair carefully nuturing a clutch of eggs. And eggs are the season's emblem, each one in delicate color a perfect tribute to form and function, our symbol of future life.

The traditional Easter basket is a replica of a bird nest, which usually consists of a carefully woven outer frame of woody materials, lined with a soft bed of grasses, mosses, or hairs serving as bedding for eggs, and later, chicks.

Egg coloring has always seemed to me a satisfying tribute to spring. This year, you might like to design your eggs to match some laid by local birds.

Killdeer, juncos, redwing blackbirds, house wrens, mockingbirds, bobolinks, and rufous-sided towhees produce eggs with a nice range of color patterns. You may have to adjust the hue or intensity of some prepared colors and you need a fine brush to add dots or streaks, but you will end with a sample of nature's diversity in a basket.

The killdeer, which builds its nest among rocks in fields, lays creamy buff (pale brown) eggs, thickly streaked with blacks, browns, and lavenders, causing the eggs to resemble rocks.

Juncos, who nest near tree roots in the woods, lay eggs of grayish white, thickly spotted with lilac and brown.

Pale blue eggs, streaked, spotted, and sprawled with purple and black are found in marsh or field nests of the fiercely territorial red-wing blackbird.

The voluble house wren, who defends the nest so fiercely, lays eggs of delicate pale pink, thickly spotted with browns and lavenders.

Mockingbirds are energetic builders who nest in bushes, vines, or trees. They lay four eggs of greenish blue spotted with red-brown.

In wide meadows, bobolinks nest riskily among rye or other tall grasses. When this hay is harvested, nests are often destroyed. The eggs laid are very variable in color—gray to red-brown, spotted and splashed with umber, olive, and purple markings.

The rufous-sided towhee, who likes thickets and open woods where there is brushy cover, lays eggs with a balanced design. The background is grayish, finely dotted with brown and some lilac, with dots concentrated at the larger end.

The striking rufous-sided towhee has a black head and back, red eyes, rust-orange sides, and white breast. It scratches in ground litter for food. Its song is a trill, sounding like "drink-your-teee" and its common call is "chewink."

These are among the 124 bird species confirmed as breeders in Columbia County, according to the 550-page *Atlas of Breeding Birds in New York State* (Andrle and Carroll, Eds.), published in 1988 by Cornell University Press. This atlas establishes a current baseline of NY State breeding species in their present ranges.

It is an ambitious and useful product of cooperation among more than 4,500 participants, professional and volunteer. In Columbia County and lower Rensselaer, 60 members of the Alan Devoe Bird Club—at the time, almost half the club's membership—searched carefully over all kinds of terrain to locate and document nest sites.

THE INDEPENDENT, MARCH 23, 1989

"…eggs are the season's emblem… a perfect tribute to form and function, our symbol of future life."

Ready, willing and able

NATURE'S WAY
Marion Dusoir Ennes

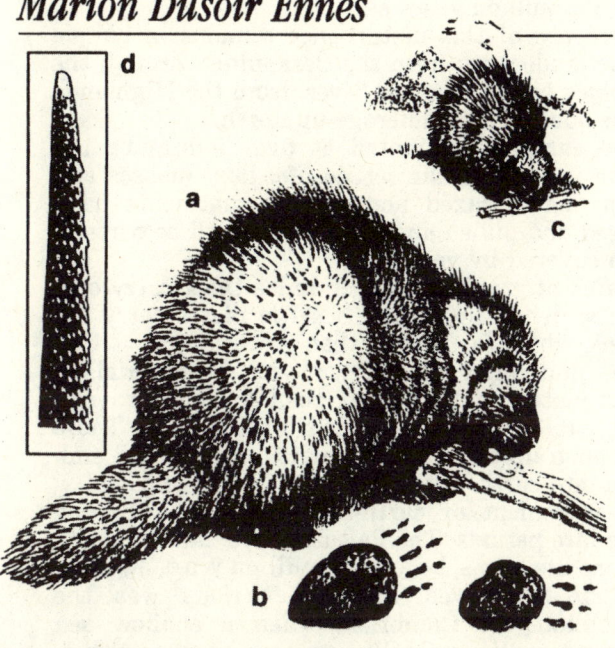

NEW YORK STATE WOODLANDS are home to porcupines. "It's not surprising to find porcupines in substantially wooded areas. Essentially passive, not territorial, they range from denser woods in winter to meadows in warmer months," says Ben Tullar of the state Department of Environmental Conservation.

When her seven-month pregnancy reaches term in April or May, mother porcupine will give birth to a well-developed infant. Active throughout winter, her den is ready in a rock crevice, burrow or hollow log.

Ten inches at birth, weighing up to 20 ounces, junior looks like a miniature adult. Eyes open, it walks immediately, though wobbly. Soft ¼-inch-long quills, hidden among a dense coat of black fur, harden within 30 minutes. This youngster is ready, willing and almost entirely able to fend for itself.

In two days baby climbs trees and can make its spines defensively erect. Little "porky" nurses 10 days, then eats an entirely green diet.

Short-legged and heavy-bodied, porcupines look clumsy on the ground but are adept climbers. They grasp tree trunks like telephone linesmen, gripping bark with rough foot soles and strong thigh muscles. The tough, fairly long, quilled tail resembles a fifth limb pressed against a tree trunk. Bristles covering its lower surface hold the climber in place as it progresses.

Herbivorous porcupines, who don't hibernate or store food, seek it constantly, feeding at dawn or dusk, sometimes by moonlight. When tree buds emerge in spring, "porky" is up at the top among the slender branches of birch, beech and maples. Here he cuts off a slender branch with large, formidable orange incisors. Sitting back comfortably, he devours young protein-rich leaves, leaf and flower buds.

Leaves of trees, whole plants with flowers and water plants keep the porcupine's protein balance high in summer. In fall, apples and acorns lure porcupines back to the trees again. They eat continuously, stuffing digestive organs that fill 75% of the body cavity.

Through fall and winter porcupines shave off outer tree bark with sharp front teeth to reach softer inner cambium, which only provides 2% to 3% protein compared to the 20% available in leaves and buds.

Despite reducing their range and minimizing travel through snow, porcupines lose weight in winter. Some die of starvation.

As tree feeders, porcupines pick up high proportions of potassium. Trees' potassium to sodium ratio is 300 to 1. The result: they crave salt, traveling miles for even minute quantities of the mineral.

Considered pests by farmers and campers, they devour objects with salt content. Perspiration permeates tool handles, shoes. Ignition wires, fan belts and hoses hold other salts, and road salt adheres to tires. Porcupines are often killed along road-salted highways.

Given his coat of 30,000 hollow, sharp-pointed quills, this North American rodent is not belligerent, although he is well-defended. When a predator—great horned owl, fox, bobcat or fisher— moves in, porcupine sticks its nose between front legs, lowering belly to the earth. Then, arching its back, rear toward enemy, it raises its quills.

Thrashing out vigorously with body and tail, it can embed hundreds of quills in the attacker's face and body. Quills are never thrown but may fly out, dislodged by muscular force.

The weasel-like fisher sometimes vanquishes a porcupine by turning it over to attack its soft white unprotected belly. But most enemies retreat, heavily peppered with painful, barb-coated quills that swell as they inch forward in the flesh, sometimes piercing a vital organ.

***a. Porcupine adult** 18 to 22 inch body, 7 to 9-inch tail. Weight 10 to 28 pounds. Covered with brownish-black hairs, some white-tipped, interspersed with hollow quills.*

***b. Tracks** rear paw at left, fore paw at right. Feet well-adapted for climbing, hairy above, bare and rough below.*

***c. Young.** Precocial at birth.*

***d. Quill** magnified. Needlesharp, hollow, yellow or white. Spines brown with microscopic diamond-shaped barbed scales. Shortest, stiffest spines on neck, rump and tail, replaced when lost or molted.*

THE INDEPENDENT, MARCH 16, 1995

"considered pests by farmers and campers, they devour objects with salt content."

NATURE'S WAY: Taconic Revolution

In this part of New York we live on or near the remnants of a great geological event, variously called the Taconic or Taconian Revolution—or the Taconic Disturbance—which lasted 110 million years, ending 335 million years ago.

Evidence of this disturbance remains in unique scenic landscapes from the Berkshires through the Taconics to the Hudson River, from the Highlands in the south to Ticonderoga up north.

The earth is estimated at over four-and-a-half billion years old. During its life, land masses and oceans have waxed and waned; continents have merged and pulled apart again, with all or parts of them covered by vast seas.

Plates of granite about 60 miles thick carry continents; dense and heavy basaltic plates carry the oceans, which float lower than granite.

The underlayer of the semi-molten material on which plates ride is heated, possibly radioactively. Heat is released like bubbles in boiling water. These may push up and separate plates, or join and sink down into earth, with consequent plate collision.

Measurement of earth-time is in eras, broken down into periods. The Paleozoic Era, named for its ancient life forms, began 600 million years ago. The first of the seven Paleozoic periods was the 100-million-year Cambrian, when a shallow sea covered New York. Continents were closer together, separated by a proto-Atlantic ocean.

Then, in the next era, the Ordovician, 445 million years ago, the plates carrying the North American and the African plates collided.

Volcanic activity and earthquakes accompanied this movement, as the gigantic ancestral Taconic Mountains were born.

Great masses of rock were pushed forward on the North American plate, causing rocks to melt or metamorphose-change texture or mineral composition. Pressure caused rock to contort into folds, creating faults and fractures. A vast mountain range grew several miles high, believed to have been as high as the Himalayas today.

Mountains grow in stages—from "youth," when they are building up and folding, to their maturity, when they start to wear down through erosion and

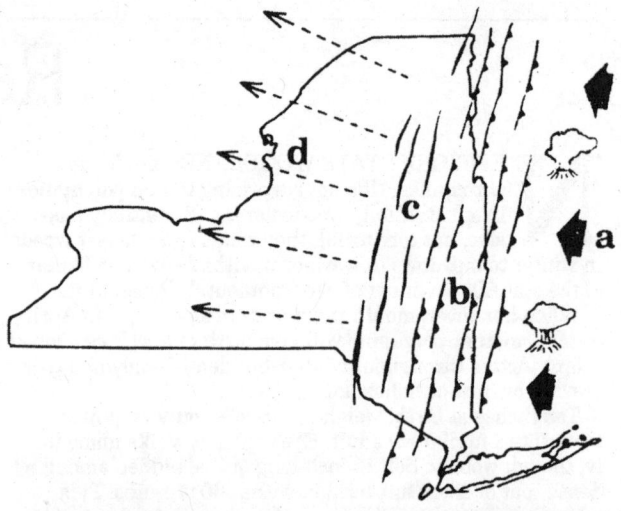

445-335 million years ago volcanic activity (a) created belts of thrust (b) and fold (c), metamorphosing rock which became the Taconic Range. By the time the plates had pulled apart, sediment flow (d) off the mountains had shifted from an easterly to westerly flow, putting down layers on the west which eventually built into the Catskills.

are said to be in old age. Building and erosion, created by different forces, occur simultaneously.

In the middle of the Ordovician Era, the steep west side of the great mountains broke loose. The Berkshires remained as stumps of the ancient Taconics.

The avalanche of rocks, called a klippe, slid down to the position of the present venerable Taconic Range, narrow, rocky, steep, wooded hills not usually higher than 2,000 feet, creating overall "a storm-tossed landscape."

The ancient forms are still fascinating, with great angled layers of rock strata, fractures, curved formations, ripples and folds. Its impressive history is documented in the rocks of distant Cambrian and Ordovician times.

The huge block of a hill that now holds Olana and serves as a mark of our own history fell off the Taconic klippe over 400 million years ago.

THE INDEPENDENT, MARCH 30, 1989

> "The ancient forms... with great angled layers of rock strata, fractures, curved formations, ripples and folds."

Wings for flight, ornament, 'love dust'

NATURE'S WAY

Marion Dusoir Ennes

NOW THAT THE SOLSTICE IS PAST, longer, lighter days tell of increased sunlight and warmth to come, anticipating butterfly days. The glory of color and pattern of these "flying petals" have thrilled for centuries. Lewis Carroll thought them delicious, saying in *Alice in Wonderland*, "observe the bread and butterfly. Its wings are thin slices of bread and butter, its body a crust and its head a lump of sugar."

Real butterflies have wings of different insect stuff, where form clearly follows function.

Though a butterfly shares many insect characteristics, the wide wings covered with microscopic scales distinguish it from all others. Part of the *Lepidoptera* order (*Lepis* meaning scales, *ptera* meaning wings in Greek) the group includes night-flying moths and butterflies, dazzling day fliers. A single medium-sized butterfly weighs as much as a paper clip.

Wings attach to the body at the second and third thorax (chest) segments. Flight results from alternate contraction and relaxation of inner and outer chest muscles. This pumping motion also helps move hemolymph (blood) around the body.

The flapping of perfectly balanced wings creates lift and forward thrust as the adult butterfly counteracts drag from behind and gravity from below.

The wings of an almost-adult are visible through the chrysalis (third stage) case. At emergence wings are so tiny and soft they must be pumped to full size immediately to prevent crippling.

Flooding the veins with blood and some air, the butterfly pumps until wings are full size. The thin double layer of transparent cuticle skin, already fitted with microscopic scales, stretches over a tubular venous network and dries hard.

The wing's shape, span, color and design, as well as the venation (blood vessel) pattern carried between the cuticles, specify a butterfly's family affiliation. Nine butterfly families each have their own design plan. Three are easily recognizable: the large swallowtails, the familiar white and yellow cabbages, and the migrating monarchs.

Tiny scales, programmed to form appropriate patterns and colors, are latched onto the cuticle, overlapping like roof shingles. Most scales are flattened and even. Some specially-shaped cells on males contain pheromones to help in courting.

In a life that lasts (except for migrators) from two to three weeks, adult butterflies have one primary purpose: to meet, mate and reproduce their species.

Attractive, well-constructed wings are vital agents in this goal. Entrancing patterns in beautiful colors and sharp contrasts are early advertisements that attract males and females to one another, often while patrolling hedgerows or woodland paths.

Wing patterns are protective also. Resting butterflies find places resembling their wings for a camouflage effect. Flying butterflies escape predators in a trice when a bird hesitates at the sight of the insect's fake but frightening eye spots.

Male monarch butterflies are among those that carry special scent pads consisting of specially-shaped scales on hind wings. In a courting dance involving fluttering, circling and stroking, a male gets close enough to release a shower of scales, called "love-dust" by some, that disburses an aphrodisiac pheromone that settles the female so their union can be consummated.

With eggs fertilized, she can fly on strong wings to find the right home for them. Testing each plant, she touches it momentarily with her foot. Chemical sensing receptors reject some, confirm the correct hosts, reassuring her as she lays her eggs that hatchlings will be well and appropriately fed.

Butterfly wings' myriad shapes. *Two pairs of wings—fore and hindwings—attach respectively to second and third segments of the body. Forewings are usually large, somewhat pointed, hindwings are smaller, more rounded.*

THE INDEPENDENT, JANUARY 4, 1996

"… a male gets close enough to release a shower of scales, called 'love-dust'…"

Spectacular scales

NATURE'S WAY

Marion Dusoir Ennes

IF THE WING PATTERNS of butterflies stir the heart, their scales—the minute structures that support these designs—dazzle the mind. The taut transparent membrane stretching over an insect's vein structure houses the tiny sockets that support thousands of complex scales.

All microscopic, most scales are 50 x 100 micrometers and come in shapes and sizes to accommodate body contours. Some are uniquely shaped, like the scent-wafting scales, able from basal scent cells to disburse pheromones, major helpers in attracting the sexes and accomplishing union.

Each scale is attached loosely to its own socket. All are placed so that scales closely overlap like a shingled roof. Direct touch, like efforts to grasp a butterfly's wings by birds, spiders or humans, quickly releases a small cloud of "butterfly dust" as multiples of minute scale pedicels (feet) slip out of their sockets.

This is small sacrifice to a butterfly slipping away from danger with its life. A large Monarch butterfly has more than 500,000 scales on its wings alone.

A butterfly's characteristic family wing design is actually a genetically-determined mosaic. Wings that start as an unpigmented double layer in the pupa are directed by genes governing wing microstructure, scale structure and pigmentation.

Each scale has its own color. Its placement is developmentally related to a focus point that carries the message as to whether the design will be perpendicularly rippled or striped, have crossbands, eyespots, large color patches or patterns dependent on wing topography.

Generally, one butterfly species carries scales with only four to five different pigments out of a selection of reds, oranges, yellows, some whites, blacks, grays, brown, tans and rusts. These blend optically by juxtaposition to produce a wide range of intensity and hue.

Not all scales depend on pigment to produce color. Iridescent blues, greens, coppers and some whites result from the effects of structural arrangement within a scale's gridwork. When we see a white butterfly, our eyes are responding to light reflected from tiny air bubbles inside the scales' grid.

Iridescent blues (like our Northeastern little blue) have a dark melanic-pigment that reflects blue and green wave lengths. The satiny sheen occurs when the angle of light on thin or vertical scale surfaces combines mechanical reflection with pigmentation.

Color mixes in butterflies can be complex. And a transparent area of a design, as in eye spots, may be due to the absence of scales, revealing clear wing membrane below.

Currently, researchers are studying the elaborate and delicate structure of scales for replication and use in industry. Iridescent material could be valuable to artists. The same technology may apply for optical purposes, for the fabrication of diffraction gratings, optical filters, coatings and certain solar absorbers.

The remarkable physical intricacy of scales has significance in a butterfly's life beyond their combined importance in locating mates, camouflage and diversionary defense.

They are vital in temperature regulation. Their mass alone, covering the wing cuticle, increases capacity to retain heat. Air-filled, scales are effective body insulators. And their complex internal grid work absorbs solar radiation with high efficiency.

Engineers trying to correct problems of damage from heat absorption during computer chip production are now looking closely at close-in-size iridescent butterfly scales. Constructed in length and thickness to offset the impact of solar energy, scales may provide a successful prototype for computer chips.

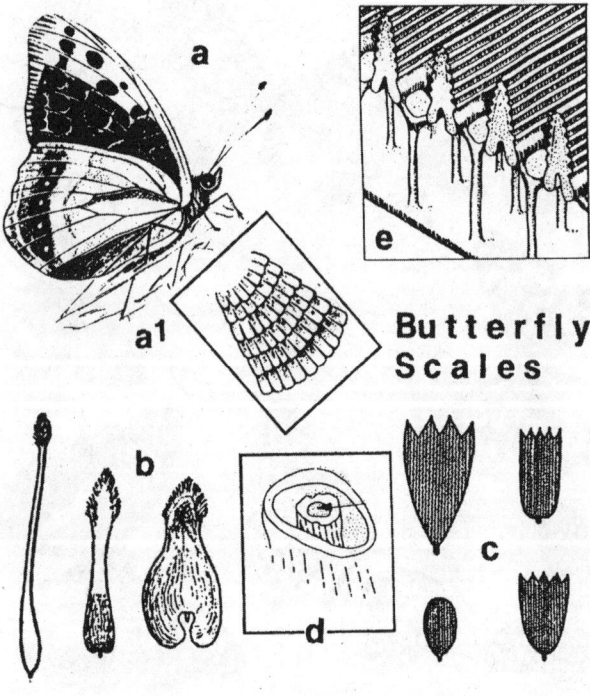

Butterfly Scales

a. Frittilary butterfly *showing one family's genetic wing patterns.* ***a-1. Inset:*** *Scales in shingle formation on wing.*

b. Scent scales, *sex-attractant carriers.*

c. Contour scales. *All scales are microscopic, displaying tiny pedicel (foot).*

d. Socket *(doughnut-shaped) for pedical at center (arrow).*

e. Vanes *on scale surface (highly magnified) which catch and reflect light rays.*

THE INDEPENDENT, FEBRUARY 1, 1996

"A large Monarch butterfly has more than 500,000 scales on its wings alone."

NATURE'S WAY
Long before flowers

Ferns with lacy, symmetrical, segmented blades are the ones most of us recognize. They include common varieties like hay-scented, sensitive, and bracken ferns, which are not protected in New York State.

All other fern species are protected by law and "may not be picked, plucked, severed, or removed and carried away without the consent of the owner thereof."

Three seriously endangered species are hard to recognize as ferns: The unusual **climbing** fern that twines around trees or other vegetation has lower leaves reminiscent of ivy.

Curlygrass ferns are less than two inches tall when mature, have threadlike leaves (from which the name is taken), and a tiny naked stalk with a few *sporangia* (spore cases) at the tip.

Hart's tongue ferns like rich soil on limestone cliffs. The descriptive name comes from broad, strap-like blades 2½ inches wide and a foot in length.

More common species, like the delicate black-stemmed maidenhair and walking ferns, also have unusually shaped fronds. Elongated arrowhead-shaped fronds of walking ferns extend pointed leaf tips. Like plant runners, the tips take root nearby and put out new shoots that intertwine with other fronds.

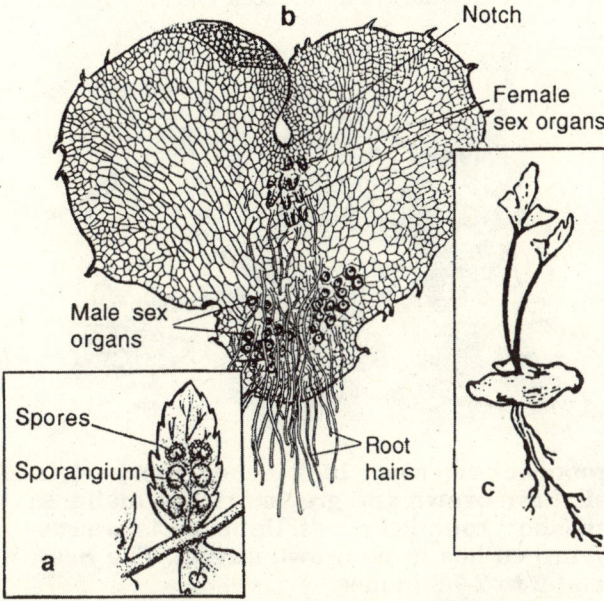

a. Fern frond leaflet with spore cases (sporangia) on underside. b. Prothallium underside, enlarged. Below notch are female sexual organs, necks protruding. Male sex organs below, among rootlike hairs. c. Tiny fern prothallium, with young plant emerging.

Without benefit of flowers or seeds, these adaptable species and many more thrive as they have for the millions of years before nature developed flowers. It took a lot of microscopic study by patient botanical pioneers to identify the ferns' "alternation of generations" system.

The plant with green fronds is one stage, easily visible to the eye. This is the sporophyte (spore carrier) with thousands of spores attached to leaf edges or undersides. Seeds contain all the components for producing a plant; spores do not. When a microscopic spore falls to a hospitable place on the soil, it produces the fern's second generation.

This generation is a flat, smaller-than-your-fingernail leaflike structure. It is a gametophyte (reproductive cell carrier) with a complete set of female and male sex organs on its underside. This *prothallium* puts down a few rootlike hairs which secure it to soil and draw up water and nourishment.

Flask-like female organs, about 20, each containing one egg and a neck through which sperm can pass, are located below the notch of the "heart."

Sperm develop in bulbous male organs near the heart apex. Once all the gametophyte's organs are mature and there is enough moisture, the male organ bursts, allowing the sperms' coiling and lashing whiplike cilia to swim toward the flasks holding eggs. Female organs are believed to exude a chemical which attracts sperm as the necks bend toward the sperm.

Usually the first sperm home wins and fertilizes the egg; all other flasks close up. The egg develops anchored to the cushiony part of the base, which provides nutrition. A stem curves upward from the notch to put out the first leaf of the new fern plant, as the root grows down. Once leaves and roots are well-established, the prothallium withers and dies.

You may never catch this microscopic sexual drama, but you might cultivate some prothallium from spores and hence a fern plant or two. I have not yet done this myself, but I have the information.

THE INDEPENDENT, APRIL 18, 1991

"You may never catch this microscopic sexual drama..."

NATURE'S WAY

Sky dancer

The dumpy little brown bird with a round body slightly larger than a man's fist, short legs, and a bill several times longer than its tail, doesn't look graceful. But environmentalist Aldo Leopold named it "sky dancer" in *Sand County Almanac* for its annual spring performance.

The woodcock's picturesque behavior and quaint looks are reflected in colorful local country names like bogsucker, timberdoodle, hokum-pake, Labrador twister.

Actually a transplanted member of the wading bird family, it hardly resembles the sleek, long-legged, long-beaked beach or marsh lovers—the sandpipers, dowitchers, and snipes.

This timberdoodle lives in moist woods, thickets, and brushy swamps where it is well camouflaged in the leaf litter and finds it main food source: worms.

Woodcocks have been returning since March from the Gulf Coast where they migrate each November. They are already "sky dancing" over their singing grounds around our county, needing large fields or swamps for the elaborate event described in the *Peterson Field Guide to Eastern Forests* by Kricher and Morrison:

"The ceremony begins on the ground as males call a very soft *cook-oo*... [then] males vocalize a repetitive nasal *preent*. Soon the male woodcock is airborne and its nasal call is replaced by a melodious high-pitched twitter, a prolonged rolling sound produced by the unique structure of the flight feathers . The bird spirals upward... [and you may] lose sight of it as it flies upward. As the male suddenly begins it slip-slide descent, it emits a high-pitched, chirping *zleep zleep*, its actual song. [Back on] earth, there is a moment or two of silence before the bird begins it's *preent* and the courtship flight is repeated."

You can take part in a woodcock vigil led by Prof.

Woodcocks measure 10-12 inches from beak to tail, have brown and grey markings on back, and short rounded wings. Underparts are rusty; crown has three brown stripes. The beak is 2-1/2 to 2-7/8 inches.

William Cook of Columbia-Greene Community College on Saturday, April 21, 5:30 p.m. at the entrance to the Fitness Trail at Lake Taghkanic State Park. Bill hopes to catch the woodcock's flight (and also look for owls). For information, call Prof. Cook, 828-4181 weekdays.

Concern about woodcock populations is mounting. There has been a 2.6% annual decline since the 1960s. In two decades, the number of singing males in the eastern U.S. fell 48%. Habitat loss is suspected as young forests mature and trees grow tall.

Woodcocks need loamy, moist soil with lots of worms for food, medium-sized young trees and bushes for cover, and large fields for courtship flights.

The U.S. Fish and Wildlife Service is on the case. At Moosehorn National Wildlife Refuge in eastern Maine—the only refuge primarily for woodcock—extensive alterations are under way to encourage growth of young woodland habitat in moist areas. By clearing some strips of old-growth forest, courtship display fields are created immediately. In about five years, these should grow into the habitat variety needed for the protection of this virtuoso performer.

THE INDEPENDENT, APRIL 19, 1990

"Woodcocks have been returning... They are already 'sky dancing' over their singing grounds..."

NATURE'S WAY

Downy partners

When last heard from in March, our downy woodpecker neighbors were beginning to court, tapping out brief messages to one another, each from its own drumming tree. A whinny-call, about two seconds of descending staccato notes, also kept them in touch, both signals bringing the pair closer and closer together.

Many birds are di-morphic: males and females of the same species have different color markings. Downies of both sexes have almost the same color markings, only differentiated by the male's red top-knot. Among birds, complex behavior is often substituted for dramatically colored plumage.

The male bird performs twists through the air, with swooping, fluttering flights.

Females signal a response by crouching, opening their mouths wide as wings spread and quiver. Looking like a nestling, the female invites feeding and the male brings her a nice fat insect.

What might look like submissive behavior to us is actually an economic signal, giving the female control. In survival terms, it is a good trade-off, with the female getting extra protein for egg production and the male genetic continuity.

Once a strong bond is formed, both partners must agree on just the right nesting tree or stub before a nest is excavated. Although both participate in excavation, the male does most of the work.

A round 1¾-inch hole is drilled into a dead tree at a point 5 to 40 feet above the ground. The tunnel hole goes in a short distance, turns downward, and further chiseling results in a gourd-like chamber 8 to 10 inches deep.

Here, on a sawdust bed, the female lays 4-5 white eggs. During 12 days of incubation, the nest is carefully guarded.

Parents take 30-60 minute turns sitting on the eggs. A returning downy often taps the tree near the nest cavity, signaling the inside bird to come out and be replaced. Males incubate the eggs at night.

The funny looking baby birds hatch in 12 days. Their naked skin looks red and is without down. Needle-like feathers soon sprout, and within 10 days the young bird is covered with black and white plumage.

From birth on, parents reach well down into the nest to feed them. Slowly, parents pull back, first to the nest top and finally to the entrance. The young call noisily the whole three weeks they are inside, and continue calling for food outside the nest for a week more.

Young birds follow their parents in downies' distinctive flight pattern, beating wings rapidly several times, then closing wings for a forward push.

When the downy begins to "sink" with gravity, the wings are flicked out, then down, making the bird appear to bounce upward like a wave-born boat.

Some downies migrate, many remain year-round. For the safety of numbers in winter, they join small foraging bands of nuthatches, titmice, and chickadees, all scouring the woodland trees for nutritious meals of hibernating larvae or masses of insect eggs.

When tree sap begins to rise in early spring, downies make "woodpecker candy" by pecking holes at the base of small branches or shallow holes through bark. In cold weather, the icicles of oozing sap are a welcome treat to the downies and their foraging friends.

Rugged individualists during non-nesting seasons, downy woodpeckers must form a secure pair bond so that a home site can be chosen.

THE INDEPENDENT, APRIL 25, 1991

"When tree sap begins to rise in early spring, downies make 'woodpecker candy'…"

NATURE'S WAY
Spring garters

This year the garter snakes, always the earliest out of all snakes, enjoyed a balmy, warm March. Some householders nervously told me of seeing quite a few.

Adult garter snakes are solitary during summer months, but are often together in bunches in spring. Sometimes they are dispersing from a communal den, which provided winter quarters to a ball of snakes, intertwined to keep warm. Other times a signal from a ready female attracts a horde of eager suitors.

Just out of the den, a female garter snake basks in the sun to gather in warmth. Soon, the epidermal layer around her mouth loosens; it is time to shed last year's skin. She rubs against a rock or rough log which "grabs" the skin as she crawls out of it.

A comfortable fit, her new spring coat has a pristine set of scales, keeled—each one with a raised center ridge front to back. The discarded skin, inside out, is left for an enterprising great crested flycatcher who likes to twine a snakeskin into its nest.

This shedding triggers the release of a hormone from a female with oviducts full of mature eggs, ready for fertilization. The scent of this hormone is picked up by eager males who flock around the female, striving to be the one she accepts. Once mating takes place, they all disperse, each finding a territory about two miles in diameter there they can eat, bask, and avoid predators.

Garter snakes often favor areas near ponds or creeks, but they live in a wide variety of habitats, including meadows, orchards, swamps, and woodlands. In an area where food sources are abundant, like a shallow pond, you will probably find more garters. They are good swimmers and enjoy the tadpoles, small fish, and young frogs that crowd such an area.

You may have a harmless garter snake as a neighbor, and should be pleased to know that it has regular, predictable habits. At night it sleeps in a rock crevice, under a log or a piece of metal, or in some debris—a place that helps maintain an even temperature. In the morning, basking on a rock, it soaks up heat from below and absorbs the sun's heat from above.

All snakes are all ecto-thermic, that is, drawing most of their heat from outside, so much time is spent adjusting locations to regulate temperature. After heat comes in they must find a place to cool off, frequently under a branch or a wide-leaved plant. A snake can be overcome by too much heat.

From such a cool spot, a garter snake can catch its prey—toads, insects, salamanders, birds, grubs, or caterpillars. Garters are especially fond of earthworms, which produce a chemical substance in the skin easily detected by the snake's sensitive flicking tongue.

With a low metabolic rate, 10 times slower than mammals, it needs a lot of down time to digest each meal, up to a week for a frog or salamander.

The same protective place keeps it hidden during daylight from predators—birds, especially raptors—and a little less accessible to medium-sized carnivorous mammals. When the sun goes down the garter snake returns to its crevice bedroom.

Mature Eastern garter snake, 18-48 inches long (average 25 inches), has three, usually yellow, stripes on darker spotted background.

THE INDEPENDENT, MAY 2, 1991

"A comfortable fit, her new spring coat has a pristine set of scales..."

NATURE'S WAY
Skunk cabbage

The six-inch tall spathe is thick and leathery, with purple and yellowish streaks. It acts as a helmet for the unusual flower complex inside. Many minute yellow florets are clustered on a rounded center structure called the spadix.

The skunk cabbage has often excited the interest of distinguished persons. That keen and observing philosopher Henry David Thoreau studied skunk cabbage in a swamp near his home in Concord.

Not satisfied with reacting to it in spring, as most do, he noted the plant's progress throughout the year. As the leaves withered and died in the fall, he detected the horns of new flowers forming for next spring's renewal and wrote of them, "They see over the brow of Winter's hill, they see another Summer ahead."

Commonly, the skunk cabbage's distinction derives from the fact that it is truly the first flower of spring, and the fact that the entire plant has a vile odor 'that combines a suspicion of skunk, putrid meat and garlic' as Blanchan observed in 1901. The fetid odor is incorporated in its botanical name, *Symplocarpus foetidus*.

It is common to the swampy wooded areas of the Harlem and Hudson valleys.

Early in spring, the tough hood (called the spathe) of the flower pokes through mud, snow, and even ice.

These flowers are warm and can reach temperatures up to 72° as the air temperature remains near 32°. The plant actually burns quantities of oxygen at a rate similar to the high respiration rate of hummingbirds.

The little florets enveloped inside the helmet of the skunk cabbage serve a very important function to the insect community. At a time when all other buds and blooms are shut up tight, the skunk cabbage is the only show in town.

The strong odor of the plant advertises it as an early nectar source for large swarms of hive bees.

Smaller woodland gnats and flies, so important in the ecology of the forest floor where they have wintered, also fertilize the plant as they take nourishment from it.

The pale green shoots which grow into the tall cabbage-like leaves that contribute to the plant's name have also been sought as nourishment.

Native American woodland Indians appreciated these early greens as food, but carefully boiled them at least twice to remove the acrid calcium oxalic which would otherwise burn the mouth. After the hunger moon, thise green vegetable tasted fine with a little maple syrup.

Skunk cabbage is a member of the Arum family, all of which have a version of the spadix/spathe construction. They thrive in damp, shady places and have acrid or pungent juice.

Among the many fascinating cousins of the "skunk" cabbage are some named for their interesting structure, like Jack in the pulpit, with its upright spadix and leafy overhanging spathe; or the green dragon, which has a long thin spadix that tapers to a whiplike end up to seven inches long. And the statuesque white calla is not a lily at all, but another Arum cousin of the skunk cabbage.

"... it is truly the first flower of spring..."

THE INDEPENDENT, MAY 4, 1989

NATURE'S WAY:
The Outdoor Conspirators

"Nature has no human inhabitant who appreciates her. The birds with their plumage and their notes are in harmony with the flowers, but what youth or maiden conspires with the wild luxuriant beauty of nature?" asked Henry David Thoreau in *Walden*.

As a country child, I lived with the world outside, felt linked with it, as if it were my extended family, but I must confess to taking nature for granted for a long time.

My husband, on the other hand, a lifelong city dweller, recently told me he hardly ever thought of nature as a reality, much less something central to his very existence. He is still amazed (and now delighted) to get acquainted with his outdoor neighbors—birds, deer, small animals—and ponders how they all manage to survive "out there."

If you are the least bit susceptible to nature's invitations—contemplation, observation, or just being with the earth—living in the country makes engagement just about inevitable.

Catherine Kazlo came here about 20 years ago and lives now in Greenport, though she spent many years in Claverack. She knows the back roads, ponds, woodlands, and just where to find the delicate early wildflowers and returning birds.

"I walk a lot, and I go to the places where plants and birds might be," she says.

About a week ago, she took me on a brief excursion in the Martindale hills where we saw several spring charmers.

First we spied the delicate white blossom of the bloodroot, a member of the poppy family which gets its name from the red alkaloid in the root which served as a pigment for Native Americans many years ago.

The trailing arbutus, a protected plant for more than 50 years because of attempts to dig it up and transplant it, is one I had seen in pictures but never growing. It has small, bell-like pink clusters nestling among lobed leaves.

On the gentle slopes of western banks which get the long afternoon sun, we found clusters of purple hepatica. The ¾-inch bloom is spring's first flower, labelled "the gem of the woods" by John Burroughs.

Presiding over this promising, if somewhat delayed, season was a bright male bluebird, who sat still for us on the edge of a tree for at least five minutes.

Catherine Kazlo uses the discovery of each beautiful treasure as a springboard to learn more, turning to books to add to her knowledge.

As a keen observer, she notes the habitat of each new plant she spots—whether it grows on banks, meadows, or woods, whether the soil is dry or wet. She can tell you whether you are more likely to find a bird in a wetland, a meadow, or a hedgerow.

So you see, we have located a conspirator, Mr. Thoreau—at least one!

There are more who would conspire "with the wild luxuriant beauty of nature," and many more of us are trying!

Hepatica

"...living in the country makes engagement just about inevitable."

NATURE'S WAY

Grass subways

For a random observer, it is easier to see a meadow vole in winter than in summer. I watched one in January, popping in and out of its undersnow tunnel leading directly to the bird feeder. It emerged about a foot from the base, gathered some fallen seed, and slipped quickly back to its tunnel.

Though chances are slim that this particular vole survived its enemies through a long, hungry winter, I like to think it did, for this little creature is industrious and resourceful and summer brings better times.

The name "meadow vole" is a redundancy, the word "vole" coming from the Norwegian word for meadow. It is named the field or meadow mouse, or bear mouse, for its appearance.

Its chunky body with small flat ears is covered above in chestnut-brown fur, silvery grey below. These field mice reach about 6½ inches, including a 2½ inch tail.

Razor sharp, yellow cutting teeth are well adapted for living and feeding patterns under tall columns of grass, sedge, or rush plants, depending on the site they choose. They prefer damp or moist meadows, but are found in varied habitats: orchards, hay fields, pastures, grassy dunes, gardens, or high marshes.

Active both day and night—though busiest at dawn or dusk—they devote great energy to adapting their territory to their social needs. They construct a community: a maze of covered paths where they eat, groom and comb themselves, mate, and raise families. They are clean and have specific communal sites for fecal pellets.

Meadow voles in "runways," tunnels they construct in grass.

Their work is so extensive, scientists calculate that voles can build up to 100 miles of paths in one square mile of grassland.

Voles may work together. One snips a grass stem at its base; if it remains upright, supported by other stems, the mouse reaches up 2-3 inches, cuts again, and repeats the pattern until the seed head falls and the inch-wide path is cleared. Another mouse bends tall grasses to arch overhead and, using its shoulders, shapes the passage until a grass subway is formed.

Males traverse the paths, looking for a receptive female who is also eager to mate. The female meadow mouse goes into estrus and often breeds immediately after the young are born, gestating a new litter while she is still suckling the first.

"The whole life of the...animal," says naturalist Edwin Way Teale, "appears speeded up—its heartbeats, activity, growth, feeding, reproduction."

The vole's fertility has been described as unequalled in the animal kingdom. Over five years, for example, a colony could, without predation and with females producing four litters of six young a year, reach a population of one million.

But predation takes a tremendous toll. Weasels, skunks, bobcats, fox and coyote, many snakes, crows, gulls, and herons are among these favoring these mice for food. They form 85% of the diets of some owls and hawks. Good swimmers, voles may also be eaten by bass or pickerel in the water.

Meadow mice lead full, energetic lives in the wild. A female vole will ultimately contribute about three litters to the population before her short life ends—in two to three months.

THE INDEPENDENT, MAY 10, 1990

"...voles can build up to 100 miles of paths in one square mile of grassland."

NATURE'S WAY:

Small creature —big signals

The female red-backed salamander attaches its eggs under the top of a hollow stump, staying nearby to guard them and keep them moist.

Population depletion and loss of activity in small amphibians like the red-backed salamander are early warning alarms to humans in this time of global warming.

The salamander family consists of mostly small mammals from one-and-a-half inches long to the giant five-foot salamander of Japan and China. All are victims of many misconceptions.

They are not lizards, with scaly skin. Salamanders have smooth, moist skin, which is not poisonous, although some secrete an unpleasant, smelly slime as a defense against their being eaten.

Salamanders cannot bite, scratch (no claws), or sting, and defend themselves by hiding. Although andirons and fire bricks have been called by their name, contrary to the old myth about them, they certainly cannot pass through fire unharmed. They even prefer cool to hot weather.

The red-backed salamander is a terrestrial species, very common in northeastern forest, occurring at the rate of 5,000 every 2½ acres.

They are important in the food webs of the forest floor, consuming detritus and helping to recycle nutrients which provide food to trees and strengthen forests. The red-back eats insects and worms, some snails, and sow bugs.

"The alteration or destruction of this food web would result in poor health of forest trees and eventual loss of many species," says Dr. Richard L. Wyman, executive director and biologist of the Edmund Niles Huyck Preserve and Biological Research Station in Rensselaerville.

Only 3½ to 4½ inches long, the red-backed salamander is slender and flat with two sets of short legs. It is voiceless. Its mouth and eyes are relatively large, and it has no external ear opening. Usually it has a brick-red stripe from head to end of tail, but is also found in a lead-grey phase.

Searching for this salamander involves turning over rocks or logs in moist areas, near brooks, or in shady places. When found among these cool, damp leaf molds, it wriggles away to avoid capture.

Its main aim is to keep its skin moist, for the red-back is lungless. It's the only vertebrate above fish without lungs, and breathes through the skin. The outer skin must be moist to take in oxygen from the air and discharge carbon dioxide. If it gets dry, it suffocates.

This makes the red-backed salamander vulnerable to climate change, especially repeated and intense droughts—which are predicted as a result of carbon dioxide increase in the atmosphere and concurrent global warming.

Dr. Wyman reports that "recent analysis of data on the relationships between soil acidity and soil moisture content revealed that, as soils dry, they become increasingly acidic. An interaction [has been shown]," he says, "between the frequency of droughts and the ability of a particular forest type to house amphibians."

Dr. Wyman's studies reveal that soil acidification (which may currently be based on deposits from acid rain) has affected the density and distribution of as many as 10 species of amphibians in northeastern U.S. With the help of volunteers, he has shown that 30 percent of the Catskill area is already too acidic for the red-backed salamander which has, up to now, been abundant and ubiquitous.

THE INDEPENDENT, MAY 11, 1989

*"The red-backed salamander is vulnerable to climate change...
as a result of carbon dioxide increase in the
atmosphere and concurrent global warming."*

NATURE'S WAY
Spotted salamanders

One late afternoon this autumn, under the lights of a shopping center, I met a spotted salamander plodding steadily toward a large discount store. The full eight inches of its broad, shiny black coat were decorated with a sprinkling of sizeable, bright yellow dots. It had the perseverence of a Christmas shopper hurrying over the concrete on four sturdy legs.

Fairly common in the eastern U.S., these chunky amphibians are rarely seen except in spring, though occasionally a full-grown salamander seeks new territory in fall.

Concerned about the salamander's safety, I picked it up, supporting its full body length. Cool and moist to the touch, wiggling a little as I carried it to a grassy wooded area, it soon disappeared under some dry leaves.

Spotted salamanders belong to the mole salamander family. Adults live primarily in burrows, hollows in stumps, or under logs or boards where they hide in winter.

Warm seasons find them foraging for sow bugs, spiders, and snails above ground, earthworms and grubs below. In undisturbed areas, they can live 10 years or more.

Spring brings great communal excitement for spotted salamanders. After a rain, when temperatures reach 40°, dozens to thousands of year-old males travel towards ponds, streams and shallow bays to court and mate with females under water.

In a large pond this congress can reach 45 to 100 males, competing to get a female interested in him and his sperm.

Within two days, females arrive and slip down to the pond bottom. When a male spots a female, he sends out a pheromone (scent signal) to attract her attention, and engagement is made.

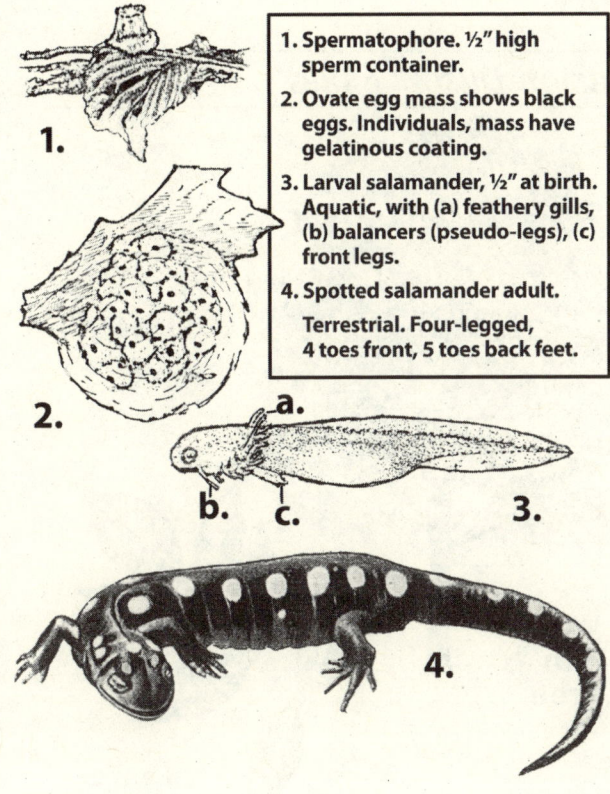

1. Spermatophore. ½" high sperm container.
2. Ovate egg mass shows black eggs. Individuals, mass have gelatinous coating.
3. Larval salamander, ½" at birth. Aquatic, with (a) feathery gills, (b) balancers (pseudo-legs), (c) front legs.
4. Spotted salamander adult. Terrestrial. Four-legged, 4 toes front, 5 toes back feet.

Activity picks up. Facing each other, they circle around, nuzzling and shoving. The male may rub his chin along the female's back. Both try to push their heads under the other's body near the base of the tail.

Soon the male moves away from her and twitches his tail. She has to be stimulated to do her part, and if she demonstrates readiness by going toward him, he will extrude a half-inch-high spermatophore on a nearby leaf. This sperm sac, looking like a glass push-pin, has a broad jelly base with cup on top filled with hundreds of sperm. More than 90 spermatophores may be deposited during each courtship.

Like birds, amphibians have an all-purpose opening at the base of the tail. This is the cloaca, from which body discharges are made and mating is effectuated.

She moves quickly to the spermataphore, covers it with her own cloaca, and draws it into her body where the sperm fertilizes her eggs. Within the week she lays several tiny egg masses with 20 to 200 eggs each on underwater foliage.

These soon swell to tennis ball size, and during two-month's gestation some are devoured by newts, leaches or insect larvae.

Hatchlings—tiny, active fish-like swimming larvae—gorge on mosquito larvae and fairy shrimp. Depending on temperature, larval growth takes one to four months, a time when they risk death from hungry herons or diving beetle larvae. Survivors absorb their tails, develop legs and lungs, get new mouths, teeth and digestive systems.

Now, two-inch juvenile salamanders crawl up to the pond's edge to begin a long life on land, hopefully not to hazard shopping at the mall.

THE INDEPENDENT, DECEMBER 10, 1992

"This sperm sac, looking like a glass push-pin..."

Nature's last word

NATURE'S WAY

Marion Dusoir Ennes

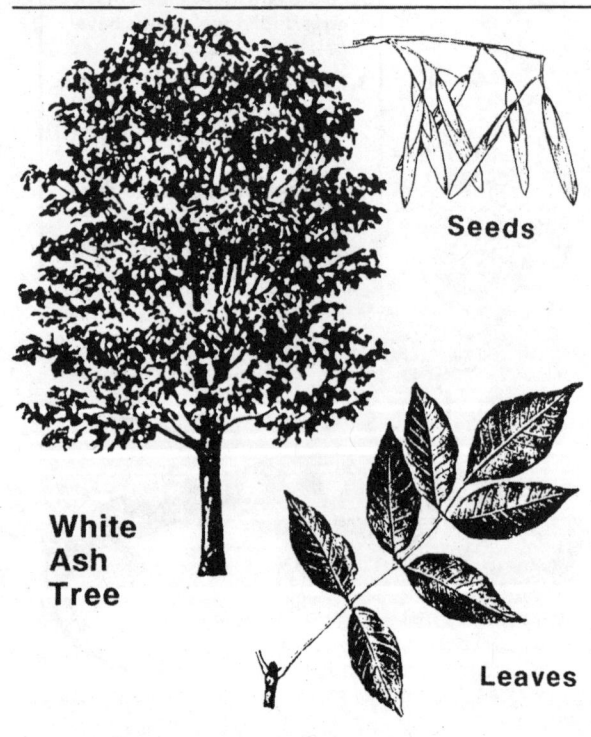

IN TIMES PAST, naturalist and tree lover Donald Culross Peattie could say, with conviction, about the white ash tree: "Every American boy knows a good deal about white ash wood. He knows the color of its yellowish sapwood, and the pale brown grain of the annual growth layers in it. He knows the weight of the white ash, not in terms of pounds per cubic foot, but by the more immediate and unforgettable sensation of having lifted and swung a piece of it, of standard size. He even knows its precise resonance and pitch, the ringing *tock* of it when struck, for it is the white ash, and white ash only that good baseball bats are made."

Today youngsters are less in tune with the virtues of different woods, but some still know the grain, heft and resonance of a white ash bat, without knowing much about the tree that produced it.

The virtues white ash wood brings to the baseball bat includes toughness and pliancy: just pliant enough and too tough to break under stress. Medium-heavy at 41 pounds for each cubic foot, it is perfect for sporting equipment like hockey sticks, oars, polo mallets and bowling alleys.

May-blooming ash trees bear flowers before leaves appear. Clusters of tiny bell-shaped purplish blossoms, males on one tree, females on another, are cross-pollinated by wind.

One tree produces up to 100,000 plump, one-winged fruits called "samaras" in pendulous clusters every season. They are an important food source for purple finches and evening grosbeaks as well as small mammals whose heavy seed consumption controls seedling spread.

By the time they reach 12 inches, seedlings develop extensive root systems which control erosion. Given sun and room to spread, fast-growing ash trees have the highest nutrient uptake of any tree. They grow best with other hardwoods in rich deep loam where they find abundant groundwater and good drainage.

The gleaming dark-green foliage and broad airy crown make it an attractive shade tree. Many are planted in small towns like Williamstown, MA. In fall their color varies from gold to bronze, mauve to royal purple.

White ash trees belong to the olive family of shrubs, trees and vines. Besides cultivated olive trees, these include some favorite ornamentals, forsythia, lilac, jasmine and privet.

Botanically-named *Fraxinus Americanus*, it also grows in Europe and Asia. Early Islandic visitors recorded its presence here in 1475. It was believed untouchable by "lightning or tempest."

Native Americans treated various conditions with its leaves, buds, inner bark or sap. They placed leaves in their moccasins or around camps to deter snakes, and drank a decoction of buds and inner bark "to prevent the pernicious effects of rattlesnake bite."

The wood was used for snowshoe frames, sleds, cradle boards, fish spears and back rests.

But the favorite use was in splint basketry. Basketry classmates and I at Eastfield Village in Rensselaer County were once confronted with a seven-foot trunk of white ash, with all its bark removed. That this could be made into a splint basket seemed unbelievable. My doubts increased as I grasped a heavy club, but I decided to follow the Iroquois way.

Wetting it down, we battered the log with clubs, then pulled up long strips. These were separated further, then cut into even splints. My woven ash basket celebrates the tree Donald Culross Peattie describes as "Nature's last word."

WHITE ASH TREE, 80 to 100 ft., 3 ft. diameter. Ash-gray bark, ridged diamond pattern.

COMPOSITE LEAVES, 4 to 12 inches, consist of 5 to 9 dark green ovate leaflets, each 3 to 5 inches, 1½ to 3 inches wide.

SAMARAS, rounded seed body topped by single tapered wing, one to 2½ inches long, ¼ inch wide.

THE INDEPENDENT, MAY 11, 1995

"Native Americans treated various conditions with its leaves, buds, inner bark or sap."

NATURE'S WAY
Well-feathered nests

No matter what the weather—cold, cloudy or windy—tree swallows return to their northern breeding grounds by about mid-April, the earliest of the six sparrow species in the county.

These birds build nests in natural tree hollows or nesting boxes 5 to 10 feet above ground, always within a short distance of water. They find insects above ponds or streams in the warmest seasons. This food is supplemented by some seeds, bayberries and blueberries, and the fruits of juniper and Virginia creeper.

Tree swallows are serious homemakers, strongly defending the nest. After rapidly repeated *chee-dee-dee-dee-deep!* calls, they dive at an invader's head, veering off just before contact. The message is clear, and however innocent, the wise trespasser leaves quickly.

Watch a small flock of a dozen or more tree swallows over a pond, and you can see them chase each other for possession of a white feather. The feather may change bills three to four times in seconds. The winner is the one who returns to his nest with the feather, where it is used as lining.

It is not really a game, reports Cornell University researcher David Winkler, in *Living Bird* magazine, Spring 1993. In his study of tree swallows in a nearby nesting area that is home to 75 nesting pairs, he focussed on breeding behaviors. "Nests lined with more feathers fledged earlier," he reports.

Female swallows first bring straw and dry grass into a tree hollow or nest box, form it into a cup by body pressure. The male helps collect materials and feathers.

Each feather is stuck in the nest base, quill down, until the soft feather base forms a curving canopy over the eggs, later the chicks. The pace of collection continues during egg laying and incubation and tapers off after chicks hatch.

Mr. Winkler wanted to be sure feather collection made the difference in early chick fledgling. It could be that parents who were the most successful feather collectors also brought the largest amount of food, making good parenting the reason for rapid growth.

In 1989, he and his team divided swallows into a removal group and a control group, keeping groups carefully matched for clutch size, breeding times and parental experience.

Then, over the breeding season, researchers checked nests daily, because birds kept adding feathers. One nest's peak number was 114.

Handling all nests and chicks in similar fashion, they removed every feather from the removal group nests and left the feathers in the control nests.

They compared weight, wing and leg length of 12-day-old chicks in the two groups and found significant differences. Chicks from the feather removal groups weighed less, their legs and wings were noticeably shorter.

It was clear that the feather-lined nests had a marked beneficial effect on chick development. Their increased insulation under and over the chicks reduced nest cooling. Needing less energy to keep warm, chicks can use more energy for growth.

For early arrivals like tree swallows, the extra effort to feather the nest helps parents speed chicks' development, reducing the time they are vulnerable to cold weather and dependent.

John James Audubon captured these tree swallows in flight as they vie for a white feather. Shorter than their swallow-tailed barn cousins, trim tree swallows, 6½ inches long, are shiny blue-green above, white below. Long wings spread 13+ inches and, at rest, reach tail's tip. Tail slightly forked.

THE INDEPENDENT, MAY 13, 1993

"…you can see them chase each other for possession of a white feather."

NATURE'S WAY

Sylvan leaper

Despite the vagaries of this spring's weather, wood frogs were probably first to reach their ephemeral pools to breed early in March—even before the peepers. This diurnal frog's botanical name, *Rana sylvatica*, means the same as its common name—for this is a true forest dweller.

Sleek as bandits, in black mask and chocolate-colored coat, wood frogs creep out of woodland debris and leaf litter, where they survive temperatures as low as -21° F. Large quantities of glycol in body tissues during winter make possible their tolerance of this low temperature up to five days, even while 35% of the frog's body fluids are frozen.

Most of us were probably huddled inside while the small but eager (and otherwise silent) male wood frogs set up their raucous mating calls, distending throats and sides to produce a hoarse clacking chorus. This sound, like the quacking of ducks, lures the larger females to water for spring breeding rituals.

Fertilized egg masses, containing up to 3,000 eggs, are often attached to twigs in water. They survive in very cold water because temperatures within the cluster can reach 11°F. higher than the water.

Nevertheless, freezing weather will destroy eggs caught in surface ice. Egg masses are also vulnerable to a fungus disease that infects and kills large numbers of eggs. Fewer than 40% of fertilized eggs become young adults.

Soon the gelatinous egg masses flatten and take on the green color of microscopic plants growing among the eggs. Once hatched, new tadpoles exhale carbon dioxide that feeds the plants, which, in turn, give off enough oxygen to support more than 2,000 breathing tadpoles.

Tadpoles hatch anywhere from 10 to 30 days after the eggs are deposited, and tadpoles can take 6 to 15 weeks to develop. Al Breisch, senior wildlife biologist of the Department of Environmental Conservation's Endangered Species Unit, explains: "The tremendous variation in rate of growth of wood frogs, eggs, and tadpoles is temperature determined. They seem to figure out their own timetable. When weather is warm, the process speeds up. In Canada, wood frog tadpoles may overwinter and metamorphose into frogs the following season."

The small black tadpoles start out by eating the green jelly that held their eggs, and then continue as scavengers of dead animal matter in water. In the multitiered mouth structures, the tadpole can strain particles that are then directly funneled into the esophagus.

By late May in our area, metamorphosis has changed the tadpoles into ¾ inch, baby wood frogs with tails, swarming at the edge of woodland pools. Soon tails will be absorbed, and skin color will fade into the mature coat. The slippery skin contains mucous glands that create a moist coating necessary for cutaneous respiration.

In great leaps, their long legs (more than 2½ times longer than head and body combined) will take them great distances from the breeding grounds. Here, for the balance of the year, they make a home among mixed hardwoods or in conifer swamps.

"Wood frogs are middle-level carnivores that thrive on a diet consisting of a wide variety of smaller invertebrates, including insects. In turn, they are prey to salamanders, raccoons, birds, and snakes," says Al Breisch.

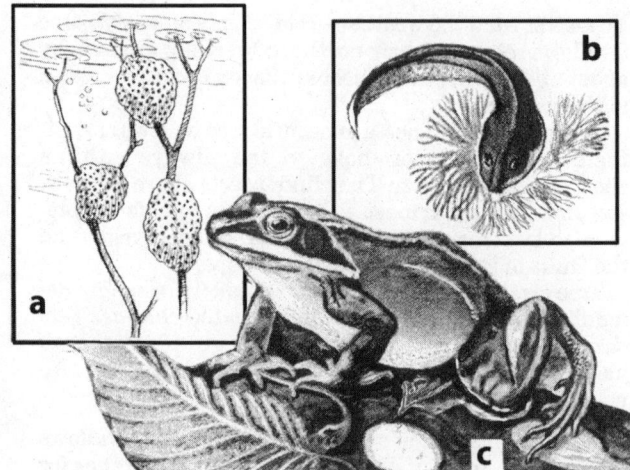

a. Wood frog egg masses. Each up to 4 inches across, attached to sedge stems. b. Wood frog tadpole. Black coloring absorbs sun's heat during growth. c. Wood frog. Male, about 2 inches, female 3 inches. Pinkish, medium or dark brown with prominent black mask ending behind eardrum. Light strip on upper jaw. Belly white.

"Populations can survive in this balance, but population losses occur as a result of human activity. Draining of ponds and introduction of predatory fish into seasonal ponds, and pesticides can drastically reduce breeding of this handsome terrestrial frog species."

THE INDEPENDENT, MAY 14, 1992

"Sleek as bandits, in black mask and chocolate-colored coat..."

NATURE'S WAY

Beautiful behinds

My first contact with an underwing moth was in the vestibule of a commuter train. In its demise, doubtless by collision, the wings were spread. I was impressed by the marked contrast between the dullish forewings and the vivid orange and black markings of the hindwings. I soon learned it is a member of genus *Catacola*, a Greek word meaning "beautiful behinds."

Though butterflies remain most popular of the 200,000 Lepidoptera species, moths account for nine-tenths of the total, many elegant in style and color, all fascinating.

Moth's wings are vital, active survival features, according to the work of Theodore D. Sargent of the University of Massachusetts, who published "Legion of Night: The Underwing Moths," a comprehensive treatment of *catacola* in eastern North America.

The Northeast supports about 70 to 104 closely related underwing moth species found in this country. These vary greatly in pattern, color, and size, but retain common wing features: their forewings mottled to resemble bark patterns of a tree trunk, their hindwings different, often brightly colored.

Catacola, like most moths, fly, feed, and mate at night. Then, folding bright hindwings under their bark-patterned forewings, they hide by settling head downward on compatible colored tree bark.

Catacola relicta, one of several "white underwings," can rest, almost invisible, against the birch tree's white bark and grey scars. Others have forewings mottled or

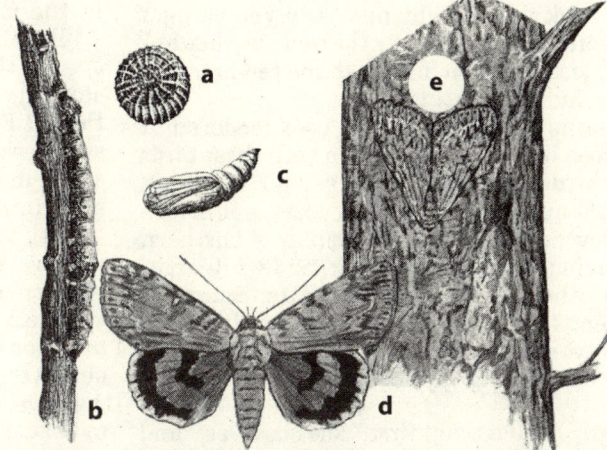

Underwing moths *(Catacola)*. (A.) Gray, sculptured egg. (B.) Camouflaged larva hidden on twig. (C.) Pupa case. (D.) Adult moth, mottled forewings and vivid banded hindwings. (E.) Camouflaged *catacola*, against tree bark showing forewings, hindwings tucked below.

marked to match their host trees—oak, beech, hickory, walnut, willow, blueberry.

Humans usually prefer pretty fluttering moths, but that brief adult stage in a Lepidoptera's existence is only one-quarter of its life span.

Like butterflies, moths are plant eaters, and start as eggs carefully placed somewhere on host plants, which provide food once the eggs hatch.

Underwing moth eggs, small and well-camouflaged, are subject to predation by woodpeckers and nuthatches searching tree branches and trunks for these overwintering delicacies in bark crevices. Egg contents are highly concentrated and impenetrable to water, preventing freezing.

Larvae les than 1/12-inch in length hatch and start feeding when host plant buds open in spring.

They have five molts, called instars. In the first they are almost transparent and blend with the leaf edge background. In successive instars, as they move toward the leaf center and on to the twig, each new coat conforms to the changed background.

After all its heavy eating and changing of coats, it takes a brief rest, spins silk to secure some leaves into a loose cocoon, then molts again to become the encased pupa. In three to four weeks the "miraculous transformation" to the adult underwing comes about.

Careful camouflage at each step has reduced loss to predation so far, but the adult needs some additional tricks to avoid the beaks of flying birds. When a *catacola* is disturbed in its hiding place, the bright flash of its hindwing can startle its predator long enough to allow the moth to fly, perhaps to a nearby tree where it becomes invisible again.

In the air, the bright hindwings are defensive pennants misdirecting a bird's beak to keep it away from the moth's vulnerable body. Many *catacola* still fly and find mates, with one hindwing torn or even lost.

THE INDEPENDENT, MAY 16, 1991

"... the bright flash of its hindwing can startle its predator long enough to allow the moth to fly."

NATURE'S WAY:

Feeder watchers

Evening grosbeaks, voracious seed-eaters, flock at feeders some winters. Almost robin-size but with short black tail, wings are black and white on yellow body for the male, female more duncolored. The male's forehead is yellow.

Many bird lovers who keep feeders full from September to June are seeing the dramatic spring influx of birds in their own back yards right now. And you can get a discussion going about whether the cool weather has brought some less common birds like the red-breasted grosbeak and indigo bunting.

Dorothy Saums of Hillsdale who uses feeders but also spreads food in her yard, has seen both these birds and believes birds are showing up earlier this year, some in sizable numbers. She has a dozen golfinches in bright yellow summer dress and a pair of northern orioles, the male in his orange, black, and white coat.

Like many other feeder watchers, Mrs. Saums is picking up trends in bird populations. Last winter she missed the evening grosbeaks who, in previous winters, had come in large flocks.

"They usually send a scout first," she observes, "and then they arrive in flocks, a golden yellow flash that brightens the winter sunshine—but this winter, none."

According to data compiled for Project FeederWatch, a continental bird feeder survey operated by the Cornell Laboratory of Ornithology and Canada's Long Point Bird Observatory, many birds that usually come south in the eastern third of the country stayed north last winter in the boreal forests of Canada.

This group, often called the "winter finches," includes the evening grosbeak, pine siskin, purple finch, and redpoll. Both evening grosbeaks and pine siskins showed decreases of 75-100% at feeders in the northeastern and southeastern US in the winter of '88 over previous year's numbers. These decreases were offset by dramatic increases in the numbers of pine siskins (a smaller brown-striped bird) in northwestern US and Canada and of evening grosbeaks in the northern Great Plains.

"Both siskins and grosbeaks are boom or bust species that wander nomadically across the continent, stopping wherever food is plentiful," says Erica Dunn, Project FeederWatch coordinator. The relatively mild, snowless winter and the good supply of favorite tree seeds in much of the East contributed to these birds remaining farther north than in other years.

With annual bird seed sales now topping $1 billion, the travels of "winter finches" produce economic repercussions for seed companies and farmers.

Project FeederWatch is enlisting participants to help monitor feeder birds in the winter of 1989-90. Field observers use specially designed data forms to record their weekly sightings. Completed forms are "read" by an electronic scanning device which transfers data to a computer system that records information about seasonal distributions and relative abundance of New York State birds.

Participants pay a $9 annual fee to cover the cost of data forms, newsletters, and postage, and must be able to identify the common birds at their feeder. Computer processing makes it possible to send volunteer cooperators an annual printed Project FeederWatch summary indicating which species were seen where and when.

To include the birds at your feeder, write to Project FeederWatch, Cornell Laboratory of Ornithology, 159 Sapsucker Woods Road, Ithaca, 14850. It will give you the opportunity to add your observations to the continental data pool.

THE INDEPENDENT, MAY 18, 1989

"... the travels of 'winter finches' produce economic repercussions for seed companies and farmers."

NATURE'S WAY
Foxy Neighbors

Vixen and cubs

Some of our wildest neighbors are famous in story and song, and more recently in opera, although here in the Northeast they live secluded, monogamous family lives in a habitat that combines open fields bounded by trees and brush.

Right now, in mid-spring somewhere nearby, a parent red fox is watching over a litter of young cubs who play in the sun outside their den while the other parent is out hunting food for the family.

The red fox is the most abundant and wide-ranging fox in North America. It is so adaptable that it can be found in the center of the City of Oxford, England, as well as the coastal plain in Israel.

Its reputation for trickery and craftiness has appealed to people for centuries. from the fourteenth-century Aesop's fables to the twentieth-century "The Cunning Little Vixen" in a charming opera by Czech composer Leos Janacek.

Sometime late last January or early February our foxy neighbors courted, made a home, and mated. Foxes will dig a new den, clean up an old one, or else use a cave or hollow log.

By early April (about 60 days after mating) the baby foxes are whelped in the den. The male fox brings food for the female during this time. His dedication to her and the family continues as the cubs grow. Both share parenting responsibilities.

In May, the litter of cubs, usually four to six, are lively, curious, and playful. If a female fox is discovered near the den with her babies, she will take flight to draw off any possible predator, while the little ones sneak back home.

Cubs' eyes open in two weeks. They are weaned by eight weeks. The parents, called the dog and the vixen, bring partially live prey to their young from about three weeks on. This is important for carnivores who must learn to hunt in order to stay alive.

By June, when cubs are three-quarters grown, the family goes out as a party to practice hunting. They start with little things like May beetles and mice but soon work themselves up to rabbits, lame grouse or pheasants.

The red fox has an acute sense of smell and excellent hearing. Alert and quick to move, its biting power is similar to a small dog. Although ready to take prey that is convenient and predictable like rabbits and mice, at times their hunting aptitudes are special. They can size up an unusual situation and take advantage of the prey's behavior for their own benefit.

By September the mature fox searches out its own territory. It has grown to an average of 42 inches, including the bushy white-tipped tail that accounts for a third of body length. They run on their toes in a track less than four inches wide and can cover as much as 245 miles in a day.

The red fox has long been considered a worthy opponent of humans in the famous hunt which brings out passels of dogs and well-dressed gentry to bring the fox to bay. Early settlers eager for this opportunity actually imported red foxes for this purpose. Those fox immigrants turned out to be the same species and interbred with native foxes.

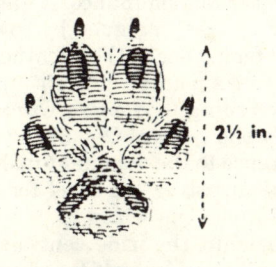

2½ in.

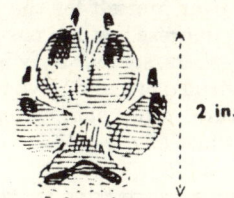

2 in.

Fox tracks. The hind feet are smaller than the front.

THE INDEPENDENT, MAY 19, 1988

"Its reputation for trickery and craftiness has appealed to people for centuries..."

NATURE'S WAY

Vagabond birds

Mysteries still surround the cowbird. *Molothrus* is its scientific name, Greek for "vagabond" or "parasite," apt description.

This common bird probably spread through our country from the southwest, first following herds of bison, later consorting with domestic cattle. Now ubiquitous, cowbirds get mixed reviews on their social habits in the world of birds.

If we think of birds as models of domestic propriety—nest builders and devoted parents—cowbirds don't fit. In 1927 naturalist Edward Forbush wrote, "Cowbirds are free lovers. They are neither polygamous nor polyandrous—just promiscuous"...and that's for starters.

From March to June, males in groups vie repeatedly with one another for dominance. A nature observer and Chatham friend was intrigued by cowbird antics.

They stand facing each other, feathers sleeked, necks arched, and beaks pointed straight up to the sky. This "bill-tilt," according to *Stokes' Nature Guides to Bird Behavior*, is a show-down. One bird withdraws enough to show deference to the dominant male, who maintains his status by thrusting his head forward as he fluffs feathers and raises his wings.

During courtship, the iridescent black male appears to be falling all over himself for the plain gray-brown female. Eager to impress her and move her to ardor, he fluffs his body feathers, spreads his wings and tail. Then he stretches his head down and forward, seeming to topple over. A guttural song, *bublowcomsee*, ends with a long, squeakly whistle.

Brown-headed cowbird, 7-8¼ inches, male above, black with dark brown head. He started wooing grey-brown female, below, by bowing. Cowbirds have short, thick bills, eat seeds and insects.

It works, over and over again, until egg-laying ends in mid-summer. It is estimated that each fertile female produces 44 eggs during this period, placing as many as possible in other birds' nests.

The highly observant female cowbird sits on a high perch where she can watch birds around her. Sometimes she scouts for nests from the ground or bushes. Occasionally she flies and flaps noisily, probably to startle nesting birds into revealing their nest locations.

In New York State at least 77 species are prey to the cowbirds' poaching, including flycatchers, thrushes, vireos, warblers, other blackbirds, meadowlarks, bobolinks, orioles, catbirds, robins.

Robins and catbirds will often remove the single, large, speckled cowbird egg. Others, like red-eyed vireos, may desert and build another nest. A cutaway view of a yellow warbler's nest shows four separate cowbird eggs, each successively roofed over until the warbler finally laid three of her own in the top layer, still crowded by a fifth cowbird egg.

Other birds incubate cowbird eggs as their own. Cowbird chicks, helpless at first, eat voraciously and grow quickly. They fledge in about 12 days.

Populations of Kirtland's warbler are seriously threatened by this brood parasite and other parental hosts may lose one of their own babies to a thriving cowbird chick. When all forms of chick loss are counted, however, bird populations are apparently not seriously diminished by the cowbird's exploitation.

As for the cowbirds, estimations are that out of 44 eggs laid annually, only 2 or 3 become adults.

Little is known about cowbirds' fledgling period, how they avoid imprinting to their foster parents, or how in late summer they locate flocks of their own species—but they do.

About 400,000 cowbirds join the gigantic mixed blackbird flocks, millions of red-wings, grackles, starlings, and others who migrate to southern U.S. or Central America each year.

THE INDEPENDENT, MAY 23, 1991

"... each fertile female produces 44 eggs during this period, placing as many as possible in other birds' nests."

SPRING — NATURE'S WAY

NATURE'S WAY

Pigeons' milk

So far as mourning doves are concerned, cooing comes before billing—and they are well-known for both. One alternate name is turtledove. Under that name the birds have earned a long-standing reputation, well-preserved in poetry and proverb, for romantic dedication. The Greeks associated doves with Aphrodite, goddess of love and beauty.

My own tribute in this vein was an early effort at Haiku:

Soothing dove call gone
unheeded—sweet bird of spring is
tragic, all alone.

Well—maybe not, though it's true that unmated males coo louder and more often than mated birds.

For mourning doves, parenting—including nest-building, incubating, feeding to fledging—is truly a cooperative affair.

It all starts with courting. The male perches—sitting erect with tail bobbing—puffs its iridescent throat, and issues a long cooing call that sounds like *ooahoo oo oo o*. Then, on the ground, he bows his head low, then raises it to give this long coo again. Soon, he rises from a perch on noisy flapping wings; then spreading his wings low, he comes down in a long, spiraling glide.

When the female is suitably impressed, they may perch close together, preen, and then preen each other. If aroused, she initiates billing—putting her bill inside his as they bob up and down.

Donald and Lillian Stokes are specialists in bird behavior and prolific writers on the subject. In this year's spring issue of the *Living Bird*, publication of the Cornell Laboratory of Ornithology, they describe some activities unique to mourning doves.

The mourning dove's nest is usually described as a loosely woven platform of sticks placed 10-25 feet above ground on an evergreen branch or in a vine tangle. Ubiquitous breeders in the U.S., nests are sited in cactus branches, hummocks, or bushes, depending on local habitat.

The rickety appearance of the unlined nest belies the careful teamwork going into its construction. The male searches out and tests as many as five twigs before finding a perfect thin, stiff, six-inch stick.

He flies to the waiting female at the nest site, hops on her back "reaching over her shoulder to give her the twig." The Stokeses state that they saw the male "fly off for more nesting material while she lodged the twig into the existing structure."

The ritual was repeated several times. This unusual behavior, common among doves and pigeons, may increase pair bonding.

Two shiny white eggs are incubated about 14 days in regular, unrelieved shifts by both parents. The female has the night shift—from roughly 5 p.m. to about 9 a.m.; the male incubates all day from 9 to 5.

Both parents feed the young "pigeon's milk," a secretion of white liquid from the crop. As each chick places its bill in the parent's bill, that parent pumps up a large portion of this 'milk'—a combination of sloughed-off skin from the crop, along with ground, partly digested seeds. Feedings are large, so less often than other birds.

Mourning doves are prolific, abundant (over 500 million in the U.S.), and adaptable. Fortunately, they are attractive, helpful to us as weed-seed eaters, and model partners.

Mourning dove, with small head, is brown above with black wing dots, tan below, and red feet, 12 inches long, 19-inch wingspread. In flight, the tail spreads wide, showing white edges. During breeding season, the male's breast is peach color and neck iridescent.

THE INDEPENDENT, MAY 24, 1990

"Both parents feed the young 'pigeon's milk,'
a secretion of white liquid from the crop."

Ancient loons—submarine divers

NATURE'S WAY

Marion Dusoir Ennes

FOR CENTURIES LOONS HAVE STRUGGLED to maintain isolated breeding territories that afford maximum protection for offspring. Considered the oldest bird in existence, with ancestors living millions of years ago, the loon family has no close bird relatives.

Come spring, handsome mated-for-life look-alike pairs hasten to their own special lake in the Adirondacks, northern New England, or Canada, ready to breed in the short time they have to raise young birds large enough to migrate.

Sounding their famous tremolo call, they speed over the surface, then brake by paddling the air vigorously, hitting water chest- first, like a seaplane.

Unlike other birds, loons' bones are solid not hollow, so their heavy weight and flight speed mean they can only land on and take off from water.

These repeated circuits are accompanied by their famous wild cry, and end in quiet copulation just out of the water on shore. Usually two olive eggs are incubated by both parents for 29 days in a shallow nest on a tiny island or bog-mat. Covered with moist dark down, chicks hatch one day after the other.

When completely dry, babies slide into the water and start to swim.

Loons are supremely fitted to their role as strong divers and marvelous swimmers. From pointed beaks to webbed toes, sleek bodies allow them to streak through water at 194 feet in 56 seconds—a rate about equal to our walking speed of 3.1 miles per hour.

Short legs ending in wide feet are securely anchored well back on the body.

They have a tremendous forward thrust. Feet fold, reducing resistance as only a narrow edge cuts through the water.

This same foot placement makes loons just about helpless on land, where their feet give them so little support they must shuffle forward, half on their bellies.

Parent loons nurture their young for three months, feeding them live fish, carrying them on their backs, keeping them warm under their wings.

In water, baby loons are vulnerable to predation by turtles and large fish, or separation caused by a motorboat wake.

Loons are endangered in New York and other states from human encroachment on breeding territories, acid rain contamination and mercury in the food chain along with other forms of lake pollution.

These strong divers are generally capable of holding their breaths for up to five minutes.

Holding wings close to their bodies, their heavy bones and lack of buoyancy help them reach depths up to 240 feet.

As summer proceeds, the family joined by some other adults frolics in the water.

Falling in line side by side, they lift their wings and raise themselves in the water to run a kind of foot race over the surface. Repeated several times, it is like a training exercise for young birds' muscles to help them in migration.

Ice forms early on northern lakes.

Loons fly 60-plus miles per hour on strong wings toward coastlines where salt waters are warmer below the surface and food is plentiful. Slowly, in plainer, more somber coats than their striking black and white checkerboard breeding plumage, they make their way to warmer southern climes on eastern coasts.

Common loon: *male and female monomorphic (looking identical). 28- 36 inches, wingspread 52-58 inches, sharp strong beak 2 ¾ inches.*

Breeding plumage black-and-white checks above, white below. Winter gray above.

Black velvety head, white-striped necklace.

Four webbed toes on wide feet.

THE INDEPENDENT, APRIL 10, 1997

"Holding wings close to their bodies, their heavy bones and lack of buoyancy help them reach depths up to 240 feet."

NATURE'S WAY
A local sphinx

One afternoon last October, members of the accounting department at COARC's Mellenville headquarters were on break when Rose Spensiero spotted what she thought was a leaf moving on the gravel nearby.

A close look revealed a sturdy, three-inch-long caterpillar moving persistently ahead in its rippling fashion.

Rose Spensiero took it to Jack Hurley who, duly impressed by the caterpillar's size and design, named it Horace, put it in a cardboard box and promised to learn more about it. After preliminary efforts, he brought Horace to me, and I took up the inquiry.

I was impressed by its sleek body—almost as thick and long as my forefinger—and its delicate color and design. It was cinnamon-brown with some thin black stripes front to rear, and almond-shaped cream-colored marks running like oval portholes along its sides.

I could see it would become a large moth and Holland's 1903 *Moth Book* had a good picture. It was a member of the Sphinx family, one of two species, *Achemon* or *Pandorus*. Both feed on vines, specifically Virginia creeper and grapes, wild or cultivated.

Further research revealed—and none too soon because Horace was thrashing about in his box—that Sphinx moths pupate underground. I hastened to provide Horace with a large plastic box with three inches of soil.

Wasting no time, he pushed the dirt aside with his head and was underneath in less than a minute.

Horace's life began as a dark green egg laid on the upper side of a host's plant leaf sometime in late summer, one of a second brood because of the season's lateness.

Once hatched, this caterpillar's body has a series of 11 segments, corresponding to the adult insect's head, thorax and abdomen.

The small, flat head with its strong chewing jaws is followed by three telescoping segments. When this larva is feeding, the segments are open, supported on a branch by three sets of small prolegs.

If the caterpillar is excited or threatened, it pulls in its head and rears up on its first six to seven segments, a position reminiscent of a sphinx, hence its name.

Thoracic (middle) segments are supported by prolegs with tips for climbing or holding onto twigs.

The eleventh (last) segment is supported by a thick prop with a very firm grasp. In young Sphinx caterpillars this segment has a projection like a horn that disappears by the last molt, thus the name "horn worm."

The larva's main function is to eat. It must consume enough to supply tissue for the chrysalis' formation, with some additional for the later emerging adult. From birth through larval growth, its weight increases more than 3,000 times.

After it feeds voraciously, it rests, then molts, shedding its skin five times before being ready to pupate. That is what Horace is still doing, though we have no assurance it has survived.

When I described Horace to the New York State Museum entomologist who identified him as *Achemon*, he warned that Sphinx pupae rarely survive captivity.

Perhaps so, but we think this larva is actually a *Pandorus*—a good name, says Mr. Hurley, considering it came from a box.

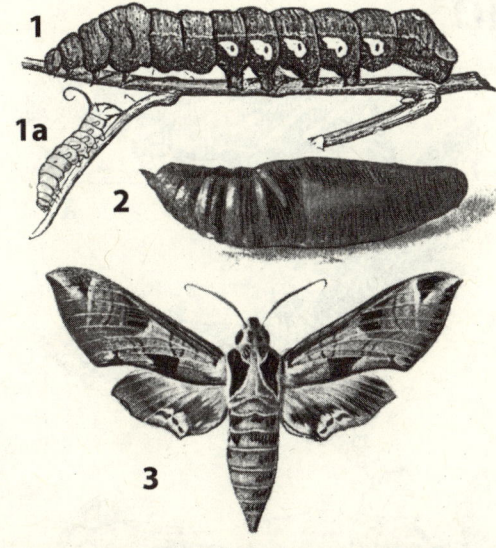

1. Full-grown *Pandorus* larva, just before pupating. Head and three telescoping segments on left. Prolegs support and carry body. 1a. Larva at emergence from egg. head on left, "horn" on eleventh segment.

2. *Achemon* pupal case. Bright chestnut-brown, 2½ inches long, contains all structures of adult.

3. *Achemon* moth, 3 to 4-inch wingspread. Head, thorax, and abdomen pinkish-tan. Forewings pinkish-tan, with dark brown lines and spots. Hind wings pink at base; tan, dark brown-dotted margin. Rust colored underside, flushed with pink.

THE INDEPENDENT, MAY 27, 1993

"From birth through larval growth, its weight increases more than 3,000 times."

NATURE'S WAY
Denizens of the dim world

The reason most of us have missed seeing moths of the Sphinx family is that most are crepuscular, flying at twilight or in the hours before dawn. At first glance, these twilight flyers are often mistaken for humming birds.

Though Sphinx moths exist worldwide, in North America most members of this insect family are medium to large, with wingspans as wide as four inches. They have stout, cigar-shaped bodies that extend well forward of the wing and far past the rear margin of the hind wings.

The slender pointed wings seem small compared to the size of the body. But the wing muscles are powerful, and their wings beat 25 to 45 times a second, so quickly it is a blur to the human eye. Because of their strength and speed as fliers, they are commonly hawkmoths.

The primary goal of the caterpillar of any member of the *lepidoptera* family (moths and butterflies) is to eat, to provide enough substance for ensuing forms. From the time the caterpillar hatches from the egg, only a centimeter or two long, till it is six weeks old, it does its job.

Sphinx caterpillars, like the light green tomato hornworm well-known to many gardeners, can ruin rows of tomato plants unless quickly picked off and discarded. The few survivors must continue the species.

The pupa, relatively quiescent in its relations with the environment, is full of internal changes. Inside its newly-formed, hard chitinous cover, the caterpillar's tiny wing buds grow, great compound eyes and segmented antennae form, and the chewing jaws give way to an extensible sucking proboscis.

In favorable conditions, this major metamorphosis culminates in the emergence of a winged adult moth.

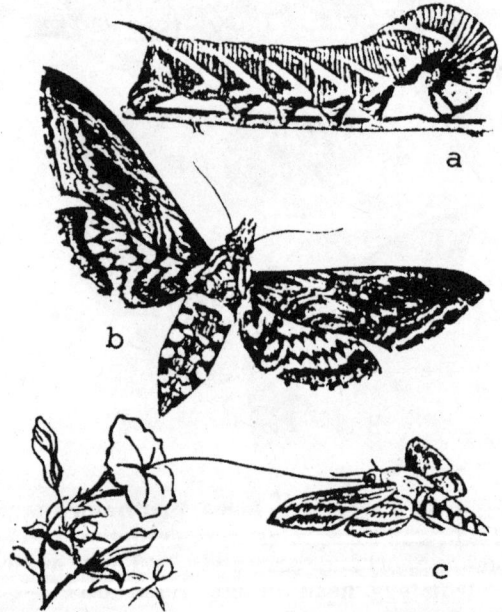

Tomato Hornworm a. Caterpillar (actual size) light green with white arrowhead markings. Harmless rear horn, function unknown. b. Adult moth (actual size). Wings brown shades in wavy lines, dark and white accents. White band center body, graduating yellow spots towards rear. c. Moth sucking up nectar.

The handsome Sphinx caterpillar brought to me last autumn crawled into three inches of soil in a plastic box at my house and never emerged.

Ronald Hodges, an entomologist for the U.S. Department of Agriculture, is writing a comprehensive series on all moths of North America north of Mexico.

When I talked with him at the Smithsonian Institution, he said that a larvae from a late batch of eggs like the one found here rarely makes it, even in natural circumstances. Adults usually emerge in summer, and then disperse over considerable distances.

In its adult form the insect has wings to take it in search of a sexual partner, for that is the main function of full-grown moths, to fertilize and produce the eggs that will become the next generation.

The adult hawkmoth's sensing equipment locates the opposite sex by smell. Its large head has a pair of spindle-shaped antennae tapering to a fine hook. Along with short feelers on either side of the mouth (the palps), these two organs are central in touch and smell, the antennae for hearing.

During their brief lifespans, Sphinx moths must take nourishment. Unlike other adult moths that have no mouthparts and never eat, this moth loves nectar.

It is endowed with a long, coiled tongue, actually a hollow proboscis that is up to three inches long, often longer than its body.

In the dim light it hurries to fragrant white, yellow or pink cupped flowers, unrolls its proboscis, and drinks deeply, brushing against and collecting enough pollen to fertilize the next flower.

THE INDEPENDENT, JUNE 10, 1993

"Wings beat 25 to 45 times a second…
a blur to the human eye."

NATURE'S WAY

Sturdy bluets

To a casual gardener like myself, the appearance of an unaccountable new bloom is a special pleasure. Though it seemed magical, it was probably an abundance of wet weather that brought a bluet seed to life on my garden ledge in mid-May last year, reappearing this year in greater profusion.

Only three to six inches high overall, bluets have delighted writers and naturalists for centuries. In his book *Nature in Miniature*, Richard Headstrom says:

"To my way of thinking, one of the most delightful of the early spring flowers is the bluet. By itself it is not a showy flower, but when massed together in countless numbers, bluets trace a milky path beautiful to see in fields and meadows."

They grow in clumps, sending up five stems with tiny oblong leaves out of a fine, feathery, basal tuft. Each stem is topped by a flower with four light blue or lavender-blue petals around a white ring, with the golden yellow center crowning a funnel-shaped cup that holds nectar at its base.

The delicate flower faces, only a half-inch across, are said to "reflect the serenity of heaven in their pure, upturned faces." Bluets have inspired several poetic names: eyebright, innocence, Quaker ladies, and Quaker bonnets.

Helen McClallen, of the Columbia County Historical Society, confirmed that Quaker women wore bonnets with wide, stiff brims and that their clothes in general were noted for simple elegance. And 'simple elegance' certainly describes bluets.

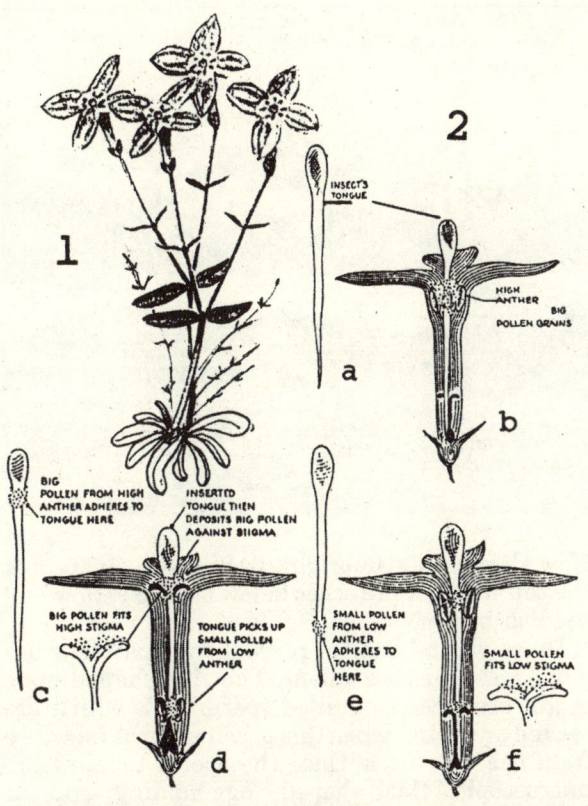

1. Bluet plant, three to six inches, flowers atop thin wiry stems, slender, light-green leaves, basal tuft. 2. (a to f) Complementary cross-pollination process. Bees' tongues transfer big and small pollens between different flowers.

This is a member of the *madder* family: all plants with petals fused to form funnel-shaped corollas with lobed margins. Included among its many tenacious cousins with grass-like leaves is the ubiquitous bedstraw, bane of many gardeners.

Bluets are small meadow perennials, surprisingly hardy and resilient. Every year 100% cross-fertilization is guaranteed because plants carry two different, but complementary, reproductive structures that capitalize on the snug fit of an insect's tongue to do the job. Small bees and several butterflies, like the meadow fritillary and clouded sulfur, do the pollinating.

One half of the flowers (all in one plant patch) have big pollen grains resting on the high anthers topping a long male stamen. The same plant has short pistils holding the stigma (female organ for receiving small pollen).

The other half (in another patch) have small pollen grains hidden inside the flower cup on short (male) low anthers. This same plant has tall stigma to receive large pollen.

The bee or butterfly thrusts its long tongue deep into the cup of the bluet to find nectar. As it does so, big pollen grains from the high anthered plant stick near the tongue base.

At another, alternately-structured bluet, big pollen sticks to the high pistil as small pollen grains adhere to the tongue near the tip, ready to be deposited in the plant with a short stamen.

The efficient system which maintains the bluet's sturdiness has helped it gain popularity in home gardens. If you have a friend with a rock garden, as I do, you may find patches of these small sky-blue blossoms covering an earth-filled crevice.

THE INDEPENDENT, MAY 30, 1991

"… the appearance of an unaccountable new bloom is a special pleasure."

NATURE'S WAY

Quaking bogs

The rare beauty of bogs is little observed by most of us. Mystery often surrounds these watery places, primordial pools trapped between two hills 10 or more thousand years ago when glaciers receded.

Local bogs are probably brimming now, for, without any natural drainage, water levels are maintained by the substantial rains we had. This makes bogs one type of wetland which serves as a flood deflector, holding weather which might otherwise create heavier creek or stream overflow.

Within its own unique ecosystem, a bog is a living biosphere which grows and changes over long periods of time. It is home to many plants, called "pioneers," which grow in water. Bog development is an anaerobic process (without oxygen) where frogs and snakes are rare.

It starts with a good-sized pond in an isolated pocket left thousands of years ago. Low-growing, rootless sphagnum moss became established around its edges, and a peaty black organic soil eventually filled in. The central pool grew smaller as the mass enlarged and thickened.

This thick mat of sphagnum usually dominates the bog, while other plants like the bog asphodel (a yellow lily) and various shrubs—some from the blueberry family, some bunchberry—seed themselves in the moss. The roots of these plants strengthen the mat further.

Like other mosses, sphagnum is a tough plant.

New shoots grow in bright, light green clusters at the top, as older branches below fade to yellow and reddish brown.

These plants' ancient reproductive patterns use a dryness/moisture valent. The club-shaped male organ produces two-tailed sperm cells which are ejected and burst when this organ absorbs moisture from the wet moss. Once the sperm touches the microscopic, flask-shaped, egg-holding cup, it breaks, opening a canal for the sperm's passage to the egg.

The resulting mature spore capsules look like small brown eyeballs. They must dry and shrink before they explode with a faint popping sound. The scattered spores grow into new rootless plants.

The bog mat prospers and grows thicker in the cool, moist atmosphere, becoming strong enough to support the weight of a person. But it is spongy and quakes under your feet, so caution is advised for those venturing out. Explorers of one bog poked through 17 feet of mat without ever touching bottom.

Bog waters, with limited drainage, start off as acidic, and become more so as the sphagnum takes minerals from the water and exchanges them for acidifying hydrogen atoms. Sphagnum served Native Americans as an antiseptic.

Most forest decomposers cannot survive this acid environment, so decomposition is very slow. Two-thousand-year-old bodies dug out of the Tollund bog in Denmark were entirely preserved in the cool, acid environment.

These conditions favor carnivorous plants like the sundew and the pitcher plant. Colonies of sundew, 4-10 inches high, attract insects. Glistening drops of a sticky substance on leaves catch, enwrap, and then digest the victim. The insects provide nitrogen not otherwise available to sundew or tall pitcher plants in the bog's acid soil.

Over eons of time a bog grows and changes—sometimes expanding if more water is added—otherwise contracting to become a swamp as ringing trees move in. Bogs offer a glimpse of another biosphere, and another sense of time.

THE INDEPENDENT, MAY 31, 1990

"Within its own unique ecosystem, a bog is a living biosphere…"

NATURE'S WAY:

Pleased to meetcha

The chestnut-sided warbler has a yellow crown separated from its white cheeks by a band of black across the eyes. Another black streak runs from the beak to the neck. Black and yellow feathers cover back and wings, which also show yellow wing bars. A streak of chestnut color runs alongside the white breast.

Thirty-three species of warblers breed in New York State and at least 16 do it in the many terrains of Columbia County.

During May most birds located their preferred nesting sites and are now well into breeding. Only the most skilled (and fortunate) bird watchers are able to catch glimpses of these quick and elusive small birds, despite the brilliant color combinations of their coats—yellow, blue, white, orange, black, brown.

Warblers are strong flyers, though only 4-6½ inches long, and migrate great distances from the West Indies, Central or South America, across or alongside the Gulf of Mexico. They can cover 100 miles in one night in good weather.

Birds tend to find a niche for themselves that maximizes food supplies and reduces competition. In a study of five warbler species which nest in a spruce forest, each species used different sections of the living space, some near the treetop, some at the middle, some low down. And also, these warblers allocated the available food supply, with each species subsisting primarily on different insects, or insects at different growth stages.

Warblers don't really warble, they buzz, twitter, trill, and tweet. A partial catalogue of their sounds includes: *bz, char, chee, churr, me, miss, orrr, see sir, switch, teach, tea, tiz, tory, tsee, way, weet, which, wont, zhee, zip, zray, zree, zur*—in many combinations.

In a recent issue of *Natural History* magazine, Don Kroodsma, University of Massachusetts zoology professor, tells of his study of chestnut-sided warblers among the brambles and azaleas in the Berkshire Hills.

In early May, the chestnut-sided warbler wakes at dawn to sing his loud emphatic "please-please-pleased to MEET cha" over and over, as often as 300 times per hour. He is trying to attract a mate. "These songs," says Don Kroodsma, "which I call primary songs, seem to have evolved mainly for communication with females.

But the chestnut-side has other concerns, too. He wants to protect his territory. So he uses his repertoire of "as many as 10 other, more rambling songs with unaccented endings" which are sung in rapid fire sequence. This delivery seems aimed at establishing himself and his new bride as a pair.

As they get acquainted he continues singing his primary song over and over to the female, even when she is crossing the boundaries of their established territory, where he would usually use his secondary songs to keep rivals away.

After their first mating he stays with the secondary songs. "For the first hour...every day, he delivers a nonstop barrage of secondary...songs."

Though the female is now content to remain in the territory, "intruding males pose a serious threat." Another male could mate with his chosen female at her fertility peak, and he would be raising another bird's young.

Once incubating, the female, no longer fertile, is safe—and the colorful chestnut-sided male returns to "please-please, pleased to MEET cha"—and sometimes attracts a second mate.

THE INDEPENDENT, JUNE 1, 1989

"Warblers don't really warble, they buzz, twitter, trill, and tweet."

NATURE'S WAY:
Some Rare Birds

Getting familiar with birds and introducing them to others is almost a reflex for many of us. In spring, we eagerly point out the first robin to the nearest child. In fall the call of the chickadee brings us to the window to watch its energetic antics. On a city street in winter, we sympathize with the house sparrow searching for crumbs after a light snow. Right now, each of us could list several birds we recognize as old friends. As we get more time outdoors, many more new friends will reveal themselves.

Mrs. Eleanor Shook and her mother have attracted many species with the fine flower garden they have created on their Livingston land.

Here, about three miles east of the Hudson, Mrs. Shook spends lots of time outdoors. "I feel comfotable outside, going through the meadows, past the creek through the old orchards and into the woods. I've done this so long, I know the small animals and birds and where to find them—and I love the quietness and peace."

More than an observer, she is a gentle acquaintance of the creatures most of us never see. She makes a note of specific dates for many bird species and has provided me with a list of more than 70 birds she spotted during the past year.

Dr. Edgar A. Reilly of Old Chatham, senior scientist, zoology (emeritus), NYS Museum, and honorary advisor to the Alan Devoe Bird Club, was most helpful in identifying several rare and diminishing species on her list.

Five birds she listed are seen here in decreasing numbers, says Dr. Reilly. The barn owl, helpful because it controls the rodent population, in the past was killed in large numbers because it flies silently and was thought to be a ghost with its wraith-like face. The red-shouldered hawk, bob white, hairy woodpecker, and snow goose are also not as common as once they were.

Among the rare birds, Mrs. Shook can count the hooded warbler, the northern shrike, the red-shafted flicker, the yellow-bellied sapsucker, the orchard oriole and especially, the bohemian waxwing.

All waxwings are playful, gregarious birds. Commonly seen here in flocks, cedar waxwings are often found eating and twittering in a bush filled with berries. Occasionally, when fruit is overripe, they get drunk from too much of a good thing.

They are sleek, seven-inches long, chocolate to fawn colored birds with a swept-back crest, a black eye-mask, pale yellow belly, touch of red about two-thirds down the wing, and a bright yellow bar across the base of the tail.

Their rare cousins, bohemian waxwings, are a little larger, eight plus inches, and greyer all around (no yellow on the belly). Bohemians can also be distinguished by the added bright yellow stripe running from the middle to the tip of the wings, and cinnamon color under the tail. Male and female have the same coloration.

Years ago this mild, attractive bird was common in large flocks, eating berries or catching insects. Now, Dr. Reilly says, "It is very rare and is found occasionally travelling with flocks of cedar waxwings. Over the years only 30 to 40 birds have been seen in New York State."

Though it is satisfying to know the rare birds are still with us, Eleanor Shook is not making distinctions. The peace and contentment she finds in the woods is enhanced by the company of wild friends—rare, infrequent, or commonplace.

Cedar Waxwing

Bohemian Waxwing

THE INDEPENDENT, JUNE 2, 1988

"The peace and contentment she finds in the woods is enhanced by the company of wild friends..."

NATURE'S WAY

Our home team

Columbia-Greene Community College with a team in a World Series?

Sure! It's the Hudson Valley Ospreys, a team of five ace birders in their second year of competition, representing the college's Institute of Natural History.

This annual event is in New Jersey, where teams vie throughout the state to identify the greatest number of bird species in 24 hours. Last year, the winners sighted 201 birds.

Forty teams from the U.S., Canada and Great Britain participated in this year's World Series of Birding, and our own Ospreys moved up in the success rating. While most teams tallied fewer birds, Ospreys improved their position from 26th last year to 19th this year.

Strategy was crucial. Captain and "top gun" Richard Guthrie (New Baltimore), treasurer and "levity chairperson" Peter Feinberg (Albany), and Bill Cook (Claverack), record-keeper and "team conscience," did extensive scouting.

At 12:01 a.m. on May 18 the full complement of Hudson Valley Ospreys, nicely rounded out by Betsy Franz (Saratoga Springs), team ears and "survival chairperson," and Jory Langner (Delmar), team eyes and "offbeat humor chairperson," were on the mark in a northern New Jersey swamp.

"First bird to greet us was a very vocal catbird," reports Mr. Cook, associate professor of biology at Columbia-Greene and director of its Institute of Natural History.

"Lots of rules govern World Series competition. All team members have to see or hear 95% of all species identified; 5% can be spotted by less than two members.

"Sound identifies birds at night. Team members must hear *and* know the bird's song, then call its name. You can try to lure a bird in, but *only* through voice imitation of the bird's call. Tapes are never used.

"Before we left the swamp," Bill reports, "we located our target species: screech, great horned, barred owls; sora and Virginia rails; whip-poor-will and many passerine [perching bird] marsh denizens such as swamp sparrow, willow flycatcher, and marsh wren."

Heartened by early success, Ospreys piled into their van, sharing space with box lunches and dinners, thermos containers with cool or hot drinks.

Last year's plan kept them in the southern part of the state. This year they decided to do it all, woodlands and meadows, fields, marshlands, and shore, about 20 stops. Not for them a respite gourmet champagne dinner break planned by one team; our Ospreys slogged right through.

After many birding stops, their records showed them at only 82 species at 11 a.m. Saturday, 30 behind the same time last year.

"At that point things looked bleak for the home team. There was a weather barrier. The day was cold, migrants weren't coming in, and earlier birds passed through during spring's warm spell.

"Despite that, we clocked about 5-6 species every afternoon hour in southern New Jersey, where we found anticipated specialties like prothonotary warbler, Acadian flycatcher, horned lark, red knot, purple sandpiper, piping plover, and blue grosbeak.

At Brigantine Wild Life Refuge on the Atlantic, the Ospreys added 33 species (28 last year), including shorebirds: American oystercatcher, black skimmer, gull-billed tern, whimbrel (a peregrine falcon), and barn owl.

"Encouraged by 146 species at dusk, a few more night species would beat last year's total of 149," Bill concluded. "We missed 1990's sharp-tailed sparrow and American bittern, but picked up solitary sandpiper, clapper rail, least bittern, chuck-will's-widow, and finally, black rail—total 151 this year!"

The big World Series of Birding is characterized in this logo of the Cornell University Laboratory of Ornithology's Sapsuckers, one of the teams competing against our Hudson Valley Ospreys. Funds from pledges earned for each reported species support conservation activities of team sponsors.

THE INDEPENDENT, JUNE 6, 1991

"Forty teams from the U.S., Canada and Great Britain participated in this year's World Series of Birding..."

Red efts and true newts

NATURE'S WAY

Marion Dusoir Ennes

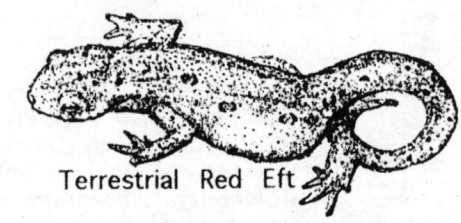
Terrestrial Red Eft

Aquatic Red-spotted Newts

ORANGE TO BRICK-RED from head to tail-tip, with black dots along each side, red efts are out among leaf litter after a rain, appearing precious as an animated jewel. Moving slowly with awkward steps, salamanders look very like the earliest fossilized amphibians.

I often wondered where red efts came from, only recently learning they live a double life. In adult form they look quite different, live in water, are properly named red-spotted newt. Newts are members of the salamander family. Some are completely terrestrial, some aquatic, and some, like red-spotted newts, are half and half.

Mother newt attaches her eggs underwater to the joint of a submerged water plant. Hatching into tiny greenish-brown, tadpole-shaped, larval salamanders with flowing feathery gills, they eat small animals. They grow steadily, and those that dodge the rapacious jaws of diving beetles, adult newts and dragonfly larvae metamorphose in three months.

Ready for land life, it is now a red eft. Its smooth larval skin is rougher and dryer. It has functioning lungs and four digit legs.

The bright skin color is a clear warning to predators like birds and most mammals, warning that the skin produces a toxin strong enough to kill a small mammal, or to burn the mouth of others.

Taking up residence several kilometers away from its natal pond, the efts' protection makes daytime hunting possible. Small animals like slugs, snails, worms, beetles and spiders are pulled in by the long sticky tongue.

The red eft grows slowly, remains on land for three to five or more years, until it reaches 3½ inches in length. Now, with olive-colored skin brightened by a row of black-ringed scarlet dots, it is ready to return to water, where it will live most of its life.

Red efts and adult newts are both well-equipped to travel. Juveniles leave ponds in summer, others return as adults in spring. In autumn, adults migrate to hibernation burrows on land, back to ponds in spring.

Besides good vision and an excellent sense of smell to give them clues, these salamanders have special homing skills. Perceiving polarized light through the pineal body in the brain, they identify the sun's position and use it as compass. They can also detect the earth's magnetic field as a directional reference system.

With tails grown broader and flatter for swimming, and smooth skin, adult red-spotted newts are prepared for pond life. Smooth skins absorb some oxygen, but as animals with lungs, they must rise to take gulps of air as needed.

Both sexes are now physically ready to mate. The male's sex organ is enlarged, holding sperm supplies, the female plump with eggs. The growth of dark ridges inside the male's hind legs facilitates sexual embrace.

In a ceremony that lasts up to four hours, he swims toward her, clasping her with hind legs just behind her front legs. Holding her firmly, he rubs his cheek and snout against her head, hoping to stimulate and encourage her with glandular secretions.

Then, slowly, continuously waving his tail, he releases his grip, walks before her on the pond bottom and deposits a spermatophore package. If she is ready, she picks it up with her own sex organ and soon releases eggs, fastening each one to a pond plant.

Red eft, juvenile form, 1 to 3½ inches, salmon-colored, rows of black-rimmed vermilion spots on upper sides. Pale below, black-dotted.

Red-spotted newt, adult. 3½ to 4 inches. Dark green above, yellowish below. Black-circled red dots sprinkled over sides, back, tail, legs. Tail broad and flat, hind legs sturdy.

THE INDEPENDENT, JUNE 6, 1996

"Moving slowly with awkward steps, salamanders look very like the earliest fossilized amphibians."

NATURE'S WAY

Creatures of air

For years dragonflies have survived the charade that they are fierce and dangerous. This impression has given them picturesque names like "devil's darning needle," "horse killer," "snake doctor," and helped maintain human myths about their dragon-like qualities. Many people fear they bite, but they don't.

Dragonflies have several features that promotes this impression. Their wing power is great. They move in strong bursts of speed and can hover in the air, stopping to look at you with enormous eyes.

Last summer I made acquaintance with one in my flower garden. It lit atop a nearby plant and stared at me. This dragonfly's long, slender, segmented body glowed iridescent blue, and the transparent, heavily veined wings held out horizontally were marked by a narrow, front-to-back black stripe. Each individual long, narrow wing may contain as many as 3,000 separate cells.

Colors of body and wings range over the spectrum, varying from one species to another, each species with its own delicately coordinated design.

The dragonfly's aesthetic appeal spans centuries: Its image illuminated medieval manuscripts, decorated Dutch tiles and Japanese stamps, and was used as a nose ornament in other oriental countries.

Emerging steadily now from their pupal cases, dragonflies will continue to come out until fall. They love the sun and become quiescent in cloudy weather. During this short season, they keep very busy, flying and eating, defending a territory, and, eventually, mating.

Newly-emerged iridescent dragonfly, average body length 2.5 to 3 inches, wingspan 3.5 to 4 inches, in common habitat: pond, stream, or lake, sometimes garden or meadow.

These ancient and best of all insect flyers are exceedingly well engineered for their activities. They have two sets of wings which beat alternately: front wings move downward as rear wings rise, and vice versa.

Two sets of indirect muscles attached to the thorax (chest) of the insect create the power to move wings. Inside the thoracic box, large vertical muscles make wings rise. Lengthwise muscles bend the thorax roof up, making wings go down.

At the same time, direct muscles help wings rotate. In this combination of motions the wingtips describe a flat, figure-eight which pushes the insect downward and forward.

This efficient system results in a remarkable air speed, ranging from 15 to 40 miles per hour, with a relatively slow wingbeat rate of 38 per second. By contrast, a mosquito, one of the dragonfly's favorite meals, must beat 280-580 times per second to travel 2.5-5.5 miles per hour.

Dragonflies are voracious eaters, taking all their prey—flies and other insects—in full flight. They accomplish this with the help of their uniquely-designed head and eyes.

Naturalist Edwin Way Teale describes the eyes as containing "as many lenses as the eyes of 15,000 men. Its head, resembling half of a hollowed-out marble, is attached to the slender body by a sort of ball-and-socket joint that enables the dragonfly to turn its head almost completely around and see below as well as above."

The legs of the insect are connected at the front end of its thorax, right behind the head. Dragonflies never walk, but bunch their legs together in flight to make a net-like container.

Swooping and darting in the sun, dragonflies catch their food live in these small leg baskets, stuffing the bodies into large, sharp-toothed jaws. By summer's end, they will reach their peak and be ready to find a mate.

THE INDEPENDENT, JUNE 13, 1991

"The dragonfly's aesthetic appeal spans centuries…"

NATURE'S WAY:

Weatherfrog

With large bright eyes wide open, the grey treefrog is ready for an agile leap to catch a careless fly or mosquito.

The vibrant trill outside my kitchen window was not, as expected, an off-course woodpecker, but a gray treefrog sending a message. After a careful search, I found it tucked neatly between two layers of suspended garden hose, a favorite place to which it often returned.

Hyla versicolor, its lyrical scientific name, is a friendly common tree frog and ranges from the East Coast west to North Dakota and Texas. Its scientific name reflects this tree frog's mastery of camouflage.

Usually the frog's rough back and legs are pearly to dark ashy grey, with darker in-spot type blotches. Its legs and "hands" are banded; it has a yellowish white spot below each eye, and the inside of the hind legs are a bright orange "flash color."

Like many amphibians, the gray treefrog can change color quickly from grey or brown to a delicate green when in leafy or grassy surroundings. In the speed of this color change it rivals the chameleon.

Its skin color is also affected by air temperature: it is darker when cooler and gets lighter when it is brighter. It even changes by the degree of roughness of the surface it sits on: rough surfaces make it darker.

These friendly 1¼ to 2¼ inch frogs live almost nine years. They go back to the Miocene period—at least 20,000 years ago—time enough to have developed some highly adaptive organs.

It has three toes on each foot with sucking disks at the tips of the toes that facilitate climbing and enable it to cling to vertical surfaces. A series of glands and a network of fine grooves in each disk help the disks work by friction and make them adhesive. The glands actually cause the cytoplasm shape and texture to change, so that cells can catch in the surface irregularities.

Larger frogs climb higher than smaller frogs, but it is believed that smaller ones with less skin surface need to stay near the ground for moisture. Amphibians "drink" by absorbing moisture through their skins.

Hyla versicolor has a single external vocal sac which balloons out when it calls. It has two separate calls: a weak bleating sound made with a half-inflated pouch and a loud, melodius trill when the pouch is fully inflated.

To do this, a treefrog shuts mouth and nostrils tight and pushes air back and forth between the lungs and mouth. Air is forced through two slits on the floor of the mouth into the expanded, resonating sac under the neck.

I may have been hearing a mating call the end of May answered by some other treefrog farther up the hill. But the calls could actually have been a forecast, for they usually came before the many frequent May showers of this year.

Treefrogs have, for centuries, been considered harbingers of rain and often have been used as charms. From Orinoco to British Columbia and the provinces of Central India, the frog has been protected or beaten, idolized or propitiated to encourage its magical power to bring needed rain.

THE INDEPENDENT, JUNE 15, 1989

"Tree frogs have, for centuries, been considered harbingers of rain and often have been used as charms."

NATURE'S WAY:
Flashy flyer

The American kestrel is beginning to be known for what it is. For years it was called the Eastern sparrow hawk, though it is a falcon rather than a hawk and rarely feeds on sparrows. It is in the same family as the sleek merlin and the noble peregrine.

The smallest member (9-12 inches long) of the local falcon family, the kestrel is worth looking for. "The most common and widely distributed raptor in the state," according to the *Atlas of Breeding Bird Birds of NYS*, it favors areas with open fields and woodland edges, but it is adaptable and may also live in cities or villages.

Kestrels are returning north, and recently I spotted one cruising along. Its curved, swept-back wings caught my eye. At first glance, the silhouette resembled a mourning dove, but the strong horizonal flight pattern contradicted this. When the bird perched at the top of a tall tree in a meadow, I could see the markings with my binoulars.

The kestrel was hunting and flew over the meadow looking for small game. Several times the bird hovered in the air to check out one particular spot.

Faced into the wind when hovering, its body is tilted upward and head slightly forward of the tail as the bird beats its wings easily and lightly. When the force of a gust proves strong enough, it may stop the wingbeats and hang suspended in air, apparently without support.

April is the month for mating, a time when the birds perform a wonderful aerial ballet. At first they sit in a tree top—near one another. The male mounts high in the air flying rapidly in a wide circle over the

The kestrel is strikingly marked. Both sexes have a white face, with curved black vertical stripes on both sides of the large black eyes. It has a rusty cap edged in slate blue. The back and tail are mottled red-brown, the buff breast spotted with black.

The male has slate-blue wings and one wide black tail band, while the female has mottled red-brown wings and narrow black bands on the tail.

perched female. He then swoops down in a flutter-glide while sounding a "klee, klee" call. Then both fly in great sweeps and curves, in a kind of chase, sometimes seeming about to touch the earth.

A strong pair bond results, and mating proceeds over a period of six weeks, sometimes as often as 15 times a day. During this time, the male brings food to the female and he continues this for 10 or more weeks, until a few weeks after the chicks hatch.

During the mating period the couple explores nesting sites together: old woodpecker nests on a woodland edge, natural tree hollows, or they may use a prepared bird box or nest in a building.

The male takes the lead in the search with special flutter-glides, calls, and carrying food to his mate to indicate his preferred site.

Arthur C. Bent, writing comprehensively of kestrels early this century, observed "by their attention to each other, which strongly suggests affection, they display the connubial character of their association."

THE INDEPENDENT, APRIL 6, 1989

"April is the month for mating, a time when American kestrels perform a wonderful aerial ballet."

NATURE'S WAY

The timber rattlesnake

The timber rattlesnake, a shy but venomous snake that is native to Columbia County, is currently undergoing a reduction of its geographic range and a population decline, says Dr. Kathryn Schneider, program director/zoologist of Natural Heritage, a cooperative program of The Nature Conservancy and the state Department of Environmental Conservation.

She points out that the timber rattlesnake is protected as a "threatened species" in New York State and the public should be aware of the importance of protecting this ecologically valuable creature.

A comprehensive fact sheet sent to Dr. Schneider by William S. Brown, professor of biology at Skidmore College, Saratoga Springs, is excerpted here.

Timber rattlesnakes used to occupy extensive areas with large populations. For many years they were heavily exploited for their oil, for bounty, and for the live animal trade. Bounties paid by local governments only became illegal in New York State in 1971.

Over the past 20 years an often illicit network of collectors, dealers, and buyers took snakes for the live animal trade, causing a sharp decline in timber rattlesnake population. Man is the most serious, persistent threat to the species' survival. Populations today have dropped 50 to 75%, well below the carrying capacity of the environment.

In northeastern New York, timber rattlesnakes occur today in remote mountainous terrain. It is

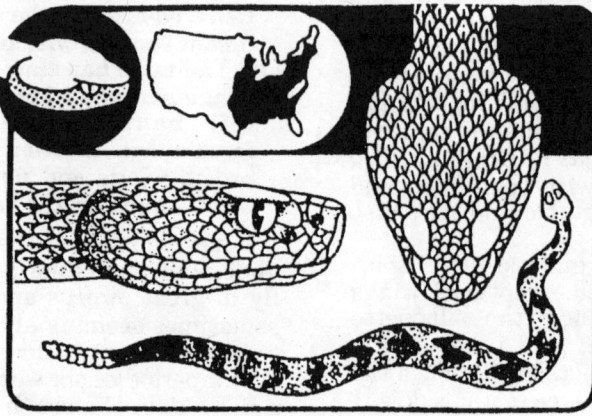

This schematic shows range, head-neck configurations, face and scale patterns of the 3-6 foot timber rattlesnake. Do not approach one in the wild; it might take defensive action. Its bite is poisonous.

a vulnerable species, particularly when aggregating for communal hibernation at winter dens.

This species' low biological replacement rate means that recovery of depleted populations takes many decades. Females mature sexually late; first reproduction occurs in the ninth or tenth year.

In any given year, only about 30% of mature females are reproductive. This low rate (three-year cycle), small litter size (about eight young per brood), and late female maturity are principal reasons for slow population growth.

The timber rattlesnake is a valuable species in the ecosystem. It is a predator of small mammals, and, like all secondary consumers, is an integral part of the food web and contributes to energy flow in the biotic community. Its "sit-and-wait" foraging behavior supplements that of actively-hunting mammals and raptors to create a more balanced prey population.

First described over two centuries ago, little is documented scientifically about this species. Its life history and behavior can contribute significantly to the science of animal ecology.

Timber rattlesnakes are insignificant threats to human life. Timid animals, they usually attempt rapid escape in nature and defend themselves only when cornered or molested. Venomous snake bites inflicted by this species are rare. The average person has a greater chance of being killed by a bee or wasp sting, choking on food, or being struck by lightning than by being killed by a rattlesnake bite.

An awe-inspiring part of our natural wildlife heritage, the timber rattlesnake clearly links us to once wild and unspoiled places on the North American continent. It is an interesting and useful part of New York's wildlife resources. As a threatened species, it deserves the full legal protection it now has, along with the interest and concern of humans.

THE INDEPENDENT, MARCH 22, 1990

"...the timber rattlesnake clearly links us to once wild and unspoiled places on the North American continent."

NATURE'S WAY

Snakes are lovers, too!

The fear and animus directed at snakes has a strong phobic quality to it, fed by traditional and picturesque tall tales.

I remember as a young teen, when I found a full-grown garter snake and started to explain some of its interesting attributes to a farmer's young sons. That farmer became so irate that he insisted on stoning the snake to death because, he said, it would get into the barn and steal milk directly from the cows' teats. That seemed a totally impossible idea to me for either the snake or the cow.

But even then, I was more confounded by the farmer's violent and irrational attack and by his inability to understand the snake's value in controlling the rodent population in his barn.

Current articles about snakes are still replete with disclaimers and explanations of old superstitions, and 41% of Americans are still afraid of snakes, though most are as likely to encounter a dragon as a snake.

Like humans, snakes have several basic needs: to get from place to place; find food; avoid danger (including predators); find environmental security to protect their bodies from extremes of heat, cold, etc.; reproduce their own species.

Just getting around on land requires a lot of muscle power for legless snakes. Consider how hard it would be to slide along the ground without knees or elbows.

Most snakes have broad, overlapping plates across their undersides. Muscular action urges a forward motion of the backward-facing plates,

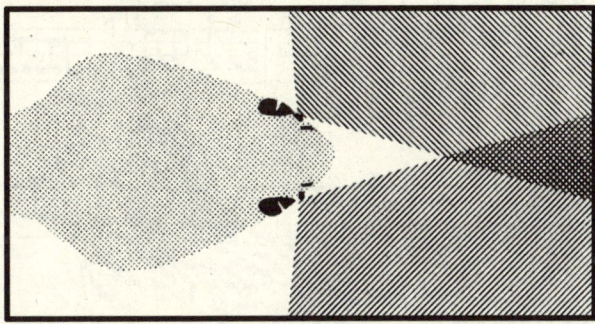

'Pit vipers' have a 180° overlapping field of sensitivity to heat, with a resultant narrow-focus target area.

which catch and hold on surface irregularities—even very slight ones—so the snake can move almost straight ahead.

On surfaces with less purchase, a snake has to loop from one side to another, pushing against stones, stems, or sand piles to make progress.

Animals need developed senses to find food and avoid danger. Snakes have fairly well developed eyesight and sense of smell but they lack external ears. They "hear" by feeling vibrations in the earth, and augment their "smell" with a delicate two-pronged tongue. By darting its tongue in the air, a snake picks up molecules on the moist surface, transfers the information for analysis to a special organ, Jacobson's, in the roof of the mouth.

Rattlesnakes have the additional benefit of special pits—one between each eye and nostril—containing cells sensitive to infrared rays that make up radiant heat, up to a tolerance of 1/1000 degree Fahrenheit.

This sensitivity makes it easier to locate and estimate the size and position of its warm-blooded prey, usually rodents. This same sense identifies that presence of predators or other enemies.

Snakes, lacking a body heat control system, must constantly find ways to keep warm or cool. In winter they cuddle together and hibernate in deep caves; summers they bask in the sun unless it's too hot, and then they crawl into a rock crevice.

And snakes are lovers, too. The timber rattlesnake mates in spring, often on a stone ledge warmed by the sun. The male touches the female with his nose, throws a loop over her and caresses her entire body. Though slow to respond, she soon reciprocates with her own caresses. When they become well-entwined, the mating is consummated.

THE INDEPENDENT, MARCH 15, 1990

"... he insisted on stoning the snake to death because, he said, it would get into the barn and steal milk directly from the cows' teats."

After tornado—song sparrows?

NATURE'S WAY

Marion Dusoir Ennes

THE FEEDERS AROUND MY HOUSE are frequented by song sparrows from time to time, but there was never any indication that they were nesting on the property—even in the shrubby yard. This abundant, thicket-loving bird is one of the most widespread breeders in the state, but it does not like to nest in forested areas, and our great hill was, until recently, covered with a mixed variety of trees 30 to 50 feet in height.

This habitat changed when the twisting fury of wind tore down 15 acres of our woodland, leaving behind a field of sorts, littered with tree trunks. Now the regular nesters—woodpeckers, chickadees, nuthatches, titmice, and owls—have lost their tree-canopy apartments. The thrushes (many threatened), flycatchers, orioles, and others must look to other wooded places for the scaffolding of branches to support their nests.

Perhaps the robins, catbirds, wrens, and phoebes will remain around the blemished buildings. It would be heartening if a song sparrow couple could join them, for that bird has been called an "unquenchable and likable little bundle of optimism", a bird whose "qualities surpass his charms".

Small and brown-coated, look alike male and female: each has its streaked, light-colored breast centered with a noticeable brown spot. Each one knows its responsibilities.

He courts her with his ebullient song—using it, too, to defend and protect their territory, their family. She builds and furnishes the nest, incubates eggs, young, using her own short calls and trills to keep in touch with him.

Once eggs are laid, the whole process, from egg production and incubation and on to fledgling, takes about three weeks. Parent divide the brood between them, each feeding and protecting its own set of short-tailed birds till they are established. Mother soon starts laying her second batch of eggs.

Despite repeated brood parasitism by brown-headed cowbirds—one nest had seven cowbird eggs—song sparrows are very successful in adding to their species' population with three or more broods a year.

Song sparrows are found across US, Canada, Mexico in many environments, as 25 different subspecies, or races, each one carefully adapted in size and coloration, to habitat, temperature, and humidity.

Male song sparrows are noted for their exuberance. Though important reasons govern his use of song, he clearly loves it, singing in any weather, any time of day, heard still in October or November.

The birdsong starts with a series (usually three) of accented, sustained notes, then about six notes in rapid succession—better described as a "group of tones separated by well-preserved intervals, and the contrasting coloring here and there of a distinct overtone", with variable rhythm.

In 1904 F. Schuyler Mathews analyzed and notated the bird's music, adding that the song sparrow's style "is unmistakably evident. He devotes himself to pure, simple melody, and is, in consequence, the best exponent of the song motif among birds".

Nowadays computer analysis has confirmed that, though these sparrows' songs follow similar patterns, each bird creates melodies of his own. Mathews recognized songs identical to the theme in Verdi's *La Donna E Mobile*, another fragment of a Chopin-like mazurka, and concludes from the variety of its productions that the bird is "nature's cleverest song genius."

Just what we need to hear on our barren, field-like hill! Three long notes, then trills from a friendly, confident being, to raise our spirits as we try adapting to our new habitat.

SONG SPARROW *superimposed on music sheet depicting song variations of four individual birds.*

Bird is about 5½-inches long. Head ruddy brown with medium gray line. Almost white underparts. Breast streaked with sepia, red-brown, joining at center of breast in distinct blotch. Tail long, brown, rounded.

THE INDEPENDENT, JUNE 22, 1995

"... though these sparrows' songs follow similar patterns, each bird creates melodies of his own."

Spring hillside in Columbia County, New York.

Run in the Meadow, Child

Run in the meadow, child.
Let the palpable wind caress your face,
                your arms, your breast.
The warmth of your inner body world
                Surging full as a passion.

Stand in the meadow, child.
Stretch arms to the sky, legs pushed
                against the earth
Arching to observe the fair moment
Driving the bird into flight.

Lie in the tall meadow grass, child.
Converse with the cricket, and
                applaud the ant
Contempate the cautious grasshopper
Leaping from his ruminations.

Roll over and over on the warm earth, child.
Study the smooth stone that bruises flesh;
A piece of the stars borrowed from
                the antique universe.
Look up at the sky.

Marion Dusoir
Big River News, April 1979
Mendocino, California

Tornado 1995

Small bulldozer at work clearing away tornado debris.

Big backhoe going after downed timber.

"Out of the blue" on May 29, 1995, an F2[1] tornado swept across the Ennes property in Columbia County. It was the first "big wind" since 1978 to hit the Hudson Valley, although locals couldn't recall a tornado in this area for half a century. Fortunately, the vortex only sideswiped two residences and other man-made structures, but it decimated eleven acres of mixed woods: yellow pine, maples, and hardwoods.

Nature has its way of reinvigorating the environment, and in good time would bring back the natural habitat. In this case, it took a bit of help from man and machines—the hills cleared of downed trees, many loads of timber removed, new meadows reseeded with grass and wildflowers.

---

1 Fujita Tornado Scale, winds 113–157 mph.

Loading logs cut from eleven acres of tornado-downed timber.

Former woods, now a new meadow ready for seeding

With a bit of help, nature replenishes a new meadow.

After Words by the Editor

A Naturalist in the Making

As Marion Dusoir's second husband, I knew her as a social work administrator, a theater and music aficionado, a mother of two young women, a gourmet cook. As I got to know her better, I found she was also a community activist, a writer, a home builder, a textile designer-weaver—then an amateur ornithologist turned natural sciences writer. After a full life of seventy-seven years she died of pancreatic cancer in the arms of her younger daughter at our home in Fort Bragg, California, on May 6, 2002.

Growing Up in New York

Marion was born in upstate New York on a small farm not yet equipped with electricity, plumbing, or central heating. Her parents were immigrants from Germany and Belgium who came to this country after World War I with two daughters.

The Dusoir family moved to New York City in 1930 where Marion received an excellent education in the public schools. While a cultural affairs reporter for radio station WNYC, she married Warren Pack, a widely known sports columnist for several New York City newspapers.

With her two daughters in public schools, Marion went back to college and earned her BS and MSW degrees from Hunter College and began a career as a psychiatric social worker. Her professional activities involved clinical social work with several NYC agencies, including the Girls Service League, Ottilie Home for Children, Jewish Community Services of Long Island, New York City Youth Board, and Jewish Child Care Association.

From 1964 to 1972 she was executive director of the Florence Crittenton League's Girl's Town, providing residential treatment for court-assigned adolescent girls in Manhattan and Brooklyn. During her eight years at Girl's Town she was active in professional and governmental groups, including the Child Welfare League of America, Federation of Protestant Welfare Agencies, and York State Welfare Conference. After retiring, she served for a year as assistant director of St. Christopher's School in Dobbs Ferry, New York, responsible for professional direction and management of foster care and residential child care for 172 "troubled" youngsters.

Second Marriages, New Lives

After her divorce from Warren Pack in 1967, Marion maintained her professional work and helped develop *Off-Off*, a magazine reporting on the off-Broadway theatrical scene in New York City. There she wrote reviews and reported on alternative theater affairs.

By happy coincidence and a bit of networking, I met Marion on a blind date, and in 1969 we were married in the ecumenical chapel at the United Nations.[1] For several years Marion and I lived on New York City's West Side. But we both wanted to get out of the city, back to the land, and in 1973 we relocated to Raspberry Ridge in Columbia County, New York, in the foothills of the Berkshire Mountains.

Marion's move back "upstate" gave her a long-awaited opportunity to rekindle her interest in matters nature, for from childhood she had a fascination with nature and its wonders. In her maturity she came back to nature as an "amateur" in the fullest sense of the word—connoisseur, motivated by a passion—and became something of an ornithologist/naturalist. That led to our connection with the Alan Devoe Bird Club, *The Warbler*, and the essays recorded in this book.

Upstate Community Participant

Upstate, Marion taught at Columbia-Greene Community College in a federally financed Foster Care Training Project in cooperation with the Social Service Departments of Columbia and Greene Counties. Later, throughout the East, she conducted a series of "Circuit Seminars in Child Care" for staff of child and foster-care agencies.

---

1 Marion knew I was a widower but had been told I was a banker. Actually, I was a public health educator by training, and a vice president of the Equitable Life Assurance Society of the US, a US Navy and Public Health Service veteran, a former national president of the Society for Public Health Education and of the International Union for Health Education of the Public, an NGO affiliated with the World Health Organization.

She was a member of the Federal Title XX Advisory Committee for Columbia County, New York, and in the City of Hudson served as consultant to the YWCA's Women's Counseling Center. She became president of the YWCA, at the time the only integrated program in Hudson. She coordinated the daily snack-bar service for Amtrak commuter train riders, the income of which supported the Hudson Day Care Center, also an offshoot of the YWCA. Marion served on the Board of Directors of the Hudson Community Chest and, as a member of the Teen Parent Advisory Council, helped a foundering YWCA-spawned program revive, get funding, and shift to the umbrella of Columbia Opportunities, the local Community Action Program (CAP) agency.

Living temporarily in Albany while I was doing volunteer work in New York City with the National Center for Health Education after my retirement from The Equitable, Marion became consultant in child and family services for the State Communities Aid Association of New York. She was, as well, president of the Regional Food Bank of Albany and a member of the board of directors of WMHT public television.

A hands-on enthusiast of textile arts, all this time Marion was honing her skills as a weaver. She won awards at the New England Weavers Seminar and the Weavers Guild of Boston. She was president of the Weavers Guild of Southern Berkshire, founding member of Thirteen Hands Craft Cooperative in Chatham, New York, and Board Member of AROW, Art Resources Open to Women, in Schenectady, New York.

Marion leading discussion of "Nature and Senses," Columbia-Greene Community College, 1983.

Along with these and other professional and community activities in rural upstate New York, she was, at the same time, intimately involved in remodeling our home and enhancing its gardens and wooded property—while, of course, editing *The Warbler* and writing *Nature's Way!*

Broadening Our Horizons

Since we both wanted to "see more of the country," we made numerous cross-country excursions in our "Big Thunder" motor homes, traveling extensively throughout the States, visiting our children and friends—and, especially, nature preserves. On professional assignments we also visited Europe, Africa, Japan, and China. But after both of us went through open-heart surgery it seemed prudent to avoid the stress of cold winters and we began spending our winters in Florida.

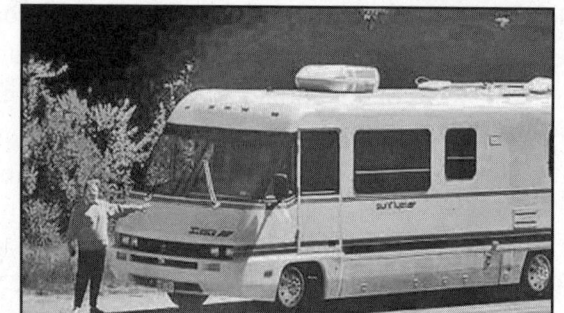
On the road with "Big Thunder," the third motor home of our "Nature's Way" travels. See "Big Thunder–Then and Now" page 173.

Finally we decided to migrate to northern California. We had, after all, been sampling the region's remarkable land and seas and climate for twenty-five years in visits to Marion's younger daughter. In 1997 Marion and I moved to Fort Bragg in Mendocino County—known to many from movies made there, and television series like *Murder, She Wrote*. This area is a hotbed of writers and artists, graphic and performing, and the climate, so far, is less capricious than that back East.

On the West Coast Marion held to her weaving—in fact, during the first of our cross-country trips in a converted van, she had all along the way spun her home-dyed yarn on a portable wheel. Now in Fort Bragg she hooked up with Pacific Textile Arts and other weaving groups.

She and I also worked with Gloriana Opera Company on organizational matters, and connected with the Mendocino Music Festival and the Fort Bragg Center for the Arts—both of us being avid supporters of theatrical and musical efforts. We became members of the Mendocino Coast Audubon Society and the Mendocino Botanical Gardens, while at the same time participating in activities of Amnesty International in Mendocino.

Since childhood, Marion's abiding interests were in writing fiction and poetry, cooking, textiles, caring for others—and persistently, nature. She always looked forward to her many ongoing writing and weaving projects, and in being with her children and relatives and her many friends.

This book is published in loving memory of her time with us, and in furtherance of her wish to contribute to the understanding and appreciation of the wondrous natural world of which each of us is a vital part.

Methods, Models, Mentors

The columns collected here were the happy result of fifteen years of a unique collaboration. It worked this way: Marion read, observed, talked, read some more, and then wrote. In the case of *The Warbler*, the mechanics she left to me. I typed, pasted up copy, placed the illustrations, and oversaw the duplicating. For both *The Warbler* and "Nature's Way," we shared the fun and the adventures and took pride in our work together. Truly, it was a labor of love.

Methods

We've often been asked how she did it. Her actual writing of *The Warbler* and for *The Independent* was in longhand, on narrow-lined white pads. She simply sat and wrote, usually at one sitting. In a sense, the *Nature's Way* columns were written "on computer"—that is, Marion's handwritten manuscripts were "word processed" by me to an exact word count required by Vicki Simons, the editor. The artwork was usually assembled by photocopying from a variety of sources in public domain, later by scanning.

When we traveled in the US, it was mostly by motor home, an early one of which we had fitted with a desktop (Macintosh!) computer. This, of course, was in the days before laptops and widespread use of the Internet, when computers were, at least to us, but sophisticated typewriters.

Marion met every deadline, no matter where we happened to be; in fact, she missed writing only two columns over the entire decade, and that was when she was hospitalized for open-heart surgery.

How Marion managed to absorb the information and insights gained from all her readings and field observations always amazed me. After all, she brought forth sixty monthly issues of *The Warbler* and produced some 190,000 words fashioned into 359 newspaper columns.

On our move across country in 1997 Marion insisted on bringing with us all her *Nature's Way* source materials—anticipating preparation of a book. Only recently, when I had occasion to delve into these files, did I realize how extensive her probing had been—just for her columns, there were five full file drawers and four large file boxes of papers, plus thirty shelf-feet of books!

Besides being an indefatigable reader (especially in this phase of her life) of the work of naturalists, past and present, Marion kept up-to-date with current professional journals, popular magazines, and newsletters in a wide range of topics—and this was before Google!

I expect she would have been pleased to have had the access that I have to the electronic treasure-troves of information now available on the Internet. In editing this book I have particularly made use of websites like the "Electronic Newsletter" of the Roger Tory Peterson Institute of Natural History, the Science Reference Section of the Library of Congress, the National Wildlife Federation, and the "About Birding" website of Christine Tarski.

Marion used field guides not only of birds, but of reptiles, mammals, insects, lichens, trees and flowers, rocks and shells. She insisted that for an amateur naturalist to have the field guides of the specific geographic area being investigated was as essential as it was to have a good pair of eyes and binoculars, sharp hearing, sturdy footwear, a notebook, patience, and an acute sense of curiosity.

Models

I know from observation that Marion savored the works of established naturalists, and she made a point of searching out the remarkable women among them. Edith Holden's *The Diary of an Edwardian Lady* (1906) was a particular delight of Marion's, as were the writings of Neltje Blanchan. She delved into Rachel Carson's books, of course, agreeing with Linda Lear that she was a "witness for nature," which perhaps Marion thought of herself as well.

Naturally, the bedrock naturalists were on her reading list: Henry David Thoreau, Carolus Linnaeus, John Muir, Luther Burbank, and so many more. She was intrigued, for example, with Gerard's 1633 *Herbal*, a 1640-page reproduction of which we bought and now is with my

Jokhanah finds Gerard's Herbal still useful after three centuries.
Photo by Renny Reep

younger daughter, a landscape designer, in Seattle. When Marion was reading Edwin Way Teale's *Wandering Through Winter*, we visited "Trailwood" in nearby Connecticut. And often she mentioned Donald Cutross Peattie and his biography of John James Audubon—whose book of plates held a special place on our coffee table.

Mentors

Marion's way of working was not, by any means, limited to reading. She was very much a hands-on, field-focused observer, and an active participant in the meetings and field activities of the Alan Devoe Bird Club with its 145-acre Powell Wildlife Sanctuary.[1]

Alan Devoe, 1944

The *Nature's Way* columns are splattered with references to naturalists of all stripes, many of national and international reputation, and some local—like Dr. William Cook of the Natural History Museum of Coumbia Greene Community College, Dr. Katherine Schneider of the New York State Natural Areas Inventory, and Betsy Blair of the Hudson River National Estuarine Sanctuary and Research Reserve.

In *The Warbler* of January 1994, Marion ran an extended commentary about Alan Devoe (1910–1955) by the late Kate Dunham, then president of the Alan Devoe Bird Club. Kate noted that the famous Roger Tory Peterson said Devoe was "one of the finest nature writers our country has ever produced." Peterson, Devoe, and Edgar M. Reilly, Jr., were close friends—and Marion had the privilege of working closely with the late Ed Reilly, curator of zoology of the New York State Museum, also a longtime member of and consultant to the Bird Club.

Edgar M. Reilly, Jr.
Drawing by Wayne Timm

The spirit of Marion's *Nature's Way* is reminiscent of Devoe's *Down to Earth: A Naturalist Looks About*. If Marion today were doing this book, I imagine she would quote, with approval, Alan Devoe's 1937 remarks about Darwin, who

"...found, for instance, that in a single acre of ground there may be 50,000 worms, and he found that they carry to the surface, in a single year, some eighteen tons of earth castings. The earthworms in an acre, Darwin learned, would in twenty years carry from the subsoil to the surface a layer of soil three inches thick; and it became evident to him that the honeycombing of the earth by its earthworms was what aerated the soil and made it porous and rendered it fit for man's agriculture.

It is good sometimes to be reminded that the ephemeral shifts of politics and ideologies are not the things on which our human welfare actually depends. The ultimate welfare of our tribe depends on things like worms."

Anna Bostford Comstock

Marion had a native and irrepressible curiosity, which she applied to all of her endeavors. Perhaps this was an inherited characteristic—her parents were adventurous and determined; her sisters intellectual achievers, one in literature, the other in science and art. Marion seemed to combine these traits. That she found inspiration and outlet in nature writing is not surprising.

Like one of the naturalists she most admired, Anna Bostford Comstock (1834–1930), Marion understood that the new ecological sciences were actually a formalized version of nature study. But beyond merely study, Marion realized that delving into these disciplines offered an experience of life that ultimately became for her a rich and sustaining philosophy.

Marion's purpose in her writing was to invite her readers to drink deeply of this elixir of delight and wonder by enticing them with small sips from the vast wells of scientific observation and research.

---

1 I was "associate editor" with Marion of *The Warbler* and, in 1991, also president of the Alan Devoe Bird Club.

"Big Thunder" Then and Now

THE ANTI-RENT WAR IN NEW YORK STATE.—ATTACK ON THE SHERIFF OF ALBANY.

Why were the motor homes we drove across country in our "Nature's Way" travels named "Big Thunder"? Not because of engine roar (although the first one did 'thunder' a bit) but because the term evoked an obscure episode in our democracy's history that occurred right where we were living. The quirkiness of the term appealed to us, and being citizens, social-activists, and history buffs we felt some "obligation" to spread the story.

Perhaps because of her Belgian-German immigrant parents' dedication to their new homeland, Marion had a natural interest in early American history; she searched out stories of early residents and took a special interest in the ethnobiology of Native Americans. Howard's Scotch-Irish-French-Huguenot family background—presumably including Nathan Hale and Dewitt Clinton and with roots in the Deep South and the Midwest—heightened his interest in the American story.

These latent links were enlivened when we took residence in upstate New York near Smoky Hollow, an area bristling with colonial and pre-Civil War events and personalities—the overbearing Dutch patroons and English landowners; the Six Nations (Iroquois) Confederacy with its matriarchy and seminal impact on our Constitution; persistent Tory-Patriot conflicts; the circumstances of the presidency of Martin Van Buren, 1837–41, and the shenanigans of his son, "Prince Henry"; the travesty of the 1877 Tilden-Hayes election, when the popular vote winner was denied office—shades of 2000! It was, of course, only later that we discovered we were next door to the birth town of Col. Oliver North of Iran-Contra fame.

Actually, the Big Thunder story has overtones of today's headlines. In 1839 the catalyst was a student activist named Smith A. Boughton, descended from a long line of French Huguenots. A young doctor from Rensselaer County, he *"had heard his father curse when he loaded his wagons with wheat for the Van Rensselaers."*[1] Later he was to tell his wife of *"the history of the settlement of the manor, an island of Old World tyranny in the New World of free men."*[2]

The spirit of anti-rentism expressed by Boughton in his role as "Big Thunder" was not new. It had risen even before the Revolution. In the 1750s, tenants of Livingston Manor[3], followed by those of Van Rensselear, had revolted against the primogeniture concept. Livingston had even raised a one-hundred-man military company under the guise of the French and Indian Wars but actually to maintain control of his properties. The issues at stake are outlined in the "History of Columbia County, 1878."[4] The tenants

"argued that they and their ancestors had already paid in rents far more than the value of the lands, even including the buildings and improvements that they themselves, and not the landlords, had put upon them, and that the degrading and perpetual nature of the tenure was inconsistent not only with the principles of republican government, but with all proper feeling of self-respect. They asked upon what principle it was that their fathers left the oppressive, aristocratic governments of the Old World, to find here, in the New, and upon the banks of the Hudson river, a system of land tenure that was overthrown in England so long ago as the year 1290, and in France in the Revolution of 1787? Could they believe that such things were right or legal? And should they by their submission allow them to become permanent?"

The story of what came to be known as the "anti-rent wars" is told in colorful detail *Tin Horns and Calico* by Henry Christman[5]. Riled-up farmers in the Helderberg mountains and Berne Township, in Hoags Corners and Alps (Boughton's hometown), and in Albany, Rensselaer, and Columbia Counties were organized. They stopped paying rent to the manor owners. Big Thunder traveled to gatherings to spread the word. Landowners invoked the law. Sheriffs pursued

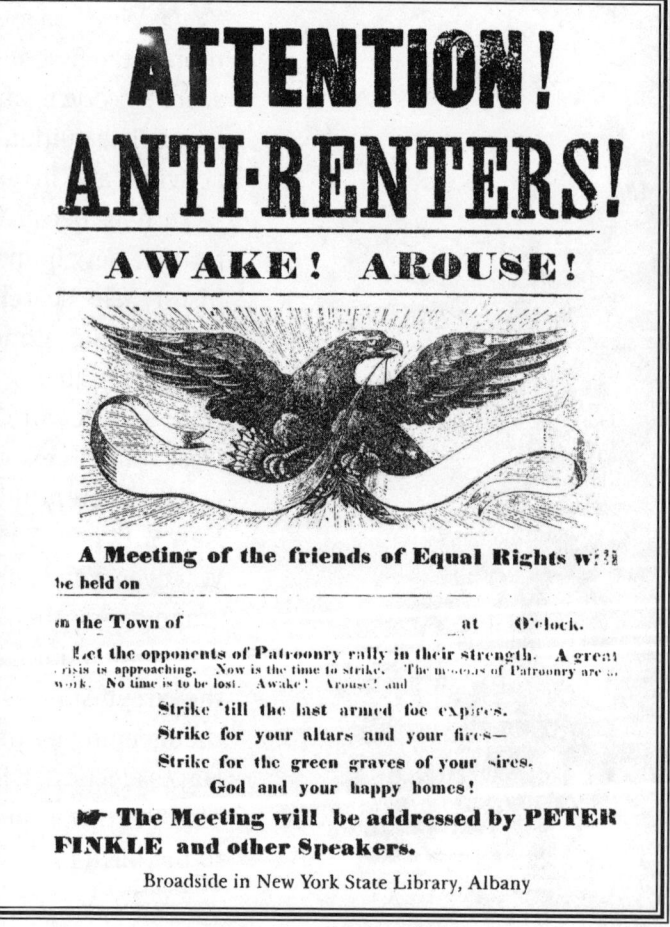

1838–44 broadside in New York State Library, Albany

"Let the opponents of Patroonery rally in their strength. A great crisis is approaching. Now is the time to strike. The minions of Patroonery are at work. Arouse! Awake! and

    Strike till the last armed foe expires,
    Strike for your altars and your fires,
    Strike for the green graves of your sires,
God and your happy home!"

AFTER WORDS — NATURE'S WAY

"Calico Indians" who signaled with tin horns from one hill to another.

Confrontations came. "Indians" kidnapped deputies, threw sheriffs' papers into blazing tar barrels. There were killings of bystanders as well as deputies. Finally, by trickery, Big Thunder was captured in Smoky Hollow, only a couple of miles from our Raspberry Ridge home. Amidst much hysteria of landowners and residents, Big Thunder was taken to jail in Hudson eight miles away.

What ensued would make good soap opera. Fearful of attacks by Indians—which, of course, never materialized—troops were called in by the governor. A long stand-off occurred, enlivened by full-dress parades of the Albany Burgesse Corps and a splendid fancy-dress ball. Several abortive trial attempts were stage-managed by State Attorney General Henry Van Buren, the ex-president's son. Judges favored manor owners and overruled juries. Eventually Big Thunder was convicted and was spirited away by night steamboat to Albany.

Direct action against authority having failed, a State Anti-Rent Party emerged and elected a governor who pardoned Boughton and other Calico Indians. In 1852 the case of De Peyster vs. Michael was decided unanimously by the appeals court—"*a legitimate close to the anti-rent controversy in favor of the anti-renters.*"[6]

Even so, landlords persisted and caused a

"wave of ejectments [which] culminated in the anti-rent outbreaks of 1865 and 1866, when again the hooded 'Indians' ranged through the Helderberg townships shouting 'Down with the rent!'... the last vestiges of the leasehold system were finally worn away in the 20th century."[7]

Dr. Smith A. Boughton—who as Big Thunder had even gone to Daniel Webster for a legal opinion on anti-rentism—returned to his medical practice and carried on until his retirement at seventy. Shortly before his death in 1888 at seventy-eight he wrote:

"The man who attempts to overthrow an existing wrong or revolutionize a principle of government that is tyrannical must not expect any reward—only in conscience and the satisfaction of knowing this his individual efforts bring a benefit to thousands. In this I am fully rewarded."[8]

And so it was Marion proposed for our "Nature's Way" travels that we call our motor homes "Big Thunder." To balance the scales, we referred to our granny unit at Raspberry Ridge as the "van Buren House." During the 1986 Bicentennial, as we undertook some bird watching in the Helderbergs, we attended the Hoags Corners 3rd annual Big Thunder reenactments of the Rent Wars on July 4.

Notes

1. Henry Christman, *Tin Horns and Calico*, p. 83.
2. Ibid, p. 83.
3. Manner of Robert Livingston, who sat on the committee that wrote the Declaration of Independence, but did not sign because he was not authorized by New York State.
4. p. 43, Facimile Edition, Sachem Press, Old Chatham, N.Y., 1974.
5. Henry Christman, *Tin Horns and Calico—A Decisive Episode in the Emergence of Democracy*, republished by the Berne County Historical Society, Hope Farm Press, Cornwallville, New York, 1975. Henry Holt and Company, Inc., 1945. Copyright, 1961, and 1975, by Henry Christman.
6. *History of Columbia County,* 1878, p. 45
7. David Maldwyn Lewis, *The Chatham Courier*, 1986.
8. *Tin Horns and Calico*, p. 319

Photograph of anti-rent reenactment during Bicentennial celebration at Hoags Corners, N.Y., near the village of Alps where "Big Thunder" was born.

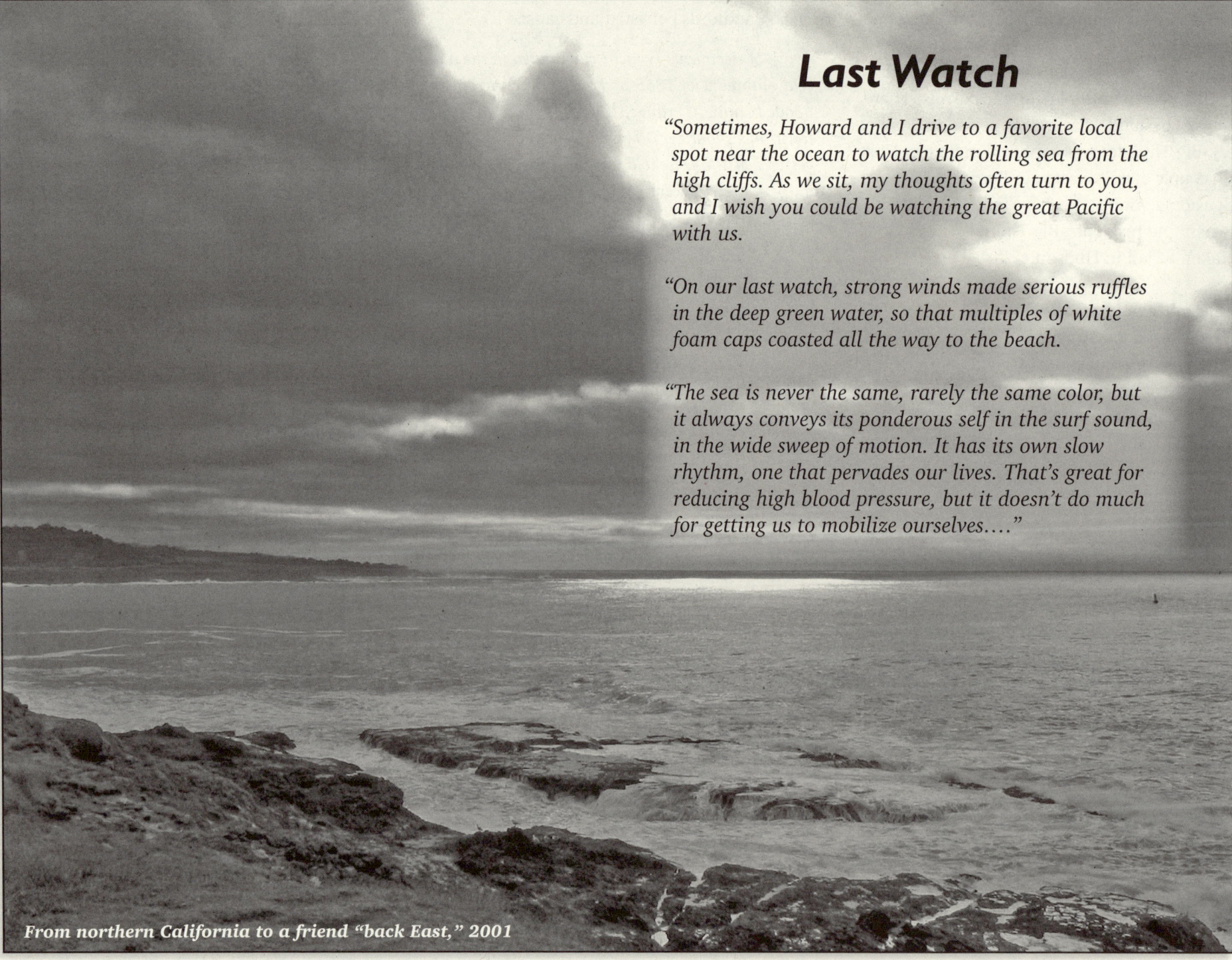

Last Watch

"Sometimes, Howard and I drive to a favorite local spot near the ocean to watch the rolling sea from the high cliffs. As we sit, my thoughts often turn to you, and I wish you could be watching the great Pacific with us.

"On our last watch, strong winds made serious ruffles in the deep green water, so that multiples of white foam caps coasted all the way to the beach.

"The sea is never the same, rarely the same color, but it always conveys its ponderous self in the surf sound, in the wide sweep of motion. It has its own slow rhythm, one that pervades our lives. That's great for reducing high blood pressure, but it doesn't do much for getting us to mobilize ourselves...."

From northern California to a friend "back East," 2001

Index

A

Able, Ken, 50, 51
Able, Mary, 50
adaptation, unique. *See* unique features/adaptation
Alan Devoe Bird Club, 6, 110, 130, 158, 172
Algonquin (Algonkin) tribe, 68, 76, 87
Alice in Wonderland (Carroll), 133
Amanita muscaria, 33
amaryllis, 4
American bittern, 60
American chestnut, 32
American elm, 82
American Indians. *See* Native Americans
American kestrel, 163
American toad, 72
amphibians
   American toad, 72
    frogs, 11, 146, 162
    salamanders, 142, 143, 160
Anderson, Barth, 19
Anderson, Hans Christian, 103
animal communication, 29, 75, 166
ants, 15
aphids, 56, 81
Apollo butterfly, 52
Arctic tern, 51
Aristotle, 27, 47
arthropods, 12
As You Like It (play, Shakespeare), 18
ash, white *(Fraxinus Americanus),* 144
Astor, John Jacob, 76
Atlas of Breeding Birds in New York State
   (Andrle and Carroll), 14, 54, 95, 130, 163
Audubon, John James, 57, 172
Audubon magazine, 24, 60, 111
Audubon Society, National, 14, 66
Audubon Society, New York State, 112
Austin, Ralph, 64
Aztecs, 62

B

backswimmer, 129
bald eagle, 38, 55
Ball, Gregory, 29
banded killifish (killefish), 19
Barbour, Spider, 7
barred owl, 104
bats, 27
bears, 9, 118
Beaudo, Dan, 92
beavers, 70, 76
bees, 20, 58, 59
beetles, 81, 129
Bent, Arthur C., 163
Berchielli, Lou, 9
Berry, Margaret Sheridan, 25
Biedermann, Ilse, 16
big brown bat, 27
"Big Thunder" story, 170, 173–175
bioluminescence, 10
biomedicine, 73, 76, 79, 88, 107
bird migration
   fueling up for, 46
   impulses prompting annual, 47
   navigation and flight paths, 41, 48, 50,
   neotropical migrants, 49
   reasons for, 45
   study of, 51
birds
   coloring of, 61, 113, 137
   communication amongst, 29, 75
   eggs of, 130
   individual species/types of (*See also* raptors;
      wading birds)
      Arctic tern, 51
      bluebird, 3, 112, 140
      bobolink, 50, 130
      cowbird, 150
      golden plover, 46
      golden seabright chicken, 29
      goldfinch, 61
      grosbeak, 148
      grouse, 101, 102
      house wren, 3, 130
      hummingbird, 22, 46
      junco, 45, 130
      killdeer, 130
      loon, 152
      mockingbird, 130
      mourning dove, 151
      phoebe, 18
      ring-necked pheasant, 71
      seagull, 92
      sparrow, 3, 50, 166
      thrush, 103
      towhee, 130
      tree swallow, 3, 145
      warbler, 48, 49, 150, 157
      waterfowl, 17, 110
      waxwing, 25, 113, 158
      wild turkey, 75
      wood duck, 5, 126
      woodcock, 117, 136
      woodpecker, 15, 80, 121, 137
   museum bird study, 117
   Neotropical Migratory Bird Conservation
      Program, 49
   New York's Breeding Bird Atlas, 14
   parenting fledgling, 23
   Project FeederWatch, 148
   songs of note, 103, 157, 166
   World Series of Birding, 159
   See also bird migration; mating and breeding
      characteristics; nesting/nest building
bittern, American, 60
black and white warbler, 48
black bears *(Ursus americanus),* 9, 118
Blair, Betsy, 19, 172
Blanchan, Neltje (later Doubleday), 120, 139, 171
bloodroot, 140
blue crab, 12
blue heron, great, vi, 53
bluebird, 3, 112, 140
bluet, 126, 155
bobcat, 37
bobolink, 50, 130
bogs, 156
bohemian waxwing, 158
Boletus spectabilis, 100
Boughton, Smith A., 173–175
breeding characteristics. *See* mating and
   breeding characteristics
Breisch, Al, 146
British Royal Navy, 64
Brown, William S., 164
brown creeper, 117
brown-headed cowbird, 150
bryophtyes (mosses and liverworts), 6, 96, 156
bulbs, flowering, 4
Burbank, Luther, 171
Bush, George, 30
butterflies, 7, 52, 111, 133, 134

C

Caldwell, Mark, 52
Calhoun, James, 30
"Calico Indians," 175
Canadian lynx, 98
cardinal, Northern, 117
Carlson, Shawn, 52
carp, 19
carpenter bee, 20
Carreiro, Margaret, 8
Carroll, Alice, 133
Carson, Rachel, 19, 82, 171
Cartier, Jacques, 76, 102
Cartin, Anita, 30
caterpillar, silkworm, 26
   See also butterflies; moths
cattails, 35
cedar waxwing, 113, 158
chestnut, American, 32
chestnut-sided warbler, 157
chicken, golden seabright, 29
chipmunks, 118
Christman, Henry, 174
Christmas trees, 123
cicadas, 69
climbing fern, 135
Cobb, Boughton, 34
cold-weather survival, 94, 115
color pigmentation, 113, 134
Columbia County Environmental
   Management Council, vii
Columbia-Green Community College Natural
   History Museum, 117, 172
commercial use of plants/animals
   biomedicine, 73, 76, 79, 88, 107
   eels as food, 119
   great egret plumes, 66
   milkweed silk and pods, 111
   mountain laurel as "spoonwood," 79
   painted turtles as pets, 24
   shagbark hickory wood, 40
   skunk musk, 17
   soybeans for food, 99
   timber rattlesnake's various uses, 164
   white ash for baseball bats, 144
   white pine timbers, 64
   witch hazel astringent, 107
   See also hunting/trapping/fishing
communication amongst animals, 29, 75, 166

Comstock, Anna Botsford, viii, 21, 116, 172
Conservationist (magazine), 90
Cook, William, 110, 117, 136, 159, 172
Cooper's hawk, 120
corms, flowering, 4
corn, 21, 31
Cornell Laboratory of Ornithology, 148
Country Journal, The (magazine), 35
cowbird, 150
coyotes, 62
crab, blue, 12
crane, sandhill, v, 39
crustaceans, 12
crystallographic orientation, 91
cultural beliefs. *See* historical/cultural reflections
curlygrass fern, 135

D

dark-eyed junco, 45
Darwin, Charles, 26, 74, 124, 172
DeBary, Heinrich Anton, 73
declining species, 14, 164
deer, 109
Delmar Wildlife Resource Center, 9
Department of Agriculture, U.S., 92, 99, 111
Department of Environmental Conservation, 37, 38, 57, 95, 146
Devoe, Alan, viii, 25, 172
Diary of an Edwardian Lady, The (Holden), 171
Different Forms of Flowers on Plants of the Same Species (Darwin), 26
Doubleday, Neltje Blanchan, 120, 139, 171
dove, mourning, 151
Down to Earth: A Naturalist Looks About (Devoe), 172
downy woodpecker, 121, 137
dowsers, water, 107
dragonfly, 63, 161
Drowne, Roland, 34
Druid priests, 124
ducks, 5, 17, 110
Dunham, Kate, 110, 172
Dunn, Erica, 148
Dutch Elm disease, 82

E

eagles, 23, 38, 55
Easter eggs, 130
Eastern phoebes, 18
Eastern turkey, 75
ecological impact
  American chestnut fungus, 32
  American elm/Dutch Elm disease, 82
  Canadian lynx and snowshoe hare, 98
  estuary food chain, 19
  fungi partnering with plants, 8, 16, 73
  of invasive loosestrife, 26
  of mosses and liverworts, 6
  Northern Flickers and ant overpopulation, 15
  of poisoning coyotes, 62
  skunk for seed dispersal/aid to duck population, 17
  turtles as pets, 24
  wetlands conservation, 30
  See also environmental issues
Edge of the Sea, The (Carson), 19
eels, 119
eft, red, 160
egrets, 25, 66
elm, American, 82
Emerson, Ralph Waldo, 79
endangered species
  amphibians as, 72
  bald eagle, 38
  ferns, 135
  ladyslipper orchid, 16
  loon, 152
  species of special concern, 14, 164
environmental issues
  disappearing habitat, 3, 14, 49, 71
  general human settlement, 120
  seagulls at landfills, 92
  thinning ozone/global warming/acidic conditions, 72, 142
  use of pesticides, 3, 14
equinox, vernal and autumnal, 104
estuary, Hudson River, 19
Evans, Christopher, 29
evening grosbeak, 148
evergreens, 123

F

falcate orange-tip butterfly, 7
falcon, 53
"Feathers" (newsletter), 60
features, unique. *See* unique features/adaptation
Federation of New York State Bird Clubs, 110
"Feeding Birds" (poem; Ennes), 83
Feinberg, Peter, 159
ferns, 34, 135
Field Guide to Ferns (Cobb), 34
finch, "winter," 148
firefly *(Photinus pyralis)*, 10
fish, 19, 119
Flicker, Northern *(Colaptes auratus)*, 15
flycatcher, 18
flying squirrel, 28
food chain, 19, 97, 164
foraging honeybee, 58, 59
Forbush, Edward Howe, 5, 150
forest food chain, 97
fox, 104, 149
Franz, Betsy, 159
Frazier, James, 124
freshwater eel, 119
Frisch, Karl von, 59
frogs, 11, 146, 162
fungi
  Amanita muscaria, 33
  American chestnut attacked by, 32
  Boletus spectabilis, 100
  decompositional properties of, 8
  Dutch Elm disease, 82
  fruiting of, 33, 73
  mycorrhizal relationship with plants, 16, 79
  National Fungus Collection, 73
  New York state mycological herbarium, 100
  as third kingdom, 73

G

garter snake, 138
Gary, Asa, 26
geology, 132
Gerard, John, 171
Glooskap (Algonkin spirit), 87
glowworm, 10
Golden Bough, The (Frazier), 124
golden plover, 46
golden seabright chicken, 29
goldfinch, 61
Good Earthkeeping Award, vii
goshawk, Northern, 106
grasses, 31
gray squirrel, 65
great blue heron, vi, 53
great egret, 66
great horned owl, 77
green-backed heron, 54
grey tree frog *(Hyla versicolor)*, 162
grosbeak, 148
groundhog, 118
grouse, 101, 102
Guthrie, Richard, 159

H

Hadcock, Steve, 99
Hagen, Kenneth, 81
Haines, John, 100
Handbook of Nature Study (Comstock), 116
hare, snowshoe, 89, 98
Hart's tongue fern, 135
harvesting plants, 32, 35, 40, 111, 116
  See also Native Americans
Hawk Mountain, 120
hawks, 29, 45, 120
Headstrom, Richard, 155
heath plants, 79
hepatica, 140
Herbal (Gerard), 171–172
hermit thrush, 103
herons, vi, 53, 54
hibernation, 68, 118
hickory, shagbark, 40
Hilton, Joan, 9
historical/cultural reflections
  on the American Elm, 82
  ancient Greeks on owls, 77
  beliefs around mistletoe, 124
  "Big Thunder," 173–175
  Chinese use of soy, 99
  the Christmas tree, 123
  connections to the "little people," 78, 96
  crabs given zodiac sign by the Babylonians, 12
  cultivation of corn, 21
  dragonflies as dragon-like, 161
  fox as trickster, 149
  French naming the muskrat, 122
  frogs as rainmakers, 162
  on great blue herons, 53
  intoxicated seagulls, 92
  ladybugs as good luck, 81
  milkweed in WWII, 111
  on mistletoe, 124
  on the shrew, 114

INDEX

squirrel vices, 93
stories about coyotes, 62
superstitions surrounding snakes, 165
white pine politics, 64
witch hazel as magical, 107
See also commercial use of plants/animals
History of Columbia County, 1878 (Ellis), 174
History of Virginia (Smith), 28
Hodges, Ronald, 154
Holden, Edith, 171
Holland, William Jacob, 153
Holmes, Oliver Wendell, 82
honeybee, 58, 59
house wren, 3, 130
Houston, David, 74
Hudson, Henry, 76
Hudson River Foundation, 6
Hudson River National Estuarine Sanctuary and Research Reserve, 19, 55, 119, 172
Hudson Valley Ospreys, 159
Hudson Valley Raptor Center, 14
Hudsonia, Ltd., 6, 26
hummingbirds, 22, 46
humus, 97
Hunt, Peg, 28
hunting/trapping/fishing
  beavers, 76
  black bears, 9
  by bobcats, 37
  Cooper's ("chicken") hawks, 120
  coyotes, 62
  great egrets, 66
  grouse, 102
  muskrat, 122
  of/by bald eagles, 38, 55
  of/by Canadian lynx, 98
  of/by herons, 53, 54
  perching ducks, 5
  pileated woodpecker, 80
  prohibitions on, 3
  ring-necked pheasants, 71
  skunks for musk, 17
Hurley, Jack, 113, 153
Huth, Paul, 16

I

Independent, The (newspaper), vii, 171
Indians. See Native Americans
insects

ants, 15
aphids, 56, 81
bees, 20, 58, 59
beetles, 81, 129
bioluminescence of, 10
butterflies, 7, 52, 111, 133, 134
caterpillars, 26
cicada/cicada-killer wasp, 69
dragonfly, 63, 160
firefly, 10
metamorphosis of, 36, 52, 147
moths, 78, 147, 153, 154
pond life, 36, 129
unique mating/breeding habits, 7, 20, 69, 78
in winter, 115
"Insects—Their Ways and Means of Living" (article; Snodgrass), 56
Institute of Ecological Studies, Cary Arboretum, 8
insulation, animal, 68, 94, 109
invasive plants, 26
Iroquois tribe, 21, 144, 173

J

Jimmys and Sallys (blue crab), 12
Jorling, Thomas, 38
juncos, 45, 130

K

Kalm, Peter, 79
Kautz, Marie, 62
Kazlo, Catherine, 140
kestrel, American, 163
Kieran, John, 3
killdeer, 130
Kingbird, The (periodical), 53
Kirtland's warbler, 150
Kiviat, Eric, 6, 26
Koqut, Ken, 37
Kricher, John, 136
Kroodsma, Don, 157

L

ladybugs, 81
ladyslipper orchid, 16
landfills, 92
Langner, Jory, 159
"Last Watch" (letter excerpt; Ennes, Marion), 176
leaf litter, 8, 97
Lear, Linda, 171

Legion of Night: The Underwing Moths (Sargent), 147
Leonardi, Lorinda, 6
leopard frog, 11
Leopold, Aldo, 39, 102, 136
Lewis, Scott, 70
Lewis and Clark expedition, 76
Life in the Cold (Marchand), 94
lightening bug, 10
Linnaeus, Carolus, 16, 73, 79, 99, 171
liverworts (bryophytes), 6
Living Bird (magazine), 145, 151
Livingston Manor, 174
loons, 152
loosestrife, purple (*Lythrum salicaria*), 26
luna moth, 78
lynx, Canadian, 98

M

mammals
  bat, 27
  bear, 9, 118
  bobcat, 37
  Canadian lynx, 98
  coyote, 62
  deer, 109
  fox, 104, 149
  groundhog, 118
  hibernation by, 118
  insulation of, 68, 94, 109
  otter, 57
  raccoon, 67, 68, 104, 118
  shrew, 114
  skunk, 17, 118
  snow tracks of, 90
  snowshoe hare, 89, 98
  star-nosed mole, 13
  tiger, 25
  vervet monkey, 29
  See also rodents
maple sugar, 116
Marchand, Peter, 94
Marshall, Peter and Ursula, 18
marshes. See wetlands
Massachusetts Audubon Society Pleasant Valley Sanctuary, 70
Mathews, F. Schulyer, 103, 166
mating and breeding characteristics
  American kestrel, 163

blue crab, 12
bluebird, 3
carpenter bee, 20
cicada, 69
cowbird, 150
falcate orange-tip butterfly, 7
goldfinch, 61
green-backed heron, 54
grouse, 101
luna moth, 78
mating season, 104
Northern Flicker, 15
phoebe, 18
reproduction as sexual, 25
sandhill crane, 39
spotted salamander, 143
woodcock, 136
See also nesting/nest building
May, John Bichard, 5
mayfly, 129
McClallen, Helen, 155
medicinal use of plants/animals, 73, 76, 79, 88, 107
metamorphosis, 11, 36, 52, 119, 147
Mettler, Elinor, 68
Mettler, John, 89
migration of birds. See bird migration
Mildner, Dennis, 12, 55, 119
milkweed, 111
mistletoe, 124
mockingbird, 130
mole, star-nosed, 13
monarch butterfly, 52, 111, 133, 134
Monhonk Preserve, 16
monkey, vervet, 29
Moore, Frank R., 46
Morrison, Gordon, 136
mosses (bryophytes), 6, 96, 156
Moth Book (Holland), 153
moths, 78, 147, 153, 154
mountain laurel (*Kalinia latefolia*), 79
mourning dove, 151
mouse, white-footed, 108
Muir, John, 171
Murchie, Guy, 91
mushrooms. See fungi
muskrat, 122
Myths of the North American Indians (Spence), 76, 87

N

Nagaya, Okichiro, 91
National Audubon Society, 14, 66
National Fungus Collection, 73
National Geographic (magazine), 50, 54
National Geographic Society, 47
National Science Foundation, 100
Native Americans
   admiration of beavers, 76
   Algonquin (Algonkin), 68, 76, 87
   bows from Shagbark hickory, 40
   Iroquois, 21, 144, 173
   mythology of, 62, 87, 122
   names for animals, 28, 68, 93
   Ojibway, 40, 93
   plants for pigment, 140
   use of plants for food, 21, 32, 40, 111, 139
   use of plants medicinally, 79, 156
   various uses of cattails, 35
   various uses of mountain laurel, 79
   various uses of white ash, 144
Natural History (magazine), 7, 74, 157
Natural History Museum of Columbia-Green Community College, 117, 172
Natural History of American Birds of Eastern and Central North America (Forbush, May), 5
Nature in Miniature (Headstrom), 155
"Nature's Night Lights" (article; Zahl), 10
Neefus, Wendy, 5
Neotropical Migratory Bird Conservation Program, 49
Nest Box Network (Audubon Society of New York State), 112
nesting/nest building
   beaver, 70
   bluebird, 3, 112
   downy woodpecker, 137
   factors involved in, 22
   hummingbird, 22
   mourning dove, 151
   muskrat, 122
   pileated woodpecker, 80
   spring's colored eggs, 130
   tree swallow, 145
New York Association of Conservation Districts, 30
New York City Turtle and Tortoise Society, 24
New York Department of Environmental Conservation, 37, 38, 57, 95
New York State Audubon Society, 112
New York State Museum, 95, 100
newts, 160
North American Bluebird Society, 112
Northern, cardinal, 117
Northern Flicker *(Colaptes auratus)*, 15
Northern Goshawk, 106
Northern Saw-Whet Owl, 95
nymph, dragonfly, 63

O

Ojibway tribe, 40, 93
orange-tip butterfly, 7
orchid, ladyslipper, 16
Origin of Species (Darwin), 124
otter, 57
ovenbird (wood warbler), 49
owls
   barred, 104
   great horned, 77
   Saw-Whet, 95
   screech, 117
   short-eared, 14

P

Pack, Linda, 125
pagan beliefs/customs, 124
Pahountis-Opacic, Julia, 41
painted turtle, 24, 88
Parker, Karl E., 95
Pasteur, Louis, 73
Pearson, Hayden, 60
Peattie, Donald Culross, 40, 144, 172
Peck, Charles, 100
Pell, Morris, 70
perch, white, 19
perching ducks, 5
Peterson, Roger Tory, 49, 120, 171, 172
Peterson Field Guide to Eastern Forests (Kricher and Morrison), 136
pheasant, 71
phoebe, 18
pigeon, 151
pigmentation of wings/feathers, 133, 134
pileated woodpecker, 80
Pinchot, Gifford, 123
pine, white, 64
pine siskin, 148
pink ladyslipper, 16
plant lice, 56
plants
   Arum family, 139
   bloodroot, 140
   bluet, 126, 155
   cattail, 35
   corn, 21, 31
   fern, 34, 135
   flower bulbs and corms, 4
   as food, 21, 32, 35, 40
   hepatica, 140
   invasive, 26
   ladyslipper orchid, 16
   milkweed, 111
   mistletoe, 124
   moss and liverwort, 6, 156
   mountain laurel, 79
   pollinated by bees, 58
   purple loosestrife, 26
   reproduction in, 4, 16, 135
   skunk cabbage, 139
   soybean, 99
   trailing arbutus, 140
   See also trees
Point Pelee (Ontario), 52
ponds, 36, 129, 143
porcupine, 131
Powell Wildlife Sanctuary, 34, 172
Power, Sandra G., 19
Preusser, Ken, 92, 112
Project FeederWatch, 148
purple loosestrife *(Lythrum salicaria)*, 26

Q

Quakers, 155

R

rabies, 27
raccoons, 67, 68, 104, 118
raptors
   eagle, 23, 38, 55
   hawk, 29, 45, 120
   kestrel, 163
   Northern Goshawk, 106
   turkey vulture, 74
   See also owls
rattlesnakes, 164, 165
red-backed salamander, 142
red eft, 160
red squirrel, 93
red-tailed hawk, 45
Reilly, Edgar A., 158, 172
reproduction, animal. *See* mating and breeding characteristics
reproduction, plant, 4, 16, 135
reptiles
   snakes, 138, 164, 165
   turtles, 17, 24, 26, 88
ring-necked pheasant, 71
Roberts, Mervin, 19
rodents
   beaver, 70, 76
   chipmunk, 118
   muskrat, 122
   porcupine, 131
   squirrel, 28, 65, 93
   vole, 141
   white-footed mouse, 108
Rood, Ron, 108
Roosevelt, Theodore, 123
Rosenberg, Vivian, 111
Royal Navy (British), 64
ruby-throated hummingbird, 22, 46
ruffed grouse, 101, 102
"Run in the Meadow, Child" (poem; Ennes), 167
Ruskin, John, 96

S

salamanders, 142, 143, 160
Sallys and Jimmys (blue crab), 12
Sand County Almanac (Leopold), 136
sandhill crane, v, 39
Sargasso Sea, 119
Sargent, Theodore D., 147
Saums, Dorothy, 148
Savannah sparrow, 50
Saw Kill River, 19
Saw-Whet Owl, 95
scales, butterfly, 133, 134
Scandinavians, 124
Schneider, Kathryn, 164, 172
Schwartz, David M., 111
Scientific American (magazine), 52
seagull, 92
Shagbark hickory, 40
Shakespeare, William, 18, 72

INDEX

Shook, Eleanor, 158
shore birds, 51, 92
short-eared owl, 14
short-tailed shrew, 114
Silent Spring (Carson), 82
skunk, 17, 118
skunk cabbage *(Symplocarpus foetidus)*, 139
Smith, John, 28
snakes, 138, 164, 165
snapping turtles, 17
Snodgrass, Robert, 56
snow, 90, 91
snowshoe hare, 89, 98
"Song of Myself" (poem; Whitman), 31
Song of the Sky (Murhcie), 91
song sparrow, 166
Sotis, Jim, 60
Southey, Robert, 78
soybean, 99
sparrows, 3, 50, 166
species of special concern, 14, 164
Spence, Lewis, 76, 87
Spensiero, Rose, 153
sphagnum moss, 6, 156
Sphinx moth, 153, 154
spotted salamander, 143
"Spring is creeping over the landscape" (letter excerpt; Ennes), 125
"Springtime" (poem; Pack), 125
squirrels, 28, 65, 93
Stager, Kenneth, 74
Stangel, Peter, 49
star-nosed mole, 13
stickleback, fourspine, 19
Stokes, Donald and Lillian, 45, 151
Stokes' Nature Guides to Bird Behavior (Stokes), 150
Storey, Janet and Kenneth, 88
sugar maple, 116
swallow, tree, 3, 145
swamps. *See* wetlands

T

Taconic Revolution, 132
Teale, Edwin Way, 141, 161, 172
Teenage Mutant Nija Turtles (film), 24
"Telltale Tail, The" (article, Witmer), 113
tern, Arctic, 51
This Fascinating Animal World (Devoe), 25
Thoreau, Henry David, 15, 103, 139, 140, 171
thrushes, 103, 112
Tidemarsh Guide (Roberts), 19
tigers, 25
timber rattlesnake, 164, 165
Tin Horns and Calico (Christman), 174
toad, American, 72
Tollar, Ben, 57
tomato hornworm, 154
tornado of 1995, 80, 166, 168
towhee, 130
Tracy, Dona, 120
trailing arbutus, 140
trapping. *See* hunting/trapping/fishing
tree frog *(Hyla versicolor)*, 162
tree swallow, 3, 145
trees
  American chestnut, 32
  American elm, 82
  Christmas, 123
  commercial uses of, 40
  shagbark hickory, 40
  sugar maple, 116
  white ash, 144
  white pine, 64
  in winter, 105
  witch hazel, 107
tulips, 4
Tullar, Ben, 131
turkey, wild, 75
turkey vulture, 74
turtledove, 151
turtles, 17, 24, 26, 88

U

"Under the Washington Elm, Cambridge" (poem; Holmes), 82
"Underachiever of the Plant World" (article; Schwartz), 111
underwing moth, 147
unique features/adaptation
  bat flying and hunting techniques, 27
  bird migration, 47, 48
  cicada tymbal membranes, 69
  downy woodpecker body, 121
  flying squirrels, 28
  honeybees, 58, 59
  owls nictating membrane, 77
  painted turtles, 88
  star-nosed mole tunneling, 13
  turkey vultures, 74
  turtle migration, 24
  underwing moth camouflage, 147
University of Kansas (Lawrence) Monarch Watch, 52
U.S. Fish & Wildlife Service, 30, 136
USDA (U.S. Department of Agriculture), 92, 99, 111

V

Van Buren, Henry, 175
varying hare, 89
veery thrush, 103
vermillion flycatcher, 18
vervet monkey, 29
viceroy butterfly, 111
Virgil, 124
vole, 90, 141
vulture, turkey, 74

W

wading birds
  American bittern, 60
  egret, 25, 66
  heron, vi, 53, 54
  sandhill crane, v, 39
Walden (Thoreau), 140
Walker, William, 35
Wandering Through Winter (Teale), 172
Warbler, The (newsletter), vii, viii, 171, 172
warblers, 48, 49, 150, 157
wasp, cicada-killer, 69
water dowsers, 107
water scorpion, 129
waterfowl, 5, 17, 110, 126, 152
waxwing, 25, 113, 158
Webster, Daniel, 175
wetlands
  cattails, 35
  Hudson River National Estuarine Sanctuary and Research Reserve, 19
  invasive loosestrife, 26
  life of a bog, 156
  moss and lichen research, 6
  restoration and conservation, 30
  transformed into ponds, 36
  winter waterfowl in, 110
Weymouth, George, 64
whirligig beetle, 129
white ash *(Fraxinus americanus)*, 144
white-footed mouse, 108
white perch, 19
white pine, 64
Whitman, Walt, 31
whooping crane, 39
Wild Birds and Their Music (Matthews), 103
wild turkey, 75
wildcrafting, 32, 35, 40, 111, 116
  See also Native Americans
Williams, Steve, 9
Winkler, David, 145
winter
  hibernation, 118
  insects in, 115
  Native American mythology of, 87
  snow, 90, 91
  survival in, 68, 94, 115
  trees in, 105
  waterfowl of, 110
  winter solstice, 104, 124
"winter" finches, 148
"Winter Roosting and Food Habits of Northern Saw-Whet Owl in Columbia County, N.Y." (report; Parker), 95
"Wired Butterfly, The" (article; Caldwell), 52
witch hazel tree, 107
Witmer, Mark, 113
Wolcott, Charles, 50
Wonder Stories (Anderson), 103
wood duck, 5, 126
wood frog *(Rana sylvatica)*, 146
wood thrush, 103
wood warbler (ovenbird), 49
woodchuck, 118
woodcock, 117, 136
"woodpecker candy," 137
woodpeckers, 15, 80, 121, 137
World Series of Birding, 159
Wyman, Richard, 142

Z

Zahl, Paul, 10

Thank you, Marion